A  SHEARWATER  BOOK

*The* UNNATURAL HISTORY *of the* SEA

*The*

# ❧ UNNATURAL ❧

# HISTORY

## ~ *of the* ~

# SEA

Callum Roberts

**◑ ISLAND**PRESS / Shearwater Books

*Washington · Covelo · London*

*A Shearwater Book*
*Published by Island Press*

Copyright © 2007 Callum M. Roberts

First Island Press cloth edition, July 2007
First Island Press paperback edition, December 2008

SHEARWATER BOOKS is a trademark of
The Center for Resource Economics.

*Library of Congress Cataloging-in-Publication data.*
Roberts, Callum.
The unnatural history of the sea / Callum M. Roberts.
p. cm.
ISBN-13: 978-1-59726-102-9 (cloth : alk. paper)
ISBN-10: 1-59726-102-5 (cloth : alk. paper)
ISBN-13: 978-1-59726-577-5
ISBN-10: 1-59726-577-2
1. Ocean and civilization. 2. Ocean—History. I. Title.
CB465.R63 2007
909'.09—dc22      2007001841

*British Cataloguing-in-Publication data available.*

Printed on recycled, acid-free paper ♻

Design by David Bullen

Manufactured in the United States of America

10   9   8   7   6   5   4

*Keywords:* Marine, fish, fishing, whales, coral, seafaring, reserve,
exploratory conservation, maritime, extinction.

To Julie, with love and thanks

# ~ Contents ~

PART THREE: The Once and Future Ocean

# Preface

LATE ON A hot June night in 1798, Captain Edmund Fanning was roused from sleep by urgent pounding on the deck above his cabin and the clamour of sailors running to their stations. He reached the deck just as the lookout called out "breakers close aboard." Fanning's ship was running fast ahead of the wind and by the time danger was spotted in the darkness, they were almost upon it. A clearing shower revealed a shadowy necklace of islands wreathed in an almost continuous sheet of foam where Pacific swells exploded onto submerged coral.

Fanning and his crew barely escaped destruction. His men tacked the ship and followed the line of thunderous breakers until they found calm water to the lee of the islands. As they breakfasted the next morning, the relieved sailors could see some fifty islets circling three shallow lagoons, none more than two meters above sea level. Most were forested with tall *Pisonia* trees while their shores were fringed with coconut palms below which nuts had accumulated and decayed over the course of years, untouched by any human hand.

Palmyra Atoll lies almost in the dead centre of the Pacific Ocean. For 180 years following the first successful passage by Ferdinand Magellan in 1519, it remained unknown to the adventurers who criss-crossed the Pacific. Fanning found it because the atoll lay on a direct line between the Isle of Juan Fernández, off the coast of Chile, and China, where he was headed. Fanning and his men, originally from Stonington, Connecticut, had just spent four months on Juan Fernández, slaughtering fur seals for their pelts to sell in Canton. When he finally set sail the skins so crammed the hold, the cabin, and the forecastle that there was barely room for the crew. At noon, Fanning embarked in a row boat with a shore party to explore Palmyra. He was stunned by the great abundance of fish they saw, he later recounted.[1]

> The sharks here are very numerous, and while the boat was on her passage into the bay, before she entered the pass, they became so exceedingly ravenous around her, and so voracious withal, as frequently to dart at, and seize upon her rudder and her oars, leaving thereon many marks of their sharp teeth and powerful jaws; but so soon as she left the pass and entered within the bay, they deserted her, their stations being instantly occupied by multitudes of fish, less rapacious, but infinitely more valuable.

While his men collected coconuts ashore, Fanning occupied himself catching mullet that crowded the sides of the boat so thickly that he could spear them without letting go of the harpoon shaft. He took over fifty of 2 to 5 kilograms (5 to 12 pounds) before deciding that any more would spoil before the crew could eat them.

More than two centuries have passed since Fanning's discovery. Palmyra passed from American to French, then to Hawaiian hands, but it was never colonized, perhaps because it was too remote even by Pacific standards. It was briefly a U.S. Naval air command base in World War II and the debris of conflict still litter the islands and lagoons. But underwater, it remains much as Fanning described it. Palmyra is one of the last places on this planet where shallow water marine life is still as varied, rich, and abundant as it was in the eighteenth century. A diver stepping into the seas around this atoll today is able to take a trip back in time to an age when fishing had not yet touched life in the sea. Beneath the swells, great coral-built ramparts front the open ocean, crusted with spreading colonies that cover the reef in bright colored plates, mounds, knobs, bushes, and folds. Above them countless tiny fish pick plankton from the water. Magnificent shoals of white and black striped convict surgeonfish, each the size of a hand, stretch into the distance, seemingly with no beginning and no end. Groups of blue-green bumphead parrot fish forty strong pass by gatherings of Napoleon wrasse as large as people. Above them milling schools of jacks cast predatory eyes over the fish below. Sharks hove in and out of view, gliding effortlessly across the reef, cutting tunnels through scattering clouds of fish as they pass.

Palmyra has more apex predators—large fish like sharks, jacks, and groupers—than any other reef known to science. Added together, there are nearly twenty times as many big fish here as on the average reef that is exploited by people for food. In the year 2000, Palmyra was bought by The Nature Conservancy to manage as a wildlife refuge for the benefit of humanity. It remains virtually unfished, apart from a small amount of catch-and-release recreational angling.

Palmyra's isolation has spared it from the scourge of human over-fishing below water. But the vigilance of conservationists is necessary to keep it pristine. There are other atolls in the nearby Phoenix Islands that have been stripped of their sharks in a few weeks by roving pirate vessels that hunt without license or permit. They operate much as Fanning and his fellow sealers and whalers once did, roaming the oceans in search of places where money waits to be caught. The grand residences of Stonington and dozens of other New England ports were built with barrels of whale oil, seal pelts, and salt cod. Throughout much of the world today, however, fishing is no longer an occupation where fortunes can be made by law-abiding captains.

In just the last fifty to a hundred years, the brief span of a single human lifetime, people have spent much of the wealth of oceans, although the effects of overexploitation can be traced back much further in time. Today's generations have grown up surrounded by the seeming normality of coasts and seabed scarred by the rake of thousands of passes of the bottom trawl, and emptied of much of their riches.

Every year I take a student class to Grimsby, on the Lincolnshire coast of England, to sift the sand and mud of the foreshore for worms. This once mighty Victorian fishing port sits at the mouth of the Humber Estuary facing the North Sea. Its fish dock juts like a wedge into the mudflats, reclaimed by nineteenth-century engineers to service hundreds of fishing vessels. In its heyday, boats crammed the harbor, five or ten abreast, and the quayside thronged with fishers, auctioneers, merchants, and carriers. At dawn, great cod and halibut covered the fish market floor, so large they were sold individually. Today the dock stands almost empty, although Grimsby is still a center for trade in fish plucked from far distant waters, like those of Iceland, Africa, and even Pacific islands.

My class comes here to look at the effects of "coastal squeeze," where today's rising sea levels press shore life into a narrowing band against the stone buttresses of the dock. Scattered rocks and seaweed fronds punctuate the blank mud, among them twisted clumps of dead oyster shells smoothed by more than a century of tides. No living oysters grow in the Humber today. These polished shells are all that is left of reefs built by thousands of generations of oysters in the tide-swept channels of the estuary. Their fragmentary remains were torn from some reef in centuries past by dredgers who destroyed the animals' habitat as they fished. Over many decades, they wore away the reefs until at last only mud remained, and the hard bottom needed by oysters was gone.

This book is an account of the history of fishing and the effects it has had on the sea. In it I take the reader from the dawn of commercial sea fishing in eleventh-century Europe to the present in a voyage through time and around the world. The media today are full of shrill stories of the collapse or imminent destruction of fish stocks that have fed humanity for hundreds of years, if not longer. My aim is to show how we have arrived at this low point in our relationship with ocean life. In doing so, I concentrate on places for which the archaeological and historical record are sufficiently complete to understand the trajectory of changes to the sea and the sequence of events that caused them. I draw extensively on examples from the New World and Europe, as well as hitching rides on the global voyages of sealers, whalers, and modern high seas fishing fleets. But I could not find sufficient material on changes in Asian seas to write about them in detail and apologize to readers looking for insights into this region. Asian seas are in much the same poor state as those in places I do describe, and readers may surmise that similar processes have been operating.

In my work as a scientist, I find that few people really appreciate how far the oceans have been altered from their preexploitation state, even among professionals like fishery biologists or conservationists. A collective amnesia surrounds changes that happened more than a few decades ago, as hardly anyone reads old books or reports. People also place most trust in what they have seen for themselves, which often leads them to dismiss as far-fetched tales of giant fish or seas bursting with life from the distant, or even the recent, past. The worst part of these "shifting environmental baselines" is that we come to accept the degraded condition of the sea as normal. Those charged with looking after the oceans set themselves unambitious management targets that simply attempt to arrest declines, rather than rebuild to the richer and more productive states that existed in the past. If we are to break out of this spiral of diminishing returns and diminished expectations of the sea, then it is vital that we gain a clearer picture of how things have changed and what has been lost.

This book is not a requiem for the sea. As I describe in these pages, we still have time to reinvent the way we manage fisheries and protect life in the oceans. I am optimistic for the future. The creation of national and international networks of marine protected areas, together with some simple reforms in the way we fish, could reverse this run of misfortune. It will take concerted public pressure and political will to change attitudes that have become entrenched over hundreds of years. But if today's generations do not grasp this opportunity, tomorrow's may not get the chance because many of the species now in decline will have gone extinct.

We cannot return the oceans to some primordial condition absent of human influence. But it is in everyone's interest to recover some of the lost abundance of creatures in the sea. Fishers, seafood lovers, snorkelers, and scuba divers are obviously high on the list of beneficiaries, but everybody has a stake in healthy oceans. For generations, people have admired the denizens of the sea for their size, ferocity, strength, or beauty. But we are slowly realizing that marine animals and plants are not merely embellishments to be wondered at. They are essential to the health of the oceans and the well-being of human society. Diverse and intact marine ecosystems are more productive, healthier, and more resilient than degraded ones. Overfishing is an important contributor to many of the adverse changes that have happened to oceans and coasts in recent times—dead zones, toxic algal blooms, flesh-eating microbes, beaches covered with slime and jellyfish explosions, to name a few. Today, we are paying the price for over a hundred years of negligence in ocean conservation. We need to restore the abundance of sea life and give marine ecosystems a chance to repair themselves if the planet is to remain healthy.

This book has been five years in the making and I owe many debts of gratitude. Jeremy Jackson's work opened my eyes to how overfishing changed the oceans in the distant past and inspired me to write this book. His generosity with knowledge and sources gave me an excellent start. A Pew Fellowship from the Pew Charitable Trusts supported me in the early stages of writing and I am grateful to Cynthia Robinson for facilitating the project. The Ernst Mayr Library at Harvard University was an invaluable source of material for the book and I thank Steve Palumbi, E.O. Wilson, the Department of Organismic and Evolutionary Biology and the Hrdy Visiting Professorship in Conservation Biology for supporting my research at Harvard. Many Pew Fellows and others have helped me through discussions, suggestions, ideas, case studies, and advice, including Angel Alcala, Jeff Ardron, Peter Auster, Bill Ballantine, Nancy Baron, James Barrett, Chuck Birkeland, Jim Bohnsack, George Branch, Rodrigo Bustamante, Chris Davis, Paul Dayton, Sylvia Earle, Jim Estes, Fiona Gell, Kristina Gjerde, Richard Hoffmann, Jeff Hutchings, Dan Laffoley, Han Lindeboom, Jane Lubchenco, the late Ram Myers, Elliott Norse, Rupert Ormond, Richard Page, Daniel Pauly, Stuart Pimm, Peter Pope, Andrew Price, Alison Rieser, Murray Roberts, Garry Russ, Yvonne Sadovy, Andrea Saenz-Arroyo, Carl Safina, Bob Steneck, Greg Stone, Amanda Vincent, Les Watling, David Wilcove, Jon Witman, and Boris Worm.

Jonathan Cobb at Shearwater Books is the editor that authors often hope for but rarely find. I am deeply grateful to him for his interest and enthusiasm for this book, and for sharing his wealth of experience and coaxing more readable prose out of me. Thanks also to Emily Davis and others at Island Press for all their assistance through to publication.

Last and most importantly, I thank my wife Julie for endless discussions, reading of drafts, love, patience, and faith. Without her continuous encouragement, I might not have made it to the end. She put up with long stretches of writing, and equally long stretches where little seemed to be achieved except the amassing of ever more old books and much reading. She now suspects that I have an incurable passion for dusty, ancient tomes and will spend the rest of my life draining her bank account in pursuit of obscure texts. Fortunately, Google Books is sparing thousands like me the expense of owning old books themselves, and in the process is promoting marital harmony.

More information about the subjects covered in this book can be found at www.york.ac.uk/res/unnatural-history-of-the-sea.

# The

## ❀ UNNATURAL ❀

# HISTORY

## — of the —

# SEA

*Part One*

## EXPLORERS AND EXPLOITERS IN THE AGE OF PLENTY

# Chapter 1

# The End of Innocence

HE SWELL lifted Bering's ship from behind, propelling it into a wall of water ahead. When the boat surged free, a torrent of green and pearl sea poured from the bow, throwing spray over a lone figure who clung to the rigging. Above him, only the topsails were hoisted, their worn canvas threatening to tear off at any moment in the savage late October gale. Despite high winds and mountainous North Pacific seas, Georg Steller preferred conditions here on deck to those in his fetid, vermin-infested quarters below.

Steller's mood was as dark as the sea around him. It was late autumn 1741 and his journey with Captain Commander Vitus Bering's expedition to North America had begun five months earlier from the Kamchatka peninsula, extreme outpost of imperial Russia. The thirty-one-year-old German naturalist and doctor was in the service of the Russian Academy of Sciences and had embarked on this voyage of discovery with high hopes: as part of Bering's expedition he would help fill in one of the few remaining blank regions on the world map. The expedition had succeeded in finding the North American coast, but day after day of dreadful weather meant that instead of returning in glory, crew members were fighting for survival. Most were wracked by scurvy, Bering having ignored Steller's advice to collect plants to ward off the disease, and now almost daily, dead were being tossed over the side. "Our ship was like a piece of dead wood, with none to direct it; we had to drift hither and thither at the whim of the winds and waves," wrote First Officer Sven Waxell, who had assumed command from the sick Bering:

> When it came to a man's turn at the helm, he was dragged to it by two others of the invalids who were still able to walk a little, and set down at the wheel. There he had to sit and steer as well as he could, and when he could sit no more, he had to be replaced by another in no better case than he. . . . Being late in the year . . . the winds were violent, the nights long and dark, to say nothing of the snow, hail and rain. We did not know what obstacles might lie ahead of us, and so had to count with the possibility that any moment something might come to finish us off.[1]

By the dawn of the eighteenth century, two hundred years of European exploration had sketched out much of the world's coastline. But the North Pacific, stretching from eastern Russia and Japan to North America, and the Southern Ocean, the name given to the waters around Antarctica, remained unknown and thereby enticing to adventurers of the day. The North Pacific was particularly intriguing, for through it might lie a "northwest passage," a shortcut for trade between Europe and China. Many explorers had already searched for such a passage from the direction of Greenland, and in 1610 Henry Hudson had paid for the attempt with his life. But no one had attempted the journey from the west, so whether Asia and North America were separate or joined was still a matter of speculation. On a visit to Paris in 1717, Peter the Great of Russia was asked by French academicians for permission to explore the lands of east Asia. He refused, announcing that he would mount an expedition to settle the question himself, and in the process map the eastern boundaries of his empire.

Nearly 8,000 kilometers (5,000 miles) separate St. Petersburg from Kamchatka, and at that time most was trackless forest, mountain, and swamp. True to his word, Peter did mount expeditions to explore this vast expanse, and on his deathbed in 1725 he drafted orders for a sea expedition to determine whether Russia and North America were joined. His wife, Empress Catherine, saw his wish through, appointing Vitus Bering, a forty-four-year-old Dane and Russian naval officer, as the expedition's leader. After three years of preparation, Bering sailed initially from Kamchatka on July 14, 1728, but fearful of becoming icebound, he turned back soon after passing the Chukchi Peninsula, Asia's easternmost point, through what would become known as the Bering Strait. Catherine's successor, Empress Anna, agreed to sponsor a second Bering expedition, one that soon grew to far exceed the first in scope, portending in scale and ambition Russia's space program of the twentieth century. In fact, Bering had taken charge of what had become four distinct expeditions: one to explore the Arctic coast of Russia, a second to chart the Kamchatka peninsula, a third to sail south from Kamchatka to Japan, and the fourth, his own voyage to America.[2] It would take nine years and the efforts of three thousand people, many of them prisoners, just to equip the various voyages.

Steller was a late addition to the expedition to America, replacing a naturalist for whom the rigors of life on the eastern frontier had proven too much. A young, energetic, and enthusiastic man, Steller quickly befriended Bering. He had a burning passion for exploration and hoped that the expedition would make his own reputation as a naturalist.

On June 4, 1740, the *St. Peter,* under Bering's command, and the *St. Paul,* a sister ship that soon was separated in a storm, finally set sail in search of America. The strain of ten years of preparation already showed in Bering, who was now fifty-nine.[3]

Keeping well south of the latitudes of the Aleutian Islands, the *St. Peter* encountered no land for nearly a month. Steller paced the deck incessantly, scanning the horizon. On July 15, he saw a great mountain in the distance, but by the time he called others it had become shrouded in mist and he was dismissed for seeing apparitions. The next day the clouds lifted, revealing what is now Alaska.

The crew were jubilant, but Bering himself remained morose. The safety of the ship and its crew, he later told Steller, weighed heavily on him. They were far from home, provisions were short, and contrary winds might delay their return. But Steller could think only of the excitement of discovery. Offshore winds prevented a landing until July 20, and then only reluctantly did Bering allow Steller to join a shore party sent for water to Kayak Island. The exasperated Steller, denied more than a brief day on land, exclaimed, "We have come only to take American water to Asia!"[4] As a joke, Bering ordered trumpets to be sounded as Steller left the ship. But Steller, with the help of his Cossack servant, made the most of the trip, collecting specimens, hiking along the coast and into the forest where they discovered a cache of provisions and a fireplace, hastily abandoned by Native Americans.

The next day, Bering rose early, came on deck, and gave the extraordinary order to weigh anchor for home, even before half the water barrels had been refilled. After a storm some weeks later drove the *St. Peter* back toward land, Bering, worried by the shallow sea near the islands, headed south, wasting many days of fair winds, according to Steller, that could instead have carried them west. Steller passed his time as best he could, making notes on the abundant life in these virgin seas:

> During the time we spent close by the land we constantly saw large numbers of fur seals, other seals, sea otters, sea lions, and porpoises. . . . Very often I saw whales, no longer singly, but in pairs, moving along with and behind each other . . . which gave me the idea this time was destined for their mating period.[5]

Toward the end of August, a violent storm impeded further progress. Water was running low, and men were falling ill from scurvy, Bering among them. On August 30, the ship dropped anchor off a group of islands where the crew buried the first of their number to die from scurvy. Steller was among the first ashore with the watering party. Finding a safe freshwater spring at a distance from the beach, he alerted the others, but, incredibly, both men and officers rejected his advice, preferring to fill the barrels with brackish water from a pool on the beach. Steller knew this could be a fatal decision and that bad water would probably intensify their scurvy, but there was little he could do. His request for a few men to assist in gathering herbs with which to fight the scurvy was likewise scorned, so he and his assistant, Plenisner, collected as many herbs as they could, which was only enough for themselves and the bedridden Bering. It was during this stopover of the *St. Peter* that the crew made their only contact with Native Americans. Steller was delighted to find people at last, and exchanged trinkets with them. But warning gunshots were fired when the natives attempted to detain two crewmen ashore, and the *St. Peter* sailed off in a hurry.

Starting in late September, storm after storm battered the ship, and sickness and death spread through the crew. It looked for a time as if Bering and his crew would perish and the tale of their discoveries never be told. Then, on November 5, they sighted land. According to Steller,

> How great and extraordinary was the joy of everyone over this sight is indescribable. The half-dead crawled out to see it. . . . The very sick Captain-Commander was himself not a little cheered.[6]

Many of the officers believed this was Kamchatka, but Steller, Bering, and some others were doubtful. They steered the ship for the only visible bay, dropping anchor by moonlight. But relief was short lived, for half an hour later heavy surf snapped first one anchor rope and then another. Miraculously, a huge wave lifted the boat over a reef that guarded the bay's mouth and into calm water beyond where they cast a final anchor. For the time being they were safe.

Having eaten herbs to protect them from scurvy, Steller and his Cossack servant were among the few able-bodied men left. The next day, they headed for shore to reconnoiter. Steller records,

> We were not yet on the beach when something struck us as strange, namely, some sea otters came from the shore toward us into the sea.[7]

To Steller this was odd because on Kamchatka, where they were hunted, otters were shy. The ones here had never encountered people, he concluded, which meant that it could not be Kamchatka. His opinion strengthened after Plenisner shot eight blue foxes, whose numbers, fatness, and lack of fear also greatly surprised him. What finally clinched the argument was their first encounter with sea cows, which Plenisner swore could not be found in Kamchatka. And so Steller realized they were stranded on an island, later named Bering Island, which turned out to be nearly 200 kilometers (125 miles) east of Kamchatka.

Their new island prison was mountainous and so barren it had not a single tree. Steep cliffs intersected by deep, narrow valleys fronted the east coast, where they landed. Apart from the bay where the *St. Peter* lay at anchor, high tide left much of the shoreline impassable and at low tide exposed 2 to 5 kilometers (1 to 3 miles) of rocky shelf. Steller remarked that it was a miracle they had survived, since attempting to land anywhere else on that coast would have destroyed the boat.

Steller and the few other able-bodied men began setting up camp. They knew the ship could not survive a major storm. Snow already capped the mountains, and winter was imminent. It was now that Steller's experiences with the native people of Kamchatka, the Kamchadals, proved invaluable. He organized shelter for the crew, copying the Kamchadals' sod-roofed, half-underground huts. This time the men accepted his advice, hollowing out crude dwellings amid the dunes and stretching canvas sails over them to keep out the weather. A hole at the center let out smoke.

While the huts were being dug, many survivors among the sick brought ashore lay in the open with little to protect them from wind and sleet. The dead and even some of the living, incapacitated by scurvy, were attacked and mutilated by blue foxes that descended on the camp. Of this dreadful time, Steller wrote,

> One screamed because he was cold, another from hunger and thirst, as the mouths of many were in such a wretched state from scurvy, that they could not eat anything on account of the great pain because the gums were swollen up like a sponge, brown-black and grown high over the teeth and covering them.[8]

Their immediate concern was survival, and hunting parties were organized to bring in meat, mainly ptarmigan and sea otter. With an urgency precipitated by the coming winter, Steller collected plants to treat the sick. Although there were more deaths, many began to recover over the following weeks, and by early December, scurvy lost its grip. There was nothing, however, that Steller could do for Bering, who lay immobile and half buried in the sand. When the men tried to dig him out, he remonstrated that the "deeper in the ground I lie, the warmer I am."[9] He died on December 8, as Steller recorded, "more from hunger, cold, thirst, vermin and grief than from a disease."[10] Of the seventy-eight men who embarked with Bering, only forty-six were left.

As winter set in, the land disappeared under deep snow. But food remained plentiful in the form of sea mammals. The naïve sea otters could still be approached and clubbed with ease. The otters, wrote Steller,

> at all seasons of the year, more, however, during the winter than in summer, leave the sea in order to sleep, rest, and play all sorts of games with each other . . . it is a beautiful and pleasing animal, cunning and amusing in its habits, and at the same time ingratiating and amorous. Seen when they are running, the gloss of their hair surpasses the blackest velvet.[11]

When the expedition first reached Bering Island, otters were abundant and encountered in groups of tens, sometimes up to a hundred. But with hunting their numbers soon thinned, and the remaining animals eventually became wary, forcing men to seek quarry farther afield, then to drag the carcasses home over difficult terrain. In November and December, they could catch otters 3 to 4 kilometers from the camp (2 miles), in January 6 to 8 kilometers (4 to 5 miles), in February 20 kilometers (12 miles), and in March and April they had to travel up to 40 kilometers away (25 miles).

Otters provided a steady food supply through winter, but their rich pelts also fueled a new disease to afflict the bored men—gambling. Steller was appalled by this development, as much for its decimation of their food supply as for what he saw as its immorality. Hundreds of otters were destroyed for the price of their pelts alone, their meat then being left for scavenging foxes. In fact, this decline in otter numbers threatened the men's chances of escaping the island. By good fortune the *St. Peter* had not been battered to pieces but driven ashore by a storm and grounded high on the beach. The expedition resolved to build a new ship out of the old when spring came, but as the snows melted, there was so little game left near the camp that the men had to spend much of their time on long hunting trips rather than helping with construction.

Other options at first appeared limited. Although sea lions, later named after Steller, were present around the island throughout the year, they were large and fierce, and the men feared to attack them. Fortunately, vast herds of fur seals arriving to breed in April and May provided an alternative food source. But because the seals gathered on the west shore of the island, their capture still required arduous treks over the mountains. It was at this time that the men turned their attention to an animal that had actually been nearby all winter—the sea cow. Steller's description of the sea cow remains one of the only eyewitness accounts, for the beast survived but a brief moment in time following its discovery.

> Along the whole shore of the island, especially where streams flow into the sea and all kinds of seaweed are most abundant, the sea cow . . . occurs at all seasons of the year in great numbers and in herds. . . . The largest of these animals are four to five fathoms long [~ 7 to 9 meters or 24 to 30 feet] and three and a half fathoms thick about the region of the navel where they are the thickest [~ 2.25 meters or 8 feet diameter].[12] Down to the navel it is comparable to a land animal; from there to the tail, a fish. The head of the skeleton is not in the least distinguishable from the head of a horse, but when it is still covered with skin and flesh, it somewhat resembles the buffalo's head, especially as concerns the lips. The eyes of this animal, without eyelids, are no larger than sheep's eyes. . . . The belly is plump and very expanded, and at all times so completely stuffed that at the slightest wound the entrails at once protrude with much hissing. Proportionately, it is like the belly of a frog. . . .
>
> Like cattle on land, these animals live in herds together in the sea, males and females usually going with one another, pushing the offspring before them all around the shore. These animals are busy with nothing but their food. The back and half the belly are constantly seen outside the water, and they munch along just like land animals with a slow, steady movement forward. With their feet they scrape the seaweed from the rocks, and they masticate incessantly. . . . When the tide recedes, they go from the shore into the sea, but with the rising tide they go back again to the beach, often so close that we could reach and hit them with poles. . . . They are not in the least afraid of human beings. When they want to rest on the water, they lie on their backs in a quiet spot near a cove and let themselves float slowly here and there.[13]

Initially, no one had attempted to kill the huge sea cows for food because easier game was readily available. But with growing scarcity near camp and the prospect of another winter on the island, necessity forced the men to attempt their capture. They fashioned a large iron hook and attached it to a long rope, which they rowed out to a grazing animal. The sea cow's thick hide was too tough to take the hook properly, however, and on more than one occasion the men lost both hook and rope as the animal fled to sea. Steller then recalled descriptions of the Greenland whalers, and, following their practice, the men made a harpoon fixed to the end of a long rope held on shore by forty men. Six men rowed the harpoon end quietly toward the animals, and as soon as a beast was struck the men on shore began to pull with all their strength to haul it to land. Meanwhile, the men in the boat thrust knives and bayonets

> into all parts of the body until, quite weak through the large quantities of blood gushing high like a fountain from its wounds, it was pulled ashore at high tide and made fast. . . . At long last, we found ourselves suddenly spared all the trouble about food and capable of continuing the construction of the new ship by doubling the workers.[14]

The sea cows, although docile, did not give up without a fight. Steller recounted,

> I could not observe indications of an admirable intellect . . . but they have indeed an extraordinary love for one another, which extends so far that when one of them was cut into, all the others were intent on rescuing it and keeping it from being pulled ashore by closing a circle around it. Others tried to overturn the yawl. Some placed themselves on the rope or tried to draw the harpoon out of its body, in which indeed they were successful several times. We also observed that a male two days in a row came to its dead female on the shore and enquired about its condition. Nevertheless, they remained constantly in one spot, no matter how many of them were wounded or killed.[15]

Perhaps by this time the men had spent too long eating ship's biscuits and their winter diet of sea mammals had grown dull, because to them the sea cow was a gastronomic epiphany. The normally restrained Steller lavished praise:

The fat of this animal is not oily or flabby but rather hard and glandular, snow-white, and, when it has been lying several days in the sun, as pleasantly yellow as the best Dutch butter. The boiled fat itself excels in sweetness and taste the best beef fat, is in colour and fluidity like fresh olive oil, in taste like sweet almond oil, and of exceptionally good smell and nourishment. We drank it by the cupful without feeling the slightest nausea. . . . The meat of the old animals is indistinguishable from beef and differs from the meat of all land and sea animals in the remarkable characteristic that even in the hottest summer months it keeps in the open air without becoming rancid for two whole weeks and even longer, despite its being so defiled by blowflies that it is covered with worms everywhere.[16]

The rest, as they say, is history. Steller and his companions completed the ship and escaped Bering Island on August 14, 1742, sighting Kamchatka just three days later. They carried with them seven hundred sea otter pelts but left behind much of Steller's painstakingly gathered scientific specimens for lack of space.

Word of newly discovered lands and their rich stocks of sea otters and seals proved irresistible, and hunting expeditions were quickly mounted. Only twelve years later, Stepan Krasheninnikov, Steller's assistant, described Bering Island as being

so well known to the Kamchatkoi inhabitants, that many go thither for the trade of sea beavers [sea otters] and other animals.[17]

Many hunters overwintered on the island, using the time to provision themselves with sea cows caught in the same way as did Bering's crew.[18]

That the sea cow herds that originally surrounded the island were huge can be gained from Steller's comment that they were so plentiful that their meat could abundantly supply all the people of Kamchatka. But such bounty would not last. In 1755, an engineer called Jakovlev visited Bering Island and the nearby Copper Island to prospect for ore. He was so struck by the speed of decline of sea cows that he petitioned, unsuccessfully, the Kamchatkan authorities to restrict their capture. Martin Sauer, writing in 1802 on Bering's expedition, said "the last sea cow was killed on Bering Island in 1768 and none has been seen since."[19]

Sadly, Steller shared the misfortunes of his sea cow. He remained in Kamchatka another three years, writing up his scientific observations and getting arrested twice for arguing against Russian oppression of the Kamchadal people. Although exonerated, he took to drinking and died of a fever in his sled on the long journey back to St. Petersburg in the winter of 1746. His grave was robbed, his body feasted on by stray dogs, and eventually the Tura River washed away all evidence of his burial. His legacy as a naturalist, however, endures to this day.

Today we know from archaeological excavations that Steller's sea cow once occurred from Japan to California. Bering Island was the last redoubt of the species, and its demise elsewhere was probably due to overexploitation by indigenous peoples and loss of the sea cow's kelp forest habitats, long before Bering's voyages. This habitat loss, as we will see, was an indirect effect of human hunting of sea otters.

To some, the disappearance of Steller's sea cow, like that of the dodo and the great auk, was an extinction waiting to happen. Their economic value, or value as food, combined with stupidity and defenselessness virtually guaranteed elimination, even by people with crude weapons. Steller's sea cow was certainly exceptional in the rate at which it succumbed to extinction. Where it was not alone, as I will show in the following pages, was in becoming depleted by people a surprisingly long time ago.

Many of us are familiar with the long history of human influence and impact on terrestrial wildlife and ecosystems. In New Zealand the human hand played a decisive role in the extinction of moas, a family of enormous flightless birds. All of the large marsupials disappeared from Australia soon after human colonization, as did huge animals like mammoths, mastodons, and saber-toothed cats that ranged across North America in Pleistocene times (the last 1.5 million years or so, ending 10,000 years ago at the close of the last ice age).

It is often thought that the impact of human activity on sea life is a modern phenomenon, a product of the last half century of pollution and industrial-scale fishing. In the following chapters, I reach much farther back in time—to the heady days of global exploration, piracy, and the pursuit of wealth—to show that people have had a far-reaching impact on marine life for centuries. In many places the oceans were transformed long before scientists first began writing papers on marine ecology, or people of today's generations first dipped their toes in the sea. The seas that we have blithely assumed to be natural and unsullied had in reality already been profoundly altered. Early accounts of ocean exploration give us a fresh view of the sea and today challenge us to rethink our entire approach to management and conservation of the marine realm. What they tell us is that we have reduced populations of sea animals by a far greater extent than imagined. The conservation targets that we have set ourselves—for rebuilding populations of fish and endangered species—are often woefully inadequate. Added to this, human activities have degraded marine habitats so thoroughly that they have undermined the productivity of fisheries and now compromise the ability of the seas to provide vital life support services to humanity. If future generations are to share the wealth of oceans that we and our predecessors have enjoyed, humanity must change its ways, and quickly, for time is short to reverse the declines.

# Chapter 2

# The Origins
# of Intensive Fishing

—— ✦ ——

LIGHT FLICKERED across wooden walls from an open fire that warmed the late March evening. Two oil lamps curled smoke into the dark roof space above. Six men were deep in conversation, between draughts of mead they talked of the metalwork business. The craftsmen of Coppergate in Yorvik, one of eleventh-century Britain's largest cities, were renowned for their workmanship, and drew traders from far afield. Two of the men this night were buyers from the continent. In celebration of their deal, a platter of fish had been specially prepared: bream, eel, and pike, much favored delicacies from local rivers and ponds, surrounded a centerpiece of something much more unusual—a great cod brought 120 kilometers (75 miles) by river from the North Sea. The men ate with relish, savoring the unfamiliar fish before casting the bones onto the dirt floor.

Nine centuries later, in the heart of twentieth-century York, an archaeologist crouches at the bottom of a deep pit. Brushing earth from a fragment of ancient bone he reveals a cod vertebra. From its size it must have come from a fish over a meter long (about 3 feet), a giant by today's standards. Archaeologists had been brought in to examine the Coppergate site after workmen digging the foundations for a shopping center unearthed remains of timber-framed buildings from the Viking era. Sifting through centuries of occupation, the archaeologists uncovered thousands of fish bones, including remnants from that eleventh-century meal. These bones and others like them, supplemented with diaries, occasional printed chronicles, and other evidence, over time give voice to the past's rhythms of everyday life. From them, we can chart changes in the importance of fish as a food source, our preferences for different species, how trade patterns developed, and the details of fish availability.

James Barrett a University of York archaeologist, and his colleague Alison Locker have, for example, compiled records of fish bones from 127 digs across England, including Coppergate, allowing them to trace patterns of fish consumption between AD 600 and 1600.[1] They made a remarkable discovery. Within the space of a few decades around 1050, there was a dramatic shift from people eating freshwater fish and fish that migrate between rivers and sea to their consumption of species that spend their entire lives in the sea. Fish resident in rivers and ponds, like pike, trout, tench, bream, and perch, together with migratory species like salmon, eel, smelt, and sea trout, dominated bone records from the seventh to the tenth centuries. But from the eleventh century onward they are supplanted by finds of herring, cod, and other cod-like fish such as whiting, haddock, and ling. A sea-fishing revolution had swept through England. Although records from continental Europe are less complete, they also suggest an abrupt rise in sea fishing more or less coincident with its emergence in England. Today's intensive sea fisheries have their origins in this shift a thousand years ago.

What made European fishers go to sea in such numbers ten centuries ago? The end of the first millennium was a period of extraordinary change in medieval Europe, and not just in fishing patterns. For several hundred years, populations had been growing rapidly as people developed mastery over their environments. Hacking into the forests, farmers ploughed land to grow more crops. The ensuing production of surplus grain and meat supported development of larger settlements that obtained their needs by trade in goods, services, and money. Within this emerging economy, workers began specializing in trades like fishing, metalwork, and tanning leather. At the political level, the feudal mosaic of warring clans and chieftains began to give way to more centralized political authority, as for example in tenth-century Britain, which was ruled by descendants of Alfred the Great.

Alongside these changes, Christianity had taken hold throughout most of northern Europe by the dawn of the second millennium. Fish had always been an important and desired source of protein, but Christian prohibitions against eating meat from quadrupeds on certain days fueled a growing demand for fish. Benedictine philosophy held that fish were less "fleshy" than other animals and so less likely to incite sexual passion. Some Christians, such as the Benedictine monks at Tegernsee Abbey in Bavaria, abstained from eating any meat except fish;[2] for most Christians, though, meat prohibitions were limited to Fridays and vigils for major feasts, such as the forty days of Lent. Depending on the brand of Christianity followed, the prohibitions totaled between 130 and 150 fish-eating days per year.

Fish was also a prestige food whose consumption was a mark of status. This was perhaps a distant legacy of Roman occupation. Roman noblemen would vie with each other to serve the most lavish fish banquets at incredible expense. Many kept ponds stocked with rare and desirable species, and the best fish would sell for their weight in silver. The cost to the Roman general Lucullus for holding a typical fish banquet in the Hall of Apollo in Rome was, for example, 50,000 drachmas (Greek coins equal to 48,000 pounds sterling[3] or ~ US$80,000 in today's money). The desirability of sea fish among the Roman elite supported a large commercial sea-fishing effort in the Mediterranean in classical antiquity, attested to by exquisite mosaics and frescos depicting tunny, octopus, scorpion fish, dolphin, bream, and a multitude of other species.

Sea fishing came much later to countries farther north, and it was some time before medieval Europeans gained a taste for marine life. Northern Europeans were not quite the extravagant epicures of imperial Rome, but they were still prepared to pay highly for good fish. While fishing for their own needs had long enabled many peasants to eat fish, by the eleventh and twelfth centuries they were also able to make some money by supplying fish for rich people's tables.[4]

Demand for fish ran high by the eleventh century, with people eating them for protein, through religious obligation, and for prestige. The development of urban markets meant that people soon began fishing for a living. Commerce in fish and the development of towns seem to have gone hand in hand: fish markets are among the earliest identifiable focal points of medieval towns. Barrett and Locker's archaeological evidence confirms that spread of the trade in fish to inland regions was principally to supply towns. By 1200, for example, a fast horse relay system delivered fish from the Norman coast to Paris, covering the 150 kilometers (94 miles) in six to nine hours. In inland rural areas, marine fish bones didn't show up until much later—in the case of cod, not until the fourteenth century.

But why was there a shift from freshwater fish to marine fish in the eleventh century? Several possibilities come readily to mind, including increased availability of marine fish, introduction of new fishing technology, and rising demand for freshwater fish outstripping supply. Abundance of cod and herring are closely tied to climatic conditions—might that have something to do with the shift? Both species thrive in cool, northerly waters and reach the southern limits of their distributions along the shores of the North Sea and the Baltic. The marine-fishing revolution occurred in England, however, at the height of what is now called the Medieval Warm Period, when Europe was basking in mild weather. Warmer conditions promote cod production in the far north but depress it in the southerly parts of the fish's range, the parts most accessible to early English fishers. Herring production was probably similarly reduced in these parts. So we can rule out the idea that an increased abundance of marine fish lured fishers to sea.

Some historians have suggested that the rise of sea fishing in medieval times coincided with the invention of drift nets, which hang like mesh walls from a line of floats to snag passing fish. While herring are susceptible to this gear, cod are not. In any case, drift netting had been used for hundreds of years prior to the eleventh century, so this could not have sparked the sudden sea-fishing revolution. There is evidence that the capacity of boats in northern Europe increased concurrently with the expansion of marine fishing, growing from approximately 18 tonnes* displacement around AD 1000 to 55 tonnes by 1025.[5] But

---

*A U.S. ton is equal to 1.016 metric tonnes. Because the two measurements are so close in size, only the metric measure is given.

this was probably a consequence of the expansion of sea fishing rather than its cause.

Perhaps the practice of sea fishing was imported before the eleventh century, paving the way for a sudden expansion in fishing effort? Between the ninth and the eleventh centuries the Vikings swept out of Scandinavia, bringing their maritime culture to Iceland, Britain, Ireland, and Normandy (Norse land). Scandinavia is in fact the one place in northern Europe where intensive sea fisheries can be traced back deeper in time, to the eighth and ninth centuries.[6] When the Vikings reached Britain and Normandy, they were already skilled sea fishers.

James Barrett has pieced together changes in fish exploitation and consumption in northern Scotland following the Viking invasion between AD 800 and 1050.[7] Iron Age sites dating from before about AD 800, had relatively few marine fish bones, and they mostly consisted of species like wrasse, bull-rout, and flatfish that could be caught from the shore. The Viking Age heralded the appearance of deeper-water fish—animals like large cod, torsk (tusk), ling, and

*Fishing for herring around 1550. Herring schools were reputed to be so dense in the Baltic that an axe thrust into their midst would remain upright. Source: Magnus, O. (1555)* Historia de Gentibus Septentrionalibus. Description of the Northern Peoples. *Volume III. Translated by P. Fisher and H. Higgens. Hakluyt Society, London, 1996.*

haddock—which would have been caught using hook and line from boats. In addition, rising numbers of fish bones in deposits indicate a steep increase in the intensity of fishing from the Iron Age into the Viking period; at the same time increased ratios of fish to animal bones reveal a shift toward a more maritime diet. These trends have been confirmed by analyses of the elemental composition of human remains, which show a growing marine chemical signature. From the eleventh century onward, the intensity of exploitation continued upward. Northern Scotland probably began exporting cod to other parts of Britain by the early 1300s.[8]

So Britain had the opportunity to turn to sea fishing in the eleventh century, but we still have to establish a motive. Demand for fish was certainly growing fast, but why was this not satisfied from traditional freshwater sources? According to historian Richard Hoffmann of York University in Toronto, Canada, supplies of freshwater fish faltered in this period through a combination of environmental change on land and overexploitation of species. Hoffmann has sifted through centuries of written records and archaeological evidence to build a detailed understanding of fishing in medieval Europe. His work provides a fascinating window into the changing conditions that led to those prevailing when the sea-fishing revolution occurred.

For the first centuries after the collapse of the Roman Empire about AD 400, there are few written records and little archaeological evidence from which to reconstruct events. We know that substantial areas of forest were cleared during the Bronze and Iron Ages prior to this era. When Caesar came to Britain in 55 BC, he described the population of southern England as "exceedingly large" and "the ground thickly covered with homesteads."[9] But by early medieval times, forests, scrub, and brushland once more covered huge tracts of Europe, isolating the scattered settlements and homesteads. Population growth stagnated, and then plague devastated Europe in the seventh century. From an estimated thirty-five million people in 200 BC, numbers fell to around eighteen million in AD 650.[10] Agricultural land contracted as people abandoned marginal lands—the hillsides, swamps, and forest edges. Extensive forest cover protects soil from erosion by absorbing rainfall and then releasing it slowly into watercourses. While forests were intact, rivers ran cool and clear, and their flows were relatively stable. The Gallo-Roman writer Ausonius wrote of the Moselle River in late fourth-century Gall as "bright as water in crystal goblets," and noted that his "vision, when it pierces this stream, finds the open secrets of the bottom."[11] At this time the main species that people fished for thrived in rivers with such conditions, particularly fishes that migrated between rivers and the sea. Throughout Europe runs of salmon, shad, and whitefish numbering hundreds of thousands of individuals would return to rivers to spawn. Vast numbers of eels moved in the opposite direction toward marine spawning grounds in the mid-Atlantic. Giant sturgeon migrated into estuaries and the lower courses of rivers to breed. In the first century, Pliny the Elder describes sturgeon from the River Padus as a fish that "sometimes reaches almost half a ton (450 kilograms) and is dragged from the water only by teams of oxen."[12] All of these species were targets for fishers, who caught them using nets, spears, basket traps, weirs (low dams built across rivers), and hook and line.

Rapid human population growth and the rise of agriculture toward the end of the first millennium had profound effects on freshwater life. Forest clearance and deep ploughing of farmland greatly increased soil erosion. The growth of settlements and their connecting tracks exposed more soil. Sediment cores taken from ponds, bogs, and estuaries show that rapid siltation occurred at this time. Ports used in Roman days became landlocked as mud was swept downstream, and formerly navigable rivers became clogged. By the eleventh century, silt had closed the Oude Rijn mouth of the Rhine in Holland, and deltas such as the Vistula in Poland expanded through additions of tens of millions of tons of upstream mud.[13]

With agricultural development came demand for power, and water mills were constructed along almost every watercourse. The spread of corn mills across the medieval landscape was explosive, according to Hoffmann, rising from perhaps 200 in England during the time of Alfred the Great (~ AD 880) to the 5,624 recorded in the Domesday Book of 1086. Similar trends were evident in continental Europe. On the Aube River in France, there were 14 mills in the eleventh century, 62 in the twelfth, and over 200 by the early thirteenth century.[14] Mill dams blocked waterways, creating bodies of slow-moving water within which silt could accumulate. Added to changes to freshwater

habitats brought about by land clearance, dams had a dramatic, dele-
terious impact on fish populations.

Migratory species like salmon require cool, clear, fast-running
waters and gravel streambeds in which to spawn. This kind of habitat
went into steep decline as a result of damming and siltation; furthermore, all migratory species suffer if their routes between sea and
spawning sites become blocked by dams and weirs. The fact that
weirs provided new sites where people could easily trap, net, and spear
migrating fish further contributed to freshwater fish decline. In this
respect, weirs were more numerous and effective in diminishing fish
populations than natural barriers like waterfalls had ever been in the
past.

An emerging crisis in freshwater fish supply is evident from the
written record of the medieval period. In 1210, the bishop of Trento in
Italy required milldams to be removed from the River Sarca at Arco
because they were blocking runs of fish from reaching Lake Garda. A
Scottish statute of 1214 required milldams to have an opening sufficient to allow salmon clear passage and for all barrier nets to be lifted
on Saturdays.[15]

The mention of barrier nets in the statute is significant. It marks an
intensification of fishing effort in rivers and estuaries as people moved
from subsistence use to providing a commercial supply. Barrier nets,
as their name implies, can be spectacularly effective in blocking the
passage of migrant fish. Set across the paths of fish moving up- or
downstream, they are periodically emptied and can prevent the passage of fish entirely if set across the full width of rivers. For example,
in Pinzgauer Zellersee, high in the Salzburg Alps, a settlement of
professional fishers grew up in the mid-1300s that was attracted by
the huge runs of whitefish. Each year the fishers paid the archbishop
twenty-seven thousand whitefish and eighteen lake trout for the right
to catch still more fish, which they would then sell. Such intensive
exploitation could not be sustained, however, and catches collapsed
after people had been fishing there for only a single generation.[16]

Falling stocks stimulated the first legal moves to tackle overfishing
even at this early date. In 1289, Philip IV of France banned the use
of a dozen different kinds of nets and barrier traps and imposed seasonal restrictions on two other methods of fishing. More than seven

centuries after it was made, his medieval proclamation has a familiar ring:

> Today each and every river and waterside of our realm, large and small, yields nothing due to the evil of the fishers and the devices of [their] contriving, and because the fish are prevented by them from growing to their proper condition, nor have the fish any value when caught by them, nor are they any good for human consumption, but rather bad, and further it happens that they are much more costly than they used to be, which results in no moderate loss to the rich and poor of our realm.[17]

Adding to the problems caused by dams and barrier nets, draining and reclamation of marshland could also have a devastating effect on migratory fish. Dikes constructed in the Rhine delta during the eleventh and twelfth centuries, for example, caused major losses of sturgeon.[18] Details of this collapse throughout Europe can be traced from numerous sources. For example, archaeological bone records show that sturgeon was once a key item in the European diet, but then its presence declined rapidly. Data from seventeen Baltic states show that sturgeon fell from being 70 percent of the fish eaten to just 10 percent between the eighth century and the twelfth/thirteenth centuries. The bone record also reveals a fall in the average size of sturgeon eaten in central Europe from the tenth century to the twelfth century. In thirteenth-century France and England, laws reserved all sturgeon for the monarch—and the British law remains in force today! By the fourteenth century, a recipe circulated in England explaining how to "make sturgeon" from veal, a convincing sign of the high regard still afforded to a nearly extinct food fish.[19]

That supplies of freshwater fish were dwindling can also be inferred from a second development that occurred soon after the beginning of the second millennium. The practice of culturing fish in ponds, known as aquaculture, was invented in France at that time and rapidly spread throughout Europe. Few people today realize the scale and importance of medieval freshwater aquaculture, Hoffmann suggests, because ponds were largely abandoned by the end of the Middle Ages. A possible reason: the availability of cheap supplies of marine fish supplanted the need for freshwater farming.[20] Aquaculture, as evidenced by the construction of fish ponds and their management in a multiyear stocking and harvesting cycle, emerged in eleventh-century France, and through the twelfth and thirteenth centuries a wave of pond building swept Europe. At the height of this building, ponds covered 25,000 hectares (62,000 acres) in upper Silesia and 40,000 hectares (99,000 acres) in central France. There were at the time twenty-two thousand ponds in upper Franconia and a further twenty-five thousand in Bohemia.[21]

Aquaculture ponds were created by damming streams and rivers. This process of converting long reaches of riverine habitat into lakes had the unintended side effect of rendering Europe's rivers even less able to support species of migratory fish. It blocked their access, increased water turbidity, and buried spawning habitats deep under mud. While ponds helped ensure stable supplies of fish to the elite who owned them, they could not compensate for the plummet in populations of migratory species such as salmon, trout, sturgeon, shad, whitefish, and lamprey that was caused by the transformation of Europe's waterways. This loss in productivity occurred despite the fact that species that favor warm, still, turbid waters actually thrived in the ponded and silted-up watercourses. Examples of such year-round resident species include bream, tench, roach, dace, pike, eel, and an exotic species introduced from the Danube basin in Eastern Europe to stock ponds, the carp.

Species that breed in freshwaters and then migrate to the sea support very productive fisheries because these fish benefit from the rich and far more extensive food sources available in the ocean. Although the amount of freshwater spawning habitat limits numbers of young entering the sea, when the survivors eventually return upriver to breed, their bodies have been fattened by ocean food. Few animals feed on these migrating fish, enabling even modest-sized rivers to support astonishing spawning runs containing hundreds of thousands of fish. In this way migratory fish transported bounty from the sea to the doorsteps of poor medieval peasants in inland Europe.

Europeans continued to transform their waterways from the thirteenth through the fifteenth centuries. The proliferation of dams was unrelenting as new industries hungry for power emerged, such as fulling cloth (beating and finishing it), metalworking, and paper manufacture. Diking and continued marshland reclamation in lower river reaches further restricted fish access and diminished estuarine spawning habitats. And to all of this, the rising human population poured into rivers an ever-growing quantity of sewage and toxic effluents from tanneries, textile dying works, and mines.

Deteriorating freshwaters, then, stimulated rapid growth in marine fishing well beyond the eleventh century. By the fourteenth and fifteenth centuries, cod, herring, and other marine fishes constituted 60 to 80 percent of fish bones in archaeological deposits.[22] The first people going to sea in boats found abundant fish for the taking. Dipping their hooks and nets into these virgin seas rewarded them with giants. Fish remains in Viking Age deposits from the north of Scotland are dominated by cod 80 to 120 centimeters long (32 to 48 inches), saithe (pollack) that reached 150 centimeters (5 feet), and ling of 180 centimeters (6 feet).[23] The enormous numbers of these animals at first more than satisfied local demands.

In the far north, fishers developed a method of drying cod in the freezing conditions of arctic Norway that greatly increased the durability of the product, opening up possibilities for long-distance trade. The bleak and mountainous Lofoten islands point like a skeletal finger into the North Atlantic above the Arctic Circle. Churning currents surge through narrow passes, and the islands are warmed by the Gulf Stream, keeping them free of ice all year round. (The Moskenstraumen whirlpool between two of the islands was immortalized by Edgar Allen Poe in *Descent into the Maelstrom*). The relative warmth of the sea here, together with the strong currents, fuel great plankton production. Every winter this attracts mighty shoals of cod from throughout the Arctic to spawn. In medieval times Lofoten fiords were packed with migrating cod, and early Norse inhabitants would seasonally abandon their farms to fish them. Cod would be gutted, beheaded, sliced open, and spread over rocks and on wooden racks to dry in the wind and frost. Treated this way, they lose 80 percent of their weight within a few months, becoming hard as wood and able to be kept for years. Stockfish, as the dried fish were called, was an ideal food for long-distance transport in medieval Europe.

Trade links between Scandinavia and the rest of Europe developed early, which accelerated the commerce in fish. The town of Bergen was founded in the eleventh century and quickly became the main trading center between north and south.[24] Northerners traded timber, hides, furs, walrus ivory, falcons, butter, and, of course, stockfish and cod liver oil. As the trade developed, there was a shift from domestic production of grain—never easy in the harsh Scandinavian climate—to production of fish and other commodities that could be exchanged for the necessities of life, and Norway became dependent on grain imports.

Trade relations between England and Norway in the twelfth century were particularly warm, which seems remarkable given the long history of Norwegian looting and plunder along the British coast. King Sverre of Norway made a speech in Bergen in 1186 that reveals the strength of trade ties at that time:

> We thank all Englishmen because they came here, those who brought wheat and honey, flour and cloth. And we further thank all those who have brought linen and flax, wax and kettles. And we also mention amicably those who have come here from the Orkney or Shetland or Faroe Islands or Iceland, and all those who have brought to this country such things as we cannot do without and are of use to this country. But the German men who have come here in great numbers and in great boats wish to take away butter and codfish and their export is of great ruin to the country. Instead of these they bring wine, which the people have begun to buy, both my men and men of the town and merchants. Much ill has resulted from such purchases, but no good. Owing to this, many have lost their lives, some their limbs, some are damaged for their entire life, others have suffered disgrace, have been wounded or beaten, and all this comes from too much drink. I owe these German merchants much ingratitude for their behaviour, and if they wish to retain their lives and property they had better leave at once.[25]

Such warnings not withstanding, trade prospered over the ensuing centuries. The kings of Norway conducted all trade through Bergen to maximize profit (and presumably to simplify taxation) and banned direct trade with northern ports, including Iceland, which had been under Norwegian control since 1262. By 1310, customs records suggest exports of stockfish from Norway were 3,000 to 4,000 tonnes per year, of which about half went to Britain,[26] and by 1368, stockfish made up 90 percent of the city's exports.[27] Fish processing in the

Lofotens and some other sites took place on an industrial scale. Olaus Magnus the Goth, a medieval cleric traveling in northern Sweden in the early 1500s, described one processing site:

> From the foot, then, of this crowned mountain there rises such a stench of fish hung up to dry that far out at sea sailors as they approach are aware of it flying out to meet them. As soon as they perceive that smell when struggling beneath the darkness of a storm, they realize it is necessary to preserve themselves and their cargo from impending shipwreck.[28]

We have no eyewitness accounts of the abundance of Lofoten cod from this time, but a mid-twentieth-century description gives the flavor of the extraordinary abundance of fish that gathered there and at other frontier sites of Europe:

> Spawning cod arrive in Lofoten waters in jam packed shoals often 150 feet (46 meters) thick. The short-lived Lofoten season accounts in normal years for 55 percent of Norway's catch of cod. . . . [The] cod average three to five feet in length [90–150 centimeters]. . . . So compact are cod shoals arriving in Vestfjorden that a dropped sounding lead may rest on the silvery mass.[29]

Cod fisheries flourished across the northern edges of medieval Europe and trade was brisk. However, during the thirteenth century, Britain's favored status with Norway came under threat from an emerging trade alliance among continental towns, known as the Hanseatic League.[30] Initially, the alliance was formed for mutual protection against pirates, but as it expanded to include about a hundred towns at its peak in the mid-fourteenth century, the league sought to monopolize northern European trade. Eventually, British merchants were excluded by force from trading in Bergen in the late 1300s, effectively cutting off their access to cod from the lucrative Icelandic and Norwegian fishing grounds. By this time, many cities in Europe had grown so large that they had outstripped the capacity of local sources of food. Long-distance trade in grain, livestock, and fish were now essential.[31]

It is not certain when the English first switched from obtaining their fish by trade at northern frontier towns to catching it themselves. Deteriorating trade conditions must have been a strong stimulus.

Men from Blakeney and Cromer on the Norfolk coast are recorded fishing off Norway in 1383.[32] English boats are first reported fishing off Iceland in 1408, and by 1413 there were thirty boats involved. Iceland passed to Denmark in 1397, and Danish administrators complained in 1425 that the English were establishing whole settlements "building houses, putting up tents, digging ditches, working away, and making use of everything as if it was their own."[33]

But why did fishers travel so far and risk the fury of northern seas when there were supplies of fish of desirable species much closer to hand off the British coast? There is little doubt that what tempted them was a possibility of far greater profits than could be obtained from fishing locally. When virgin fish stocks are first exploited, they quickly yield their greatest bounty as the largest fish are caught. However, these initial catches often far exceed the long-term production that can be sustained once the accumulated biomass of old fish has been diminished. Indications from twentieth-century fisheries suggest that intensive fishing can remove 80 percent of the virgin stock in just fifteen years.[34] Medieval fisheries were much less intense than those of today, but they were clearly capable of fishing down local stocks. Frontier fisheries in pristine seas would have enticed medieval merchant adventurers and fishers just as gold and diamonds would later draw people to brave extremes of danger in Africa and the Americas.

The English were probably not welcomed by early fifteenth-century Icelanders when they began to fish in that region's waters.[35] They were accused of violence, murder, and looting, not to mention stealing fish. In the 1470s and 1480s the Hanseatic League began flexing its diplomatic and naval might to exclude the English from Icelandic cod fishing altogether. Armed fleets from Hamburg confronted naval vessels escorting the English fishing fleet and, according to Icelandic sources, clashed with them eight times between 1486 and 1532. History has a way of repeating itself. The cod wars of the 1960s and 1970s, when Iceland asserted its rights over domestic fisheries to exclude the European long-distance fleet, falls within recent memory. That the first cod war was fought off Iceland five hundred years earlier is less well known!

By the late fifteenth century many English merchants had grown wealthy from long-distance fishing and trading, but their exclusion from Iceland now forced them to look for new opportunities. In 1492, a Genoese navigator named Christopher Columbus turned the interests of Europe in a completely different direction. Following his lead, wealthy merchants from the port of Bristol in the west of England decided to hire someone to explore these new western horizons for commercial opportunities. They appointed Zuan Caboto, more often remembered as John Cabot, a citizen of Venice and resident of Bristol. Armed with a warrant from King Henry VII to seek new lands in his name, he set sail across the North Atlantic toward the setting sun in 1497. Europeans would discover an astonishing abundance of fish and other marine life in North America, triggering a transatlantic migration of fishers from across the continent to reap the newfound wealth. It shifted the north–south axis of medieval commerce in fish that had prevailed for four hundred years, to an east–west trade that would dominate in centuries to come.

## — *Chapter 3* —

# Newfound Lands

— ◆ —

*T*HE LATE FIFTEENTH century heralded the onset of Europe's global ocean exploration. Overland trade routes to India and China were already well established, and in 1488 Portuguese explorer Bartolomeu Dias rounded the Cape of Good Hope at the southern tip of Africa, establishing the possibility of a sea route to the Far East. By the end of the century, Portuguese navigators reached east Africa and India. Today, Columbus's 1492 voyage to the New World is generally regarded as the moment of birth for westward exploration. It surely is important, but rumors that the world must be round and that there was land to the west waiting to be discovered had been circulating for more than half a century before that voyage. Bristol merchants, for example, first probed the Atlantic in 1480 in search of an island they called Brasile. This continued into the early 1490s, by which time they were sending two or three ships west every year. Some scholars have concluded that these voyages must have discovered something, possibly Newfoundland, but because of a lack of firm evidence, the credit for this discovery still rests with John Cabot, whose reports would prove an important stimulus to the development of Atlantic fisheries.[1]

Bad weather, lack of provisions, and a dispute with the crew

doomed Cabot's attempt in 1496 to sail to the New World. Unde-
terred, the following May, he embarked with a company of only seventeen men in a ship called the *Matthew*. When Cabot stepped
ashore in the New World thirty-five days later, he claimed this new
country for King Henry VII. His point of landfall remains uncertain,
but it is often assumed to have been somewhere in Newfoundland.[2]

Cabot's logbook does not survive, but he evidently soon spread
word of the abundance of fish he encountered. Within a month of his
return, Raimondo de Soncino, the Milanese ambassador to England,
sent a report on what he had heard from the voyagers to the Duke of
Milan:

> They assert that the sea there is swarming with fish, which can be
> taken not only with the net, but in baskets let down with a stone, so
> that it sinks in the water. I have heard this Messer Zoane [Cabot] state
> so much. These same English, his companions, say that they could
> bring so many fish that this kingdom would have no further need of
> Iceland, from which place there comes a very great quantity of the fish
> called stockfish.[3]

Spurred by success, the following year John Cabot fitted out a larger
expedition of five ships to find a sea route to Cathay through the tropics. He and his crew disappeared without trace on the voyage, and so
it fell to his son Sebastian to continue exploring the newfound lands.
In 1508, Sebastian, probing for a northwest passage to the Far East,
sailed up the coast of Labrador and possibly reached Hudson Bay.
Like his father, he returned with extraordinary accounts of the wildlife and fish. Peter Martyr, a personal friend, later recalled the younger
Cabot's descriptions, including this one:

> Cabot himself called those lands the Baccallaos because in the adja-
> cent sea he found so great a quantity of a certain kind of great fish like
> tunnies, called baccallaos by the inhabitants, that at times they even
> stayed the passage of his ships.[4]

For some reason, the English were slow to take advantage of the
Newfoundland fisheries. Perhaps it was because the Bristol merchants' greater motive in the Cabot voyages was to seek a new trade
route to the Far East to replace the unreliable and expensive overland

route then used. Perhaps it was because there was nobody in New-foundland to trade goods with for fish, as the merchants did in Iceland. Whatever the British reasons, others in Europe were not so slow to appreciate the benefits of fishing these teeming waters. French, Portuguese, and Basque ships were among the first wave of exploiters, making commercial voyages to Canadian shores as early as 1504. By 1517, transatlantic travel had become almost routine, with some 50 ships crossing the ocean that year in pursuit of cod, and profit.[5] By the close of that century, their ranks had swelled to more than 150 a year.

By then, the English had caught on to the largesse to be had, and their vessels joined the annual race across the North Atlantic in pursuit of fish. Ships departed Europe between January and April, to return laden by late October. Initially, the men had little incentive to overwinter in Newfoundland, but growing competition for shore-based sites to dry fish eventually stimulated the English to found settlements and assert their claim to the land.[6] Cabot's extraordinary descriptions of the abundance of cod and other fish are difficult for us to believe today, except that other accounts corroborate them. John Mason, governor of one of the first colonies, at Cupid's Cove on the Avalon Peninsula of Newfoundland, wrote of his travels in 1620 in *A Brief Discourse of the New-Found-Land*:

> But of all [the land and wildlife], the most admirable is the Sea, so diversified with severall sorts of Fishes abounding therein, the consideration of which is readie to swallow up and drowne my senses not being able to comprehend or expresse the riches thereof. For could one acre thereof be inclosed with the Creatures therein in the moneths of June, Julie, and August, it would exceed one thousand acres of the best Pasture with the stocke thereon which we have in *England*. . . . June hath Capline, a fish much resembling Smeltes in forme and eating, and such aboundance dry on Shoare as to lade Carts, in some partes pretty store of Salmond, and Cods so thicke by the shoare that we heardlie have been able to row a Boate through them, I have killed of them with a Pike; Of these, three men to Sea in a Boate with some on Shoare to dresse and dry them in 30. dayes will kill commonlie betwixt 25. and thirty thousand, worth with the Oyle arising from them 100 or 120. pound [£12,800 to £15,300 sterling or US$21,300 to $25,400 in today's money[7]].[8]

Mason wrote his discourse in part to encourage settlement, and his descriptions had a propagandist tone. Nevertheless, many others with less incentive to exaggerate offered similar accounts.[9] English interests concentrated on the shore fishery and they dried their fish on land much as Norwegians and Icelanders had done for centuries. Fishers from southern Europe, however, who had plentiful supplies of salt, were able to remain at sea full time by salting fish down in the hold as they caught them. This gave them access to the riches of the Grand Banks.

> What is called the great bank of Newfoundland, is properly a mountain, hid under water, about six hundred French leagues from the western side of that kingdom . . . you find on it a prodigious quantity of shell-fish, with several other sorts of fishes of all sizes, most part of which serve for the common nourishment of the cod, the number of which seems to equal that of the grains of sand which cover this bank. For more than two centuries since, there have been loaded with them from two to three hundred ships annually, notwithstanding the diminution is not perceivable. . . . These . . . are true mines, which are the more valuable, and require much less expence than those of Peru and Mexico.[10]

So wrote Pierre de Charlevoix in 1719, a French priest traveling undercover for King Louis XIV to reconnoiter routes to the west through North America. The comparison of cod fishing with the mines of Spanish America is telling, because silver mining was by this time well established and highly lucrative. Discovered in the mid-sixteenth century, throughout the seventeenth century the silver mines of Potosí in Bolivia and Zacatecas and Guanajuato in New Spain (Mexico) supplied bullion carried twice yearly between the New World and Europe by armadas numbering tens and sometimes up to a hundred ships. By comparison, the consumption of Newfoundland cod by Spain and Portugal alone came to some 300,000 quintals per year in the mid-eighteenth century, equivalent to 30,000 tonnes of fish. One French port, Granville, fitted out more than four thousand ships for the Newfoundland fishery between 1722 and 1792.[11] The throngs of cod on the banks and shores of the New World seemed inexhaustible.[12]

Early accounts of the abundance of fish and wildlife offer us a

*Hook-and-line fishing for cod on the Grand Banks of Canada in the nineteenth cen-tury. Early fishers used smaller vessels and fished from the deck of the boat using drop-lines with several baited hooks. Dories—small rowing boats that worked away from the main boat—and longlines were a nineteenth-century introduction to increase fishing power. Source: Whymper, F. (1883)* The Fisheries of the World. An Illustrated and Descriptive Record of the International Fisheries Exhibition, 1883. *Cassell and Company Ltd., London.*

window to the past that helps reveal the magnitude of subsequent declines. They provide us with benchmarks against which we can compare the condition of today's seas. Such benchmarks are valuable in countering the phenomenon of shifting environmental baselines, whereby each generation comes to view the environment into which it was born as natural, or normal. Shifting environmental baselines cause a collective societal amnesia in which gradual deterioration of the environment and depletion of wildlife populations pass almost unnoticed. Our expectations diminish with time, and with them goes our will to do something about the losses. Seeing the world through the eyes of early travelers helps us to better understand our own environment and gives us the impetus to find better ways to protect it.

At the beginning of the seventeenth century, expeditions were mounted to explore the coasts and lands south of Newfoundland to the northern limit of Spanish colonization, then located around today's border between South Carolina and North Carolina. Commercial interests were first on the scene with a succession of voyages in the early 1600s to search for fish and other economic opportunities. New England, as the northern part of this region came to be known, was a revelation, rich in wildlife and timber.

Captain Bartholomew Gosnold, an Englishman, was one of the first to explore New England. He made land somewhere off the coast of Maine in May 1602 before turning south to discover a great hook of land. Gabriel Archer, who sailed with Gosnold, wrote,

> Neere this Cape we came to anchor in fifteene fadome, where wee tooke great store of Cod-fish, for which we altered the name [from Shole-Hope], and called it Cape Cod.[13]

In pushing back the frontiers of the known world, these sailors once again found seas that had seen little exploitation. Native Americans caught fish and shellfish in nearshore areas. Their boats, made of birch bark and crewed by seven or eight men, could travel only short distances. But because there was so much fish near shore, the local people had no need to fish in deeper water farther from land.

The first descriptions of New England fish stocks recalled those of Newfoundland in their magnitude a century before. John Brereton, who also sailed with Gosnold, reported that

> in five or six houres . . . [the fishing party] . . . had pestered our ship so with Cod fish, that we threw numbers of them over-board again: and surely, I am persuaded that in the moneths of March, April, and May, there is upon this coast, better fishing, and in as great plenty, as in Newfound-land: for the sculles of Mackerell, herrings, Cod, and other fish, that we dayly saw as we went and came from the shore, were woonderfull; and besides, the places where we tooke these Cods (and might in a few daies have laden our ship) were in but seven faddome water, and within less than a league of the shore: where, in Newfound-land they fish in fortie or fiftie fadome water, and farre off.[14]

If Brereton was impressed by the ease of fishing off New England compared with that around Newfoundland, he was also struck by the greater size of the animals: "Fish, namely Cods, which as we encline more unto the South, are more large and vendible for England and

France, than the Newland fish."[15] Others made similar remarks. James Rosier, who described the New England cod as "so much greater [than from Newfoundland], better fed, and abundant with traine [oil]," penned this description in 1605:

> Thomas King boatswaine, presently cast out a hooke, and before he judged it at ground [i.e., touched bottom], was fished and haled up an exceeding great and well fed cod: then there were cast out 3 or 4 more, and the fish was so plentifull and so great, as when our Captaine would have set saile, we all desired him to suffer them to take fish a while, because we were so delighted to see them catch so great fish, so fast as the hooke came downe: some with playing with the hooke they tooke by the back, and one of the Mates with two hookes at a lead at five draughts together haled up tenne fishes; all were generally very great, some they measured to be five foot long, and three foot about.[16]

And of the fishing near Sable Island off the coast of Nova Scotia in 1607, Robert Davies wrote that "hear wee fysht three howers & tooke near to hundred of Codes very great & large fyshe bigger & larger fyshe then that which coms from the bancke of the new Foundland."[17]

By the time of these voyages, Newfoundland cod had been intensively exploited for a hundred years, and fishing there had evidently already had an impact on fish numbers and size. Catching fish reduces their average life span. Since fish like cod continue growing throughout their life span, fishing therefore reduces the average size of individuals in a population. The Newfoundland fishery had driven down the average size of cod, and the relatively unexploited stocks in New England became a reminder of the past.

Speculators from Britain in search of profits sponsored exploration of New England. Their unabashedly commercial purpose is obvious from the things that attracted the adventurers' attention: tall, straight pine and fir trees for ships' masts, rosin, and pitch; cypress for turpentine; game animals and birds to support settlement; timber, fish, and furs for export. There were commodities aplenty in this new land, and speculators piled money into colonization. Today, what people most often associate with the early settlement of the New World is the arrival of Catholics, Puritans, and Quakers seeking to escape religious persecution in Europe. In reality, most colonies were founded as commercial ventures, and investors expected them to pay for themselves and to deliver healthy profits.

New England was far from wild and empty. The coast and lands beyond were quite densely populated by Native Americans with whom contact and trade was soon established. The notion of noble savages in balance with their environment has often been discredited. However, the first Europeans to arrive in the New World had to support themselves from fish and game, both of which they found to be extremely plentiful, even close to Native American settlements. Martin Pring wrote in 1603 of the lands around Massachusetts Bay:

> The Beasts here are Stags [elk], fallow Deere in abundance, Beares, Wolves, Foxes, Lusernes [lynx], and (some say) Tygres [mountain lions], porcupines, and Dogges with sharp and long noses, with many other sorts of wild beasts, whose Cases [pelts] and Furres being hereafter purchased by exchange may yeeld no smal gaine to us.[18]

Notably, these lands had plenty of large predators, suggesting intact food webs and a light touch from hunting by Native Americans.[19] Early travelers certainly dined lavishly on this game, and their journals are full of descriptions of the gastronomic and medicinal qualities of local animals.[20] When colonists ran into trouble, it was often through inadequate hunting, fishing, or planting skills, coupled with a failure to appreciate seasonal patterns of animal abundance. For the well-prepared colonist, who had planned ahead properly, there was plenty to eat.[21] So much so, that many good food sources were largely ignored in favor of "better preferred" meat. William Wood, for example, a colonist in 1620s Massachusetts, mentioned the abundance of one icon of today's New England cuisine, the lobster:

> Lobsters be in plenty in most places, very large ones, some being twenty pound in weight [9 kilograms]. These are taken at a low water amongst the rocks. They are a very good fish, the small ones being the best; their plenty makes them little esteemed and seldom eaten. The Indians get many of them every day for to bait their hooks withal and to eat when they can get no bass.[22]

The sea, like the land, was a place where large predatory animals sported in profusion. In the eyes of European fishers, cod were undisputed rulers in the seas off eastern North America. But they were only one part of a remarkable ecosystem. Travelers stood in awe of seas that seethed with life. The meeting of the southward-flowing, cold, and nutrient-rich Labrador Current with the warm Gulf Stream, on the Grand Banks and off the coasts of Nova Scotia and New England, fueled immense plankton production (as well as producing the notorious fog). This plankton sustained vast schools of herring, capelin, sand lance, squid, and other forage animals that in turn were hunted by grand armadas of voracious cod. The engine of production ran through much of the year, supporting huge resident and migratory stocks of fish and marine mammals. John Brereton wrote of this abundance in the Gulf of Maine in 1602:

> Whales and Seales in great abundance. Oiles of them are rich commodities for England, whereof we now make Soape, besides many other uses. Item, Tunneys, Anchoves, Bonits, Salmons, Lobsters, Oisters having Pearle, and infinit other sorts of fish, which are more plentifull upon those Northwest [sic] coasts of America, than in any parts of the knowen world.[23]

A century later, in 1709, De Charlevoix was also struck by seas bursting with large, predatory animals:

> After leaving the great bank, you meet with several lesser ones, all of them equally abounding in fish, nor is the cod the only species found in those seas. And though you do not in fact meet with many Requiems [sharks], scarce any Giltheads [dolphins] and Bonettas [tuna] or those other fishes which require warmer seas, yet to make amends they abound with whales, blowers, sword-fish, porpusses, threshers [killer whales], with many others of less value.[24]

It is hard today for us to picture the marine life witnessed by the people who first ventured into these waters. So much has changed since then. Early travelers to New England found enormous herds of walrus breeding on Sable Island off the coast of Nova Scotia, for example. The white Beluga whale of the Arctic was then common as far south as Boston. Both also thrived in the Gulf of St. Lawrence along with many other species of marine mammals. Curious flightless birds called "Pengwinnes" were among the first sentinels heralding landfall to transatlantic sailors and were found from Labrador to the Carolinas.[25] The great auk, as this bird is more familiarly known, was an early victim of the European onslaught on North America's wildlife. Today, a few hundred Beluga whales remain in the Gulf of St. Lawrence,[26] but the walrus and great auks are long gone.

The same rich production that sustained seals, whales, swordfish, and porpoises supported astonishing numbers of seabirds. Jacques Cartier was a native of St. Malo in France and had been to Newfoundland to fish, returning to Canada in 1534 to explore the Gulf of St. Lawrence for the French king François I. On the outward leg of his voyage, he made straight for Funk Island off the Newfoundland coast, knowing that he could stock up on provisions there. He wrote of this visit that he and his shipmates

> came to the island called the Island of Birds, which lieth from the mainland 14 leagues. This island is so full of birds that all our ships might easily been freighted with them, and yet for the great number that there is, it would not seem that any were taken away.[27]

The birds breeding at the beginning of July when Cartier visited would have included arctic terns, Leach's storm petrels, puffins, razorbills, kittiwakes, common guillemots, Brünnich's and black guillemots, and of course, the great auk.[28] Pressing on into the Gulf of St. Lawrence, Cartier's expedition stopped off at another great bird colony in the Madeleine Islands to gather more great auks and gannets:

> [W]e went down to the lowest part of the least island where we killed about a thousand of those Godetz [gannets] and Apponatz [great auks]. We put into our boats so many of them as we pleased, for in less than one hour we might have filled thirty such boats with them.[29]

The remarkable birds of these islands also captivated De Charlevoix when he passed by in 1719:

> [B]esides the sea-gulls and the cormorants, which come thither from all the neighbouring lands, there are found a number of other fowl that cannot fly. What is wonderful, is, that in so prodigious a multitude of nests every one finds his own. We fired one cannon shot, which spread alarm over this feathered commonwealth, when there arose over the two islands a thick cloud of those fowl of at least two or three leagues in circuit . . . [a French league measured 4.45 kilometers or 2.8 miles].[30]

Seabirds were of great importance to early travelers, colonists, and cod fishers. Funk Island was well known to sixteenth-century fishers, who loaded up with thousands of seabird chicks at the beginning of their cod-fishing season. Hacked into quarters, the birds made excellent bait. Similarly, fishers and early colonists in Newfoundland loaded up with and then salted great auks to use for provisions. These birds were also pursued commercially for their feathers, which were used to stuff pillows and mattresses. After hunters had killed the birds, they plunged them into cauldrons of boiling water, which allowed the feathers to strip away easily. The plucked carcasses were then boiled to remove fat, which was used as lamp oil, and the bodies were used to fuel the fires.

Eggs of great auks and all varieties of seabird were also collected in vast numbers to feed the burgeoning colonies. That this bounty lasted so long in the face of relentless persecution is tribute to the extraordinary fecundity of these birds, and the immense wealth of marine life that supported them. But it could not last, and by the late eighteenth century the great auk was living on borrowed time. The last phases of hunting these birds on Funk Island off the Labrador coast[31] are described by the fur trapper Captain George Cartwright in a lively account of sixteen years that he spent in this region at the time of the American Revolution. In his book, Cartwright predicts that the great auk will become extinct, sixty-seven years before the last one was seen in 1852:

> Tuesday, 5th July, 1785: . . . A boat came in from Funk Island laden with birds, chiefly penguins. . . . Innumerable flocks of sea-fowl breed upon it every summer, which are of great service to the poor inhabitants of Fogo; who make voyages there to load with birds and eggs. When the water is smooth, they make their shallops fast to the shore, lay their gang-boards from the gunwale of the boat to the rocks, and then drive as many penguins on board, as she will hold; for the wings of these birds being remarkably short, they cannot fly. But it has been customary of late years, for several crews of men to live all the summer on that island, for the sole purpose of killing birds for the sake of their feathers, the destruction which they have made is incredible. If a stop is not soon put to that practice, the whole breed will be diminished to almost nothing, particularly the penguins: for this is now the only island they have left to breed upon; all the others lying so near to the shores of Newfoundland they are continually robbed.[32]

The great auk, like Steller's sea cow, could be viewed as an extinction just waiting to happen. That great auks could be made to walk the plank to their deaths is a poignant symbol of their inability to survive the press of humanity into their last strongholds. Like Steller's sea cow, great auks were once much more widespread, occurring from Florida and the Mediterranean to arctic Norway and Greenland. They appear to have been progressively eliminated throughout the Holocene, the ten thousand years since the end of the last ice age, probably by human hunting. Early travelers and settlers showed almost no sentimentality toward animals. They valued wildlife as simple commodities. On the rare occasion when a writer strays into making some observation about the beauty of a particular bird or mammal, the next line almost always reveals how to kill it, what it tastes like, and how many ailments it can cure! Concerns voiced about declines in animal numbers were raised only because fewer would be left to catch. So Cartwright's warning about the fate of the great auk went unheeded.

Early European colonists of North America were surrounded by abundant wildlife, and for hundreds of years, if one species declined, they could just switch to others. The sea was a source of seemingly endless wealth to them, and the rivers and estuaries of the New World were equally important to the prosperity of the new colonies. But even in these first European centuries in the New World, there were already signs—below the surface, so to speak—of how rapidly fish and wildlife populations, once of an abundance hard to imagine, could be depleted.

# Chapter 4

# More Fish than Water

WHEN THE EARLY European explorers and settlers first sailed deep into the New World's great estuaries and rivers to explore the hinterland, they were completely unprepared for what they found. The rivers they sailed from in Europe were by this time awash with human waste, choked with sediment, and, in their upper reaches, blocked by long chains of milldams and weirs. Not since the early Middle Ages had Europe's major rivers run cool and clear. By the late fifteenth and the sixteenth centuries, the days when shimmering columns of fish fought their way upstream to spawn were long forgotten. In the rivers and estuaries of the New World, Europeans rediscovered what they had lost at home.

Among the first travelers to comment on this were those to the Chesapeake Bay region, beginning with the settlers of the earliest lasting British colony in the New World, Jamestown, founded in 1607. The vast Chesapeake estuary drains over 165,000 square kilometers (64,000 square miles) of the eastern United States and is today bordered by the Virginias, Maryland, New York, Pennsylvania, Delaware, and Washington, D.C. It penetrates 300 kilometers (190 miles) inland and its labyrinthine islands and waterways include 18,500 kilometers of coast (11,500 miles).

The enterprising twenty-seven-year-old Captain John Smith and his companions located their colony of Jamestown along the James River one of the southern tributaries of the bay. Sailing up this river, they were captivated by its freshness and beauty and the fertility of the surrounding lands. "The river," Smith wrote, "is enriched with many goodly brookes, which are maintained by an infinit number of small rundles and pleasant springs that disperse themselves for best service, as do the veins of a mans body."[1]

Shortly after their arrival, the council of the colony wrote to their backers in Britain:

> wee are sett downe 80. miles within a River, for breadth, sweetnes of water, length navigable upp into the contry deep and bold Channell so stored with Sturgion and other sweete Fishe as no mans fortune hath ever possessed the like, And as wee think if more maie be wished in a River it wilbe founde, The soile [is] moste fruictfull, laden with good Oake, Ashe, wallnutt tree, Popler, Pine, sweete woodes, Cedar and others, yett without names that would yeald gummes pleasant as Franckumcense.[2]

To the new colonists, Chesapeake Bay seemed a vision of Eden.[3] First impressions were later confirmed by exploration of the rivers feeding the Chesapeake. The Potomac River, which runs through today's Washington, D.C., was explored in 1608 by Smith and a small party. Smith wrote,

> Patawomeke . . . is 6 or 7 miles in breadth [~ 10 kilometers]. It is navigable 140 miles [224 kilometers], & fed as the rest with many sweet rivers and springs, which fall from the bordering hils. These hils many of them are planted [by the Native Americans], and yeelde no lesse plenty and variety of fruit than the river exceedeth with abundance of fish.[4]

The James and the Potomac were not the only rivers that captivated Smith and his company. The Susquehanna River, the largest of the Chesapeake tributaries, feeding the northern reaches of the bay, inspired Smith to write, "Heaven and earth seemed never to have agreed better to frame a piece for man's commodious and delightful habitation."[5]

Like the rivers in early medieval Europe, those of the New World ran pure and clear through thickly wooded valleys and floodplains that protected the soil from erosion. This newfound clarity must have dazzled people of the seventeenth century used to rivers like the Thames whose refuse-thickened waters slopped London's bridges and embankments. No wonder, then, that they filled their journals with eulogies on crystal rivers and sweet springs. New World rivers shared another characteristic with those of early medieval Europe: they seemed almost overflowing with fish. Walter Russell and Anas Todkill accompanied Smith on his 1608 reconnaissance of the Chesapeake tributaries:

> Some Otters, Beavers, Martins, Luswarts [lynx], and sables we found, and in diverse places that abundance of fish lying so thicke with their heads above the water, as for want of nets (our barge driving amongst them) we attempted to capture them with a frying pan, but we found it a bad instrument to catch fish with. Neither better fish more plenty or variety had any of us ever seene, in any place swimming in the water, then in the bay of Chesapeack, but there not to be caught with frying pans.[6]

Later, sailing out of the Potomac into the bay, they grounded on one of the many oyster reefs as the tide ebbed:

> [W]e spied many fishes lurking amongst the weeds on the sands, our captaine sporting himself to catch them by nailing them to the ground with his sword, set us all a fishing in that manner, by this devise, we tooke more in an houre then we all could eat.[7]

Gabriel Archer, whom we met with off the coast of New England in his 1602 voyage, was also among the Jamestown colonists. He wrote back to England in 1607, describing the abundance of life in the river and estuary:

> The mayne river abounds with Sturgeon very large and excellent good: having at the mouth of every brook and in every creek both store of exceeding good fish of divers kindes, and in ye large soundes neere the sea are multitudes of fish, banks of oysters, and many great crabbs rather better in tast then ours, one able to suffice 4 men.[8]

Smith also described the great bounty of the Chesapeake in 1608:

Of fish we were best acquainted with Sturgeon, Grampus, Porpus, Seales, Stingraies, whose tailes are very dangerous. Brettes, mullets, white Salmonds, Trowts, Soles, Plaice, Herrings, Conyfish, Rockfish, Eeles, Lampreyes, Catfish, Cocles and Muscles.[9]

Significantly, Smith and other seventeenth-century writers name animals that are today extremely rare in the bay. Pilot or killer whales (grampus[10]) and other even larger whales were then regular visitors to the Chesapeake. A 54-foot whale (16.6 meters) was cornered and killed in the James River in 1746, for example. One of the earliest efforts to control pollution in the New World was a petition by the Council and Burgesses of Virginia to the Governor in 1698 "to issue a proclamation forbidding all persons whatsoever to strike or kill any whales within the bay of Chesapeake in the limits of Virginia." They argued further that pollution caused by rotting remains was poisoning fish and making the rivers "noisome and offensive."[11]

Porpoises too were widespread. Francis Louis Michel, a Swiss traveler visiting the Chesapeake in 1701, claimed that the porpoises were "so large that by their unusual leaps, especially when the weather changes, they make a great noise and often cause anxiety for the small boats or canoes. Especially do they endanger those that bathe."[12] And John Lawson, surveying the Carolinas in the early 1700s, reported that porpoises "are frequent, all over the Ocean and Rivers that are salt; nay, we even have a Fresh-Water Lake in the great Sound of North Carolina that has porpoises in it."[13]

Diamondback terrapins also bred prolifically in the Chesapeake and other bays and rivers and were esteemed as food. Hammerhead sharks were also present in the Chesapeake if the paintings of John White are to be believed. A companion of Sir Walter Raleigh and in the 1580s governor of Roanoke, the first English settlement in North America, White had ample opportunity to study the bay and its inhabitants and left many beautiful paintings of the flora and fauna, as well as of Native American inhabitants. Among the animals he painted was the alligator, also an inhabitant of estuaries as far north as North Carolina, stopping just short of the Chesapeake.[14] Like White, Lawson was also a keen observer of Native American life and customs:

These Dwellings are as hot as Stoves, where the Indians sleep and sweat all Night. The Floors thereof are never paved nor swept, so that they always have a loose Earth on them. . . . yet I never felt any ill, unsavoury Smell in their Cabins, whereas, should we live in our Houses, as they do, we should be poison'd with our own Nastiness; which confirms these Indians to be, as they really are, some of the sweetest People in the World.[15]

Among megafauna, sturgeon ranked at the time of colonization as one of the most impressive Chesapeake spectacles. At this time, they measured up to at least 18 feet long (5.5 meters) and weighed as much as 800 kilograms (1,800 pounds). Sturgeon had not been seen in large numbers in Europe since the end of the first millennium, and the New World gave seventeenth-century colonists an opportunity to taste the fish long since reserved by law for the monarchs of England and France. They relished the opportunity. In season, sturgeon migrated from the sea into estuaries and rivers in extraordinary numbers, and the early colonists at Jamestown had depended on them to survive a difficult early period when other foods were scarce. They also quickly became an important commodity, and barrels of pickled sturgeon and their caviar roe were among the first exports from the New World. As early as 1612, Thomas Dale, governor of the Jamestown colony, proclaimed that all sturgeon caught and caviar cured should be declared to him, on penalty for a first offence of the reprobate losing his ears, and for a second offence being condemned to a year in the galleys![16] A century and a half later, sturgeon fishing in the Potomac River was the subject of a striking comment by the English visitor Andrew Burnaby:

Sturgeon and shad are in such prodigious numbers that in one day within the space of two miles only, some gentlemen in canoes caught above six hundred of the former with hooks, which they let down to the bottom and drew up at a venture when they perceived them to rub against a fish; and of the latter above five thousand have been caught at one single haul of the seine.[17]

Sturgeon were abundant not only in the Chesapeake but throughout the rivers of eastern North America as far north as the St. Lawrence and the Great Lakes. Here was another echo of rivers in early med-

*A day's catch of sturgeon in the late nineteenth century on the Columbia River of Washington State, USA. Sturgeon fisheries developed later on the west coast than the east, but scenes like this would have been common around Chesapeake Bay and other eastern estuaries between the seventeenth and nineteenth centuries. Source: Contemporary postcard.*

ieval Europe. As Burnaby and many others made clear, species that migrated from the sea to spawn were prolific, stretching the capacity of some witnesses to believe what they saw. Most important among them were shad and alewife, relatives of the herring family. Come the spring, fabulous numbers of these fish poured into the rivers from the sea. In his natural history of Virginia, William Byrd II wrote of herring (alewife) in 1728:

> When they spawn, all streams and waters are completely filled with them, and one might believe, when he sees such terrible amounts of them, that there was as great a supply of herring as there is water. In a word, it is unbelievable, indeed, indescribable, as also incomprehensible, what quantity is found there. One must behold oneself.[18]

Shad and alewife fell easy prey to the nets, weirs, and traps of the settlers. George Washington caught them in vast numbers from the Potomac River at his Mount Vernon estate. Thousands of fish could be taken at a haul of the seine. Records from just one of Washington's fishing sites, Johnson's Ferry, for 1774 show 9,862 shad and 1,591,500 alewife taken.[19] This was but a drop in the bucket for the Potomac as a whole. By 1832 there were 158 fishing sites on this river, nearly eight thousand fishers, and 450 boats. They landed an estimated 22.5 million shad and 750 million alewife.[20] Other Chesapeake rivers also supported great fisheries and the amount of fish extracted yearly was staggering.

When George Washington chose the site for the U.S. capitol in 1790, his motivations went beyond simply finding a convenient place not far from home. He noted later that he was influenced by the "many fine Clearwater springs at ground level suitable for drinking, and the many fast flowing streams to power griste mills . . . and at the head of a river plentiful with fish the year round."[21]

Virginia was far from unique in having clear rivers and abundant fish. Estuaries and rivers all along the coast supported huge spawning runs of fish. In the New England colonies, sturgeon was joined by other species like striped bass and salmon. Of striped bass, one enthusiast wrote,

> The bass is one of the best fishes in the country, and though men are soon wearied with other fish, yet are they never with bass; it is a delicate, fine, fat, fast fish, having a bone in his head which contains a saucerful of marrow, sweet and good, pleasant to the palate and wholesome to the stomach. When there be great store of them we only eat the heads and salt up the bodies for winter, which exceeds ling or haberdine [cod]. Of these fishes some be three and some four foot long [90 to 120 centimeters], some bigger, some lesser. At some tides a man may catch a dozen or twenty of these in three hours.[22]

By the mid-seventeenth century, New England was already Britain's most successful experiment in overseas colonization. William Wood, the enthusiast of striped bass just quoted, spent four years living in the new colonies and in 1634 wrote an account called *New England's Prospect: A True, Lively, and Experimental Description . . .* addressed to would-be colonists and "the mind travelling reader." He took his readers on a whistle-stop tour of the Boston region, dropping in on many places well known today, such as Salem, Charlestown, Brookline, and Boston itself, listing the advantages of each. But

Wood's descriptions of the rivers and estuaries are so different from today's conditions as at first to seem scarcely believable. Page after page of his book is filled with matter-of-fact reports of numerous kinds of fish and shellfish that paint a picture of overwhelming fecundity and wealth.[23]

Wood leaves us in no doubt of how important the rivers and their fish, and particularly the migratory fish runs, were to early settlers. For example, describing the Charles River near Boston, he wrote,

> A mile and a half from [Watertown and Newton] is a fall of fresh waters which convey themselves into the ocean through the Charles River. A little below this fall of waters the inhabitants of Watertown have built a weir to catch fish, wherein they take great store of shads and alewives. In two tides they have gotten one hundred thousand of those fishes. This is no small benefit to the plantation. Ships of small burden may come up to these two towns, but the oyster banks do bar the bigger ships.[24]

The rivers of Massachusetts also impressed by their abundance of salmon, a fish long since scarce in much of Europe, and reserved there largely for the elite. It was in Maine and eastern Canada, though, that salmon reached the remarkable abundances that must have characterized the rivers of Europe in the early Middle Ages. Captain George Cartwright made repeated references in his diaries to the salmon of eighteenth-century Labrador—and to the scale of their slaughter by New World colonists.

> Monday, August 21st, 1775 [A] little higher, there is a most beautiful cataract, the perpendicular fall of which is about fourteen feet, with a deep pool underneath. It was so full of salmon, that a ball could not have been fired into the water without striking some of them. The shores were strewed with the remains of thousands of salmon which had been killed by the white-bears, many of them quite fresh; and scores of salmon were continually in the air, leaping at the fall; but none of them could rise half the height. The country all round is full of bear paths. . . .
>
> Sunday, July 18th, 1779 Fish were still in prodigious plenty; a new salmon house of ninety feet by twenty was built. . . . Only ten nets were put out at first, and in a few days the fish were in such abundance

that the people were obliged to take four of them [the nets] up again; and when they had taken up some of those yesterday, having neither salt nor casks to cure more fish, they were killing thirty five tierces, or seven hundred and fifty fish a day, and might have killed more with more nets. Six hundred and fifty-five fish were killed to-day. Clear fine weather.[25]

The bounty of New World rivers and estuaries provided reliable supplies for generations of colonists, helping them survive brutal winters, drought and periodic crop failure. Alewife and shad penetrated far upstream on their spawning runs—as far as the Blue Ridge Mountains in Virginia, 250 kilometers (150 miles) from the sea—bringing the abundance of the sea to settlers deep inland. These fish were often caught in such immense numbers that they were left to rot in heaps, especially during shortages of the salt needed for their preservation. The more enterprising settlers used surplus fish as fertilizer.[26]

So plentiful was fish that settlers could afford to be choosy about what they ate. Early New Englanders evidently thought little of halibut, according to William Wood:

> The halibut is not much unlike a plaice or turbot, some being two yards long and one wide and a foot thick; the plenty of better fish makes them of little esteem except the head and fins, which stewed or baked is very good. These halibuts be little set by while bass is in season. Thornback and skates is given to the dogs, being not counted worth the dressing in many places.[27]

Of the New World's bounty, one early eighteenth-century visitor remarked, "I have sat in the shade at the heads of the rivers angling and spent as much time taking the fish off the hook as in waiting for their taking it."[28] The situation could not last. It was all but inevitable that the problems that afflicted medieval Europe would reappear in the New World. As the colonies grew, demand for food and mill power increased. The land was cleared for crops and timber, clear waters grew turbid, and the rivers began to choke with silt. Milldams sprang up along every watercourse, fish weirs spanned every suitable bend and fall of the rivers, and run after run of spawning fish was blocked.

The story of the St. Jones River that runs into Delaware Bay, northern neighbor of the Chesapeake, typifies the problems residents experienced by the early nineteenth century. The problem wasn't just decline in fish numbers but access to fish. The tidal section of the St. Jones snaked 32 kilometers [~ 20 miles] upriver from the bay to the Delaware state capital of Dover. In the early 1800s, it was bordered by farms, like the one belonging to the irascible Judge Richard Cooper, a justice in the Delaware Supreme Court. In 1816, Cooper enraged his upstream neighbors by constructing a fish weir across the river to intercept migrating shad and alewife. By blocking the spawning runs, Cooper denied his neighbors access to fish, and they marched on his house to demand the weir's removal. Judge Cooper was ready for them, with a swivel gun he had mounted on the weir. Failing to get satisfaction, sixty-three people took their case to the legislature, petitioning to have the weir removed on the grounds that it left many of the "poorer classes destitute of meat."[29]

Fish weirs had been illegal on public land in Delaware since 1736, but Cooper's was on private land. Despite Cooper's legal connections, the court sided with his neighbors. In 1817, the court outlawed all weirs on the St. Jones River, demanding their immediate removal. This should have solved the problem, but times were hard. The country was recovering from the War of 1812 and a string of cool, wet summers had led to low crop yields. By 1819, over a hundred people petitioned the legislature, this time to legalize fish weirs. Many were the same signatories of the earlier petition to ban them! The petitioners noted that the St. Jones had become so muddy that fishers could not see the fish any more to catch them. Weirs, they contended, were the only practical way to catch fish. The legislature agreed, allowing weirs to be built once more—provided they conformed to specified size and spacing criteria. They also had to be removed once a year to allow currents to scour sediment from the river bottom.

The requirement for periodic weir removal was intended to tackle the growing problem of siltation. Weirs trapped sediment on both rising and falling tides. But the law was inadequate to the scale of the problem. By 1816, around two-thirds of forests had been cleared from the St. Jones watershed. The exposed soil was easily eroded, especially during storms. Fish weirs then greatly accelerated the transformation of the St. Jones from navigable channel to a maze of shallow sandbars, swamp- and scrub-smothered "cripple" land that could no longer be farmed. By 1824, the town of Dover was cut off from the mainstream by nearly 10 kilometers (6 miles) of unnavigable river. Suddenly, the issue shifted from being one of fishing rights to an urgent need to keep the river open to boat traffic. By 1830, weir fishing was abandoned, partly because of siltation but also because there were fewer and fewer fish to catch.

The St. Jones experience was repeated elsewhere. In the late nineteenth century, an old-timer from Virginia was asked about his earliest recollections of fishing, dating back to around 1800. Although he recalled an era of much greater abundance than prevailed in his old age, he said that old people in his youth spoke of more fish still than he had experienced: "The supposition was that the clearing of the country and consequent muddying of the streams had destroyed them."[30] Just as in medieval Europe, the habitats sought by fish that migrate from the sea to rivers—cool, clear, swift-running waters— were being replaced by slow, muddy watercourses, ponds, and lakes.

Fish declined in consequence river by river, spreading scarcity along the coast. As stocks dwindled, longer nets were set to intercept spawning runs, in some cases 4 or 5 miles (7 kilometers) across and stretched from bank to bank. They simply hastened the losses. Regulators woke up to the problems too late, repeatedly implementing legislation placing more and more stringent limits on net sizes and fishing sites. For example, the Delaware state legislature imposed a heavy tax on gill and seine nets set on the Delaware River in 1829, taxing them by length to keep their sizes down.[31] Farther north, the General Assembly of Connecticut passed a law in 1719 permitting town councils to prevent obstructions being constructed across rivers to preserve the fishing.[32] They passed a second law in 1735 requiring mill owners to construct fish passes around their dams and to keep the dams open during the alewife spawning season. But under pressure of declining fish catches and growing industrialization, the efforts of legislators lagged behind the declines, always falling a little short of giving the fish enough of a break that they could recover as their habitats changed for the worse. More notable, perhaps, than the eventual decline of fish spawning runs was that they should have lasted so long given the colonial onslaught. By the early nineteenth century, many runs had collapsed and others faltered. The industrializing economy of the eastern United States speeded up losses thereafter. Surveying the state of North American fisheries for the U.S. Treasury Department in the mid-nineteenth century, Lorenzo Sabine was clear as to where the blame lay for declines. Speaking of the New Brunswick salmon fisheries, as one example, he wrote,

> The loyalists and other early settlers found the salmon in almost every river and stream in the colony. At present it is never seen in some, is becoming scarce in most, and is of importance as an article of export in the St. John alone. . . . The catch at Salmon Falls, in the St. Croix [a river bordering New Brunswick and Maine], thirty years ago was two hundred a day, on the average, for three months in a year. . . . But such has been the decline that it is said only two hundred were taken during the entire year of 1850 by all who engaged in the business on the river. It is stated that the dams erected across the river have produced this change in the fishery, and facts appear to sustain this position. . . . In two or three streams of minor size, where no obstructions exist, and where the water is not muddy, the pursuit is still attended with some success and profit.[33,34]

As stocks of fish declined, fishers turned their attention to other marine species for sustenance and commerce. One such was the oyster. Travelers had remarked on oysters ever since the first arrivals in the New World. Probably what attracted their attention was the fact that oyster banks in estuaries and rivers were so extensive they posed hazards to navigation. John Lawson noted in the early eighteenth century that Native Americans added a small keel to their canoes "to preserve them from the Oyster-Banks, which are innumerable in the Creeks and Bays."[35] The Swiss traveler Michel was impressed by the size of the oyster population in the Chesapeake when visiting in 1701: "The abundance of oysters is incredible. There are whole banks of them so that ships must avoid them."[36] He and others also delighted in their gastronomic qualities: "They surpass those in England by far in size, indeed, they are four times as large. I often cut them in two, before I could put them in my mouth."[37] Lawson, too, enjoyed them: "Oysters, great and small, are found in almost every Creek and Gut of Salt-Water, and are very good and well-relish'd," he commented. "The large oysters are excellent, pickled." And of another shellfish species he remarked for different reasons:

> Man of Noses [steamer or long-neck clams] are a Shell-Fish commonly found amongst us. They are valued for increasing Vigour in Men, and making barren Women fruitful; but I think they have no need of that Fish; for the Women in Carolina are fruitful enough without their Helps.[38]

By the late nineteenth century, oyster fishing was in full swing. A casual observer looking at the estuaries of Europe and North America during the 1960s, prior to recent cleanup efforts, could be forgiven for thinking that it was pollution that destroyed the utopia described in medieval and early American writings. But habitat alteration and loss, combined with overfishing, long predated the worst impacts of pollution. In fact, as I will soon show, overfishing, particularly of oysters, increased the severity of later pollution problems. The bountiful Eden of rivers teeming with every kind of fish and shellfish could not long survive the European colonization of North America, and the rivers of the New World soon followed the course of those in the Old World.

# — *Chapter 5* —

# Plunder of the Caribbean

— — —

HE INDIAN facing them was evidently hostile. After three days' march into the jungle of the Panamanian Isthmus, William Dampier and his party were desperate to find a guide who could lead them to the Caribbean coast, and this man was not being cooperative. It was early May 1681, and they were on the run after a disastrous attempt to sack Arica, a Spanish settlement in today's Chile close to the border of Peru. Twenty-eight pirates had been killed, eighteen desperately wounded, and their three surgeons taken prisoner. The action brought to an end, for now, their campaign of buccaneering along the Pacific coasts of Spanish South and Central America. The Spanish were on high alert and the pirates anxious to find safer waters.

Dampier later recalled their confrontation in a book relating his exploits:

> All [of the Indian's] Discourse was in such an angry Tone, as plainly declared he was not our Friend. However, we were forced to make a Virtue of Necessity, and humour him, for it was neither the time nor place to be angry with the *Indians*; all our Lives lying in their Hand. . . . We were now at a great Loss, not knowing what Course to take, for we tempted him with Beads, Money, Hatchets, Matcheats, or Long Knives; but nothing would work on him, till one of our Men took a

sky-coloured Petticoat out of his Bag and put it on his Wife; who was so much pleased with the Present, that she immediately began to chatter to her Husband, and soon brought him into a better Humour.[1]

Dampier was an extraordinary man. Born in the west country of England around 1650, he was in the course of his colorful career a planter, logwood cutter, pirate, navigator, hydrographer, sea captain, diplomat, explorer, naturalist, writer, and relentless traveler. By the age of sixty, three years before his death, he had circumnavigated the globe three times. Dampier took great interest in every aspect of his surroundings and was an astute and accurate observer. He kept a detailed journal of his exploits and observations throughout even the most dangerous periods of his life, protecting it from river crossings and the ravages of tropical fungus and termites by sealing his notes in lengths of hollow bamboo plugged with wax. We owe to his diligence an invaluable window into the world of the late seventeenth century. Dampier's descriptions reveal much about the wealth of marine life at this time, especially of large animals like turtle, manatee, and jewfish that buccaneers relied on for food.

The Caribbean of the day swarmed with European settlers and adventurers, and Dampier was not the only chronicler of this lawless era. Other pirates and privateers published their memoirs in England as well, helping us to build a broad picture of the state of marine life at the time. Notable among them are John Esquemeling's *The Buccaneers of America*,[2] and Basil Ringrose's *The Dangerous Voyage and Bold Attempts of Captain Bartholomew Sharp, and Others; Performed Upon the Coasts of the South Sea*.[3] It seems strange to us today that piracy should have been looked upon so leniently that people could openly admit to it in print. Indeed, an infamous pirate of the day, Henry Morgan, was even knighted and in 1674 made deputy-governor of Jamaica. But at the time, piracy was seen as a means of harrying Spanish settlers in their New World colonies. It was tolerated or in times of war even given official approval, in which case buccaneers were referred to as privateers. When sanctioned by the Crown, vessels engaged in piracy were given Letters of Marque allowing them to attack enemy vessels and settlements at will and keep the spoils.

To understand why the Spanish were so hated, we must look back to the time soon after Christopher Columbus discovered the Caribbean. Spain acted immediately to secure advantage on its find. The Spanish monarchy pressured Pope Alexander VI, a Spaniard, to issue a series of papal bulls securing Spain's right to

> all islands and mainlands whatever, found or to be found . . . in sailing or travelling west and south, whether they be in regions occidental or meridional and oriental and of India.[4]

Portugal, another preeminent seafaring country at the time, quickly secured an agreement with Spain to divide the spoils. In 1494 they signed a treaty giving Spain the right to all lands west of a line of longitude approximately 1,700 kilometers (1,100 miles) west of the Cape Verde Islands, and Portugal all newly discovered lands to the east. Not surprisingly, other countries were outraged by these blanket claims, England, France, and Holland foremost among them. So Spanish and Portuguese colonial interests, and their monopolization of trade with their colonies, frustrated but also fueled the expansionist ambitions of others.

Spanish colonies quickly took root in Central and South America, principally Mexico and Peru, following energetic and brutal campaigns by the conquistadors. The primary aim of those colonies was to supply wealth to Spain, initially of plundered gold and silver. Then in the 1540s, rich silver mines were discovered in today's Mexico and Bolivia. The settlers also created vast cattle ranches and sugar plantations on their lands. People in the new colonies quickly developed huge purchasing power, and by the mid-sixteenth century a two-way trade had developed. Ships sailed from Spain laden with European goods of clothing, weapons, glass, wine, paper, and the like, and returned with bullion, cacao, cochineal, sugar, and tobacco. From 1550 to 1610, the number of ships sailing between Seville and the colonies averaged over sixty a year.

Given Spain's jealous guarding of trade with its colonies, the vast sums of money being shipped, and the perceived injustice of its territorial claims, it was hardly surprising that piracy and smuggling took root.

Dampier was among the first of a new breed of traveler. In England it was the dawn of an era of scientific enlightenment. The Royal Society had only recently been formed, in 1660, by the likes of chemist Robert Boyle and polymath Robert Hooke. They espoused as principles the search for truth and knowledge. Celebrated travelers from earlier times, like Sir John Mandeville, who made it at least as far east as China in the fourteenth century, wrote fantastical accounts of their experiences.[5] Dampier's style, by contrast, was to report things exactly as he saw them. He was a writer of rare ability, and the mix of exotic tropical environment with high adventure was irresistible to the reading public—his books were instant best sellers.

William Dampier's only portrait hangs in Britain's National Portrait Gallery, just off Trafalgar Square in London. From a dark corner, he surveys the unimposing room with a wry and knowing look, perhaps amused to find himself among such company. Beside him is the seventeenth-century beauty and socialite Venetia Stanley, who died at thirty-three after drinking viper wine in the hope of preserving her beauty, the wine a great success since she never grew old. Surrounding them are leading intellectuals of the day: Robert Boyle, Thomas Hobbes, John Bunyan, John Milton, William Harvey, and others. Dampier is an oddity here, his ruddy complexion that of an outdoor man of action in contrast to the pale faces of society beauties and indoor thinkers with whom he shares the walls. His coarse sailor's clothing and rough brown hair are very different to their elaborate ruffs, wigs, and togas.

By Dampier's time, two hundred years since Columbus's voyages, the West Indies had become thickly populated with European settlers and their African slaves. Larger colonies, like Jamaica, Porto Rico, Hispaniola, and Barbados each supported tens of thousands of white settlers and similar numbers of slaves. Mainland colonies were similarly populous. Over the same period there was a corresponding collapse in native populations, especially in the insular Caribbean. Persecution by the settlers played its role, but epidemic diseases brought from Europe had greater impact. Three hundred thousand natives are believed to have inhabited the Hispaniola Columbus discovered, for example, of whom only sixty thousand were alive in 1508. Forty years later, Oviedo, one of the first historians of the New World, estimated that there were as few as five hundred left.[6] The new colonies needed food, which they got by planting crops and introducing domestic animals. But they also obtained a significant amount from hunting and fishing. Freshwater fish and land game were in short supply, especially on the islands. There were few large game animals, and their populations were swiftly decimated by a combination of habitat modification and hunting by people and their introduced dogs. Hogs, goats, and cattle devastated island ecosystems, rooting up and stripping vegetation. For a supplement to agriculture, people turned to the sea for food.

With no settled abode, pirates and other mariners had always depended heavily on seafood. From time to time, pirates supplemented their diet with maize, flour, sugar, beef, and the like from trading vessels taken as "prizes" and shore raiding. Traders could buy supplies in ports of call. But plentiful seafood for free was taken for granted by sailors, as it had been for centuries. The pirates of Dampier's day recognized their inferiority compared to native peoples in the art of fishing and quickly co-opted them as crew members to help supply the ships. Dampier wrote in admiring terms of the Mosquito Indians of the Caribbean coast of Central America:

> [T]hey are very ingenious at throwing the Lance, Fisgig, Harpoon, or any manner of Dart, being bred to it from their Infancy; for the Children imitating their Parents, never go abroad without a Lance in their Hands, which they throw at any Object, till use hath made them masters of the art. . . . Their chiefest Employment in their own Country is to strike Fish, Turtle, or Manatee. . . . For this they are esteemed and coveted by all Privateers; for one or two of them in a Ship, will maintain 100 Men: So that when we careen our Ships, we choose commonly such Places where there is plenty of Turtle or Manatee for these *Moskito* men to strike.[7]

Until recent times, navigators were constantly "careening" their boats; in other words, scraping fouling organisms from the bottom. Careening involved taking boats into shallow water, or running them ashore if small enough. The crew would then use ropes attached to the masts to winch them sideways, one side at a time, to expose the bottom for cleaning. Careening also provided the opportunity to replace rotten or worm-infested wood. Sailors would have to careen every few months, but pirates careened almost monthly to reduce drag and maintain their boats in peak sailing condition. Speed was critical to success, in both pursuit and flight! Dampier had plenty of time to observe Mosquito Indian hunting techniques while his ship was laid up. They hunted with great skill from small canoes that seemed impossibly unstable, sometimes killing as many as two manatees a day, for days on end. The Mosquito Indians were not slaves to the pirates but respected and valued members of the crew.

Reading the accounts of Dampier and other pirates, it is obvious they had little trouble in supplying their needs from the sea. Turtle, monk seal, and manatee were abundant, especially if you knew where to look. There were great multitudes of manatees around the mainland coastal swamps of South and Central America, and many also around islands like Jamaica and Cuba. Caribbean manatees were greatly admired as food, as Steller and his companions would later relish their northern relative. Steller is known to have read Dampier's book. Turtles were scattered throughout the Caribbean and Gulf of Mexico, but gathered to breed in colossal numbers at rookeries dotted across the region. Those concentrations inevitably attracted hunters, setting the scene for what would become one of the great wildlife exterminations of colonial times.

The best places for hunting larger marine life were well known and much frequented by pirates. Dampier comments on two of the most famous places for turtle:

> The most remarkable Places that I did ever hear of their breeding, is at an Island in the *West-Indies* called *Caimanes,* and of the Isle *Ascension* in the *Western Ocean* [South Atlantic]: and when the breeding Time is past there are none remaining. Doubtless they swim some hundreds of Leagues to come to those two places.[8]

A later inhabitant of the Caribbean, Jamaican planter Edward Long was also impressed by the Caymans and their association with turtles. Writing of them in his *History of Jamaica*, he commented,

> The instinct which directs the turtle to find these islands, and to make this annual visitation with so much regularity, is truly wonderful. The greater part of them emigrate from the gulph of Honduras, at the distance of one hundred and fifty leagues, and, without the aid of chart, or compass, perform this tedious navigation with an accuracy superior to the best efforts of human skill; insomuch that it is affirmed, that vessels, which have lost their latitude in hazy weather, have steered entirely by the noise these creatures make in swimming, to attain the Caymana Isles.[9]

When the English captured Jamaica from the Spanish in 1655, they quickly appreciated the strategic significance of the Cayman Islands and their turtles. From then on, turtle hunting expeditions were mounted at regular intervals from Jamaica to supply meat for the garrisons stationed there and the wider populace. Turtles and manatees were also in high demand because, being marine animals, they could be considered fish and therefore eaten on holy fasting days when the meat of quadrupeds was forbidden.

Columbus originally named the Cayman Islands "Las Tortugas," on account of the turtles, when he discovered them on his fourth voyage in 1503. He appears to have concerned himself little with marine life and made only passing comments on terrestrial wildlife of the New World, though occasionally his evident appreciation of the beauty of the Caribbean creeps through. We must instead look to others for insight into the environment. The discovery of the Cayman Islands is recorded by Ferdinand Columbus, Christopher's son, who was with his father on the voyage, "[W]e were in sight of two very small and low islands, full of tortoises, as was all the sea about, insomuch that they looked like little rocks."[10] This description echoes that of the priest Andrés Bernáldez, who wrote an account of the second voyage. Coasting among the islands of the Jardin de la Reina in southern Cuba, Bernáldez reports that Columbus and his crew were stunned by the great abundance of turtles:

> [T]hroughout that voyage they saw that there were many turtles and very large. But in those 20 leagues, they saw very many more, for the sea was all thick with them, and they were of the very largest, so numerous that it seemed that the ships would run aground on them and were as if bathing in them. The Indians value them highly and regard them as very good to eat and as very healthy and savoury.[11]

Columbus did not land in the Cayman Islands, but Sir Francis Drake did, decades later, in 1585. Drake and others in his flotilla were struck not only by turtles:

> The 20. of Aprill we fell with two Ilands called Caimanes, where we refreshed our selves with many Allagartas and greate Turtoises, being very ugly and fearefull beasts to behold, but were made good meate to eate.[12]

*Green turtles were easiest to catch when females left the water to lay their eggs. Dozens or even hundreds could be caught in a night by a few men turning them onto their backs. Source: Whymper, F. (1883)* The Fisheries of the World. An Illustrated and Descriptive Record of the International Fisheries Exhibition, 1883. *Cassell and Company Ltd., London.*

Drake's account is corroborated in the descriptions of two others in the party, one of them aboard Martin Frobisher's ship, the *Primrose*. This unidentified author adds that they killed more than twenty "Alligatos," some of which "weare ten foote in lengthe."[13] There is a magnificent painting of the Isle des Caimanes in a sixteenth-century manuscript in New York's Pierpoint Morgan Library. In it, turtles and crocodiles swarm across the island and its beaches. The island is heavily wooded and at the time uninhabited. Dubbed the Drake Manuscript because of its reference to Drake and his landfalls, this painting and many others in the book are believed to be the work of two French Huguenots who sailed with Drake. Following Columbus, later visitors renamed Las Tortugas as Lagartos (another form of Allagartos), and finally the Caimanas around 1540, from the Carib word for crocodile.

By Dampier's time, the crocodiles were still there but in reduced numbers. Archives in the Cayman Islands indicate that crocodiles were present up to the 1840s, with sporting hunts for them a Sunday pastime. Today, they are extinct on the islands. Turtles, although sufficiently abundant to provide reliable meat, were also less common in Dampier's time than they had been at the time of Columbus. Indeed, so much had turtle numbers fallen that it was clear something had to be done to limit the slaughter. Colonial administrators in Bermuda were first to act, perhaps because in this isolated mid-Atlantic island, there were few other options for food, and the losses were felt more keenly than elsewhere. They passed an act in 1620, stating,

> In regard that much waste and abuse hath been offered and yet is by sundrye lewd and impudent psons inhabitinge within these islands who in their continuall goinges out to sea for fish doe upon all occasions, And at all tymes as they can meete with them, snatch and catch up indifferentlye all kinds of Tortoyses both yonge and old little and greate and soe kill carrye awaye and devoure them to the much decay of the breed of so excellent a fishe, the daylye skarringe of them from our shores and the danger of an utter distroyinge and losse of them.
>
> It is therefore enacted by the Authoritie of this present Assembly That from henceforward noe manner of pson or psons of what degree or condition soever he be inhabitinge or remayninge at any time wthin these Islands shall pseume to kill or cause to be killed in any Bay Sound

or Harbor or any other place out to Sea: being wthin five leagues round about of those Islands any young tortoises that are or shall not be Eighteen inches in the Breadth or Dyameter and that upon the penaltye for everye such offence of the ffforfeyture of fifteen pounds of Tobacco whereof the one half is to be bestowed in the publique uses and the other upon the informer.[14]

Jamaican authorities soon followed the Bermudan example. Edward Long, in his *History of Jamaica*, mentioned that in order to preserve the supply, a law had been passed in 1711 that stated "no person shall destroy any turtle eggs upon any island or quays belonging to Jamaica."[15]

The persecution of turtles for meat continued well into the twentieth century. Eating turtle is still permitted in a few Caribbean countries, despite the fact that all marine turtles are listed as endangered or critically endangered by the World Conservation Union. Today, there are an estimated two hundred thousand nesting female green turtles worldwide, and only about eight thousand nesting female hawksbill turtles left in the Caribbean.[16]

I first heard about the decimation of turtles in the Caribbean at a conference of coral reef scientists in Panama City in 1995. I was in a vast, darkened auditorium whose humid atmosphere was redolent with the smell of moldering carpet. At the podium stood a tall, lanky man in his fifties, his shock of curly red hair tied back in a ponytail. A reading light cast shadows upward over a deeply lined face. In sonorous tones, Jeremy Jackson unveiled his ideas about how Caribbean coral reefs had been transformed by hunting and fishing since Columbus first sighted them.[17] The stage from which he spoke seemed as huge as the auditorium, and for some reason the acetate projector was set in the middle, far from the podium. Jackson's talk was periodically interrupted as he changed acetates, each time pacing across the floor accompanied by the squeak of new shoes on tired floorboards. As the talk progressed, it began to seem like he was pacing out five centuries of ruin before me.

Jackson has done more than any other scientist to explore the history of human impacts on the sea. In his talk he tried to build a picture of the Caribbean as it was five hundred years ago. Just how many turtles were there when Columbus first hailed land in 1492? Jackson used two approaches to estimate numbers. In one he calculated how many turtles were hunted from the Cayman Islands, and in the second he asked how many turtles could be supported by the food available to them in the Caribbean. Eighteenth-century Jamaica when it was taken over by the British had no agricultural infrastructure and only about five thousand inhabitants.[18] Early on, the colony had to rely heavily on hunting turtles for provisions. By Dampier's time, the turtle fishery was at its peak, with forty sloops and up to 150 men employed catching and shipping turtles to Jamaica. Between 1688 and 1730, they killed around thirteen thousand turtles per year. Because they were caught while laying eggs, all were female. Using estimates of the sex ratio of turtles and assuming that only around 1 percent of the population was removed each year, Jackson calculates that the population using the Cayman Islands for nesting numbered 6.5 million. He then extrapolated to the rest of the Caribbean, assuming five additional turtle rookeries about the same size as the Cayman Islands, suggesting a total of 33 million to 39 million animals.

Jackson applied the second approach to green turtles, which feed on sea grass. Using estimates of the area of seagrass meadows and the production of grass, he came up with an even larger number. There would have been enough food for up to 660 million green turtles. Predators like sharks, groupers, and birds would have kept numbers below this, but the figure serves as an upper limit to the realm of possibility. More recent work by Jackson and his students suggests a figure between 50 million and 100 million turtles.[19] As Dampier noted, pirates sought out places to careen their boats where they could find ample food. A close reading of his books and those of many who came before and after, suggests that there were other important turtle rookeries that have since disappeared, raising the numbers from the earlier estimate.

As well as turtle and manatee, Caribbean waters abounded with fish in Dampier's time. Pirates constantly speak of success in fishing. At the Isle of Pines (now Isla de la Juventud), off the south coast of Cuba, Esquemeling describes a typical careening and provisioning stop. In the fishing they "were so successful as to take in six or seven hours as much fish as would abundantly suffice to feed a thousand persons."[20] This seems like flippant exaggeration today, but when

Columbus landed with his party of twelve hundred hungry men at a village on the coast of Espaniola, they were able to obtain plentiful fish from the Indians and by fishing themselves.[21] And, like Dampier, Esquemeling had expert help: "We had in our company some Indians from the cape of Gracias à Dios, who were very dexterous both in hunting and fishing."[22] Goliath groupers, huge mottled fish that reach 2 meters (80 inches) in length, were abundant and in Jamaica were a staple food for people in buccaneering days.[23]

Together with a group of colleagues, Jeremy Jackson would later repeat his analysis for other regions of the world, like the Gulf of Maine and Chesapeake Bay, finding a pattern common to all regions. Colonial expansion from Europe signaled the onset of a mass slaughter of marine megafauna that accelerated over the following centuries.

The great quantities of marine life encountered by early explorers and colonists of the Caribbean, like William Dampier, should not be construed to imply that native peoples had no impact on the sea. The Caribbean was settled by peoples from South America who island-hopped up through the Lesser and Greater Antilles beginning about 400 BC. Most of the region had been settled by AD 700, and by the time of European discovery, the islands were thickly populated.[24] Elizabeth Wing of the Florida Museum of Natural History has picked over native middens on islands throughout the Antilles.[25] Marine organisms dominate the deposits, suggesting that island peoples obtained most of their animal protein from the sea, much of it from coral reef fish. Wing found distinct patterns in the middens that reveal shifts in food availability that have the hallmarks of overexploitation. Archaeological remains from early phases of settlement are dominated by land crab fragments, for example, which over time are replaced by West Indian top shells. Easily caught and lacking significant refuges, crab populations declined as the human population grew. Likewise, the size of fish caught declines over time, and the evidence also indicates a shift from easily caught predatory fish in early phases of settlement to more herbivorous fish later on. Despite this evidence that fishing had affected some species in some places, natives of the Caribbean, like Native Americans to the north, still had large reservoirs of seafood on their doorsteps.

On his return to Spain, Columbus recalled breathing in the magic of this New World. Standing at the rail of his caravel on a sultry Caribbean evening as the water jogged and swashed the boat, he smelled the perfume of soil and flowers wafting on a land breeze from the island of Cuba. A dense blanket of trees swept from the sea up the mountainsides, fading from greens to blues with distance. Beneath the caravel, the shadowed forms of huge groupers slunk among reefs that rose like castles from the seagrass plain, their evening hunt revealed by the rush and turn of shimmering fish. As the evening deepened, the flash and wink of fireflies punctuated the shore and the nighttime chorus of the tropics drifted over the water. What, I wonder, did he think the future held for this place?

## — *Chapter 6* —

# The Age of
# Merchant Adventurers

⁓—⁓

T HE MORNING of January 31, 1709, was fresh with a stiff breeze from the southwest. Ahead, an island rose from the sea as the men sailed closer, its contour gradually resolving into the ragged skyline of Juan Fernández. At the helm was Woodes Rogers, captain on the flagship of a privateering voyage to plunder the Spanish colonies and their supply ships. Although other boats were fair game, their main quarry was the Manila galleon that sailed from Peru to the Philippines and back once a year laden with newly mined riches of the Spanish empire. But before they fell in with the Spanish, the flagship and its two companions needed to replenish their own supplies of food, wood, and water and give their sickening crews respite from scurvy. For people whose intentions were not entirely honorable, this island was perfect.

Juan Fernández is a speck of land, just 22 kilometers (14 miles) from end to end, one of a small group of islands in the South Pacific, 800 kilometers (500 miles) from the Chilean coast. Although well known to buccaneers, it was always hard to find, and a few days before landfall Rogers complained that not one chart agreed with another as to its location. But Rogers was in good hands, for with him was a regular visitor to the island—or at least as regular as anybody got in those days—his pilot, William Dampier. Dampier had visited in 1681 and 1684 and knew the island had all they needed. Juan Fernández was well stocked with goats, left there by a Spaniard of the same name who discovered the place in 1563 and lived there for a time. The waters were thick with fish,[1] and the island was also remarkable for its seals, as the sailors became aware when they came to anchor, the acrid stench and incessant clamor assaulting them from the shore.

The seals had impressed Dampier on his previous visits, and he mentioned them in his *New Voyage Round the World*:

> Seals swarm as thick about this Island, as if they had no other place in the World to live in; for there is not a Bay nor Rock that one can get ashore on, but is full of them. Here there are always thousands, I might say millions of them, either sitting on the bays, or going and coming in the sea round the island, which is covered with them (as they lie at the top of the water playing and sunning themselves) for a mile or two from the shore. . . . A blow on the nose soon kills them. Large ships might here load themselves with seal-skins, and Trane-oyl [oil extracted from blubber]; for they are extraordinary fat.[2]

Rogers was taken by the sheer spectacle of the seal herds, writing in his account of the voyage,

> When we came in, they kept a continual noise day and night, some bleating like Lambs, some howling like dogs or Wolves, others making hideous noises of various sorts; so that we heard 'em aboard, tho a mile from the Shore. Their fur is the finest that I ever saw of the kind, and exceeds that of our Otters.[3]

Although Rogers and Dampier were unaware of it, this was a species of fur seal found only at Juan Fernández, and later named *Arctocephalus philippii*. Rogers also commented on a second species that used the island to breed, the South American sea lion, an altogether more formidable beast.

> I saw several of these vast creatures . . . upward of 16 foot long [4.8 meters], and more in bulk, so that they could not weigh less than a Tun weight. The Shape of their Body differs little from the Sea-Dogs or Seals, but have another sort of Skin, a Head much bigger in proportion,

and very large Mouths, monstrous big Eyes, and a Face like that of a Lion, with very large Whiskers, the Hair of which is stiff enough to make Tooth-Pickers. . . . I admire how these Monsters come to yield such a quantity of Oil.[4]

Unknown to those aboard Rogers's ships, a man on shore watched the arrival of the privateers with growing excitement. Alexander Selkirk had spent the last four years and four months alone on the island, each passing day marked only by another notch cut into a tree at his camp. His captain had marooned him there after a disagreement, leaving him only a firelock, a pound of gunpowder, bullets, tobacco, a hatchet, a knife, a kettle, a bible, some mathematical instruments, and his books. A shore party picked up Selkirk the next day, and Rogers described him memorably as "a Man cloth'd in Goat-Skins, who look'd wilder than the first Owners of them."[5]

Selkirk had been master of the vessel that had marooned him, and Rogers immediately took him on as mate. He remained with them for the rest of the voyage. Selkirk was not the first to have been marooned on Juan Fernández, it turns out. On Dampier's first visit a Mosquito Indian who was out hunting was abandoned when the ship had to leave in haste. He was collected three years later on Dampier's next visit. Woodes Rogers's recollection of these incidents later inspired Daniel Defoe to write *Robinson Crusoe*, basing Crusoe on Selkirk, although Man Friday and Crusoe met only in the author's imagination.

Three and a half months later, after much adventuring along the coast of Spanish South America, the ships in Rogers's party rendezvoused in another favorite haunt of buccaneers, the Galápagos Islands, some 1,000 kilometers (625 miles) off the coast of Ecuador. By this time, seventeen of his party were dead, lost from illness or killed in clashes with the Spanish.[6] They badly needed to regroup and refresh their supplies. A scattered archipelago of thirteen large islands with many smaller islets and wave-swept rocks, the Galápagos were ideal for provisioning. Well, almost. They were remote enough from the mainland to escape the Spanish, and the seas around them thronged with fish, shellfish, and turtles. Moreover, they had the perfect convenience food for sailors in days before refrigeration—giant tortoises, for which the islands were named. What these equatorial islands lacked much of the time was easily accessible freshwater, and after a few weeks of recuperation and provisioning the ships were forced to sail for Gorgona, a wetter island close to mainland Colombia.

Generations of travelers to the eastern Pacific, including Dampier and his companions, were struck by the great profusion of sharks there. Sharks swarmed in the bays, followed boats, and frequently interrupted fishing by taking all the hooks. James Colnett, on a voyage to these seas prospecting for sperm whales in 1793, gave a typical accounting at a stop off the Colombian coast:

> At Rocka Partida was a prodigious quantity of fish, but we caught only a few, as the sharks destroyed our hooks and lines, and no one on board, but myself, had ever before seen them so ravenous. One of our men reaching over the gun-whale of the boat, a shark of eighteen or twenty feet in length, rose out of the water to seize his hand, a circumstance not uncommon at the Sandwich Isles [Hawaii], where I have seen a large shark take hold of an outrigger of a canoe, and endeavour to overset it. This was in some degree the case with our boat; a number of them continually seizing the steering oar, it became of no use, so that we were obliged to lay it in.[7]

Reports of sharks of this size are common in the literature of the time. An 18- to 20-foot (~ 6 meters) shark would be exceptional today and might appear easy to discount as exaggeration. But the men who reported them had the opportunity for close comparison between the length of their boats and the length of the sharks. Two years later, George Vancouver also commented on the abundance of sharks, "the most bold and voracious" he had ever seen:

> These assembled in the bay in very large shoals, constantly attending on our boats in all their motions. . . . The general warfare that exists between sea-faring persons and these voracious animals afforded at first a species of amusement to our people, by hooking, or otherways taking one for the others to feast upon, but as this was attended with the ill consequence of drawing immense numbers round the ship, and as the boatswain and one of the young gentlemen had nearly fallen a sacrifice to this diversion, by narrowly escaping being drawn out of the boat by an immensely large shark, which they had hooked, into the midst of at least a score of these voracious animals, I thought proper to

prohibit all further indulgence in this species of entertainment. . . . These sharks appeared to be of three distinct sorts; the most numerous were of the tyger kind, these were beautifully streaked down their sides; the other sorts were the brown and the blue sharks.[8]

Today, tiger sharks are scarce in most seas and rarely reach more than a few meters long. But occasional giants of 5 to 7 meters (17 to 23 feet) are recorded. Evidently, they were abundant in the little-fished waters of the eastern Pacific in the seventeenth and eighteenth centuries.

Rogers and his ships were back in the Galápagos a few months later after another interlude of plunder and six more men lost to fever, scurvy, and snakebite. His log gives enough detail of their provisioning efforts to allow an estimate of the number of turtles and tortoises taken. Tortoise, and to a lesser extent turtle, were ideal foods for seafarers. Giant tortoises are found only in the Galápagos and, at that time, a few remote islands in the Indian Ocean.[9] Galápagos tortoises possess the remarkably adaptive ability to survive for months without food or water, their bodies going into a state almost of suspended animation during the periodic droughts that afflict the islands. Sailors would corral tortoises on deck for a few days while they cleared their bowels, and then stack them on their backs below deck like so many barrels of food, slaughtering them as needed for months thereafter. Turtles fared less well. If taken from the beaches before laying their eggs, they would last only a matter of weeks before dying.[10] Over a period of several days, Rogers and his companion ships repeatedly sent their pinnaces (small sailing tenders) to shore to stock up with tortoises and turtles. In his log he tallies their success, noting that he had about 170 sea turtles and 55 tortoises, while another boat had approximately 135 sea turtles and 75 tortoises. This, he states, was as much as they could use before spoiling. A few weeks later, they added another 100 turtles from the Mexican mainland. Boats setting forth on long voyages typically carried large stocks of provisions, but they were unwholesome and substituted with fresh foods wherever possible.

Over centuries of seafaring, sailors must have eaten simply staggering quantities of seafood and game.[11] Explorers, buccaneers, colonists, and traders all took their toll on marine life, although their impacts were modest compared to what would come in the twentieth

*Sailors often amused themselves catching sharks. In past centuries, the numbers and sizes of sharks that swarmed around ships were much greater than today. Source: Figuier, L. (1891)* The Ocean World. *Cassell and Company, Ltd., London.*

century. However, hunters would soon launch a systematic onslaught against an animal that occurred farther north—the sea otter.

By 1776, when Captain James Cook set sail on his third voyage, the gap between Baja California and Alaska loomed large and enticing.[12] Cook did not sail direct for America, but headed first for the Pacific. For two years he surveyed northward from New Zealand, passing through Tonga, Tahiti, and Hawaii before finally setting course for the North American continent in early February 1778. He sighted land on March 7 somewhere on the Oregon coast. Bad weather prevented Cook from landing, and he worked his way north, missing the Strait of Juan de Fuca and passing up the west coast of Vancouver Island. On March 29, the *Resolution* and *Discovery* entered Nootka Sound and were greeted by a large and friendly group of people in canoes, eager to trade. Cook later discovered from some Spanish silver spoons traded to him, that a Spanish explorer, Juan Pérez, had been there four years earlier. But it was Cook's voyage that was to have the most lasting impact, for word of his discoveries soon began a process of rapid exploration, exploitation, and settlement of the northwest coast. Cook wrote in his journal of trade with the native people:

> A great many Canoes filled with the Natives were about the Ships all day, and a trade commenced betwixt us and them, which was carried on with the Strictest honisty on boath sides. Their articles were the skins of various animals, such as Bears, Wolfs, Foxes, Dear, Rackoons, Polecats, Martins and in particular the Sea Beaver, the same as is found on the coast of Kamchatka.[13]

The sea beaver was the same sea otter that had so captivated Steller during his 1741–1742 sojourn on Bering Island and that brought on many of his companions the lust for furs. Trade on Cook's vessels was brisk: an American traveling with him later estimated that they left Nootka with around fifteen hundred sea otter pelts.[14] At the time, Cook was unaware of the value attached to these skins, but they had long been cherished in the East, especially in China, where mandarins wore robes trimmed with otter fur. Steller notes that so valuable were the furs seen to be that some of the sailors from their shipwrecked crew suggested spending another winter on Bering Island in order to catch more otters![15] Cook's expedition headed north to Alaska, eventually entering the Arctic Ocean through the Bering Strait. During this time, they contacted Russian hunters and fur traders, the northern legacy of Bering's expedition. This encouraged the crew to think of trading their skins, and they sold around a third of them to a Russian trader at a relatively modest price. They would later regret their haste to sell, because on the voyage homeward, the ships stopped at Canton. There they disposed of the pelts for the fabulous sums of fifty to one hundred dollars each, one fine specimen even fetching three hundred dollars.[16] When word got out, initially by word of mouth and then in Cook's posthumous account of the voyage,[17] the sea otter gold rush expanded quickly along the west coast of North America.

Within two years of Cook's ships returning to England in 1779, vessels from England and America were fitted out for voyages to trade for pelts with native peoples. Initially, ships passed along the coast, picking up skins from animals that had already been caught, many of which had been made into cloaks and other items of clothing. This supply was soon exhausted, and natives started to hunt otters for barter. At first, hunters used traditional methods. Throughout the northwest coast and Aleutian Islands, they pursued otters in

*The sea otter in Nootka Sound, Canada. After an engraving made on Captain Cook's third voyage of discovery in 1778. Source: Cooke, C. (1802)* Modern and Authentic System of Universal Geography. Volume II. *MacDonald & Son, London.*

kayaks or canoes, attempting to get close enough to harpoon them with a javelin.[18] The spears were tipped with detachable bone points to which a piece of line made of whale sinews was attached. This line was in turn attached to inflated bladders to slow the progress of a wounded animal and allow the harpoon to be retrieved if the hunter missed. Groups of hunters in kayaks would often chase otters, forcing them to submerge by shouting and splashing each time the animal surfaced to breathe, until, exhausted, the otter could be dispatched by harpoon. Within twenty years of Cook's voyage, instead of cloth and iron, muskets were being traded to the natives for pelts—to kill their enemies, as the early trader William Sturgis grimly observed[19]—but the weapons were soon turned on the otters, to great effect.

In 1799, Sturgis was a seventeen-year-old employed by a Boston company in a trading voyage for otter skins to the northwest coast. He kept a journal detailing his impressions of the region, its people, and the practicalities of trading. Enormous numbers of skins were purchased and shipped to the Far East in those early years. The *Eliza*, with which Sturgis traveled, for example, picked up 2,800 skins and a similar number of tails, which were purchased separately. On arrival at a new place for trading, Sturgis wrote, the people were

> always a great while before they will make a bargain for the first Skin, that generally settling the price for the whole tribe. When once this preliminary article is adjusted to their satisfaction, you can buy them as fast as you can pay for them while their stocks last. . . . What makes it most difficult to get the Skins is that you must first please the mistress of the family, for, if she insists upon it, the husband will quarrel for a needle for hours and dare as well be shot as silent before the lady is willing that he should.[20]

The *Eliza*'s skins fetched an average of twenty-five dollars apiece in Canton, the price having been depressed since Cook's day by greater supplies. Sturgis tallied up the skins traded by American vessels alone between 1799 and 1802, as coming to a total of 60,800.

The trade for otter pelts spread rapidly south and north along the North American coast. The French explorer La Pérouse stopped in California in 1786 and remarked on the commercial opportunities possible from a Spanish trade in otter pelts. The Native Americans in Monterey Bay, he observed, hunted otters only on land by beating them with sticks or catching them in snares. The Spanish had never traded any otter pelts, and nobody used them locally as it was too hot. But this would soon change, La Pérouse predicted correctly. The Spanish had already established links between the New World and the Far East with their Manila galleon,[21] and it was a simple matter to load up with otter skins on the return voyage, especially now they were extending their settlements north into the sea otter habitats of California. Hunting using simple reed canoes and guns supplanted the primitive snares and clubbing methods described by La Pérouse as otters grew more wary. The Spanish trade in otters was controlled by colonial officials, and pelts were exchanged in China for mercury, a commodity in short supply in South America and much needed for extracting silver from ore. By 1790, nearly ten thousand furs were exported to China, which reputedly fetched over three million dollars for the Spanish treasury.[22]

The early trade in California otters was limited by difficulties of supply, as Native Americans lacked either hunting methods or inclination to catch as many otters as the Spanish wanted. At the beginning of the nineteenth century, American traders sensed an opportunity and went into partnership with Russians to realize it. They shipped in skilled Aleut hunters with kayaks to pursue otters and were soon able to export thousands of skins year after year. But Spanish troops and hostile native peoples harassed the Russians and Americans, and their enterprise petered out around 1815. In 1821, Mexico gained independence from Spain, and California became its northernmost province. Otter trading was liberalized, and Russians now went into partnership with Mexico, an arrangement that lasted for the next decade. After this, hunting licenses were issued to residents and itinerant fur trappers who had made it to the coast from the interior of America. Otter hunting greatly intensified as hundreds of people were lured by the prospect of quick money.

When Mexico became independent, otters were still abundant, and were present in San Francisco Bay in great shoals. One observer reported that from San Francisco to the Santa Clara estuary, "the ground appeared covered with black sheets due to the great quantity of otters which were there."[23] But in the years leading up to 1850, when California became a part of the United States, otters were persecuted to the edge of extinction. Farther north, sea otters also declined, but hunting intensity remained high as scarcity drove up the price paid for pelts. For many years after Cook's voyage, otter pelts sold for twenty-five to forty dollars a skin in the Chinese markets. By the late nineteenth century, however, this had reached nearly two thousand dollars. In 1911, it was estimated there were only one thousand to two thousand otters left between Alaska and Baja California. Today, they are extinct throughout the whole west coast up to Alaska, except for a small population that survived near Monterey Bay and a population reintroduced to Vancouver Island from Alaska in the 1960s and 1970s. (Although still small, both populations are growing, and the range is gradually expanding.[24])

Sea otters prey heavily on sea urchins and abalones; the latter are grazing mollusks that feed on seaweed and are much esteemed for their beautiful iridescent shells. Urchins also graze seaweed, and abundant sea otters and large fish and lobsters keep prey animals, especially urchins, scarce. If grazing pressure is low, seaweed can flourish and dense kelp forests cloak rocky coasts. Near San Diego, George Vancouver in 1793 reported the presence of kelp forests extending 2 miles (3 kilometers) offshore.[25] The kelp there grew in water up to 30 fathoms deep (~ 55 meters; 180 feet), and plants reached 50 fathoms in length (~ 90 meters; 300 feet). Francisco de Ulloa, cruising through the California Channel Islands in 1539, was also struck by the kelp:

> Among these Islands are such an abundance of those weedes, that if at any time wee were enforced to sayle over them they hindred the course of our ships. They grow fourteene or fifteene fadome deep under the water, their tops reaching four or five fadome above the water. They are of the colour of yellow waxe, & their stalke groweth great proportionably. This weed is much more beautifull then it is set foorth, and no marvell, for the natural painter and creator thereof is most excellent.[26]

Sea otters did not eliminate abalones in the southern part of their range. So many abalones still thrived in the shallows that one eighteenth-century observer of Baja wrote, "On the beach of the Pacific Sea, from 27° to 31° [N] there is an unbelievable multitude of univalve shellfish which are considered the most beautiful of all that are known." [27] Farther north, however, large abalones were so scarce [28] that Spanish traders bringing shells from Monterey found that they were the most highly valued goods with which to barter for otter pelts with tribes in Nootka and its vicinity. [29]

The disappearance of Steller's sea cow from Bering and Copper Islands has long been blamed on intensive hunting. But its extinction took only twenty-eight years, a remarkably short time for hunting alone to depopulate the islands, especially given the large numbers reported by Steller. Their extinction is easier to understand in light of the role sea otters played in maintaining kelp forests. Russian hunters swiftly reduced otter populations on these uninhabited islands where the animals had not learned to fear people. This would have triggered an ecological disaster for sea cows as urchin populations expanded and grazing pressure increased. Based on what we know today, it seems likely that kelp forests would have started to disappear within ten years of the onset of otter hunting. Steller mentioned in his journal that at the end of winter, sea cows looked half starved with their ribs visible through their skin. Sea cows were totally dependent on kelp for food and relied on summer seaweed growth to rebuild their strength and reproduce. Without kelp, they were doomed. Starvation was perhaps more important than hunting in their decline and certainly helps explain the extraordinary rate at which they succumbed. [30]

There is a common theme in European expansion and exploitation of the sea. First, the explorers—Columbus, Cabot, Drake, Bering, Cook, and others—set sail for God, country, fame, and wealth. They returned with tales of strange seas teeming with wildlife. Through books written by Dampier and people like him, the possibilities for exploitation became known in Europe, stimulating a second wave of travel financed by merchant adventurers in pursuit of profit. Those voyages, although commercially motivated, were instrumental in extending the boundaries of the known world. As well as the animals slaughtered for commercial ends, sailors and travelers had major impacts on the fauna of islands and the sea, butchering millions of animals for provisions.

Charles Darwin reached the Galápagos in 1835, over a hundred years after Rogers's privateering days. In their primordial desolation the islands must have seemed like the end of the world. But Darwin knew they had been much visited before, for he carried copies of Dampier's and Rogers's books with him and was particularly keen to discover the famous tortoises. It took him two days of hiking to find one, so badly had populations been depleted by centuries of provisioning visits.[31] Intriguingly, it was not Darwin who first wondered how such distinctive tortoises came to be there. Rogers posed the question in 1712:

> [T]here are . . . Land Turtle almost on every Island: 'Tis strange how the latter got here, because they can't come of themselves, and none of that sort are to be found on the Main[land].[32]

It is easy to imagine Dampier and Rogers discussing the finer points of Galápagos natural history as the boat rocked at anchor in some sheltered cove. This far-flung scatter of land has been an inspiration to naturalists for centuries.

As I write this chapter, from the corner of my desk a Galápagos tortoise stares at me with sightless mother-of-pearl eyes. The distinctive shape of its shell shows it was a native of Santa Cruz, from which some souvenir-hunting seaman plucked it in the late eighteenth century. The passing years have given the shell a deep black luster, and the leathery skin is shriveled and cracked with age. When once it breathed cool air sweeping off the Pacific and tasted dew on morning leaves, the era of piracy had ended. Commercial interest had turned from galleons to much larger and more reliable prey.

## — *Chapter 7* —

# Whaling: The
# First Global Industry

◆—◆

CLOUDS PRESSED low and grey over the ice, merging imperceptibly with frozen sea on the northern horizon. The desolate sweep of the Arctic ice pack was broken only by the grotesque architecture of ice slabs twisted into pressure ridges by storms. At the prow of a slender wooden dory, a harpooner stood motionless, staring intently at leaden waves ahead while four men behind him sat hunched over their oars. Near exhaustion, they had been pursuing the whales for five hours, rowing into the wind from their ship, now 10 kilometers distant. Their reverie was shattered by a loud blow that raised a column of spray ten boat lengths away; with a shout from the harpooner, the men bent to the oars.

As the gap closed, the man at the prow hoisted his harpoon, balancing it for a moment or two before lifting one end high above his head. With practiced flourish he unleashed the iron in a graceful arc. When the harpoon struck, the whale roared and dived, snatching rope from the coil in the boat. As the line thundered over the gunwale, one of the men poured water on the wood raising clouds of steam in the freezing air. Another reefed a second coil of rope to the end of the first. Maddened by pain, the whale continued to dive until all eight coils were spent. As the last, tied off to the bow, went taut, the boat sped off dangerously, punching through the waves as the helmsman struggled to prevent capsize and the whale threatened to drag the bow under. This headlong charge could last for thirty terror-stricken minutes or more until the whale was forced to surface for breath. At that moment, the men must try to get another harpoon in before the whale dives again and the ride begins once more. They hoped the whale would tire before the lines snapped or disaster struck, and then they could close in for the kill. This time, their luck held, and a second boat fixed a harpoon in the whale on the first breath. By the time it surfaced a second time, they moved in for the kill.

The moment of victory for whalemen was also the time of greatest peril. To kill the whale they must get close enough to plunge their lances deep into its belly, probing for vital organs. The harpooner's shoulders flexed and twisted as he worked the lance into the whale. The oarsmen pressed the boat close—but ready at a moment to pull away when the death flurry came. Soon the whale began spouting blood, giving boat and men a hellish aura as crimson spray froze over them and the sea turned red. The whale shuddered and convulsed, warning the men to stand off as its great tail slapped the water with a cannon-shot sound. Minutes later, the leviathan gave a final heave and expired.

Nobody is certain when people first began to hunt the whale. In the ninth century, England's King Alfred entertained a traveler called Ohthere from the northland of Scandinavia. The traveler spoke of a voyage he had made far beyond the northern limits of habitation in Norway into the White Sea and the land of the *Finnas*. There he hunted for *hrosshvalr* (the horse whale, or walrus), coveted for its white tusks and for hides from which the strongest rope could be made. He told the king,

> This whale is much smaller than other whales; it is no more than seven ells long [3.2 meters; 11 feet]. . . . The best whale hunting is in his own country; those are forty-eight ells long, the biggest fifty ells long [22 to 23 meters; 77 feet].[1]

*The death flurry of a Greenland right whale. In the background, smoke belches from whale ships where the blubber from previous kills is being boiled down. Source: Whymper, F. (1883)* The Fisheries of the World. An Illustrated and Descriptive Record of the International Fisheries Exhibition, 1883. *Cassell and Company, Ltd., London.*

Ohthere's tale is the first written record of whale hunting, but the earliest known record of the practice comes from rock art in Korea. Detailed rock carvings at the Neolithic site of Bangu-dae in South Korea date from 6000 to 1000 BC.[2] They show Pacific gray, northern right, sperm, killer, and minke whales. They also show the pursuit and capture of whales by people in small boats, using harpoons and ropes to which air-filled bladders were attached to help secure the whales. The resistance of the bladders tired the whale, allowing hunters to track its position from the surface, homing in for the kill when the whale was exhausted.

About the time of Ohthere, whaling was also under way farther south in Europe, and traces of medieval whaling can be found in archaeological remains from the Bay of Biscay (offshore of today's France and Spain), Normandy, and Flanders. *Ælfric's Colloquoy* on fishing, written in the late tenth century, includes mention of a fisherman who says that he has caught porpoises and sturgeon, among other fish, but he doesn't attempt to catch whales because they are dangerous and can sink the many boats sent to hunt them. The fishing master with whom he speaks replies "many catch whales and . . . make great profit by it."[3] By this time, it seems, whaling was well established and highly organized.

Early whaling was conducted from shore with boats sent in pursuit once an animal was spotted. Remains of watchtowers on the Biscayan coast suggest that spotters were on the lookout for whales for extended periods during the hunting season.[4] French and Basque whalers used harpoons attached to lines for catching whales, whereas Scandinavians and Icelanders used spears and lances. The superiority of the southern technology led eventually to its adoption worldwide. Whalers pursued animals that came close inshore, killing them at sea and towing them to land for processing, or driving them into bays for slaughter.[5] During the eleventh and twelfth centuries, whaling was frequently practiced in the southern North Sea and the English Channel. There is a possibility, based on records of stranded animals, that whale numbers fell over this period. Certainly, historical records indicate that whale hunting declined in Flanders, Normandy, and England into the fourteenth century, suggesting a fall in abundance.[6]

Basque whalers possibly pursued rorqual whales like the finback. These whales have a series of grooves in the skin below the mouth and throat that expand and enable them to take huge gulps of water as they engulf schools of small fish such as the sardines, pilchard, and mackerel that frequent Biscayan coasts. However, it is also likely Basques hunted the slower-moving northern right whale and Atlantic gray whale.[7] The latter was a coastal species that is now extinct; the former is extremely rare today and no longer occurs in either the Bay of Biscay or the North Sea. The bones of both species have been found in archaeological remains in Holland, France, and England, and a sketch depicting a gray whale was made in seventeenth-century Iceland. In New England, a species matching the description of the gray whale was known as the "scrag" by whalers, but they were hunted to extinction by the early eighteenth century.

Basque and Biscayan whaling efforts along the western coast of Europe seem to have peaked in the twelfth and thirteenth centuries,[8] but by the sixteenth century they were probably struggling to find enough animals locally. Certainly, they were extremely quick to cross the Atlantic to exploit whales in Canada once the discoveries of Cabot and Cartier became known in Europe. These explorers were stunned by the abundance of whales they saw. Cartier, exploring up the Gulf of St. Lawrence in 1535, reported,

> There are also many Whales, Porposes, Seahorses, and Adhothuis, which is a kind of fish that we had never seene nor heard of before [the beluga whale]. They are as great as Porposes, as white as any snow, their bodie and head fashioned as a grayhound, they are wont always to abide betwene the fresh & salt water, which beginneth betweene the river of Saguenay and Canada.[9]

Passing along the northern coast of the gulf, he continued,

> I beleeve that there were never so many Whales seen as wee saw that day.[10]

Basque and Biscayan whalers would also have received news of the whales from the fishermen who followed hard on the heels of Cabot to exploit cod. By the middle of the sixteenth century, whaling stations were well established on the Labrador coast opposite the Strait of Belle Isle.[11] Some thirty galleons carrying two thousand crew made the Atlantic crossing every summer to hunt Greenland and northern right whales passing through the strait.

The Basques would not stay long in these waters. Increasing risk of piracy from English, French, and Dutch vessels made the ventures too risky by the late sixteenth century.[12] But explorers, merchants, and travelers were at the time discovering fertile new hunting grounds in more northern latitudes. It was in these northern latitudes that Dutch and English commercial interest in whaling was reawakened. Anthonie Jenkinson, writing of a voyage from the city of London to Russia in 1557, reported,

> Thus proceeding and sailing forward, we fell with an Island called Zenam, being in the latitude of 70 degrees. About this island we saw many Whales, very monstrous, about our ships, some by estimation of 60 foot long: and being the ingendring time they roared and cried terriblie.[13]

The supply of whales was plentiful in the north, and Olaus Magnus the Goth alludes to whale hunting on the Norwegian coast in the sixteenth century:

> When sea monsters or whales have been hauled out of the sea thanks to the fishermen's skill, resourcefulness and strenuous toil, or driven on beaches by violent wind and storm, or by the wrath of hostile fish, the people of the neighbourhood divide their booty with axes, and hatchets in such a way that with the meat, blubber and bones of a single whale or monster they can fill between 250 and 300 carts. After they have put the meat and fat into vast numbers of large barrels, they preserve it in salt, as they do other huge sea-fish. They use it for home consumption according to need, or sell it to others who will export it to distant lands for the same purposes.[14]

Magnus continues,

> On the giant fish discovered on the shore of northern England in the year 1532. Although this enormous beast was regarded as a prodigy by the people of the neighbourhood, and men were staggered when they gazed at its extraordinary size [28 meters (93 feet), probably a blue whale from the description], nevertheless the Norwegian coasts between the fjords at Bergen and Trondheim have similar creatures as their ever present, familiar guests.[15]

The real concentrations of whales had not yet been found. Toward the end of the sixteenth century, oceangoing explorers set forth to look for northwest and northeast passages to the Far East: Martin Frobisher, William Baffin, John Davis, Willem Barentz, and Henry Hudson led exploration of northern seas. Their names are frozen for posterity on maps of the inhospitable world they discovered. Today, in one of the world's whale-watching hotspots, a tourist might hope to see two or three whales on a good day, ten or so on an unforgettable day. Before the era of commercial whale hunting began, such numbers barely attracted notice. In the hotspots for whales, places where the animals resorted to feed and breed, there could be such astonishing numbers that even these well-traveled observers reached for their logbooks. George Best, describing the third voyage of Martin Frobisher to Baffin Island in 1578, wrote of one memorable encounter: "On Monday the laste of June, wee mette with manye greate Whales, as they hadde beene Porposes."[16] At this time, groups of porpoises often numbered in the hundreds or thousands, so the comparison is telling.

Although Arctic explorers discovered no shortcuts to China, they returned with news that had merchants scrambling to equip vessels to hunt far and wide for whales and seals, as these animals provided commodities of growing value in the more populous and urbanized world of seventeenth-century Europe. Both produced oil in abundance that could be extracted by boiling up the blubber and carcasses and was used for lighting and cooking. Whalebone—the hundreds of flexible bony plates that baleen whales use to filter food from the sea—was also highly valued, providing stiffening ribs for corsetry and skirts. Ambergris, a waxy material from the intestines of sperm whales, formed a base for mixing perfume and medicines.

Early seventeenth-century merchants in Holland and England could smell wealth on the northern breeze. There was just one problem: nobody among them knew how to catch and process whales. Luckily for them, the tradition of whaling remained alive among the Basques and Biscayans, and they hired skilled workers from those groups, with instructions to their captains not to miss any opportunity to learn methods of whaling from these men.[17] The earliest images of whale fishing around the island of Spitzbergen (one of the island group now called Svalbard), which is north of Scandinavia and was discovered by Barentz in 1597, show Dutch ships—but the people directing operations, harpooning whales, and overseeing processing of the carcasses are dressed in Basque clothing.

The Dutch fishery prospered, and by 1684 there were 246 vessels catching whales around Svalbard.[18] Initially, they adopted the same approach used since the origins of whaling—hunting whales close to the coast and processing them onshore. But soon whales became scarce near shore, and an offshore fishery developed that spread farther afield. Vessels would set sail for the Arctic toward the end of the European winter, aiming to arrive as the ice broke up and the whales gathered to mate and fatten up on the spring plankton bloom. One Yorkshire whaler of the nineteenth century rued the fact that in seventeen years,

> I never saw either blossom or fruit upon the trees, and my eyes and senses were never blessed with the scent of growing flowers, the sight

of ripening corn, or the subsequent harvest operations . . . my most constant surroundings during those years were ice, snow, fogs, or the boundless expanse of ocean.[19]

Sailors developed methods to process whales at sea. Carcasses were strapped alongside the ship with chains and the blubber stripped and winched aboard. Instead of boiling blubber onshore to extract the oil, ships in the Arctic fishery would barrel up the blubber direct, and the oil would be extracted in home ports (a fearsomely smelly operation given the rancid state of the blubber).

Riches could be made by bold adventurers willing to travel far afield, but whaling was a notoriously brutal, bloody, and hazardous business. In the Arctic, ships had to get close in among the ice floes in pursuit of whales. When the wind turned, or a sudden storm got up, the ice could close in minutes, crushing vessels as if made of match-wood. Many ships were lost, and many seamen died. For example, a ship destroyed by ice off Greenland left sailors stranded on floating wreckage for a week, buoyed up by casks of blubber. After five days they begged the surgeon to bleed them so they could slake their thirst on their own blood. The surgeon obliged, but half died before another whaling ship rescued the survivors.[20]

Fortunately, help was often closer to hand. Eighteenth- and nine-teenth-century paintings of the northern whale fisheries are often filled with boats stretching from foreground to horizon. Thinking today of the empty desolation of northern seas, such scenes appear contrived more for artistic effect than meant as accurate representations of reality. But the numbers of ships involved was extraordinary. In a forty-six-year period up to 1722, the Holland whaling fleet alone numbered 5,886 ships.[21]

Around the time that Europeans began sailing north for Arctic whales, the settlement of New England got under way. Early explorers and colonists there found waters surging and blowing with whales. The Reverend Richard Mather, sailing with a ship of colonists for New England in 1635, kept a diary of their passage. Passing onto the banks of Newfoundland, he wrote,

In y$^e$ afternoone wee saw mighty whales spewing up water in y$^e$ ayre like y$^e$ smoake of a chimney, and making y$^e$ sea about them white and hoary as it is said Job [xli. 32] of such incredible bignes y$^t$ I will never wonder y$^t$ y$^e$ body of Jonas could bee in y$^e$ belly of a whale. At evening o$^r$ seamen sounded and found ground at 50 fathom.[22]

The pages of Mather's diary are filled with similar entries. A few days later, approaching the North American coast, he wrote, "This day in y$^e$ afternoone wee saw multitudes of great whales, which now was grown ordinary and usuall to behold."[23]

The New England whale fishery began by taking whales that had stranded,[24] but the abundance of whales close inshore—so close they would sometimes enter Nantucket harbor in Massachusetts—soon drew people to sea with harpoons. By the late seventeenth century, shore whaling was well established from Long Island to Maine. The offshore fishery first grew from Nantucket, when in 1712 a boat was blown offshore and managed to secure a sperm whale. This stimulus quickly led to an offshore fleet that over the next sixty years gradually spread through the North Atlantic, going farther afield as the population of sperm whales declined. The sequence of exploitation went from the New England coast, to the Carolinas, Bahamas, West Indies, Gulf of Mexico, Caribbean Sea, Azores, Cape Verde Islands, and the west coast of Africa. Only in 1774 did American whalers first pass south of the equator to hunt off Brazil, in response to dwindling whale numbers in the North Atlantic. Throughout the eighteenth century they also engaged in whaling to the north, on the Grand Banks and in Davis Strait to the west of Greenland, hunting northern right whales.

Whales swiftly assumed great value in the industrializing economies of North America as well as Europe. By the eighteenth century, whale oil lit the streets, salons and parlours of Europe and America. Uses for whales diversified as the industry prospered. Whales helped lubricate the wheels of industry, cleanse the bodies of a newly hygiene-conscious society, and suppress the waists of its ladies. It was vital to maintain supplies. With local stocks much depleted by the eighteenth century, New Englanders sought fresh grounds. In 1726, George Shelvocke, a British navigator, alerted them to possibilities in the south Atlantic. In a book documenting his voyage round the world, he described the extraordinary numbers of whales seen in places not yet reached by whalers:

[W]hales, grampusses, and other fish of a monstrous bulk, are in such numbers off the coast of Patagonia that they were really offensive to us very often. For they would come sometimes so close to us as to stifle us with their stench when they blew, and would lie so near us that I have frequently thought it impossible to escape striking upon them on every send of a sea. I am a stranger to the Greenland fishery, therefore cannot say why a trade for blubber might not be carried on here. I may venture to affirm it is a safer navigation, and I am apt to believe that here is a greater certainty of succeeding.[25, 26]

To Patagonia's south, near Tierra del Fuego, another traveler, La Pérouse, was also impressed by the abundance of whales in 1786:

Throughout our navigation through the Strait at a half league from the shore we were surrounded by whales; it is evident that they are never disturbed—our ships did not frighten them, they were swimming majestically half a pistol shot from the frigates; they will be sovereigns of these seas until such time as whalers come to make the same war against them as in Spitzbergen or Greenland. I doubt there is a better place for this type of fishing anywhere in the world. . . . The only inconvenience is the length of the voyage which requires about five months of navigation for each crossing [of the Atlantic].[27]

A little later, cruising the coast of Chile, he continues,

Throughout the night we were surrounded by whales—they swam so close to our frigates that they threw water on board as they blew.[28]

As northern stocks thinned, American whalers turned to these southern regions to pursue fisheries in more productive waters, and by the early nineteenth century, whaling had become the first global business. La Pérouse's "inconvenience" of a five-month crossing had been eclipsed. New Englanders embarked in enormous vessels on voyages three to four years long. They reached every corner of the globe where whales were known to resort, and explored places where few had ventured before. As one nineteenth-century writer put it, "The duration of the voyage is protracted to a length which would justify our calling it an exile."[29] Whalers hunted the southern counterparts of the northern right whales preferred by Arctic whalers. But sperm whales were prime quarry by the late eighteenth century. They were known as great fighters and would thrash the sea to foam in their death flurries. Herman Melville chose a sperm whale as antihero of *Moby Dick* for a good reason. By the early nineteenth century, sperm whale oil had become the fuel of choice for candles and lamps because of its bright and near smokeless flame. (Candlepower, a unit of illumination still in use today, is based on the light produced by a candle made from the oil of the sperm whale.)

Sperm whales were found mainly in tropical latitudes. By the time of Darwin's 1835 visit to the Galápagos Islands, the place was overrun with American whalers in pursuit of sperm whales. One early scientific account of this species, written the same year, gives an idea of their numbers that lured men to undertake such lengthy voyages.

> The sperm whale is a gregarious animal, and the herds formed by it are of two kinds, the one consisting of females, the other of young not fully grown males, and the latter are again generally subdivided into groups, according to their ages. . . . These herds are called by the whalers "Schools", and, occasionally, consist of great numbers; I have seen in one school as many as five or six hundred.[30]

Explorers along the west coast of North America also found new stocks of coastal whales. On his 1786 voyage that took him to Monterey Bay, California, for example, La Pérouse remarked, "One cannot put into words the number of whales that surrounded us nor their familiarity; they blew constantly, within half a pistol shot of our frigates, and filled the air with a great stench."[31] George Vancouver was struck by the large numbers of whales near California's Cape Mendocino in 1792, and later, in his exploration of the waters around Vancouver Island, he was equally impressed by whales in Desolation Sound: "Numberless whales enjoying the season, were playing about the ship in every direction."[32]

Shore fisheries for whales soon sprang up along the west coast of North America, notably in California and the Baja Peninsula. Pacific gray whales were hunted along their migration route from Baja, where they calved in the sheltered lagoons of Mexico, north to the feeding grounds in the Bering Sea. Captain Scammon, a nineteenth-century whale and seal hunter, discovered one of these calving lagoons in Baja, a place that still bears his name. There the females would congregate to give birth where the whales "collected at the most remote extremities of the lagoons, and huddled together so thickly that it was difficult for a boat to cross the waters without coming into contact with them."[33]

Scammon wrote a book in 1874 recording the rise and progress of the gray whale fishery. Bay whaling began in 1846 and expanded quickly, with fifty ships involved two years later, he reports. Records made from shore-based watchtowers in the early 1850s showed that about a thousand whales a day passed along the shore between December 15 and February 1. At first they were hunted by men who waited in boats, concealed among the kelp, for a whale to approach close enough to get a harpoon in. The whales soon became wary and had to be pursued away from the kelp forests. The bomb lance, an improvement on the traditional harpoons, was introduced in the 1840s. These harpoons exploded a shot into the whale on contact, killing the animal or at least hastening its end. By the mid-1850s, boats hunted whales from every navigable bay and lagoon along the entire coast of California and the Baja Peninsula. Their pursuit was intense and relentless. By 1872, the daily passage of migrating whales seen from shore had fallen to around forty.

*California gray whales in their Arctic summer feeding grounds illustrated in the whaler Captain Scammon's 1874 book on Pacific mammals. Source: Scammon, C. M. (1874)* The Marine Mammals of the North-western Coast of North America. *Dover Publications Inc., New York, 1968.*

Scammon was a whaler hardened by the slaughter he took part in. But by the time, he wrote his book, he had become concerned at the depletion of the gray whale:

> The civilized whaler seeks the hunted animal farther seaward, as from year to year it learns to shun the fatal shore. . . . [T]he large bays and lagoons, where these animals once congregated, brought forth and nurtured their young, are already nearly deserted. The mammoth bones of the California Gray lie bleaching on the shores of those silvery waters, and are scattered along the broken coasts, from Siberia to the Gulf of California; and ere long it may be questioned whether this mammal will not be numbered among the extinct species of the Pacific.[34]

Whale stocks were rapidly depleted in every new whaling ground discovered. By the mid-nineteenth century, there were some 650 American whaling ships alone in the Pacific, manned by 13,500 seamen. Whalers were desperate to discover new grounds and would follow any fresh lead. In 1848, an American whaling captain penetrated the Bering Strait into the Chukchi Sea and found abundant bowhead whales for the taking. Unlike sperm whales, bowheads could be lanced with ease, dying like sheep, as one chronicler put it.[35] A year later, 154 ships hunted bowheads in these icebound and dangerous waters.

The industry as a whole prospered only because whalers constantly sought and found new grounds where whales had not yet been slaughtered. It was kept up so long because whalers progressively switched from more desirable to less desirable species as stocks of the former dwindled. Looking back, it is easy to see that whales were extirpated place by place and species by species through the seventeenth to twentieth centuries. Yet at the time, many people preferred to believe that the whales moved somewhere else rather than confront the reality that whalers were eliminating the very basis of their industry. Herman Melville represents this collective myopia in *Moby Dick*:

> [E]qually fallacious seems the conceit, that because the so-called whale-bone whales no longer haunt many grounds in former years abounding with them, hence that species also is declining. For they are only being driven from promontory to cape; and if one coast is no

longer enlivened with their jets, then, be sure, some other and remoter
strand has been very recently startled by the unfamiliar spectacle. . . .
[S]o, hunted from the savannas and glades of the middle seas, the
whale-bone whales can at last resort to their Polar citadels, and diving
under the ultimate glassy barriers and walls there, come up among icy
fields and floes; and in a charmed circle of everlasting December, bid
defiance to all pursuit from man.[36]

The reality was very different. A late nineteenth-century map of
whaling grounds shows half of their total area already abandoned
because the whales had been hunted to the point of commercial
extinction. As whales dwindled, whalers became indiscriminate in
their killing. In his memoirs, a whaler writing in the late nineteenth
century contrasts the old days with more recent times:

> Off Pond's Bay [in Greenland] we saw a large number of whales but
> they were of a small description. Some ships caught many, but our cap-
> tain gave orders to his men not to strike a whale unless it was large.
> These instructions are very proper when you can pick and choose, but
> now all must be taken which comes first.[37]

But demand for whales had by this time begun to decline. In the mid-
nineteenth century, whale oil lamps were supplanted by mineral oils
and natural gas.

It is peculiar that many modern accounts leave out much of what
went on during four centuries of intensive commercial whaling. The
graphs I show my students of declines in whale catches stretch back
only to the early twentieth century, since these are all that are readily
available. Partly, this is because there was a twentieth-century revival
of whaling. Now equipped with steam and diesel power, whalers
could pursue finback whales like blue, sei, and minke that were too
swift for crews in rowboats. Until then these species had mostly
escaped exploitation. They disappeared one by one in a continuation
of the previous pattern until a halt was called to all whaling in the
early 1980s. But the serial depletion of whales stretches back to medieval times in Europe. That story is seldom told.

Scientists at the International Whaling Commission have
attempted to estimate the number of whales before whaling began in
earnest in the seventeenth century. This commission oversaw management of whale fishing and now struggles to enforce the morato-

rium agreed in the 1980s, although Japan, Norway, and Iceland continue whaling in defiance of the ban. Based on logbook and other historical records, the commission calculated that there must have been around twenty thousand humpback whales and between thirty thousand and fifty thousand fin whales in the North Atlantic. Two

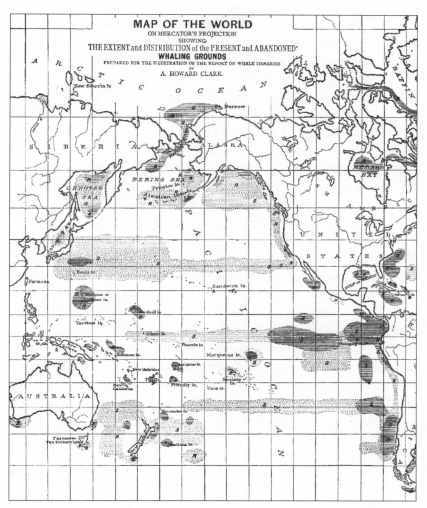

*Whaling grounds of the Pacific around 1880. Dark shaded areas indicate places still fished at the time, while light shaded areas were abandoned whaling grounds. The letters refer to different whale species. S = sperm whale, R = right whale, B = Bowhead whale, G = California Gray, and H = humpback. Source: Unknown.*

American academics, Joe Roman and Steve Palumbi, have challenged their conclusions using genetic data from present-day populations of these species, suggesting that the early populations were far larger.[38] Genetic variability increases with the size of a breeding population. This enables population size to be estimated from analysis of genetic material in tissue samples. Because whales have a long generation time, it takes a very long time for genetic variability in their populations to equilibrate after a change in population size. The genetic heterogeneity of today's whale populations still reflects population sizes from days before large-scale commercial whaling. Genetic estimates by Roman and Palumbi put prewhaling population sizes at 360 thousand for the fin whale and 240 thousand animals for humpback, nine to twelve times the estimates from whaling records.

To me, these genetic estimates seem much more in accord with the kind of whale numbers seen by early travelers. Population sizes estimated from logbook records could underestimate true numbers for several reasons. The most obvious are that many logbooks have been lost, and that many whales were struck and lost and later died but weren't recorded. In the twentieth century, furthermore, many whales killed were not declared to the International Whaling Commission. Whatever the reason for the difference, genetic data and historical commentaries from eyewitnesses suggest we may greatly overestimate recovery of whale populations since the moratorium was implemented. Our best estimates put present-day numbers of humpbacks at nine thousand to twelve thousand and fin whales at fifty-six thousand. Using whaling commission estimates, this suggests fin whales are fully recovered and humpbacks are well on the way. The truth could be very different. If the genetic estimates of population sizes are accurate, then early resumption of whaling based on a false assumption of recovery could imperil whales once more.

# — *Chapter 8* —

# To the Ends
# of the Earth for Seals

— ◆ ◆ —

O
N A REMOTE island in the southern Indian Ocean in 1817, New Englander William Phelps squared up for battle:

I knew nothing of the habits of the elephant [seal], had never seen one killed, and there I was, with a lance two feet long on a pole-staff of four feet, and seal club, a butcher's knife and steel, with orders to kill, butcher and cook one of those enormous beasts, the smallest of which looked as if he could dispose of me at a meal. After the boats' crews were out of sight I took a survey of the amphibious monsters, and selecting the smallest one, commenced the battle according to orders. When I hit him a rap on the nose he reared up on his flippers, opened his mouth, and bellowed furiously. This gave me a chance at his breast; plunging my lance into it, in the direction of where I thought his heart ought to be, I sent the iron in "socket deep." This was all right so far, but I was not quick enough in drawing it out again, and stepping back. He grabbed the lance by the shank with his teeth, and drawing it from the wound, gave it a rapid whicking round; the end of the pole hit me a rap on the head, and sent me sprawling. . . . My next resort was the seal-club. With this I managed to beat the poor creature's eyes out, and then, fastening my knife on the pole, I lanced him until he was dead.[1]

If Phelps himself was a novice at such slaughter, for others seal hunting was already big business by 1817. Hundreds of ships fitted out for sealing plied the remote reaches of the oceans in search of their prey. For as long as people have hunted, seals have been fair game. Seal bones turn up in coastal middens thousands of years old wherever seals occurred. The animals furnished the Inuit of Greenland with almost all they needed: meat and blubber for food; oil for cooking, light, and heat; skins for clothes and bedding, kayaks and rope; sinews for twine; the stomach and intestines made windows and curtains for their huts, waterproof clothes, and bladder floats for hunting; bones were used for tools, fish hooks, and harpoons.[2] Seal populations coped well with these low levels of hunting, but they were completely unequipped to survive the intensive commercial exploitation that developed in the eighteenth and early nineteenth centuries.

The earliest sealing for commercial ends targeted walrus. The medieval Scandinavian traveler Ohthere and his people hunted walrus in the ninth century, probably using their carcasses in much the same ways as the Inuit, but the ivory tusks and hides attracted much wider commerce. Walrus carry a pair of tusks that curve downward 30 to 80 centimeters (12 to 32 inches) from a small, wrinkled face, out of which eyes like black grapes peer over a dense moustache. The whiskers are used to sense shellfish on the seabed, while the tusks signify social status and are occasionally used as a lever to help haul out onto ice floes and to "walk" up rocks. (The Latin name for walrus, *Odobenus rosmarus,* means "tooth-walking seahorse.")

The collapse of the Roman Empire in the fifth century had choked off northward trade in African ivory. By the early Middle Ages walrus ivory was traded south by northern peoples like Ohthere and was carved into exquisitely figured casks for religious ceremonies and into game pieces such as the tenth-century chessmen found on Scotland's Isle of Lewis.[3] Walrus hide, one of the strongest leathers known, was used for high-performance rope. To make rope, a walrus would be skinned in a spiral, winding from tail to neck. A large animal might produce an unbroken strip 28 meters long (90 feet). Walrus ropes powered siege catapults in the sixteenth century.[4] In the nineteenth century, the leather was used for drive belts in industrial machinery, but by the twentieth century, walrus hide found a more mundane role as billiard cue tips.[5]

The Norsemen found walrus when they colonized Greenland in the tenth century. In summer they hunted them northward into the Davis Strait, trading tusks for goods from Iceland and Scandinavia. Norse seafarers from Greenland also found them in more temperate

*Walruses were a prized item of commerce from the early Middle Ages on, valued for their tusks and tough hides. But catching them could be a dangerous business. Source: Hamilton, R. (1839)* Jardine's Naturalist's Library. Mammalia Volume VIII. Amphibious Carnivora Including Walrus and Seals, Also of the Herbivorous Cetacea, &c. *W. H. Lizars, Edinburgh.*

waters when they discovered North America. Perhaps walrus hunting was one motivation for their brief settlement of that continent.[6] L'Anse aux Meadows in Newfoundland, the only confirmed Norse settlement in North America, fronts the Strait of Belle Isle, an important migratory route for seals and whales between the Gulf of St. Lawrence and the Labrador Sea. This settlement is generally believed to be a base from which the Norse made forays south into the St. Lawrence where they would have found walrus. When the next wave of European explorers and fishers reached North America in the late fifteenth and sixteenth centuries, walrus were still plentiful around the islands and rivers of the Gulf of St. Lawrence and as far south as Sable Island off Nova Scotia.[7]

Walrus hunting was an early motivation for European expeditions to the New World, alongside cod fishing and whaling. The walrus is among the largest of the seals, big males weighing nearly 1.5 tonnes and reaching 3.5 meters in length (12 feet) As well as tusks and hide, the average walrus produces half to three-quarters of a barrel of prime oil (at that time a barrel contained 31 gallons or 120 liters of oil). In 1591, a ship from France stopped at Sable Island and killed fifteen hundred walrus. Hearing of this, Bristol merchant Thomas James wrote of the discovery to the Lord High Treasurer of England, Sir William Cecil, no doubt wishing him to support further commercial ventures to the region. In addition to other uses, walrus hide was excellent as a shield in battle, he claimed, and the tusks were "as soveraigne against poyson as any Unicornes horne."[8]

Basque whalemen working the Gulf of St. Lawrence took many walrus over ensuing decades. By the time of the expedition by Pierre de Charlevoix up the St. Lawrence in 1719, however, few were caught anymore.[9] But this hardly mattered to sealers, since abundant new stocks of walrus had been discovered in the far north and were soon being exploited alongside whales. At the time of its discovery by Willem Barentz in 1597, the Arctic Ocean archipelago of Svalbard on its own is estimated to have supported twenty-five thousand walrus.[10] They were slaughtered by the thousands and boiled up for oil on shore by industrious Dutch and English whalers. Walrus and other seals were easy game for hunters, although killing seals was not always so easy as William Phelps found in his 1817 encounter with the elephant seal. François Péron, a naturalist traveling on a French voyage of discovery around the world in 1800, put it succinctly:

> In making it necessary for seals to come and rest on land, and there to bring forth their young, Nature seems to have wished to dedicate them to death and destruction. As a result, without any means of defence, scarcely able to drag themselves over the ground, the seals everywhere must fall victim to the larger animals and, above all to man. Thus, fleeing alike from these two types of enemies, their timid herds are to be found in large numbers only on these distant islands, on lonely rocks, and in the midst of the eternal ice where savage beasts do not exist, where man, even more formidable, has not made his permanent home.[11]

Péron's insight sums up why the sight of seals in vast herds so astonished early travelers. For millennia, people had hunted seals around inhabited coasts, thinning their numbers and driving them to remoter shores. Modern peoples discovered their breeding strongholds only when they took to the sea in ships, finding the most spectacular colonies in the farthest-flung regions. John Davis, for example, was taken aback by seals near Baffin Island in 1585: "We saw about this coast marvelous great abundance of seales skulling together like skuls of small fish."[12]

Walrus hunting was always closely associated with whaling. Whale ships throughout much of their history would make up cargoes with seals when they couldn't catch enough whales. But the sealing trade soon branched out in a different direction, moving on to fur seals as walrus became scarce, and as a new market for high-quality fur opened up.[13] This move was stimulated by trade in sea otter pelts with China. Fur seal skins were also sought after in China. The fur could be used directly, but the hair was also pressed into felt. Russians working the Aleutian Islands for otters already traded fur seal pelts into China. These pelts sold for a small fraction of the price of otter fur, but the animals were far more abundant. It did not take long for European and American traders to see the opportunities for profit from places like Juan Fernández, off the Chilean coast, whose vast fur seal rookeries had so impressed William Dampier and others.

The first serious commercial sealing expeditions to Juan Fernández took place in the late 1780s and early 1790s. By this time,

European seafarers had plied the world's oceans for three centuries. Atlantic seal colonies had been exploited for oil and skins in the seventeenth and early eighteenth centuries, largely as an adjunct to whaling or to supply local needs. But the opening of the China market for skins quickly took the industry to a new level. In the space of three decades, from 1790 to 1820, seal hunting exploded across the globe. Suddenly, seals were seen in a new light. To the merchants of the day, the barking, clamoring masses heaved out on the beaches must have seemed like piles of money for the taking. Fur seals bore the brunt of this onslaught.

There are two main groups of seals: seals with external ears, the Otariidae, and the true seals, or Phocidae. To sealers, these groups were distinguished as fur seals and hair seals, respectively. (Walrus is in a family of its own.) Fur seals possess a deep, double layer of hairs. Long outer guard hairs protect a thick layer of fine hairs with up to 57,000 hairs per square centimeter (350,000 per square inch). These hairs trap a layer of air, keeping the skin dry. Fur seal pelts were therefore highly valued, whereas hair seal pelts had poor-quality fur and were useful only as leather. Hair seal pelts were often discarded from seals slaughtered for oil; by contrast, fur seal carcasses were left to rot and only the skins taken. Hair seals were passed over in the first wave of hunting but acquired value for oil later on as whale fisheries declined.

The extreme vulnerability of seals to capture proved instrumental in their downfall. The first sealing expeditions to Juan Fernández, for example, killed them in droves. In 1792–1793, the New York–based *Eliza,* the first American sealing vessel to visit the islands, carried away thirty-eight thousand skins to China. Over the next seven years, ten or twenty boats a year loaded up from Juan Fernández. Amasa Delano, a participant in this trade, estimated that some three million fur seal skins were shipped from these islands and others nearby over this period.[14] In 1805, the Spanish closed the islands to foreign sealers, but by that time most of the fur seals were gone and the hunters had moved elsewhere.

Early on in the spread of large-scale, commercial sealing, François Péron and his men spent twelve days stranded by a storm on King Island in the Bass Strait of southern Australia. With little food of their own, Péron's party were forced to share the hospitality of a seal-ing crew who had been left there for the past thirteen months to kill and process elephant seals for oil (their pelts were little valued as this species is a hair seal). Seeing the sealers at work, Péron knew that the trade, and the seals, could not last. Writing of his visit in 1802, he pre-dicted the end of the elephant seals:

> [T]his great species of seals is going to find itself attacked on all sides at once; it is going to suffer everywhere frightful losses, which will become more and more irreparable. It will not even have left the means of escape open to the whales, that of being able, by taking refuge in the midst of the polar ice, to surround themselves, against man, with the horrors of nature. Indeed a warm temperature is absolutely necessary for the seals: the land is their habitual abode; after having been the cradle of their existence, it becomes the theatre of their love-making, it receives their last breaths. . . . With such needs, how could they escape the pursuit of their principal enemy? In their case, more so than for the whales, must doubtless be realized, this elo-quent prediction of one of my first and dearest teachers: "This great species will be wiped out like so many others; discovered in its most hidden retreats, reached in its most distant places of asylum, defeated by the irresistible force of human intelligence, it will disappear from the surface of the globe: one will only see some remnants of this huge species; its remains will become a dust that the winds will disperse. . . . It will live on only in the memory of men and in the pictures of the species." (Lacépède, *Histoire Naturelle des Cétacés,* 1804).[15]

At its peak, there were hundreds of ships in the seal fishery, lured by the large profits possible for quick and bold captains. Sealers reached every corner of the globe, depleting seal populations as they went. In the late 1700s the Falkland Islands were worked over and ships then moved south, braving the rugged coast of Staten Island, now called Isla de los Estados, off the far southern tip of South America. South Georgia at the fringes of the Antarctic seas was reached about the same time as Juan Fernández. By the time it was worked out, it had produced at least 1.2 million pelts. During the early 1800s sealers also worked their way north and south into the Pacific, stripping the Galápagos and the coasts of Baja and California. Though seals were scarcer in these less productive warmer latitudes,

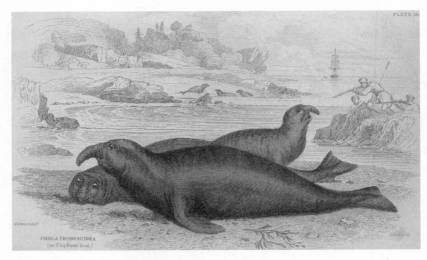

*When fur seals and whales became scarce in the early nineteenth century, hunters
turned their attention towards elephant seals whose carcasses were rich in oil. Source:
Hamilton, R. (1839)* Jardine's Naturalist's Library. Mammalia Volume VIII.
Amphibious Carnivora Including Walrus and Seals, Also of the Herbivorous
Cetacea, &c. *W. H. Lizars, Edinburgh.*

in only a few years American and Russian sealers took 150,000 fur
seals from the Farallon Islands off San Francisco. Galápagos, Baja,
and Guadeloupe Island off the Mexican coast collectively yielded at
least the same number.

During the first decade of the 1800s, sealers also reached the southern outposts of the Indian Ocean: Kerguelen, Heard, Prince Edward
Island, and the Crozets. These isolated specks of land lie around
2,000 kilometers (1250 miles) from the edge of Antarctic, far south of
trade routes. They had been missed by explorers until necessity drove
sealers and whalers into unknown waters. Within a few years of the
discovery of new rookeries, they could be stripped from tens of thousands to a few hundred animals. Sealers saw no sense in leaving any
animals behind because the next ship to visit would take them. What
happened to these seals was an early manifestation of what Garrett
Hardin called the "tragedy of the commons," which may arise where
many people have access to a desired but limited resource that nobody
owns or nobody can control. If each person using the resource acts

selfishly, rather than for the common good, all will eventually lose as the resource is depleted. In an influential study published in the 1960s, Hardin explained how this concept applied to grazing of animals on common land.[16] Individuals seeking to profit from this free resource try to maximize the number of animals they graze on the land; in combination, though, their flocks overgraze and all the animals may starve in the end. If instead the farmers acted cooperatively and agreed to keep overall flock size within the limits of the land, all would be better off.

By 1810, the sealers were well aware that what had seemed like an infinite resource was dwindling fast. Exploration of unknown seas for unexploited rookeries became an increasing necessity for profits to be had from sealing, and secrecy became the capital stock of companies hunting seals. Nonetheless, aside from François Péron's lamentation on the elephant seal, in writings of the day it is hard to find any sense of remorse over the decimation other than in purely utilitarian terms. An entry on sealing in *Jardine's Naturalist's Library* volume *Amphibious Carnivora* speaks of recent events in the South Shetland Islands:

> On this barren spot their numbers [fur seals] were such that it has been estimated that it could have continued permanently to furnish a return of 100,000 furs a year; which to say nothing of the public benefit, would have yielded annually, from this spot alone, a very handsome sum to the adventurers. But what do these men do? In two short years, 1821–2, so great is the rush, that they destroy 320,000. They killed all, and spared none. The moment an animal landed, though big with young, it was destroyed. . . . So is it, we add, with other localities, and so with other Seals; so with the Oil-Seals, and so with the Whale itself, every addition only making bad to worse. And all this might easily be prevented by a little less barbarous and revolting cruelty, and a little more *enlightened* selfishness.[17]

The South Shetlands of which Jardine spoke had proved a late bonanza for the sealing industry. In the austral summer of 1819, William Smith, captain of a trading boat between Buenos Aires and Valparaíso, rounded Cape Horn further south than usual in a search for more favorable winds. Nine hundred kilometers (560 miles) southeast of the Horn, he sighted distant ice-covered peaks shrouded in fog and cloud. On reaching Valparaíso, he reported his discovery to a British naval officer in the port, who dismissed his findings as probably just ice. Later that year, Smith made landfall, claiming the islands for Britain. This time, when he reported his discovery, a naval expedition was quickly dispatched to reconnoiter the islands, taking Smith as pilot.

Imagine Smith's surprise when on arriving he found two sealing vessels already on the South Shetlands! Despite all his care in concealing the location of his find, word of Smith's earlier discovery had leaked out. A ship from Buenos Aires and a Connecticut ship called the *Hersilia* that had been in the Falklands were already assaulting the islands' fur seal rookeries. The *Hersilia* managed to take on nine thousand skins in only fifteen days. (The captain later lamented that he had seen three hundred thousand seals and could have taken three times the number of skins if only he had had enough salt.) The Buenos Aires vessel was better prepared: it went away with fourteen thousand skins after five weeks' work.

An 1821 *Edinburgh Philosophical Journal* account by the ship's doctor of the naval surveying voyage included this prediction:

> The fur of the [seal] is the finest and longest I have ever seen; and from their now having become scarce in every other part of these seas, and the great demand for them both in Europe and India, they will, I have no doubt, become, as soon as discovery is made public, a favourite speculation amongst our merchants.[18]

And speculation there was. Sealers elsewhere reacted quickly to news of the discovery. In the 1820–1821 season, some thirty American sealers and two dozen British vessels descended on the islands, stripping the beaches of their breeding colonies and coming increasingly into conflict with each other as numbers of seals dwindled.[19] Over the season, the vessels spread out among the islands, searching for undiscovered haul-outs, profit their desire and their reward. They were back the following year, but found few fur seals and were forced to resort to hunting the much less valuable hair seals to fill their cargoes. Only three years after the islands were first discovered, the South Shetlands seal rush was over, with some 250,000 pelts taken and thousands more seals slaughtered. The self-interest shown by sealers was anything but the enlightened kind that Jardine had wished in his *Amphibious*

*Carnivora* that sealers would show. The tragedy of the commons had played out to devastating effect in this desolate corner of the world.

The South Shetlands represented one of the last major "finds" for the fur sealing industry, but it did not signal the end of sealing. There were still large numbers of elephant seals to be hunted for oil. In the early days of sealing, elephant seals had been hunted by a few vessels that specialized on this animal, but more often were caught to make up cargoes of oil from whaling, or as an adjunct to fur sealing. After the decimation of fur seal herds, elephant sealing became big business, at least until the mid-nineteenth century when elephant seals also became scarce. As these preferred species declined, sealers turned to other sources of oil, such as sea lions and monk seals. The three species of monk seal are warm-water specialists and were never as abundant as the seals that inhabited the rich polar waters. Of the three populations of monk seals, the Caribbean population was common fare for pirates in Dampier's day (although considered much inferior to manatee flesh), but it is now extinct, and the Hawaiian and Mediterranean populations hover at the brink of extinction. Even the scattered populations of these species were fair game for sealers, and today's low numbers are partly a legacy of their zeal.

Why didn't fur seals bounce back from their population collapse in the early nineteenth century? They in fact did so in a handful of places, but when those spots too were discovered, boats were briefly able to load up on skins once more. But the general pattern was for fur seals to be taken whenever they were encountered by people engaged in other activities, such as whaling and fishing or even by cargo carriers. Typical of the kind of mixed cargoes seen in the mid-nineteenth century was that Captain Graville returned to Hull in 1848; it included 225 barrels of blubber, 10 hundredweight of baleen [~ 500 kilograms; 1100 pounds], 1 unicorn (a narwhal), 1 seahorse (a walrus), 8 bearskins, and 7,510 seal skins. But such good fortune could quickly turn in this trade: the following year Graville's ship was wrecked in Greenland, although all of the crew was saved.[20]

Growing scarcity drove up the price of pelts, so hunting remained worthwhile even with smaller numbers—another reason the seal population couldn't bounce back easily. A seal skin that once fetched one dollar could sell for seventeen dollars in the early twentieth century.[21] The sealers found other values for the less desirable seal species, which also kept them in business. The "trimmings" trade involved the sale of dried seal penises and gall bladders for use in oriental medicines, and whiskers for toothpicks and opium-pipe cleaners.[22] Sustained persecution caused numbers to dwindle further, and by the early twentieth century all eight species of southern fur seals were on the edge of extinction. The rookeries of Juan Fernández had fallen silent, and the native fur seal there was thought extinct. Also believed extinct were the Galápagos fur seal and the Guadeloupe fur seal, formerly a resident of the Baja Peninsula and islands off the California coast.[23]

There were two final pockets of abundance though, on the east and west sides of North America, in Newfoundland and the Pribilof Islands in the Bering Sea. Hunting of seals in both places had been more controlled than the free-for-all massacre that characterized remote and uninhabited islands at the extremities of the earth. The Newfoundland seal hunt came under the jurisdiction of Canada, while that of the Pribilofs was initially Russian but transferred to the United States when the latter purchased Alaska in 1867. The Newfoundland seal hunt was based mainly on harp seals that haul out on the ice to pup during an improbably short season of about three weeks each year. There they could be clubbed to death and skinned in the tens of thousands. The harp seal hunt is still profitable today (and controversial). But the seals of the Pribilofs nearly succumbed to overexploitation in the late nineteenth century.

Northern fur seals (*Callorhinus ursinus*) were the target in the Pribilofs. This was the species Steller came across on Bering Island in 1742, but their real stronghold was in the Pribilofs. When these islands were discovered in 1786, their seal rookeries were as thickly populated as those of Juan Fernández, probably numbering 3 million seals. Initially, the hunt was uncontrolled, like those elsewhere. However, from around 1800, efforts were made to regulate the kill to avoid waste and ensure long-term profitability. By the time Alaska passed into American hands, the annual take had stabilized between 30,000 and 40,000 skins.[24] Under American jurisdiction, hunting intensity increased, with an annual take of 100,000 skins a year by the Alaska Commercial Company between 1870 and 1890. This alone was sufficient to endanger the herd, but there was also a growing problem from pelagic sealing—that is, the hunting of animals at sea.

The northern fur seal is a migratory species. After pupping is over, the Pribilof population heads south, following the west coast of North America. Females travel farther than males, getting as far as California, while the latter remain in the Gulf of Alaska. Seals breeding on Bering and Copper Islands and the Kurils head south toward Japanese waters. While America was able to regulate hunting on its shores, it could not stop sealers taking animals at sea. Offshore sealing killed indiscriminately: male, female, or immature, all were fair game. What made matters worse was that females leave their rookeries to feed several times during a three- to four-month breeding season, so could be shot by sealers and their pups left to starve. Washington Coulson, an American naval captain, in 1896 gave evidence to the U.S. Congress on the condition of seal life in the Pribilof Islands:

> I visited the Reef and Garbotch rookeries, St. Paul Island, in August, 1891, and saw one of the most pitiable sights I ever witnessed. Thousands of dead and dying pups were scattered over the rookeries, while the shores were lined with emaciated, hungry little fellows, with their eyes turned towards the sea uttering plaintive cries for their mothers, which were destined never to return.[25]

Numbers of pelagic sealers increased rapidly, from four boats in 1880 to sixty-eight in 1890.[26] The killing was highly wasteful, since many seals sank immediately when shot and were lost. Some estimates put the number lost as high as 96 percent of those shot, but the more likely average was about two out of three seals lost. With four nations involved—Japan, Russia, Britain (representing Canada), and the United States—it wasn't long before relations soured as arguments flared over what to do about the declines.

Pelagic sealing undermined U.S. management of the herd and robbed the Treasury of valuable revenue. For their part, countries involved in pelagic sealing recognized the need for management, since seal numbers were in freefall. Something had to be done. In the early 1890s, a partial agreement among these nations was reached through international arbitration in Paris, limiting the activities of pelagic sealers. It soon became clear though, that nothing short of an outright ban on pelagic hunting could save the dwindling herds. Finally, in 1911, a treaty was signed prohibiting all pelagic sealing and dividing up the terrestrial catch among the parties. By this time, the Pribilof herd numbered just 130,000 animals, and the treaty came only just in time to prevent complete disappearance. The agreement was the first international environmental treaty.[27]

It is easy to forget, in these days of reliance on petroleum, that the origins of our dependence go back much further than the times in which we first learned to pump oil and gas from the earth. It was in the seventeenth and eighteenth centuries that we first forged econ-omies dependent on oil for light, heat, and many other uses. Most of that oil came from the sea, grown in the bodies of whales and seals. Over four centuries the whale and seal hunters slaughtered on an astonishing scale, killing millions of animals to feed demand for oil, skins, whalebone, and ivory. They stripped the seas, place by place, species by species, killing the largest and most spectacular megafauna left on the planet. In the late nineteenth century, the hoary old British whaler William Barron reflected with an optimism hard to muster today on how matters had changed in his lifetime:

> At one time it was almost thought that the world would stand still if the supply of fur of seals, and bone and oil of whales should cease. The supplies did cease, but still the world goes on, and what was half a century ago so highly valued is now scarcely missed.
>
> Science and nature have ministered to man's necessities, and a far better oil of illuminating purposes . . . has been supplied in such abundance that the homes of the poor are supplied with a better, cheaper, and more healthy illuminator than whale oil. Thus we have an assurance that the needs of man will always in some form be supplied by a bountiful providence.[28]

The depredations of sealing and whaling stretched beyond the shores and beaches of the places visited. Remote islands in particular supported many other species that had adapted to the isolation and comparative safety of their haunts, some of them unique. The islands had dense populations of ground-nesting birds such as penguins, albatrosses, and shearwaters. They were slaughtered as provisions and decimated by introduced rats, cats, and dogs. In some places, birds became new targets for exploiters, albatrosses slaughtered for feathers and penguins boiled up in the hundreds of thousands for oil. The verdant, tree-clad slopes rhapsodized by early visitors were soon converted to overgrazed and eroding scrub by goats and pigs introduced for food.

It is easy to see how people on land have altered the ecology of islands, eliminating some species, introducing others, and changing the landscape. Beneath the sea, the alterations must have been just as dramatic though much harder to see. The destruction of fur seals on Juan Fernández removed a major fish predator from these seas and a food source for the 6-meter-long (20 feet) sharks seen plucking seal pups from the surf by early visitors. The complete removal of Greenland right whales and walrus, from around the islands of Svalbard in the Arctic Ocean, whose prediscovery populations have been estimated at forty-six thousand and twenty-five thousand, respectively, surely precipitated a dramatic shift in the Arctic ecosystem.[29] Loss of the whales freed up some 3.5 million tonnes of plankton yearly, probably benefiting little auks and fish like capelin and cod. The obliteration of walrus would have reduced predation on shellfish, giving a boost to species like eider duck and bearded seals. Removal of predators probably also had negative consequences that reverberated through food webs, perhaps knocking out as many species as they benefited. When today travelers stand on a lonely strand in the South Shetland Islands and hear the shriek of a skua bending to the wind, it is not the same place that William Smith discovered. When they smell the ocean on the salt breeze, it is not the same breeze that ruffled the fur of countless seals in the early nineteenth century. The signs of hunters and fishermen long since gone are still written in the seas all around. We are only now learning to read them.

# Chapter 9

# The Great
# Fisheries of Europe

S A TEENAGER I lived in Wick, a remote fishing port of seven thousand inhabitants located at the far northeast extremity of Scotland. The land is low and for much of the year the climate bleak. My favorite weekend pastime was to hike along the ragged cliffs fronting Wick Bay to a ruined tower, and there contemplate nature and life. Old Wick Castle was thick walled and crouched on a narrow, rocky promontory, three sides sea and one land. I would sit on the headland, the wind billowing waves through the grass and spreading windrows across the bay, enjoying my solitude. Aloft, effortless fulmars rode the wind, and kittiwakes returning with food wheeled and shrieked before finding their ledge among the thousands of others crammed with birds. Occasionally, a trawler would chug from the bay, headed for some far distant grounds, perhaps the Barents Sea or Iceland. There was little to suggest how different the scene had been a hundred years earlier when, in terms of catch, Wick was the world's largest fishing port.

Wick's fortunes were founded on herring. Each year vast empires of fish converged upon the shores of Britain and Europe. In the north, herring and sprat reigned; in the south, the legions comprised pilchard, sardine, sprat, and anchovies. All these species are members of the same family of fish, the Clupeidae or herringlike fish.[1] The sardine is the juvenile stage of the pilchard, as its Latin name *Sardina pilchardus* reflects. The sprat is a smaller version of the herring that occurs near shore and around estuaries in tightly packed schools. Herringlike fish occur in huge schools and feed on tiny planktonic organisms drifting in the open sea. Among fish in this family, the herring itself was by far the most important in economic terms. It was the most abundant of all the fishes around northern European shores, each year coming within reach of coastal fishers when the great schools pressed inshore to breed. Their oily flesh is firm and succulent and afforded vital protein to rich and poor alike. Moreover, they could be salted in barrels and transported long distances from the sea to markets without spoiling. As one early twentieth-century writer put it, "In value and renown the herring takes an unassailable position as the lord of fishes."[2]

Since the dawn of commercial fishing, the great coastal fish schools that swirled around European coasts were a mainstay of fishing. In turn, the bounty drew other species, like whales, seabirds, sharks, and seals, creating magnificent spectacles the like of which no longer exist in Europe. But the schools were capricious, too, sometimes bringing great plenty, at other times abandoning their familiar haunts altogether. Across Europe, fisheries rose and fell to the pulse of the unseen environmental signals that controlled the fish, and with them went the fortunes of people and nations.

James Bertram, an expert on fisheries, described the scene in Wick during the herring season in the late nineteenth century. The boats left the harbor en masse as evening approached, fishing at night when the herring schools came to the surface.

> Soon the red sun begins to dip into the golden west, burnishing the waves with a lustrous crimson and silver, and against the darkening eastern sky the thousand sails of the herring-fleet blaze like sheets of flame.[3]

Each skipper would tack up and down on the wind, searching for signs of herring before shooting the nets and letting the herring and tides do the rest.

*A great catch of mackerel landed at Lowestoft Harbor, England around 1905. The hold is full and the fish fill the deck to the gunnels. This catch sold for £200, equivalent to around £10,000 or US$20,000 today. Source: Wright, S. (1908)* The Romance of the World's Fisheries. *Seeley and Co. Ltd., London.*

Surrounding us on all sides was to be seen a moving world of boats; many with their sails down, their nets floating in the water, and their crews at rest. . . . Others were still flitting uneasily about, their skippers, like our own, anxious to shoot in the right place. By-and-by we were ready; the sucker goes splash into the water; the "dog", a large inflated bladder to mark the far end of the train, is heaved overboard, and the nets, breadth after breadth, follow as fast as the men can pay them out, each division being marked by a large, painted bladder, till the immense train is all in the water, forming a perforated wall a mile long and many feet in depth; the "dog" and the marking-bladders floating and dipping in long zigzag line, reminding one of the imaginary coils of the great sea serpent.[4]

Herring fishing was most successful, and most beautiful, on the darkest nights. In the inky blackness of a summer night, beneath the boats great herring schools ignited around them a phosphorescent planktonic glow that flickered and flashed off mirrored scales. Occasional streaks of light revealed the passage of predatory fish plunging through the schools. As the nets were hauled, the plankton would wink and glow on the meshes and bodies of the fish. A visitor to the Hebridean Isle of Barra in the 1920s described the delight of this moment:

> I have seldom seen anything which was quite so physically and coldly lovely. For the first fifty yards or so of the nets we found nothing; then quite suddenly we began to pull on board over the tiny boat, sheets and sheets of shimmeringly ecstatic silver. My back was soon aching and my hands and arms up to the elbows slimy and wet with fishy blood, torn and bruised with the net. . . . The herrings flopped, shivered, gleamed, and died as I piled them into the hold; but innumerable thousands more emerged from the black and moving sea. It seemed to me endless, but it was lovely.[5]

Herring were caught in drifting gill nets that intercepted the schools as they passed. In an attempt to swim through, the fish would force their heads through the mesh and get held by the gills, being able to move neither forward or back. Occasionally, hundreds of thousands of fish were taken in a haul, and boats had to discard some at sea for lack of space. In fair weather, some boats crept back to port so low in the water from their catch that waves would lap over the gunwales.

As boats returned to Wick Harbor, they met a scene of prodigious activity.

> On all sides we are surrounded by herring. On our left hand countless basketfuls are being poured into the immense gutting-troughs, and on the right hand there are countless basketfuls being carried from the three or four hundred boats which are ranged on that particular side of the harbour; and behind the troughs more basketfuls are being carried to the packers. . . . All around the atmosphere is humid; the sailors are dripping, and every thing and person appears wet and comfortless; and as you pace along you are nearly ankle deep in brine. Meantime the herrings are being shoveled about in the large shallow troughs with immense wooden spades, and with very little ceremony. Brawny men pour them from baskets on their shoulders into the aforesaid troughs,

and other brawny men dash them about with more wooden spades, and then sprinkle salt over each new parcel as it is poured in, till there is a sufficient quantity to warrant the commencement of the important operation of gutting and packing. Men are rushing wildly about with note-books, making mysterious-looking entries. Carts are being filled with dripping nets ready to hurry them off to the fields to dry. The screeching of saws among billet-wood, and the plashing of the water-wheel, add to the great babble of sound that deafens you on every side. Flying about, blood-bespattered and hideously picturesque, we observe the gutters; and on all hands we may note thousands of herring barrels, and piles of billet-wood ready to convert into stave. At first sight every person looks mad—some appear so from their costume, others from their manner—and the confusion seems inextricable; but there is method in their madness, and even out of the chaos of Wick harbor comes regularity.[6]

The herring schools reached the coast of Britain in a series of waves, coming later in the year the farther south you went. The first spring schools appeared in the northerly Shetland Islands around late April. The schools came inshore at Wick and northern Scotland a month later. They arrived in northern England in July through August, and finally the great schools of East Anglia arrived in October. Along the Scandinavian coast, spring spawning herring arrived among the islands and fjords of Norway early in the year, while Sweden and Denmark had to wait until autumn. Piecing together this behavior, along with herring patterns along the North American coast, the eighteenth-century naturalist Thomas Pennant developed an elaborate hypothesis. He imagined the herring wintered as a vast mass in Arctic seas, and then, pursued by natural enemies and pressed by the need to feed and breed, set forth on an almighty migration:

> [T]the great colony is seen to set out from the icy sea about the middle of winter; composed of numbers, that if all the horses in the world were to be loaded with herrings, they would not carry the thousandth part away. . . . [T]hey are seen to separate into schools, one body of which moves to the west, and pours down along the coasts of America, as far south as Carolina, and but seldom farther. In Chesapeak Bay, the annual inundation of these fish is so great, that they cover the shores in

such quantities as to become a nuisance.[7] Those that hold more to the east, and come down towards Europe . . . begin to appear off the Shetland Isles in April. These are the forerunners of the grand school which arrives in June.[8]

Although imaginative, Pennant was mistaken, and even by the early nineteenth century his theory was being questioned. Whalers had never seen herring in the Arctic, certainly not in the numbers envisaged by Pennant. Others pointed out that herring could be caught around Europe in all seasons of the year, albeit in greatly reduced numbers in some months. More careful observations revealed that herring from different areas of Europe were distinctive and not part of a single mass; skilled traders could even tell where a fish had come from just by looking at it. These varieties, it transpired, were distinct races that came inshore to spawn in particular areas at particular times. Summing up a century of observation and research, the French fishery scientist Marcel Hérubel declared in 1912, "There are almost as many races as localities."[9]

There was no mistaking the spectacle presented by the great annual arrival. The appearance of the herring schools and their attendant armies of predators ranked as one of the world's most remarkable wildlife phenomena. The very name "herring" is thought to come from the German *heer*, meaning "army." The eighteenth-century playwright, novelist, and encyclopedist Oliver Goldsmith takes up the description in the 1776 edition of his *History of Earth and Animated Nature*:

> [The] arrival [of the grand school] is easily announced, by the number of its greedy attendants, the gannet, the gull, the shark and the porpess. When the main body is arrived, its breadth and depth is such as to alter the very appearance of the ocean. It is divided into distinct columns, of five or six miles in length, and three or four broad; while the water before them curls up, as if forced out of its bed. Sometimes they sink for the space of ten or fifteen minutes, then rise again to the surface; and, in bright weather, reflect a variety of splendid colours, like a field bespangled with purple, gold and azure. . . . The whole water seems alive; and is seen so black with them to a great distance, that the number seems inexhaustible. . . . Millions of enemies appear to thin their squadrons. The fin-fish [fin whales] and the cachalot

[sperm whale] swallow barrels at a yawn; the porpus, the grampus, the shark, and the whole numerous tribe of dogfish, find them an easy prey, and desist from making war upon each other . . . and the birds devour what quantities they please. By these enemies the herrings are cooped up into so close a body, that a shovel or any hollow vessel put into the water, takes them up without farther trouble.[10]

Fishers pursuing herring would search the horizon for signs of a school: the breach or blow of whales, the sudden leaping rush of fish scattering above water to escape attack from unseen predators below, wheeling mobs of seabirds, and the airborne pummeling by gannets plunging into water thick with fish. Along westerly coasts of Europe, people also looked for the fins of basking sharks breaking the surface, a sure sign that plankton was thick in the water. Come early summer, these giant sharks appeared in thousands, cruising and circling with mouths agape to strain the nutritious planktonic broth.

The appearance of the herring schools signaled that spawning time was near. Herring spawn in shallow water over rocks and gravel, usually near coasts. Early-season herring were often too fat and heavy with roe to be preserved by salting or smoking and had to be eaten fresh.[11] Such enormous schools could deposit vast quantities of spawn. Drifts of sticky eggs were sometimes encountered covering the seabed to depths of 1 to 2 meters (3 to 6 feet).[12] Haddock shoals finding a herring spawning ground would so gorge themselves on eggs that they became fat and acquired a distinctive flavor. So close would the herring schools approach the shore, and so thick were they in the water, that heavy seas could sometimes throw great numbers ashore where they could be retrieved by the basketful.

In the years around 1870, some eight hundred thousand barrels of herring a year were cured in Scotland,[13] bringing prosperity to a country where other opportunities were sparse. Scotland's herring fishery grew in large part from a series of government initiatives in the eighteenth and nineteenth centuries to encourage Britain's inhabitants to profit from the wealth crowding their shores. Such encouragements included funding harbor improvements, like those that made Wick great, and establishment of the first fishery subsidies, called "bounties," usually paid to vessel owners by ton of shipping.

These efforts grew from a mixture of indignation and government pragmatism. A seventeenth-century observer writing in 1633, for example, sputtered, "It maketh much to the ignominie and shame of our English nation that God and nature, offering us so great a treasure, even at our own doores, wee doe, notwithstanding, neglect the benefit thereof, and by paying money to strangers for the fish of our own seas, impoverish ourselves to make them rich."[14] And from a practical perspective, Britain depended on the fishing industry to act as a low-cost nursery of seamen to provide a ready source of trained sailors for the British navy should war come.[15] Promoting the fishing industry was thus a matter of patriotism, national pride, and economic necessity. Georg Hartwig, a Victorian author and writer on the sea, put it nicely in 1892 while giving us a sense of the magnitude of just the herring enterprise in Scotland:

> When we think of the present grandeur of British commerce, which extends to the most distant parts of the globe, and ransacks Nature for new articles of trade, it seems almost incredible that up to the middle of the sixteenth century the herring fishery on the British coasts was left in the hands of the Dutch and Spaniards, and that the acute and industrious Scotchmen should have been so tardy in working the rich goldmines lying at their gates. But if their appearance in the market has been late, they have made up for lost time, by completely distancing all their competitors. In 1855, the Scotch herring fisheries employed no less than 11,000 smacks or boats, manned by 40,000 seamen, who were assisted by 28,000 curers and labourers, exclusive of the vessels and men bringing salt and barrels or engaged in carrying on the export trade.[16]

One lesser-known effect of the sequential pattern of herring appearances around the shores of Britain was the annual migration of the fishing fleet and an entourage of gutters and curers to follow the fish. In the eighteenth century, thousands of women from throughout the countryside would walk hundreds of miles to the north of Scotland every spring to meet the herring schools. John Knox, who traveled the highlands of Scotland in the late eighteenth century, was struck by the hardships of life for these migratory herring lassies:

> The families of these poor people are in a state of constant migration; for the wives and children of fishermen are employed in gutting the fish. The women travel along the dreary coast, from bay to bay . . .

with their infants on their backs, a little oatmeal, a kettle and a few
other utensils, which an uninhabited waste [the Scottish coast] could
not supply: they commence their cold and heartless labour without
shelter for themselves or their infants, without any change of their
daily diet of fish and oatmeal, no house to screen the sick or the
dying—the heath, the cavern, or stunted bush their only bed.[7]

As the season drew on, the fishing fleet moved south with the herring, followed by women and children on shore. By autumn some
women might have traveled almost the length of the country, from
Wick to Yarmouth in the east of England. Conditions improved
slightly by the latter part of the nineteenth century, when the fish gutters traveled by train between ports, but they continued to endure
great hardship. Today, there are still migratory labor forces that criss-
cross nations following the seasons as they harvest crops, and fishers
who criss-cross oceans in pursuit of migratory fish.

Along the south coast of England, and along the shores of France,
Spain, and Portugal, where there were few or no herring, more
southerly species brought seasonal plenty to fishing communities.
Pilchards, sardines, and anchovies formed large schools close inshore,
and were pursued by large schools of predatory mackerel and other,
more formidable beasts. These schools were nothing like the mountainous herring armies, whose schools could block the light from 20
or even 40 square kilometers of seabed (8 to 16 square miles). But they
still darkened bays and coasts. Because these fish approached closer
inshore than herring, the manner of catching them was different.
Rather than use passive drift nets, the schools were encircled by
seines and then hauled into the boats or drawn up the beach. Anyone
who has tried to discover the position of a school of fish from boat
level will know how hard it can be. Fishers in the cliff-fronted shores
of western England had an answer to this difficulty, employing
cliff-top "huers" to guide them to the fish and direct their capture.
The nineteenth-century author Wilkie Collins penned a memorable
description of an encounter with a huer:

> A stranger in Cornwall, taking his first walk along the cliffs in August,
> could not advance far without witnessing what would strike him as a
> very singular and even alarming phenomenon. He would see a man

*Scottish women gutting herrings at the English port of Scarborough on the North Sea coast around 1910. From the eighteenth to the early twentieth centuries, women and children would migrate almost the length of Britain following the herring fleet as it pursued the fish schools southward over the course of the season. Source: Contemporary postcard.*

standing on the extreme edge of a precipice just over the sea, gesticu-
lating in a very remarkable manner, with a bush in his hand, waving it
to the right and to the left, brandishing it over his head, sweeping it
past his feet; in short, acting the part apparently of a maniac of the
most dangerous description.[18]

Catches of pilchards were enormous in good years. They were
salted down in great heaps for ten days or so before being packed in
hogsheads for export to Mediterranean countries. In 1871, an excellent
year, 45,000 hogsheads were exported, amounting to some 135 million
fish. More usually, exports ranged from 15,000 to 30,000 hogsheads.[19]
The fishery employed six thousand fishers and twice as many women
and children in good years.[20]

Writers marveled at the fecundity of the sea, as evidenced by the
great fisheries for these schooling fish. Writing of the herring, Goldsmith made a back-of-the-envelope calculation of their fecundity in
1776:

> This power of encreasing in these animals, exceeds our idea, as it
> would, in a very short time, outstrip all calculation. A single herring, if
> suffered to multiply unmolested and undiminished for twenty years,
> would show a progeny greater in bulk than ten such globes as that we

*Emptying a good catch of pilchards from a seine net off the southern coast of England
in the nineteenth century. Copy of an original painting by Charles Napier Henry,
now in the Tate Gallery, London. Source: Wright, S. (1908)* The Romance of the
World's Fisheries. *Seeley and Co. Ltd., London.*

live upon. But happily the balance of nature is exactly preserved; and their consumption is equal to their fecundity. For this reason we are to consider the porpess, the shark, or the cod-fish not in the light of plunderers and rivals, but of benefactors to mankind.[21]

Today, fishes of the herring tribe and species like them are known as "forage fishes." This is because they play a fundamental role in sustaining marine food webs. By feeding directly on microscopic phytoplankton and zooplankton, they convert it into flesh that larger fish, marine mammals, and seabirds can eat. The mighty schools that attracted fishers drew hosts of predators. Whaling had thinned cetacean ranks somewhat by the eighteenth and nineteenth centuries, but until the twentieth century whalers generally avoided predatory rorqual whales of the kind that eat schooling fish. Only then, when boats were faster and explosive harpoons were standard, was it worthwhile to pursue them. These whales carried too little blubber, and their heads were small, so the lengths of baleen were short and of low value. They were also muscular and lively and could put up a vigorous fight when harpooned, risking life and capital. So fin, minke, and blue whales were prominent among the ranks of predators pursuing the throngs of herring, pilchards, and sprat in European seas.[22]

Whales were joined seasonally by voracious sharks, dogfish, porpoises, dolphins, and predatory fish like mackerel, tuna, and cod. Even the giant bluefin tuna would penetrate the North Sea during warmer periods, hunting herring to the mouth of the Baltic and the north of Scotland.[23] Such predators were thus for centuries a common sight even close to shore.[24] Harbor porpoises, for example, were so named because they were so plentiful around the coasts of Europe they entered rivers and harbors. The 1810 edition of *A History of Earth and Animated Nature* says of the porpoise:

> There are great numbers of Porpoises seen on the English coasts, especially in Mackarel and Herring seasons; at which time they are wont to do very great damage to the fishermen, by breaking and destroying their nets to get at the fish; and sometimes so entangle and wrap themselves up in them, that they are often taken. . . . These fish will sometimes pursue their prey close to the shore, nay, even in the very harbour.[25]

Goldsmith, writing a few decades earlier, in 1776, says of dolphins and porpoises around Britain:

> They are found, the porpess especially, in such vast numbers, in all parts of the sea that surrounds this kingdom, that they are sometimes noxious to seamen, when they sail in small vessels. In some places they almost darken the water as they rise to take breath. . . . In times of fairer weather, they are often seen herding together, and pursuing shoals of various fish with great impetuosity. Their method of hunting their game, if it be so called, is to follow in a pack, and thus give each other mutual assistance. At that season when the mackarel, the herring, the salmon, and other fish of passage, begin to make their appearance, the cetaceous tribe are seen fierce in the pursuit; urging their prey from one creek or bay to another, deterring them from the shallows, driving them towards each other's ambush, and using a greater variety of arts than hounds are seen to exert in pursuing the hare. . . . Indeed, these creatures are so violent in the pursuit of their prey, that they sometimes follow a shoal of small fishes up a fresh water river, from whence they find no small difficulty of return. We have often seen them taken in the Thames at London, both above the bridges and below them.[26, 27]

Porpoises and dolphins were just two among the host of predators in pursuit of schooling fish. They were joined by sharks; the large porbeagle, blue, mako, and thresher sharks were common hunters of European seas and were occasionally accompanied by great white sharks. Today, the maximum length of a great white shark is listed in guidebooks as 6 meters (~ 20 feet),[28] but reports in eighteenth- and nineteenth-century literature, too numerous and detailed to be dismissed, suggest sizes of 8 or 9 meters were not uncommon.[29] Accounts at the time compare them in size with whales.[30] Sharks much annoyed fishers, ripping their nets and getting tangled in lines, often with great loss of catch. Porbeagle sharks hunted pilchards and herrings in scattered companies, while thresher sharks may have used their long and flexible tail fins to herd and possibly stun schooling fish.

Before twentieth-century industrial fishing took hold, European seas seethed with life. The British Isles sit amid a broad expanse of shallow, continental shelf stretching from Scandinavia far into the

Atlantic. Every winter, storms mix nutrients from the seabed with surface water so that in spring, when the days lengthen and sunshine warms the sea, there is explosive plankton growth. This rich planktonic soup nourished the immense schools of fish upon which the larger predators fell in endless pursuit. The sight of a herring school being attacked from all sides must have inspired awe in those who witnessed it. The herring in blind panic career in swerving rushes as packs of dogfish and cod pick them off from the edge of the school; fin whales break the surface with open mouths, spilling fish in streams of liquid flapping silver back into the sea; lithe blue sharks dart above and below the whales, some lifted clear of the water as the whales raise their heads from the water, slithering from their flanks back into the sea; and porbeagles glide like shadows, cutting deep passages through the school far below. At the surface, confusion reigns as thousands of birds bob on the oily water, picking at the dead and dying, some flapping from the water to avoid being sucked into the maw of a whale; the staccato whoosh of attacking gannets raining from above, cutting deep into the school, their passages marked by bubble trails; and the air thick with birds circling, swooping, and crying. Then there's unexpected calm when the fight passes to another quarter, leaving dark water punctuated by thousands of mirror scales twinkling and turning as they sink beneath the oily surface.

Through long centuries, the residents of Old Wick Castle must have had plenty of time to ponder the distant spectacle of herring schools fleeing the predatory pack. Herring supported almost unimaginably productive fisheries in the best seasons. When the builders of Old Wick Castle first sought solitude on that desolate northern shore sometime in the early fourteenth century, the herring capitals of Europe were in Scandinavia and Denmark, although there were plenty of herring around Wick. In Sweden, herring schools visited the fjords and rocky skerries of the Bohuslän coast, fronting the Skaggerak, to overwinter after spawning.[31] Since at least the tenth century, herring were caught close to land with beach seines that were used to encircle the schools and then pulled ashore, or with fixed gill nets set to intercept the fish. Along the southern shore of Sweden, in Scania, there was another spectacular herring fishery. The early Danish chronicler Saxo said that the herring schools along this coast were so tremendous that they blocked the passage of boats and could be taken by hand.[32] This fishery impressed Olaus Magnus in the sixteenth century:

> They [the herring] present themselves in such large numbers off shore that they not only burst the fishermen's nets, but, when they arrive in their shoals, an axe or a halberd [spear] thrust into their midst sticks firmly upright.[33]

Bohuslän and Scanian herring fisheries highlight one of the enduring problems for fishers who chase schooling fish—the capricious nature of the schools. Because they depend on plankton for food, and plankton production is highly affected by weather and sea conditions, the schools fluctuate greatly in size from year to year. The same vagaries of weather and sea influence the migratory behavior of the fish and can lead them to abandon their familiar haunts, sometimes for decades. Surviving monastic and tax records luckily give us a detailed picture of fluctuations in the Bohuslän fishery from the tenth century to the present day. Periods of abundance coincided with periods of harsh climate and bitter winters, while in times of scarcity the weather was mild. A similar, but opposing pattern can be seen in the pilchard fisheries of southern England and France. Harsh winters produced poor catches, while mild weather yielded plenty.

The erratic nature of the herring schools provided an important spur to the growth of an offshore fishing industry, with large vessels capable of pursing the fish wherever they might be. By the sixteenth century, Holland was undisputed king of the herring trade, to the envy of its neighbors. Their dominance rested partly on the discovery of a brine curing method in the fourteenth century that much improved the life span of preserved fish. It was said that Amsterdam was founded on the bones of herring. By 1681, nearly half a million Dutch were employed by the fishery, one-fifth of the population. The bounty lasted beyond the end of the nineteenth century, although fortunes shifted with the passage of time. The Danish Scanian herring fishery collapsed never to recover in the early fourteenth century, while dominance over the fishery passed to the British in the eighteenth century. By the mid-nineteenth century, 8,000 to 10,000 kilometers (5,000 to 6,000 miles) of drift nets were set every night among the North Sea herring schools during the peak of the season.[34]

As great as fish catches were, they were but a drop in the bucket compared to the amount consumed by predators. In its 1863 report, the Royal Commission appointed to inquire into trawling for herring in Scotland, estimated the consumption of herring by two of their most dedicated predators, cod and gannets. Making an allowance of two herring eaten per cod per day during a seven-month season, it estimated annual consumption of 29 billion herring, ten times more than taken by all the European fisheries put together. To this, the gannets of a single breeding colony, on the Scottish island of St. Kilda, added a further 214 million fish. Set in these terms, the take by people seemed trivial.

Throughout the history of the herring, pilchard, and sprat fisheries, people often caught more than they could save. Oily fish spoil quickly, and salt was limited. Excess fish were used as manure and fed to livestock. In the late nineteenth century, with the development of steam vessels, fishing power increased dramatically and fish often swamped the market. Before long, fishers on both sides of the Atlantic began to target schools specifically for fertilizer and animal feed, using enormous nets with tiny meshes. There was little point in worrying about selectivity or quality if the animals were only to be dumped in fields or fed to hogs. In America, menhaden, another relative of herring, became the mainstay of this fishery. With a now near limitless agricultural market for the catch, the great school fisheries expanded into the twentieth century. Just half a century later, the human take of herring would rise high enough to trigger the first superabundant fish stock to collapse. This would be followed by many others.

# Chapter 10

# The First Trawling Revolution

*T*HE REAR DECK glistens in the harsh floodlit glare. It is three in the morning and the trawl is being lowered into the sea. Fine rain sheets through the cones of light and streams from every surface. Beyond the pool of light the dark backs of waves roll by, punctuated by gasps of breaking foam. The pitching deck and shifting tones of the growling engines mark their forward progress as the boat clambers up slopes and plunges into the valleys of this unseen seascape. Taught steel cables thrum overhead as they peel off the winch, passing suspended through the towering arch at the rear of the boat before shooting downward into the black sea. Thirteen hundred meters (4,300 feet) below, the trawl mechanism descends toward the continental slope, surprising a few lantern fish in its cavernous gape and electrifying the permanent night with the spark and flash of disturbed plankton. Night is permanent at this depth, and the net is what stimulates the plankton to phosphoresce. Half an hour later, touching down on the bottom, the trawl begins to rumble across the flank of Patagonia in pursuit of toothfish, cutting a swath a hundred meters wide and four stories high.

Eight hours later, two 5-ton steel hydroplane doors, used to hold the trawl open, break the surface. There is a pause in the haul-back while they are secured. Then hauling resumes to bring the net aboard to the whining protest of the winch. First the bag of the trawl slides up the open incline at the stern, then the cod end, a mesh bag that contains the catch, emerges from the sea streaming water and bulging with fish. Men in yellow oilskins hurry around a deck slick with water and fish slime, manipulating the net over open hatch doors before slipping the knot on the cod end, cascading a part of the deep Atlantic into the open hold. It is a good haul and many dark toothfish of 1 to 2 meters long sprawl amid a chaos of broken life.

Apart from the feeble flap of a fin here and there, and the jerking death struggle of brittle starfish, the catch seems lifeless. Few animals survive ascent from such great pressures. Most fish lie with mouths agape, tongues forced from their heads by bloated swim bladders and sightless eyeballs starting from their sockets. Alongside the toothfish lies the twisted wreckage of deep-sea life—branches of pink bamboo corals, torn sponges and coiled sea fans, sea urchins, sea cucumbers, crabs with fist-sized bodies attached to long slender broken legs, deepwater sharks with humped backs and hooded silver eyes, slime-wrapped hagfish and gargoyle-faced grotesques with names only a scientist would know. The toothfish and a few other species are valued, but most of the rest is considered worthless and discarded over the side. This is modern bottom trawl fishing: destructive, wasteful, often lucrative, and now highly controversial. It is one of the most common methods of catching fish in use today.

Trawling—the dragging of nets across the seabed—has a long history. We can date its origin quite precisely because of a complaint made to the English king Edward III in 1376 requesting that he ban a new and destructive type of fishing gear:

> The commons petition the King, complaining that where in creeks and havens of the sea there used to be plenteous fishing, to the profit of the Kingdom, certain fishermen for several years past have subtly contrived an instrument called "wondyrechaun" made in the manner of an oyster dredge, but which is considerably longer, upon which instrument is attached a net so close meshed that no fish be it ever so small which enters therein can escape, but must stay and be taken.

And that the great and long iron of the wondyrechaun runs so heavily and hardly over the ground when fishing that it destroys the flowers of the land below water there, and also the spat of oysters, mussels and other fish upon which the great fish are accustomed to be fed and nourished. By which instrument in many places, the fishermen take such quantity of small fish that they do not know what to do with them; and that they feed and fat their pigs with them, to the great damage of the commons of the realm and the destruction of the fisheries, and they pray for a remedy.[1]

This is the first historical reference to a bottom trawl from anywhere in the world. Parliamentary procedures seem to have changed little over the course of centuries. The response to this petition was to appoint a commission to look into the complaint. The commissioners met in the port of Colchester on the Essex coast to give their verdict. They reported that the net was "three fathoms long and ten men's feet wide."[2] At the ends of a 10-foot (3-meter) wooden beam were two iron frames formed like a colerake (a rake used for clearing ash out of a furnace). The top of the net was attached to the beam with nails, while the bottom had a rope weighted with lead and many great stones. The lower part of the net ran along the seabed, scaring fish into the bag, held open by the beam above. The commissioners could not see their way to an outright ban of what would be easily recognizable today as the beam trawl, but they determined that it should be used only in deep water and not in the waters of coastal estuaries and bays. No law was passed to enforce this decision, perhaps because all parties agreed to the solution.

This earliest account of trawling practice provides as eloquent a statement of the drawbacks of this fishing method as any I have read. What is striking about the commoners' petition is that, even at the very beginning, the trawl was perceived as a destructive and wasteful fishing method. Also remarkable is the evident understanding of the biology of the animals people fished and of how these animals relied on biologically rich habitats for survival. Today, in its several forms, the trawl is one of the most widely used and destructive types of industrial fishing gear. The arguments put to the king in 1376 have echoed down the centuries as trawling spread and methods were adapted. They have recently flared up again in discussions of deep-sea trawling, as once again the trawl is moving into regions never before fished, with disastrous consequences for bottom-living creatures.

With the invention of the beam trawl, the fourteenth century marks the first of three trawling revolutions. The second would happen in the late nineteenth century with the addition of steam power to trawling vessels. The third came in the second half of the twentieth century as trawlers penetrated the deep sea for the first time. Intense controversy surrounded each of these trawling revolutions, with many people calling for the method to be banned, commissions of enquiry appointed, and arguments made for and against. Trawling has survived these many challenges. It remains to be seen whether deepwater trawling will survive the charges laid against it today.

Even at the time of the first trawling revolution, what is notable about the spread of bottom trawling was that its appearance was almost universally met with anger and hostility, at least by fishers not using trawls. Most of what we know about the early history of trawling in fact comes from measures taken to ban or restrict its use. In 1491, fishers from southeast England were fined for using "unlawful engines" and small-meshed nets to catch juvenile fish.[3] In 1499 the fishers of Flanders were more successful in protecting habitats and fish stocks from trawl damage. There a decree was passed that banned trawls that "rooted up and swept away the seaweeds which served to shelter the fish."[4] A century later, in 1583, the Dutch banned trawling for shrimp in their estuaries. France made the practice of trawling a capital offence the following year, and in England, the tide also turned against trawling. Two fishermen were executed for using metal chains on their beam trawls (standard issue on the beam trawl today) to help scare fish off the bottom and into the nets. Despite popular opposition to it, trawling was evidently too attractive as a means of catching fish to be abandoned.

Further complaints were made in the seventeenth century about the use of trawls with small meshes, and Britain passed a law in 1714 stating that

> as the breed and fry of sea fish has been of late years greatly prejudiced and destroyed by the using of too small a size of mesh and by other illegal and unwarrantable practices, no one shall use at sea, upon the

coast of England, any trawl net, drag net or set net, for catching any kind of fish except herrings, pilchards, sprats, or lavidnian [sand eels] which has any mesh of less size than three and a half inches from knot to knot.[5]

The practice of trawling spread slowly at first. By the late seventeenth century, trawlers were common in Great Britain only around the port of Brixham in the English Channel and around the mouth of the Thames estuary. They were small boats that towed nets with a beam only 3 to 3.5 meters wide (10 to 12 feet).[6] There was also scattered use of primitive trawls around continental coasts, but compared to other forms of fishing, trawling remained a minority pursuit. Several factors, I believe, held it back. The controversy over trawling must have discouraged many people from adopting the gear when other successful methods were readily available. But there was a more fundamental problem, as the fourteenth-century trawlers discovered: how to dispose of a plentiful catch in the days before refrigeration and when markets for fresh fish were limited to coastal towns. The discovery of curing methods for herring and pilchards was instrumental in directing early efforts to expand fisheries around Europe toward these species, using large drift and seine nets rather than trawls to snare them. There was also a ready market for dried and salted cod brought from Scandinavia, Iceland, and Newfoundland. These fisheries quickly grew to industrial scales with complex infrastructures for preserving and distributing fish. But there was still little possibility for disposing of large quantities of fresh fish from a trawl. Instead, small-scale hook-and-line fisheries typically supplied local needs.

Hook-and-line fishing prospered through two main developments. One was the switch from handlines to longlines in the eighteenth century. Longlines, as the name implies, were far longer than handlines and carried hundreds or thousands of hooks attached to the main line by short lengths of twine. The second boost came from the invention of the well-boat in Holland sometime in the sixteenth century. This was a boat fitted with watertight bulkheads blocking off a middle section of the vessel. Holes bored through the timbers allowed seawater to flood and circulate through this central well. Line-caught fish, especially hardy species like cod and halibut, would be thrown into the well as soon as they were caught. They could then

*Beam trawls consist of a bag net held open by a wooden or steel beam. They were invented in fourteenth-century England and were towed by sailing boats until the late nineteenth century when steam power was introduced. Source: Collins, J.W. (1889)* The Beam Trawl Fishery of Great Britain with Notes on Beam Trawling in Other European Countries. *Government Printing Office, Washington, DC.*

be kept alive and fresh, for weeks if necessary, for transport to coastal ports. There they were transferred to holding tanks to be slaughtered and sold as demand dictated. Well-boats were introduced to England in 1712 and quickly caught on, ensuring supplies of fresh fish to people in London.[7] By the early decades of the nineteenth century the port of Grimsby on the Yorkshire coast of England was filled with casks of live cod in temporary storage. The naturalist Frank Buckland described the scene:

> Floating in the water are a great number of immense boxes, looking like gigantic dice. They measure about ten feet long, five feet wide, and four feet deep. In one place the boxes were so thick that the water could not be seen. These boxes contain live cod, and they get renewed water as the tide goes in and out, through the holes bored in the sides of the boxes. . . . One of these boxes was hauled up alongside a barge, and the lid opened for my inspection. The sight was most interesting and curious: there appeared one solid mass of living cod, all struggling and gaping with their immense mouths. . . . According to the supply wanted for the market, the cod are taken out of the boxes and "felled" by a blow on the head with a heavy mallet. . . . In another of these boxes there was a large number of great halibuts. . . . The cod will live in the boxes eight weeks: they have no food given them.[8]

Early in the nineteenth century, trawlers from ports on the south coast of England ventured into the North Sea and took large quantities of valuable turbot and brill. These prime fish were sold to the wealthy and in London were known as "West End Fish." Like other flatfish, they lived close to the bottom and were not taken in significant numbers except by the beam trawl. Initially, these fishers struggled to get their fish to market fresh using horsedrawn carriages. Well-boats were good for getting fish close to coastal markets, but they could not solve the problem of overland transport. However, a new invention was about to change fishing forever.

The development of a steam railway engine in the late 1820s paved the way for a dramatic expansion of fishing, transforming the economics of trawling in particular. By 1840, there were 1,100 miles of railway in use throughout Britain, expanding to over 7,000 miles by the early 1850s.[9] Similarly rapid building programs were soon undertaken in Europe and America, providing quick and efficient transport between the coast and inland centers of population. The market for fresh fish suddenly expanded, and the price rose with increased demand. For a time, live line-caught fish were carried in tanks of water mounted on railway carriages, but preservation by ice imported from cold countries like Norway and Canada soon made this obsolete. The large volumes of fish landed by trawlers could now be sold at sufficient profit to cover the cost. By the early 1860s, over 100,000 tons of fish a year were carried by the railways of Britain, and the size of the fishing industry was twice what it had been twenty years earlier.[10]

Once railways were established, there was a boom in trawling in countries bordering the southern North Sea. Perhaps the biggest stimulus to English trawl entrepreneurs came in 1843. It was a bitter winter and a trawlerman from Hull was on his way back from a poor trip to the Dogger Bank. Chancing his trawl in an unfamiliar spot, he discovered an uncharted depression in the North Sea bed. He could hardly believe his luck when the net came up almost bursting with a catch of sole, another prime species in high demand. The sole had retreated to deep water apparently to escape the cold, and the spot soon became known as the Great Silver Pit, for wealth could be hauled from the water as quickly as trawlers fished: "such catches were made as the most experienced fishermen had never dreamed of."[11]

With railways spreading, any number of fish could be sold. As virgin coastal grounds became more heavily fished, pressure grew to find new fishing grounds. Fishers began to operate in fleets to extend their range, one boat carrying all of the fish to port every day to ensure the catch arrived fresh. By the 1850s, use of ice to preserve fish became routine, and the industry consumed thousands of tons per year. Ice had the dual benefit of expanding the market and increasing the area of the fishing grounds. Boats carrying ice were no longer tied to coastal waters and could hunt farther offshore.

What was it like to fish for bottom fish in the North Sea in the early nineteenth century during these heady days of explosive growth in the fishing industry? With the exceptions of large-scale herring and cod fisheries, most fishing up to then had been from small boats within a few miles of shore. As fishing power grew, vessels pushed farther offshore, encountering rich new grounds. The North Sea was astonishingly fertile and was dotted with raised banks and shoals thick with fish. Foremost among them, the Dogger Bank sprawled across more than 30,000 square kilometres (11,000 square miles) of the central North Sea, almost equidistant between England, France, Holland, Germany, and Denmark and was fished by people from all these nations. During the last ice age, when the North Sea was dry, the Dogger was a land of low rolling hills and valleys, trodden by woolly mammoth and rhinoceros. But by the nineteenth century, it was the kingdom of fish:

> If the North Sea waters were translucent, what a wondrous sight would be presented to the voyagers upon its surface! Countless myriads of fishes find existence in them, and certain portions of the Dogger and other banks would not show sand or shell, or smooth or rough ground, according to the charts; but would reveal an almost solid moving dark or silver mass.[12]

On a good day in the early nineteenth century, eight men with handlines might catch eighty score of cod on the Dogger, or two hundred fish each.[13] With ten hours fishing in a day, that is one fish per man every three minutes. It was a time, too, when giant fish still lurked in abundance in the deep. Buckland notes the sale of a halibut in London in 1874 that measured 75 inches long by 47 inches wide (188 x 118 centimeters). Common skate grew to be as large as doors. One served at St. John's College at Cambridge University in the late eighteenth century weighed 200 pounds (91 kilograms) and in the body measured 42 inches long by 31 inches wide (105 x 78 centimeters), and fed 120 people. William Buckland described an even larger skate: 82 inches long with the tail, and a body 63 inches wide (205 x 158 centimeters). In these rich waters, fishers had to compete for their quarry with an abundance of predators. Walter Wood, an early twentieth-century writer on the North Sea, describes the most pernicious:

> The dog fish is the shark of the North Sea, the past and present foe of all fishermen. He wages incessant war with their nets and catches; he never shows mercy, and never gets it. He is a game fish and usually dies fighting. He can do incalculable mischief to drift-nets and make vast numbers of herring and small fry utterly unfit for market, because he seems to kill and mangle for the mere joy of murder and lust of maul.

He is voracious and ferocious, and when he is hauled in the trawl at midnight it is needful to turn aside for settlement with him, for he will bite through any limb to the bone, and will not let go.[14, 15]

Today, there are few places left in the world where sharks are prolific. Tales of fish being stripped from the hooks by sharks as fast as they are caught have taken on the mantle of myth, or at any rate are limited to a few tropical hotspots such as Cocos Island in the eastern Pacific. To think that such scenes were once also common in Europe tests our credulity, but they were. Sharks in the North Sea even occasionally killed sailors who fell overboard.[16] Farther north, on the Arctic whaling grounds, large Greenland sharks could be so common that if a boat was delayed in flensing a whale by bad weather, the carcass could be stripped of its flesh in a day.[17]

Not all encounters with predators were bad for fishing, and fishers often took advantage of chase between predators and their prey. The herring fishers looked for signs of a struggle at sea to find the shoals. Likewise, cod fishers switched from longlining offshore to handlining inshore when packs of cod pursued the herring there. Haddock, according to Goldsmith in 1810,

> annually visit the British coasts in shoals that sometimes extend along the shore above 100 miles in length, and 300 in breadth. On the Yorkshire coast, they keep close to the shore, and such is their numbers, that two or three fishermen will sometimes take each a ton of them in a day; but, beyond their limits, he finds nothing but dog-fish, which have, no doubt a tendency to pack them together.[18]

Trawlers pushing into virgin grounds would sometimes find their nets so full of fish they would tear in the process of hauling them. Occasionally, a net would become so full underwater it would stop a boat in its tracks.

The size of the English trawling fleet expanded from around 130 boats in the early 1840s to over 800 by 1860 in response to the advent of steam rail power and increased demand. This expansion was not a welcome development to many thousands of fishers using lines, nets, and traps. Increasingly, the trawlers came into conflict with other fishers, and trouble erupted. In the 1850s there were violent protests in Ireland and parts of Britain, with nets burned and trawlermen driven

*Nineteenth-century fish market in the town of St. Ives in Cornwall, England. Fish were caught locally using hook and line. Source: Contemporary postcard.*

away by intimidation. Like their fourteenth-century predecessors, the fishers complained that the trawlers were wiping out fish stocks, especially by the destruction of fish spawn and immature fish. They argued that the trawl cleared the bottom and ruined their bait beds, such that longliners could not get enough mussels and whelks to bait their hooks. The fishers also complained that trawlers swept away their drift nets, longlines, and crab pots, and that crab populations were imperiled by soft crabs being crushed when shedding their shells. Pilchard and herring fishers also claimed the trawl broke up and dispersed schools of fish, driving them away.

With the fishing industry at boiling point, the British government appointed a Royal Commission in 1863 to inquire into the complaints against trawling, as well as other grievances. Their terms were to investigate

> firstly, whether the supply of fish is increasing, stationary, or diminishing; secondly, whether any modes of fishing . . . are wasteful, or otherwise injurious to the supply of fish; and thirdly, whether the said fisheries are injuriously affected by any legislative restrictions.[19]

The three members of the commission toured the nation, visiting eighty-six fishing communities and taking over a thousand pages of evidence from many hundreds of witnesses. One of the commissioners was the zoologist Thomas Henry Huxley, then only thirty-eight years old but already well known for his robust defense of Charles Darwin's theory of evolution by natural selection. Huxley probably already had strong views on fisheries before he embarked upon this marathon tour. He certainly had them by the time the commission reported three years later, for the inquiry came to a most extraordinary conclusion that few could have imagined at its commencement.

To appreciate the nature of fishers' grievances against the trawl, it is important to understand how beam trawls work. At the time of the Royal Commission's enquiry, the wooden beam of the trawl that held the net bag open was typically around 36 to 38 feet long (11 to 12 meters), much larger than the trawls employed by fishers in previous centuries. This was mounted on two steel frames that held the beam off the bottom as it was towed, leaving the lower side of the bag, to which a weighted ground rope was attached, to drag along the seabed. The net was shot over the side of the boat and towed for around three to five hours before being winched using a hand-operated capstan. Unlike catches obtained using drift nets, lines, and traps, trawl catches were highly variable. A nineteenth-century description gives a good flavor of a typical haul:

> The contents of the net differ according to season and locality, but generally they are of a most varied character—a wonderful exhibition of marine life. Sliding back and forth on the slippery deck, as the vessel rolls in the sea-way, are soles, turbot, brill, and plaice, giving vigorous but rather spasmodic slaps on the plank with their tails; here may be seen the writhing body of a conger eel; there the fierce wolf-fish, with its jaws armed with wicked-looking teeth, snapping at whatever comes in its way, while prominent in the crowd is one of those wide-mouthed fishing frogs [the angler or monkfish], which some one has called an "animated carpet-bag." These, together with gurnards, iridescent with beautiful color, the vicious dog-fish—always the fisherman's enemy—wriggling about, shells, sea anemones, sea-corn, etc., constituted a variety of animal life such as is rarely brought together by any other means.[20]

This description also gets to the heart of one of the most serious complaints fishers leveled at the trawl: that it roots up the bottom and destroys the habitat, food, and spawn of the fish.

In their report, the commissioners began with a rather damming caricature of the nature of their witnesses and the quality of evidence given:

> Of the many methods of taking Sea Fish . . . very few have escaped complaint from one source or another. . . . As these complaints have usually been brought against one class of fishermen by others, who, rightly or wrongly, conceived themselves to be unjustly injured in their most important interests; and as they have been rebutted by persons whose means of living largely, or wholly, depend upon their power to continue the alleged wrongful practices; it will not be a matter of astonishment that the evidence, so far as it records merely personal convictions, and assertions that can neither be proved or disproved, is of the most conflicting character. In making this remark we have no wish to reflect in the slightest degree upon the veracity of either side. . . . But fishermen, as a class, are exceedingly unobservant of anything about fish that is not absolutely forced upon them by their daily avocations; and they are, consequently, not only prone to adopt every belief, however ill-founded, which seems to tell in their own favour, but they are disposed to depreciate the present in comparison with the past. Nor, in certain localities, do they lack the additional temptation to make the worst of the present, offered by the hope that strong statements may lead the State to interfere, in their favour, with dangerous competitors.[21]

The commissioners overwhelmingly rejected the contention that the supply of fish was diminishing. In the absence of systematic fishery statistics (none were collected at the time), they were unable to see any clear trend in abundance. In some places, a species might be doing well, whereas in others fishers claimed it had fallen in numbers. In most places, some species remained productive, even if others seemed to have fallen off. The signal, if there was one, was lost in the noise of real year-to-year fluctuations in abundance and the imprecision of people's recollections.

On the contrary, the commission was strongly impressed by the contribution that trawlers made to the supply of fish in the marketplace by this time. One witness, a fish trader from Billingsgate Market in London, stated that some 90 percent of the fish he sold were from the trawl. Furthermore, the line-caught fish, being larger and dominated by prime species, fetched a higher price and were out of reach of the poor. Restricting trawling would therefore have a serious negative impact on the supply of food, he concluded.

Regarding the second complaint, that the trawl is wasteful and destroys immature fish and the spawn of fish, the commission again concluded that the allegations were unproven. In the first place, although they heard much evidence of immature fish in catches, they had no data on how mortality from fishing related to that from natural causes. They inferred that natural causes far outweighed fishing, and therefore catching young fish was regrettable but not wasteful. As for spawn, at this time, most fishers thought fish spawned on the seabed and that trawls must necessarily destroy spawn. Science was unable to help the commissioners come to a view, since little was known about fish reproduction. They were persuaded, however, that much of what fishers thought was fish spawn brought up in the trawl was actually other animals such as sponges, sea squirts, and cuttlefish eggs. In drawing their conclusions, they were also much influenced by the counterargument that trawling actually increased production from the sea. One witness referred to trawlers fishing over the same ground, and following each other to get better catches. When asked if there was any particular food the fish feed on, he replied with the essence of the counterargument:

> There is when the ground is stirred up by the trawl. We think the trawl acts in the same way as a plough on the land. It is just like the farmers tilling their ground. The more we turn it over the greater supply of food there is, and the greater quantity of fish we catch.[22]

It was in relation to their final question, whether fisheries are injuriously affected by any legislative restrictions, that the commission delivered its bombshell:

> [I]f any trawling ground be over-fished, the trawlers themselves will be the first persons to feel the evil effect of their own acts. Fish will become scarcer, and the produce of a day's work will diminish until it is no longer remunerative. When this takes place (and it will take place

long before the extinction of the fish) trawling in this locality will cease, and the fish will be left undisturbed, until their great powers of multiplication have made good their losses, and the ground again becomes profitable to the trawler. In such circumstances as these, any act of legislative interference is simply a superfluous intervention between man and nature.[23]

Having for three years heard so much evidence on fisheries "of the most conflicting character," the commissioners might be forgiven for thinking that there was little a government could do to improve fisheries through legislation. Their conclusion was as shocking as it was simple:

> We advise that all Acts of Parliament which profess to regulate, or restrict, the modes of fishing in the open sea be repealed; and that unrestricted freedom of fishing be permitted hereafter.[24]

Two years later, the Sea Fisheries Act was passed into law, expunging from the statute books more than fifty acts of Parliament accrued over several centuries. Fishing became possible whenever, wherever, and with whatever methods fishers pleased. British attitudes toward fishing at this time largely mirrored views elsewhere in the world. Set against the bounty and fecundity of nature, there seemed little harm that people could do to wild fish stocks that inhabited seemingly limitless seas. But this laissez-faire approach led to unbridled expansion of fisheries, and within a couple of decades it would have serious impacts on fish stocks and their habitats.

# Chapter 11

# The Dawn of
# Industrial Fishing

***

*I*NSIDE THE Aberdeen Sheriff Court House in late September 1883, the air is thick with tobacco smoke, in marked contrast to the chill clarity of the Scottish autumn outside. Where the judge and counsels would normally sit, five eminent gentlemen listen intently to John MacDonald, line fisherman, give evidence. The room is crowded, and latecomers still squeezing in at the back take off their caps as they enter. Mr. Marjoribanks, a member of Parliament, is putting the questions:

> Q. When you say [the trawlers] destroy the feeding grounds of the fish, how do you mean they do that? How do they interfere with the feeding ground of the fish?—A. They trawl along the bottom and tear everything that is before them.
>
> Q. Then you will not agree with a statement made at a former inquiry, that the effect of the trawl at the bottom of the sea was to increase the food of the fish by cultivating the bottom?[1]

At this point the courtroom erupts in indignation, and people shout their disapproval of the suggestion across the floor. MacDonald's reply, if he made one, is lost in the uproar. The chairman, Lord Dalhousie, is forced to intervene:

Gentlemen, I must really ask that we must not have these expressions of feeling, because there is a great deal of work to get through, and if we lose half a minute every time a statement is made we shall take a long time before getting through our work. . . . We are trying to get out evidence, and it is not at all proper, it is not at all fair to the witnesses, and not likely to help us in our work, that we should have these expressions of feeling.[2]

Mr Marjoribanks returns to his question:

Q. You would quite disagree with that suggestion that I made?— A. Yes.
    Q. Then your opinion would be that it is impossible that the trawl net by disturbing the bottom of the sea, could stir up additional food for the fish?—A. It cleans away everything before it.[3]

You can well understand the chairman's impatience. John MacDonald was only the third witness to be examined in what threatened to be another lengthy Royal Commission of Inquiry, this time focused exclusively on trawling. By the time the last evidence was taken in London, a few days before Christmas the following year, over twelve thousand questions would have been put to witnesses. Among the commissioners at Aberdeen was Thomas Huxley, veteran of the first inquiry, his face now deeply lined and with a shock of grey whiskers sprouting from each cheek. He would not be present at the last meeting, having been forced to retire from the proceedings due to severe depression and failing health, brought on by overwork and his beloved daughter's descent into mental illness.[4] But Huxley's probing questions in the early stages of the inquiry, and his mighty intellect, nonetheless strongly influenced the outcome.

What led so soon to another inquiry into trawling? With the commercial success of beam trawling, and the removal of all impediments to its use, industrious fishers quickly made improvements to increase fishing power. Early in the nineteenth century, sailing trawlers were 20 to 30 tons burden. Fifty years later, they were larger—70 or 80 tons—longer and leaner and carried a much greater spread of canvas, lending speed and power. By the 1870s, there were some sixteen hundred to seventeen hundred British trawlers, around twelve hundred of them working the North Sea.[5] Fishers using traps, hooks, and nets had come to an accommodation of sorts with the sailing trawlers. By learning to predict their movements according to conditions of wind and tide, they could set their gear where the trawlers would be unlikely to damage them. In addition sailing trawlers could not work areas of rough ground, and these places gave the best catches to line fishers and crab and lobster potters, welcome refuges from the sweep of the trawl. But in the middle of the 1870s, their world was overturned. The steam trawler was born.[6]

Reflecting on the history of fishing in his 1911 book *North Sea Fishers and Fighters,* Walter Wood calls the transition from sail to steam in fishing "one of the most amazing of modern revolutions." He wrote, "Steam, the conqueror, rules the North Sea fishing industry."[7] Steam burst the fragile truce among fishermen. Almost overnight it transformed fishing power and changed all the rules of fishing.

The fishing power of sailing trawlers was limited by wind and tide. They could not fish in calm weather for lack of motive power. To keep the gear on the seabed, rather than lifting off, they could tow only with the tide, which meant that fishing was impossible when wind and tide were set in opposite directions.[8]

Steam trawlers, to the great resentment of other fishers, had no need to wait for wind or tide. Freed at last from the yoke of weather that had held seafarers since time began, they could trawl backward and forward relentlessly. Furthermore, steam trawlers could tow larger nets than sail, and the length of beams swiftly increased to more than 50 feet (15 meters). The ground rope on beam trawls dragged by sailing vessels was made of old rope. If the trawl snagged on some obstruction, the ground rope would give way before the towing lines could snap and cause complete loss of the gear.[9] Steam power allowed chains to be wrapped around the ground rope since the vessel could now tow over larger and more stubborn obstructions, whether they be rubbish, rocks, or marine life. Steam winches could also handle steel cables, allowing trawls to be hauled over rougher ground and in worse weather than was possible using traditional hemp rope. Hauling the trawl net by steam winch also speeded up fishing, bringing in a trawl in fifteen to twenty minutes that would have taken fifty backbreaking minutes by hand crank.[10]

*Steam trawlers in the Fish Dock at Grimsby on the Lincolnshire coast of England in the early twentieth century. Steam power quickly replaced sail power for bottom trawlers after its introduction in the 1870s. Source: Contemporary postcard.*

The 1883 commission reawakened all the old arguments about trawling, as well as new ones specific to steam trawlers. Scottish fishers had resisted trawling until a few years before the inquiry, and it was partly in response to their outrage at incursions of steam trawlers from the south that the investigation took place. By the time of the hearings there were thirty steam trawlers working the Scottish coasts.[11] Many witnesses spoke of the impact of trawls newly introduced to their fishing grounds. Peter Sims gave evidence of the first experiments with trawling in the Firth of Forth, an estuary on the east coast of Scotland:

> Well one of these fish salesmen, as you call them, persuaded one of our Broughty Ferry skippers to try his trawl in the river [the estuary], saying if there was any damage done he would redeem it. The consequence was that one of them tried it, and the first drag of the trawl he got her so full that he could not get her aboard. He had to take her to the beach and let the water away from her before he got her emptied. When we saw that, first one and then another got a trawl, till every boat in town had trawls. They trawled up the whole river and they cleared it out in six weeks. Since then you would not get sixpence worth on a line now.[12]

By the time of the 1883 commission, there was growing evidence of depletion of fish stocks in areas close to the coast, which many witnesses blamed on trawling. And fishers had responded to the challenge of falling stocks by increasing fishing effort and by hunting for new fishing grounds, which made matters worse. Peter Paxton of Dunbar, for example, increased his longlines from five thousand hooks to over seven thousand within six years of the steam trawlers coming in. Crab and lobster fishers set more pots, and trawlermen and herring drifters switched to steam power, with all the advantages that gave. Concerns grew that too much was being taken too fast from the sea. Joseph Hills of the Sunderland Sea Fishery Protection Committee put it well:

> It was exactly the same with us in 1878. There was an immense quantity of fish coming in, and the very quantity that was coming in caused us to be alarmed and concerned about the matter. We knew that we were "killing the goose that had laid the golden eggs," and we thought it necessary to remonstrate against that state of affairs. The thing has gone on from that time to the present time, and whereas the trawlers at that time were able to get an abundance of fish at a very short distance from the port of Sunderland, they have had gradually to go further and further to sea; but the same class of vessels that went trawling there have been to some extent discarded. Larger, more powerful, and more scientific vessels have been brought into operation, and they have been enabled to carry more coals so as to go farther out to sea, and the result of the process has been that the whole coast of Durham, Northumberland, and Yorkshire has been destroyed, till there is nothing left but a mere remnant.[13]

Joseph Douglas of Eyemouth on the Northumberland coast had been a fisherman for forty-three years by the time of the inquiry and had lived through the fishing revolution brought on by railways, ice, and steam. He described the move offshore:

> Q. Were there many trawlers down there in those days?—A. Well when we went there they were trawling quite close in, very close to shore. . . . As time rolled on, year after year, they went out to the deep sea, and now I suppose at this present time, they go from about 200 to 300 miles.[14]

Complaints about trawl boats catching too many undersized fish were heard repeatedly. Witness after witness raged against the wastefulness of trawling. George Burgon, a onetime line-net-and-trawl fisherman of Eyemouth, on the stand:

> Q. Did you ever see a large quantity of small fish brought up, fish too small?—A. A good quantity. I am not speaking personally of what I caught myself, but what I have seen landed. I have seen hundreds and hundreds of baskets landed daily, not one day, but day after day.
>
> Q. Too small?—A. Too small, and more especially skate. I have seen hundreds of baskets of skate not bigger than the loof [palm] of your hand. I would say there would not have been fewer than 150 skate in each basket that would not have been fit for any human food at all.[15]

John Swinney, a Sunderland fisherman, recalled seeing discarded fish floating at sea:

> Last herring season I was going in a herring boat with my stepfather and he was sitting amidships looking to windward. He saw something floating on the water, and he said to me "Jack, what is that?" I said, "fish, sir." I put down the tiller and shoved her right alongside the fish. My little boy comes with the scum net, places some of the fish on the deck, and another man, when he took some of these small fish, said, "what a shame."
>
> Q. These were dead fish?—A. Dead fish, chucked overboard in the morning when the trawlers put their trawls overboard. I would willingly be my share for a set of oilskins [sic] for any gentlemen to go and see the destruction. That is what is wanted. We want men to go and see the destruction, not sit in this place and talk about it. We want it to be seen.[16]

John Craig, a Scottish fisherman from Portlethen:

> Q. What mischief do the trawlers do?—A. They destroy a great many immature fish, small fish, and they destroy the spawn. It is clear that the sea is a free fountain to every one, and every one should take as many fish as he can and go to the market and sell as many as he can, if he does not take them in a rascally way, but I consider that the trawlers take them in a rascally way because they murder more than they take.[17]

Complaints were also repeatedly made to the commission about the destruction of the bottom being caused by trawls. These fishers' testimonies allow us to begin to construct a picture of the transformation of the seabed as trawlers swept into fresh grounds.

The seabed is subject to many natural disturbances as well as those of trawling. Fish and crustaceans dig holes and grub up worms. More destructively, where seas are shallow, as they are over raised parts of the continental shelf, violent storms disturb the seabed and bring water to the surface, enriching it with nutrients that feed spring plankton blooms. Shallow banks like the Dogger are notorious during storms because waves crest across the shallows, creating dangerous breakers like those that took more than 360 fishers to their deaths in 1883. One fisherman caught in the storm described the appearance of the Dogger as a "roaring, foaming plain."[18] Every year shallow banks are reworked by storms and must be colonized by organisms anew. Wave energy falls off rapidly with depth, however. By a depth of 25 meters or so (83 feet), and shallower along sheltered coasts, conditions are sufficiently placid for fragile animals and plants to establish and persist, even through boisterous weather on the surface.

Tidal streams also scour coastal seas, moving sediment and gravel around. But delicate animals like corals, sea fans, and crinoids can also live in places where tidal flows pour strong as rivers. Over thousands of years, complex biological communities developed and grew, spreading across tens of thousands of square kilometers of seabed. These communities were not restricted just to areas of hard bottom, but carpeted mud, sand, gravel, and cobble, too. The biological structures knit together and stabilized sediments, enabling other animals and plants to colonize and grow. Across the rolling plains and hills of the continental shelves grew sponge groves of fantastic shapes and hues. Wafting among the sea whips and fans were beds of feathery bryozoans populated by gliding starfish and snails. Over long stretches of coastline, vast carpets of sea squirts extended seaward, sheltering scuttling crabs and lobster. In deeper water, delicate anemones and sea pens rose like forests from muddy fields, the creeping prawns beneath their canopy never straying far from their burrows for fear of hungry cod and haddock. Farther below, in the darkness, elaborate reefs built by the creeping growth of cold-water corals cover rubble scoured into banks by ice sheets grounding on the seabed during the last ice age. In the chill water, they afford homes for a thousand species of life.

In 1883, *The Piscatorial Atlas of the North Sea, English and St. George's Channels* was published to coincide with the International Fisheries Exhibition, held in London that year.[19] It is a magnificent quarto-sized volume of colored maps, each showing the distribution of a commercially valuable fish or shellfish of the time. There is also a map showing the nature of the seabed throughout the region. Splashed in carmine across 24,000 square kilometers (9,375 square miles) of the southern North Sea is an area marked "oysters." These oyster grounds consisted of reefs built of oysters, knitted and interlaced with countless other invertebrates. The bottom of the North Sea was hardened by a living crust, something that many scientists today find hard to believe.

Into this world, trawling came as a new and highly disruptive force. To the nineteenth-century grandees conducting the trawling inquiry, this world was barely conceived of and scarcely imagined. To the fishers, the habitats were real and critically important to the animals they caught. Although branded by earlier commissioners as "exceedingly unobservant of anything about fish that is not absolutely forced upon them,"[20] many of the fishers giving testimony had an intuitive and, given the rudimentary condition of marine science at the time, a surprisingly accurate view of the way the sea worked.

Trawlers quickly removed the communities of invertebrates accumulated through the ages. While most operators interviewed tried to underplay the impact of the trawl, for obvious reasons, some admitted the damage done. One questioned, Joseph Gravels from Brixham, recalled trawling on the edge of the Dogger Bank and other North Sea banks and filling his nets with invertebrates, once so full that it stopped his boat. Trawlermen called the invertebrate and seaweed crust over the seabed "scruff" and for a time avoided areas that clogged nets too much, such as off the coasts of Yorkshire and Lincolnshire.[21]

Another man interviewed in the inquiry, George Marshall from the port of Whitby on the Yorkshire coast of England, had been fishing forty-seven years:

> My experience is this. I believe trawling to be one of the most destructive things that goes into the sea, and I am in a position to prove that. I

have proved it time after time, year after year, that it destroys food, small fish and everything. The ground rope that is attached to the trawl clears all away with the exception of anything large enough to stop it going farther.[22]

John Meynell of Sunderland, spoke of his experience aboard a trawler:

Q. The night you were out did you see a great quantity of immature fish caught?—A. From what I saw come out of the bag it was a disgrace to look at.

Q. Tell us what it was?—A. Spawn, coals, boots, shoes, shirts, all kinds of rubbish; little trays [trees] that the fish resorts among; If you saw a little coral, I believe the bottom of the sea is something similar. There is a herbage that the fish live among; it is like a plantation at the bottom, and the trawlers bring up nothing but mud and all kinds of things in it.[23]

Other fishers noticed the change taking place as the seabed was stripped of its invertebrate life and seaweeds. Initially, they caught great mats of material torn up by the trawlers. John Swinney, a line fisherman from Sunderland, explained,

Well you have heard from Mr Hills about the seaweed. Now the trawlers as they trawl turn everything upside down, and I can prove it. We bring up from the bottom of the sea as much as a horse's waist [in thickness] or small lines of spawn[24] and seaweed mixed up.

Q. Till the trawlers appeared on the scene you never brought up this seaweed on your lines?—A. Only small quantities.

Q. Now you bring up large quantities?—A. The trawl gathers it altogether, and as they lift the trawl they leave it there.[25]

After a time, the bycatch of invertebrates and plants on the lines decreased simply because there was less left to gather. Henry Meldrum from the northeast coast of England recalled his experience of longlining:

Well, when we used to go for haddocks we used to get all kinds of curiosities, little trays [trees] of all sorts, and every description of shells, and what not. We cannot get anything on the lines now. We used to get things they called coxcombs, and the trawlers have swept them all away the same as they have swept away all the best fishing. They had a gold mine there . . . . [26]

As the trawlers worked over the seabed, they tore up the complex matrix of animal and plant life. John Driver of Newhaven said that during the eight months he had worked on a trawler, he had seen as high as three or four cartloads of horse mussels, clams, shells, and stones come up in a trawl drag. William Hunnam, a fisherman from Cockenzie on the Scottish coast, described the damage done to an area renowned as a bed for gathering bait for longlines:

> About two miles off Cockenzie, and then six miles east and west, . . . they have taken away the upper crust of the ground. And, mark you, it is the upper crust that the clams and scallops live amongst.
>
> Q. How do you know; have you seen it?—A. We know by our dredges going over it. The crust is all gone.
>
> Q. What was the crust?—A. The ground that the scallops live amongst. It is just a ground made up of broken shells, and all the like of these sort of things; and underneath that is mud. If we give our dredge half a fathom too much rope, she goes down altogether into the mud.[27]

Alexander Anderson, a fishmonger from Edinburgh:

> Q. A witness said yesterday that two or three miles north of Inchkeith the trawling had completely destroyed the ground and that there are no fish there. That is true, is it?—A. Yes.
>
> Q. To what do you ascribe the fact that these old men cannot make a living? Do you distinctly ascribe it to the trawling?—A. The fish have been taken away by the trawlers; the trawlers have destroyed the ground to which these fish came.
>
> Q. You think they destroyed it?—A. They dragged up the herbage that these fish came to feed upon at certain seasons of the year. The haddock is as fond of dulse [a seaweed] and what grows on the bottom as of any other food.[28]

Although Anderson was mistaken about haddock eating seaweed— they are carnivores—he was right about their association with more complex bottoms covered by growths of marine animals and plants. This association was well known to fishers. J.W. Collins, an American visiting Britain to investigate the beam trawl with a view to introducing it to America, wrote in 1889,

> A bottom of mud or sand, in a moderate depth of water, is the most favorable ground for the use of the beam trawl, providing, of course,

fish can be taken thereon; but it often happens that fish are much more abundant on rocky grounds, known by the name of roughs among the North Sea fishermen. Therefore, though there is always a great risk of losing the trawl when working on rough bottom, the hope of obtaining a large catch is often sufficient inducement for the fishermen to make the venture.[29]

Arguments over whether trawling increased the size of usable catch resurfaced during the new inquiry. Fishers in favor of trawling argued that the trawl dug up worms and other food from the seabed, making them available to fish. Others, such as John Murray, a fisherman from North Berwick, countered that the trawl destroyed the food of fishes:

> [A]ll along our coast . . . the ground abounded with small shell fish, particularly the cray fish, which is the chief food of large fish. I have taken out of the stomach of a cod four or five at a time; I have also taken them out of large haddocks and codlings. Now the ground is cleaned of this sort of shell fish by trawling, and now we have no large fish because their food is all taken away. I quite disagree with some of the evidence that has come before your lordships stating that the turning over of the ground makes fish more plentiful. I consider this statement is quite unnatural. The less ground is disturbed the more plentiful fish is.[30]

There were similar lengthy arguments in the new inquiry about whether trawling destroyed fish spawn. Much of the questioning hinged on whether or not fishers had actually seen spawn come up in the net. Many said they had, although on close cross-examination, they often could not be sure it was spawn and not some invertebrate or other. Surprisingly, what was obvious to many fishers, that running a huge beam trawl through a bed of spawn could break it up and disperse it, to the detriment of the eggs, was barely considered by the commissioners. As the aggregation of haddock and other predators around herring spawn was well known, it could hardly be doubted that trawlers would target areas used for spawning. Thomas Huxley, cross-examining James Marr of the port of Pittenweem on the Scottish coast, put it to him that by removing predatory fish, trawling might actually be doing the herring spawn a favor. Marr countered "Yes, but they were destroying more spawn than the fish were eating." One can imagine Huxley leaning forward and delivering his cutting riposte, "It does not appear plain to an unprejudiced reason, but still that is your opinion.—Yes."[31]

The spread of trawling caused the greatest human transformation of marine habitats ever seen, before or since. The descriptions of witnesses to the 1883 trawling commission chart the shift from biologically rich, complex, and productive habitats to the immense expanses of gravel, sand, and mud that predominate today. This change came first to Britain and parts of Europe, but by the 1920s would spread to reach the Americas, Africa, Australia, New Zealand, and seas beyond. Today, restless, shifting sands drift where once an oyster empire spread across the southern North Sea. The last oysters were fished there commercially in the 1930s, and the last living oyster was caught in the 1970s.[32]

Today there is hardly a scrap of suitable bottom in the world that has not felt the scrape of a trawl. David Boyter, a line fisher from Cellardyke in Scotland, was another witness to face Huxley's piercing gaze. The following exchange shows how fishers understood that the trawl was changing marine habitats, and reveals Huxley's ignorance of its use in the process:

> [Huxley] When you speak of muddy water, do you mean a muddy bottom?—A. A muddy bottom. If the bottom is muddy the water as a rule is muddy also.
>
> [Huxley] Are you aware that trawling takes place over a muddy bottom? All the trawling round the coast of Scotland is evidence that there is a muddy bottom there?—A. That is not so. The fact is it is quite the reverse.
>
> [Huxley] The fishermen before us the last two or three days have asserted that in certain places it was muddy and in others it was sandy?—A. It was not muddy; it was made muddy by the use of the trawl.
>
> [Huxley] The trawl does not take the mud and put it there?—A. No, but the trawl stirs up the mud.[33]

The power of the trawl to dig up the seabed was much increased by steam. With chains on the ground rope, steel cables, and engine power, trawls could drag and roll rocks along the bottom, crushing, pulverizing, and stripping the living matrix and liberating the mud and sediment beneath.

The conclusions of the 1883 trawling commission might be considered a whitewash given the nature and volume of evidence heard in criticism of the trawl. They concluded there was evidence for a falling off in stocks of only a few species of fish and only in places near to the coast. About the beam trawl, they concluded correctly that it was "not destructive to cod and haddock spawn," as they don't spawn on the seabed. More controversially they found that there was "no proof of injury to the spawn of herrings or other edible fish," which is not the same thing as no injury. Finally, they stated, "The injury done by the beam trawl to the food of fish is insignificant," and that there was "no wasteful or unnecessary destruction of immature food fishes."[34] Resentment at the latter conclusions echoed around Britain's ports until at least the end of the nineteenth century. A pamphlet published in Aberdeen in 1899 says it all:

> Dozens of witnesses swore before the commission that the trawl destroyed the food of fishes, the spawn of fishes, and the immature fishes; many declared from their personal experience that it was enough to make an angel weep to see the awful signs of destruction brought up on deck by the trawl.[35]

By this time, however, it was all over for opponents of the trawl. The 1880s saw the introduction of a new kind of trawl that could fish over rougher ground and could catch round fish like cod in addition to the flatfish the beamers were able to snare. This "otter trawl" dispensed with the cumbersome and heavy wooden beam, replacing it with two wooden boards, one on either side of the net that acted as hydroplanes in the water to keep the mouth of the net open. Otter trawls opened up huge new swathes of sea to trawling, and compensated, at least temporarily, for the reduction in catches caused by diminishing stocks. Line fishers were literally forced out of business by the trawls. Their expenses were greater—bait was costly and becoming more so as trawls tore up the bait beds[36]—and their competitive edge on prime fish was lost to the otter trawl.

The Royal Commission of 1863, when considering the supply of fish, really looked only at the volume coming to market, giving short shrift to stories of falling catches told by fishers. At that time, there was no such thing as fisheries science, and if the commissioners can be credited with anything positive, it is that they highlighted the need for better information to judge the state of fisheries. It would be some time, though, before an enterprising biologist was able to capture in statistics what the fishers experienced in their boats. Walter Garstang, who worked at the Marine Biological Association's laboratory in the west of England, devised the measure "catch per unit of fishing effort." He tallied up the fishing power of the fleet from the port of Grimsby on the North Sea, combining both sailing and steam vessels in a single measure he called "smack units." A steam vessel was taken to have four times the catching power of a sailing smack, the small sail-powered vessels that had been in use up to this time. Between 1889 and 1898, the total catch increased from 173,000 metric tonnes to 230,000 metric tonnes, a clear increase in the supply of fish according to the metric of the 1863 commission. But when the catch was offset by the increase in fishing effort, the catch per smack unit had fallen by nearly half, from 60 metric tonnes to just 32 metric tonnes. No wonder the fishers were complaining. The 1863 commission noted, "On the western part of the Dogger Bank it is not uncommon for a single trawl vessel to take, in a three hours' trawl, from two to three tons' weight of fish."[37] By the early part of the twentieth century, that had collapsed to just one ton per tow.[38]

By now, fish stocks had fallen in size so much that it was a matter not so much of choice but of necessity to use the trawl, although line-and-trap fisheries persisted in coastal areas. While the 1883 commission again concluded that the evidence against trawling was unproven, they did commission research into the question by a Professor McIntosh of St. Andrews University in Scotland. Thus began the first experiments with fishery closures. Several inshore bays and estuaries were closed to trawling and have remained so to this day. After a decade of study, McIntosh, too, exonerated the trawlers from blame in the depletion of fish stocks.[39] His research was flawed, however, because he did not, and probably could not, exclude line fishermen from areas closed to trawling. Given sanctuary from the terror of the trawl, the linesmen fished the closed areas intensively, thus preventing the expected buildup of fish.

McIntosh's research findings, although controversial, signaled the

*Blue shark, from the frontispiece of William McIntosh's 1899* The Resources of the Sea, *described as a species that "often ruins man's nets and hooks and defies his influence." Source: McIntosh, W.C. (1899)* The Resources of the Sea as Shown in the Scientific Experiments to Test the Effects of Trawling and of the Closure of Certain Areas off the Scottish Shores. *C.J. Clay and Sons, London.*

final acceptance of trawling in Britain and paved the way for global expansion of the practice. Already, Europe's steam trawler fleets, including those of Holland, France, and Germany, were fishing farther and farther afield in search of new grounds, reaching Iceland and the Mediterranean coast in the late nineteenth century. With each stage of expansion, trawlers encountered virgin stocks . . . and a virgin seabed.[40] By 1889, J.W. Collins wrote, "[A]t the present time it is pretty safe to say that there is little of the bottom of the North Sea suitable for trawling over which a beam trawl has not passed."[41] By the beginning of the twentieth century, scientists estimated that 100,000 square miles of the North Sea (260,000 square kilometers), its entire trawlable area, was hit twice every year by trawls.[42]

Ælfric, the abbot of Eynsham, near Oxford in England (AD 955–ca. 1020), wrote a tract on fishing in the early eleventh century in which he unwittingly described the end of an era in fishing. In it a fisherman is asked why he does not fish in the sea. He replies, "Sometimes I do, but rarely, because it is a lot of rowing for me to the sea."[43] A few decades later, his descendants would take to the sea out of necessity to catch fish, regardless of the hardship. Commercial sea fishing in northern Europe was born out of the world's first fishery crisis. Rising demand and massive habitat loss and transformation in freshwaters from damming and soil erosion, as we've seen, led to a collapse in the productivity of freshwater fisheries around the middle of the eleventh century.

When these fishers first took to the sea to catch fish for commercial gain, they could fish only close to shore and with rudimentary gears. Over the ensuing centuries, their art developed through a series of progressive improvements to technology, punctuated by several innovative leaps, such as the beam trawl, longline, and drift net. By the close of the nineteenth century, fishing power had been utterly transformed. Prior to this, the activities of fishers were inconsequential compared to natural forces, in all but localized areas close to coasts. But steam power gave fishers a new and lethal edge, cutting them loose from the bonds that held them close to ports. People had gained the ability to alter the oceans. During the twentieth century, they would exploit that ability to the full.

# Part Two

# THE MODERN ERA OF INDUSTRIAL FISHING

— *Chapter 12* —

# The Inexhaustible Sea

*I*N 1813, Henry Schultes, a British political commentator, set forth in strident terms the case for expanding commercial sea fishing in Great Britain. In doing so he betrayed a conception that was prevalent at the time throughout the industrializing world and its colonies, that the productivity of the seas was inexhaustible:

> In addition to a highly productive soil, the seas which surround us afford an inexhaustible mine of wealth—a harvest, ripe for gathering at every time of the year—without the labour of tillage, without the expense of seed or manure, without the payment of rent or taxes. Every acre of those seas is far more productive of wholesome, palatable, and nutricious food than the same quantity of the richest land; they are fields which, perpetually "white to harvest" [ripe], require only the labourer's willing hand to reap that never failing crop which the bounty of Providence has kindly bestowed. . . . That the mine we have to work upon is in reality inexhaustible, a transient inspection will be sufficient to satisfy the most sceptical inquirer.[1]

The good men of the 1863 Royal Commission to investigate the effects of trawling on British fish stocks concurred with Schultes's rosy view of the sea as a place ripe for fisheries expansion and never questioned the idea that nature was there to provide for people. Their main motivation for recommending the removal of all fisheries legislation was to stimulate the fishing industry to greater energy and effort. They believed that we had yet barely tapped the wealth of the oceans. And they too were impressed with the potential yield per acre, as if the sea were ground:

> Once in the year an acre of good land, carefully tilled, produces a ton of corn, or two or three cwt. of meat or cheese. The same area of the bottom of the sea on the best fishing grounds yields a greater weight of food to the persevering fishermen every week in the year. Five vessels belonging to the same owner, in a single night's fishing, brought in 17 tons weight of fish, an amount of wholesome food equal in weight to that of 50 cattle or 300 sheep. The ground which these vessels covered during the night's fishing could not have exceeded an area of 50 acres.[2]

Apart from getting their arithmetic wrong—one vessel would have covered around 50 acres, five would have fished five times more—the commissioners erred in assigning all of the fish production to the area of sea from which they were caught. Currents draw plankton and other organic matter across the seabed, enabling resident fish to benefit from a much greater total area of production. And unlike sheep and cattle on lands that are fenced in, the commissioners' fish moved from place to place, gathering food from a much wider region than the point of capture. Once planted, the rosy optimism and misconstrued productivity of the sea refused to be uprooted, even by the turn of the twentieth century when evidence of falling stocks had become hard to ignore. The bounty seemed endless, almost miraculous, and people closed their eyes to troubling signs of depletion.[3]

Alarms were beginning to be sounded, however. In the late nineteenth century, scientists had begun to gather the kind of data previous Royal Commissions on fisheries had so wished they had. Using these figures, Walter Garstang published, at the very beginning of the twentieth century, the first study of overfishing, "The Impoverishment of the Sea."[4] His evidence of a falloff in the quantity of fish was as unambiguous as his title. But Walter Wood, an enthusiast for the sea's inexhaustible bounty, had words for people like Garstang and the many dozens of witnesses to previous Royal Commissions who had predicted that the trawl would be the end of fishing:

The gloomiest of prophecies have been made concerning the harvest fields of the North Sea. Every year, for generations has brought forth its dismal seer who has foretold the utter depletion of the banks; yet these Jeremiahs have been consistently confounded, for, despite the vast growth of the fishing industry, the total quantities of fish increase annually. This is largely due, of course, to the opening of new and distant grounds.[5]

The last comment is a caveat innocently introduced, but proving so contrary to his argument. Even Wood, then, tacitly acknowledges that there must be limits to how much we can take from the sea. Throughout the first half of the twentieth century, the nascent discipline of fishery science developed around the need to "do something" about fisheries problems. The wide natural population fluctuations experienced by many marine species provided ample room for arguments over whether there was a human hand in declining stocks. In

*U.S. court at the International Fisheries Exhibition of 1883 in London. This exhibition showcased the growing might of the world's fishing fleets, but already, signs of depletion were apparent in some fishing grounds. Source: Whymper, F. (1883)* The Fisheries of the World. An Illustrated and Descriptive Record of the International Fisheries Exhibition, 1883. *Cassell and Company Ltd., London.*

recent years, climate change skeptics have raised similar arguments, contesting that natural variations rather than human activities are responsible for warming trends, so giving regulators an excuse to postpone action. However, as far as controversies around fishing went as decades passed, it became clear that fishing had major effects on stocks of exploited species. Perhaps the most compelling evidence was an unintended consequence of the First World War. Wartime hostilities led to a blockade of the North Sea, effectively shutting down the offshore fishery for four years. At the end of the war, when boats again took to the sea, they caught huge hauls. Later estimates suggest that stocks of the main fishery species trebled during the four years of the war.[6]

Throughout the nineteenth and early twentieth centuries, fishing underwent its own industrial revolution. Although traditionalist fishers often resisted new technologies, necessity soon forced them to embrace them. Declining stocks of fish rendered the old technologies obsolete, and those who refused to adapt to the new went out of business. For a long time, technological advances and the opening up of new fishing grounds concealed the extent of population declines. Aggregate landings looked healthy, because of continued growth in fleet size and catching capacity. But old-time fishers knew from their daily experience that it was getting harder to catch fish. Fishers as a profession have long been caricatured as pessimists for whom the past is always better than the present. It is easier to understand their predilection for gloom when you realize that fishery declines have been part of their everyday experience for at least the last two centuries.

The beginning of the twentieth century signaled a new era for the fishing industry all over the world. Fishing power had never been greater, and it must have felt to fishers that they had at last gained the upper hand in their fight for a living from the sea. Sailing boats were discarded wholesale in favor of engine-powered vessels that could fish far afield. There was an optimism about that, which was perhaps not justified given the declines experienced in fish stocks close to coasts, and dissent against new fishing technologies fell silent.

There are three ways to get more from the sea when the rate of fishing exceeds the rate of production of a species—catch something else, fish somewhere else, or fish less. The last of these remedies was a prescription from the new 'fisheries science,' which I will come back to later. It seems paradoxical that you can get more by fishing less, but it is a simple consequence of letting more young fish live to a marketable size. Perhaps not surprisingly, the less fishing remedy was not terribly popular. Instead, when an area's population of a fish species declined, fishers concentrated their efforts on expanding into new grounds and catching new species. The only problem with catching new species, it seemed, was lack of a ready market. In 1943, a young biologist with the U.S. Fish and Wildlife Service set out to solve this by publishing a handy guide to the seafood of New England called *Food from the Sea* that introduced unusual fish to consumers. Rachel Carson would later become well known for her book *The Sea Around Us,* published in 1951, and for her classic *Silent Spring* in 1963. In *Silent Spring,* Carson pictured a world poisoned by pesticides from which birds had been exterminated. But in her early writings on marine life, she never imagined seas without fish. Her seafood guide is full of optimism for the future in fisheries, suggesting that the solution to overfishing is to diversify. In the ringing tones of the 1940s, Carson's seafood guide exhorts the reader to try new kinds of seafood:

> Scarcely any other class of food offers so great a variety—so rich an opportunity for gustatory adventure. The housewife who experiments with new fish species and new methods of preparation banishes mealtime monotony and provides delightful taste surprises for her family.[7]

Carson accepts that some species, such as haddock, have been overexploited. The market for several species of fish, including haddock, halibut, and pollock, had received a huge boost in the early 1920s with the development of the frozen-food industry. Catches rose and then fell as fishing boats homed in. She suggests consumers substitute species such as cusk, a deepwater relative of cod that lives over rugged bottoms, and wolffish. Wolffish have bulbous toothy heads that seem ill matched to their lithe, eel-like bodies. They live among rocks and corals and make a living crushing urchins and mollusks with their powerful jaws. The wolffish is, Carson explains, "an excellent table fish that deserves to be better known."[8] Some of her other suggestions are perplexing, given the state of stocks known at the time. For example, the two species of alewife that were so important to the early settlement of America had obviously fallen to unprecedented lows. She contrasted 1940s catches with those of 1896, finding that in Connecticut, Rhode Island, and Massachusetts they had declined from 8 million pounds to under 1 million pounds a year (~ 3,600 to 430 metric tonnes). But alewife runs in 1896 were already far below those of the early colonial period. Despite this, she says,

> Threatened shortages of other, better known fishes—especially those taken on distant grounds—focus attention on the alewife as a virtually neglected potential source of millions of pounds of protein food.[9]

Perhaps wartime austerity led Carson to contemplate once again species that had provisioned American armies in previous conflicts. Her solutions to the low numbers of alewife are technical fixes: stocking new ponds and installing fish ladders to help spawning runs pass dams.

Soon after the Second World War and twelve years after the publication of Rachel Carson's guide, *The Inexhaustible Sea* was published in America. The authors of this 1955 volume asserted that "the teeming waters of the oceans . . . are virtually untapped as a source of food."[10] Continuously upbeat, the book exhorts on nearly every page for more efficient and greater use of marine fish stocks by the world's growing human population. It ends with a remarkable statement, given how deeply human societies had already drunk of the wealth of oceans:

> As yet we do not know the ocean well enough. Much must still be learned. Nevertheless, we are already beginning to understand that what it has to offer extends beyond the limits of our imagination—that someday men will learn that in its bounty the sea is inexhaustible.[11]

*The Inexhaustible Sea* was not the product of some hack journalist or ill-informed popular writer. It was written by two academics, Hawthorne Daniel and Francis Minot—the latter, the director of the Marine and Fisheries Engineering Research Institute at Woods Hole, Massachusetts, a world center for marine research; the former, employed at the American Museum of Natural History in New York.

Buoyed by growing confidence in the capacity of human ingenuity and industrial prowess, the visionaries of the early post–World War II period saw the solution to overfishing—and to human overpopulation—in technical fixes. Why simply take what the sea readily provides when with a little intervention we could get far more. The authors of *The Inexhaustible Sea* suggested stirring up areas of the bottom on Georges Bank to boost production, perhaps not realizing that by then trawlers had been doing this for nearly half a century. Others went further. In a 1964 article on the future of fisheries, two earnest-looking gents, one in black suit and dark-rimmed glasses, perhaps a veteran of the Manhattan Project, suggested sinking nuclear reactors to create nutrient-rich upwelling sites.[12] Natural upwellings bring nutrients from the dark seabed to illuminated surface waters where they can be used to fuel plankton and fish growth. Upwellings like those off the coasts of Peru and West Africa support some of the most prolific fisheries in the world. Why not create more? Sir Alister Hardy looked to the future in his 1959 book on sea fisheries. He foresaw a time when vast expanses of the sea would be farmed:

> Shall we always fish and farm the sea from ships at the surface— dragging bags below us out of sight? I doubt it. Before we explore the moon in space suits, as I am sure our great-great grandchildren will, I believe men, with improved diving apparatus, will be working on the sea-bed. Perhaps, working in two hour shifts from a mother ship above, they will be driving pressure-proof submarine tractors down below, powered by atomic energy: rounding up the fish in nets of novel design or whirring backwards and forwards over the bottom pulling the latest starfish eradicator. The tractors, driven by propellers in the water, will of course have buoyancy tanks so that they are light enough to skim the bottom on their mud-shoes without sinking in. They will all be in wireless communication with one another and with the parent ship; their positions will be accurately pinpointed for them on some new kind of portable navigation screen. With a bill for labour and fuel less than that for three or four trawlers, one mother ship may perhaps operate a fleet of tractor-trawls advancing in line across the Dogger Bank below her; with the tractors remaining on the sea-bed for long periods, the men and their bags of fish will be drawn up at intervals through an opening into a well at the bottom of the ship, just as whole whales are drawn today into the hull of a floating factory.[13]

Hardy's dreams have not yet been realized, but much of the stuff of his musings can be seen today. The methods may differ, but we farm the sea on a colossal scale. There is barely a suitable sea loch or fjord in Scotland, Scandinavia, Canada, or Chile that is not full of salmon cages. Entire bays are crammed with prawn ponds and fish cages in Southeast Asia. Half the world's mangrove forests have been felled, large swathes of it to accommodate aquaculture. In Japan, even open coastlines support fish farms, and in some places cages stretch from shore almost to the horizon. We still fish from the water's surface, but technology enables us to see much better what our nets are doing underwater. Hardy's underwater tractor analogy is telling. Our trawl nets, scallop dredges, and clam rakes plough the seabed as thoroughly as any terrestrial tractor.

The decades following the Second World War heralded a global intensification of fishing that mirrored the industrialization of terrestrial agriculture. Global capture fishery production rose steadily into the 1980s, peaking around 85 million metric tonnes per year. By this metric, fisheries looked healthy, and the predictions of the 1950s and 1960s appeared to be fulfilled. But these aggregate catch statistics concealed worrying trends. Large catches were maintained only by a steadily increasing fishing fleet with growing fishing power. Stocks were disappearing from traditional grounds, and fleets were switching to other, previously untargeted species. And boats were seeking fish farther afield in places that had largely escaped exploitation.

In the following chapters that make up Part Two, I revisit places explored in Part One of this book to look at the intensification of fishing and how the environments and species in those places fared through the twentieth century and on to present times. In telling this story, I look as well at a place that largely escaped fishery exploitation in previous centuries: the deep sea. For it is in the depths of the abyss that the endgame for modern fisheries is now being played out.

# ~ Chapter 13 ~

# The Legacy of Whaling

—◆—◆—

ARLY INTEREST in the coasts and seas of the North Pacific focused on fur, blubber, and whalebone. Following Bering and Steller's placing of Alaska and the Bering Sea on the world map in 1741, and Cook's visit to the Canadian coast in 1778, this region quickly became the familiar haunt of adventuring hunters and traders. By the end of the nineteenth century, hunting had stripped these seas of otters, seals, and many of the large whales. But sailors and settlers were also attracted by the abundance of fish, especially salmon, which thronged the rivers that opened on to coasts around the entire North Pacific rim. Stepan Krasheninnikov, Georg Steller's student assistant, commented in the mid-eighteenth century on astonishing streams of fish that seemed almost to cause rivers to reverse direction as they returned from the sea to spawn:

> In Kamtschatka the fish come from the sea in such numbers, that they stop the course of the rivers, and cause them to overflow the banks. . . . They swim up the rivers with such force that the water seems to rise like a wall before them.[1]

Salmon, together with Pacific cod and halibut, lay within easy reach of shore and were the first targets for Pacific coast settlers. To begin with, catches were limited to coastal markets, but with the advent of canning technology in the late nineteenth century, together with rail-roads and the use of ice, markets expanded inland and overseas, in turn driving further growth in fisheries. By the early twentieth century, cod had been practically fished out from nearshore banks, but fisheries for northern species of salmon and halibut had grown into huge industries.[2] In 1889, there were thirty-nine salmon canneries along the banks of the Columbia River in Washington State alone, which in that year produced 629,000 cases of salmon. By 1901, there were seventy canneries spread between the Fraser River in British Columbia and Portland, Oregon.[3] While fisheries industrialized in the North Pacific, seal and sea otter populations spent the first half of the twentieth century slowly dragging themselves out of the pit into which the blubber and fur industries had plunged them. Protection afforded under the 1911 treaty began to pay off. This agreement among the United States, Russia, Canada, and Britain limited the number of seals that could be caught and prohibited capture of seals at sea. The fur seal haul-outs that had almost fallen silent, year by year grew more clamorous. By midcentury, beachmasters once again tossed their battle-scarred heads and bellowed bloody challenges across packed bodies of females and pups. From rockbound and hidden clefts of coast shunned by even the boldest hunters, tentative sea otters reemerged. Slowly, at first, they began to reclaim seas forfeit to the fur industry, spreading through the islands like drifting summer fog. By the 1960s a population explosion was in full swing throughout the Aleutians and Alaska Peninsula. Otters numbered an estimated twenty-six thousand by 1965, up from a low of one thousand to two thousand animals globally in 1911 when hunting was stopped.[4]

About this time, interest of the Northwest fishing industry shifted toward a species that had until then attracted little attention, the Alaska pollock. This smaller relative of the cod reaches about 4 to 5 kilograms (9 to 11 pounds) in weight. In the late nineteenth century, George Brown Goode passed rapidly over it in his monumental volume on the fishery species of the United States:

> [The pollock] ranges from Monterey to Behring's Straits. It is taken with hook and line in deep water, and is never plentiful south of Cape Flattery. It feeds upon anchovies and the like. Nothing is known of its

breeding habits, enemies or diseases, and, unless it be the Beshow [of
the Makah Indians], it is not sufficiently abundant to attract any
notice as an article of food.[5]

At that time, it is obvious that the stronghold of the pollock had yet to
be discovered, for it is one of the most abundant fishery species in the
world. In the Bering Sea, pollock occurs in immense shoals that feed
on plankton, krill, and small fish. It makes up an estimated 60 percent
of the combined weight of all fish species in Bering waters. Today
Alaska pollock supports one of the world's largest fisheries, with average landings of 1.3 million metric tonnes a year.[6] Shoals are scooped
from the water into the vast mouths of midwater trawls, openings
large enough to swallow a cathedral without touching the sides. Most
pollock is not eaten as fillet fish, but is processed into fish fingers, fish-
cakes, fishmeal, and surimi. In the early 1960s, the Japanese invented
a way of making surimi paste from pollock, opening the way for a
massive expansion in catches. Now that pollock could be shaped into
fake crabsticks, shrimp, and all the other panoply of reconstituted
seafood that surimi offered, almost unlimited quantities could be
marketed.

Catches of pollock peaked in the mid-1980s, reaching nearly 3 million metric tonnes a year. About this time, strangely, the spectacular
gains made by seal populations in preceding decades went into
reverse. First, populations of the harbor seal and fur seal began to
decline, followed swiftly by that of Steller's sea lion. Numbers plummeted, and by 2000, 90 percent of harbor seals, 50 percent of fur seals,
and 80 percent of Steller's sea lions were gone. As if this were not a big
enough blow, sea otters followed, declining by 80 percent in the Aleutian Islands from 1990 to 2000.

Blame for the declines of seals and sea lions first turned upon the
pollock fishery. Pollock are a linchpin of Bering Sea food webs, cap-
turing the prolific production of plankton and converting it into food
for other fish, birds, and marine mammals. Could fisheries be depriv-
ing animals of their prey, so precipitating population collapse? Years
of research have failed to demonstrate any convincing link between
pollock fishing and sea lion decline, however. Seals in rookeries where
declines were greatest were, if anything, in better condition than in

places where declines were less pronounced, suggesting animals were not going hungry.

Jim Estes of the University of California at Santa Cruz and his colleagues have another explanation. Theirs is a tale that has peculiar twists and turns and delves backward in time. If correct, it suggests that past human activities in the North Pacific have had lasting and unforeseen consequences for wildlife in the region today. Put simply, they argue that killer whales are eating the smaller marine mammals.[7] The great whales, such as gray, blue, and bowhead whales, were once important prey of killer whales, and Estes and his colleagues contend that industrial whaling robbed them of their prey, forcing them to switch to eating smaller marine mammals. In recent decades during which the global moratorium on whale hunting has been in place, it has been easy to forget that whales were hunted ruthlessly up until the mid-1980s. Between the close of World War II and 1970, the whaling industry continued its campaign against the great whales, slaughtering at least half a million in the North Pacific and Bering Sea. In Estes's opinion, faced with a crisis in their food supply, killer whales first switched to the larger seals and sea lions and then switched to sea otters as sea lions became scarce. Killer whales were spared the depredations of whaling because, unlike almost every other cetacean, they had no commercial value. They lacked valuable baleen, carried little blubber, and were too swift for most whaleboats.

The killer whale is the ultimate top predator in the oceans. It is not a true whale, but is the largest of the dolphin tribe, reaching a length of up to 9 meters (30 feet) and weighing up to 10 metric tonnes. Its characteristic streamlined body, piebald coloring, and mastlike dorsal fin are instantly recognizable. As a child, I knew them by reputation from picture books as terrifying killers. According to these volumes, their prey included dolphins, porpoises, penguins, and seals, although they would take fish if nothing else was available. In appalled fascination, I watched nature programs where penguins teetered nervously at the edge of ice cliffs, in the certain knowledge that one would soon fall victim to the killer prowling below. Even ice floes were no secure refuge for the beleaguered birds, as the killers would "spy-hop," seeming to stand almost upright in the water scanning with beady eyes for prey. Once they spotted prey, they would tilt the floating ice by pushing from below or mounting it from above, forcing penguins to slide to their fate. Killer whales, it had to be admitted, seemed less forbidding in the confines of an oceanarium, leaping for fish and towing their trainers around the pool. But nobody seemed to have had the nerve to test their amiability by swimming with them at sea.

Over the years, patient study of coastal pods of killers in places such as British Columbia revealed a more docile creature that lived in large family groups and, like most of us, much enjoyed salmon. These animals permitted close observation, and could be approached with safety in boats as flimsy even as a kayak. Familiarity and new understanding softened their harsh reputation, and killer whales were recast as misunderstood dolphins. People even got into the water with them, filming their hunts for salmon and herring. The same studies did also reveal a darker side, at least as seen from our mammalian perspective. A few "transient individuals" came and went from the seas inhabited by these well-balanced families, and they ate mammals. But mammal eating was perceived a minority pursuit, and killing whales had almost been forgotten. "[I]t is said that a school of killers will attack a large whale and tear it to pieces like a pack of wolves," Sir Alister Hardy, the renowned British oceanographer wrote in the 1950s, "but perhaps they can only attack an old whale or one in poor condition."[8]

Like all theories that challenge cherished beliefs, the idea that hungry killer whales turned on seals and sea otters has been highly controversial. In particular, critics argue that the great whales were never important prey for killer whales in the first place. However, older sources provide ample evidence that relations between killer whales and great whales has not always been amicable. Pliny the Elder penned in the first century AD what is probably the first written description of killer whales attacking great whales:

> Whales even penetrate into our seas. It is said that they are not seen in the Gulf of Cadiz before midwinter, but during the summer periods hide in a certain calm and spacious inlet, and take marvellous delight in breeding there; and that this is known to the killer whale, a creature that is the enemy of the other species and the appearance of which can be represented by no other description except that of an enormous

mass of flesh with savage teeth. The killer whales therefore burst into their retreats and bite and mangle their calves or the females that have calved or are still in calf, and charge and pierce them like warships ramming. . . . To spectators these battles look as if the sea were raging against itself, as no winds are blowing in the gulf, but there are waves caused by the whales blowing and thrashing that are larger than those aroused by any whirlwinds.[9]

Killer whales and great whales were abundant around Scandinavia at the time of Olaus Magnus in the sixteenth century, and he describes one hunt by a killer, or grampus, thus:

Although the whale is prodigiously long, a hundred to three hundred feet,[10] and its body a colossal mountain, it has an enemy, the grampus, which is certainly smaller, yet, with its rapid leap and swift attack, a more savage brute. The grampus, a creature resembling an upturned boat, is armed with ferocious teeth, which it uses as brigantines do their prows, and rips at the whale's genitals or the body of its calf. It

*Two killer whales attack a great whale in a woodcut from Olaus Magnus the Goth's 1555* History of the Northern Peoples. *Descriptions of killer whales attacking great whales are commonplace in old literature, but the idea that they prey on large whales has met with skepticism recently. Source: Magnus, O. (1555)* Historia de Gentibus Septentrionalibus. Description of the Northern Peoples. Volume III. *Translated by P. Fisher and H. Higgens. Hakluyt Society, London, 1996.*

rushes to and fro, harassing the whale with its spiny back, trying to thrust it into the shallows or on to the shore. The whale, incapable of turning about because of its enormous bulk, is powerless to resist the cunning of the grampus and can only preserve itself by fleeing.[11]

Magnus includes a splendid woodcut illustrating the struggle between a great whale and the killer. The whale blows furiously as one killer mounts it from above while a second bites its belly from below. He later notes that in Norway, the killer whale is called *springhval,* or the leaper, for the "nimbleness and speed with which it sets upon the whale and goes for its privy parts."[12] Killer whales were evidently active in the Bering Sea, too, and Krasheninnikov reports killers preying on great whales in his history of Kamtchatka:

> The kasatki [the killer whale], (falsely called the sword-fish) which are numerous in these seas, are very useful to the inhabitants, for these fish frequently either kill or drive whales on shore. Steller had an opportunity of seeing an engagement between the kasatki and whale, both at sea and upon *Bering's* island. When the kasatki attacks the whale he makes him roar so that he may be heard some miles. If the whale makes off, the kasatki follows him at some distance 'till great numbers of them gather together, and make a general attack. It is never observed that such whales as are thrown on shore have any part eaten out of their bodies; so that this war between the whales and kasatki must proceed only from a natural enmity. The fishers are so much afraid of these animals that they not only never throw any darts at them, but if possible avoid going near them.[13, 14]

Oliver Goldsmith reported on the killer whales' predatory habits in the 1776 edition of his *History of Earth and Animated Nature,* describing their pack hunting behavior:

> There is still another and more powerful enemy [of great whales] called, by the fishermen of New England, the Killer. This is itself a cetaceous animal, armed with strong and powerful teeth. A number of these are said to surround a whale, in the same manner as dogs get round a bull. Some attack it with their teeth behind; others attempt it before; until, at last, the great animal is torn down, and its tongue is said to be the only part they devour when they have made it their prey.[15]

Many witnesses of killer whale attacks remarked on the tendency of the killers to eat only the tongues of their prey. They evidently shared similar tastes to whalers, Eskimos, and Kamtchadals, who were united in their appreciation of the epicurean qualities of whale tongues.[16] In more recent times, the camera crew filming a killer whale attack on a gray whale calf off California for the *Blue Planet* television series saw the killers satisfied by the tongue alone after a struggle that lasted several hours.

Edward Cooke, an English privateer cruising the waters off northern South America in 1709 also commented on the spectacle of battling whales:

> Abundance of young Whales and Granpusses would often come blowing in Droves very near our Ships, the Thrashers hard at Work laying them on the Back, and the Sword-Fishes pricking them under the Belly. The Spaniards say the Thrashers and Sword-Fishes often kill the Whales. It was good Sport to us to see them.[17]

Cooke's mention of swordfish attacking whales alongside killer whales was a common conception until at least the end of the nineteenth century. Swordfish are large, fast-swimming predators growing 4 to 5 meters (13 to 17 feet) long and weighing several hundred kilograms. The largest reach more than five hundred kilograms (1,100 pounds). They carry a formidable spike of a half meter to 1.5 meters long (5 feet) protruding from the nose. Swordfish hunt the high seas and aggregate in food-rich places favored by whales and other giants of the ocean such as bluefin tuna. Until relatively recently, there was much speculation over the purpose of the swordfish's blade. From ancient Greek and Roman times to the present, swordfish bills have been found embedded deep in ship's timbers, suggesting a capacity for powerful attacks on large animals like whales. But, perplexingly, swordfish have relatively small mouths and teeth, making it hard to see how they could eat large and tough prey. Underwater photography of hunting swordfish has now revealed that the swords are brandished with vigorous side-to-side chopping movements through packed fish schools. These parrying thrusts stun and chop fish into pieces that are then snapped up whole. The fish-eating habits of swordfish belie their historical reputation as whale killers.

Perhaps the confusion arose from the several names given to killer whales. They were often called swordfish after the stiff upright dorsal fin so visible to seafarers. Killers were also known as thrashers, leading to another confusion. Descriptions of attacks on whales also sometimes mention thresher sharks. Like swordfish, threshers are large, open-water predators. They reach 3 to 6 meters (10 to 20 feet) long, of which up to half consists of a tail fin that has a greatly elongated upper lobe. Threshers use their tails to stun and herd shoaling fish, sometimes appearing to hunt cooperatively. Although equipped with more formidable teeth than swordfish, they are also ill adapted for eating whales. Almost certainly, killer whales were the sole predators in whale attacks. Swordfish and threshers were often seen with killers, and may have dined well on scraps liberated by the whale feast, but it is doubtful they played any part in the attacks.

What is obvious from the number and consistency of historical accounts is that killer whales were committed predators of the great whales, not merely opportunists taking sick whales and calves here and there. Past generations who observed the species hunting in seas brimming with great whales clearly understood this.[18]

Rekindled interest in killer whale predation led scientists to reexamine their assumptions and their data. Film of attacks showed that killers left raking scars across the smooth expanses of whale flesh. Animals that had escaped death should be identifiable from this scarring. Amee Mehta of Boston University in the United States and her colleagues trawled through years of photographs and data from long-term studies of whales in twenty-four different parts of the world. They found wide variation in the frequency of unsuccessful attacks, ranging from no scarred animals to 40 percent of whales carrying scars. Interestingly, almost all of the animals with scars had them from the outset of the research. Just 5 percent of whales gained scars during the studies, suggesting that most attacks are on young whales. Mehta and colleagues concluded that the idea of killers switching prey from great whales to seals and sea otters was incomplete and misleading. I can't see that their data threaten the prey-switching hypothesis. Science is a competitive and often combative process, and to be published, papers often have to challenge others. Certainly, the suggestion that killer whales had switched from eating whales upset prevailing wisdom. But the finding that they mainly attack, and presumably eat, young whales supports the hypothesis rather than discredits it. Fewer adult whales means fewer calves, which means less prey for killers. Indeed, Mehta and colleagues have only confirmed what that venerable whaling captain Charles Scammon knew in the 1870s. After describing attacks by killers on adult whales, he then says,

> The Orca, however, does not always live on such gigantic food; and we incline to the belief that it is but rarely these *carnivora* of the sea attack the larger Cetaceans, but chiefly prey with great rapacity upon their young.[19]

Hal Whitehead and Randall Reeves of Dalhousie University in Canada have added another twist in the story of why killer whales may have begun targeting smaller mammals in the North Pacific. Sifting through old accounts of whalers, they came across many references to killer whales as scavengers. For centuries, they argued, whalers have supplemented the diet of killers with discarded carcasses and, often to the whalers' annoyance, with carcasses that have yet to have their blubber removed. A paper published in 1725 on the natural history of whales described killers dragging away a carcass:

> These Killers are of such invincible Strength, that when several Boats together have been towing a dead Whale, one of them has come and fastened his Teeth in her, and carried her away down to the Bottom in an Instant.[20]

William Scoresby, the British whaler, wrote in his logbook in the early nineteenth century of an instance of killer whale scavenging:

> Capt. Dring lost two fish [right whales], after being killed, by being carried off by the Killers. . . . These animals attacked the dead whales, it is said for the sake of its tongue, which alone they eat, and often carry them off from the fishers against every security and precaution—the boats towing them being obliged to cut them adrift to prevent their being carried down along with them.[21]

Whitehead and Reeves argue that it was scavenged whale carcasses, not living whales, that fed killer whales up to the 1970s. In support of their idea, they show that there was no sudden decrease in availability of living whales in the 1970s that could have forced killers to switch to eating smaller marine mammals. The major decline in whale abundance in the twentieth century took place between 1920 and 1960 as industrial whalers slaughtered their way through whale species that had escaped the depredations of eighteenth- and nineteenth-century whalers. But the number of whale kills made by whalers—and hence the number of carcasses—plummeted between 1960 and 1980. After the introduction of a moratorium on commercial whaling in 1986, the supply dried up almost completely.

Marine mammals are intelligent creatures and the antics of killer whales in oceanaria show them to be quick learners. From historical accounts, it is clear that they soon appreciated the relationship between whaleboats and carcasses and would follow whalers in expectation of dinner. With the development of exploding harpoons in 1865, and the addition of engine power to whale ships in the late nineteenth century, whaling operations would have become audible below water for at least tens of kilometers, sounding a clear dinner gong to any killer whales in the vicinity. Over the following century, Whitehead and Reeves argue, if anything, active predation on great whales would have declined as a surfeit of bodies satisfied the appetites of killers.

There is a second line of evidence that supports their view. Following the implementation in 1911 of the treaty prohibiting fur seal killing at sea, the Pribilof herd began to recover. By 1921, the herd stood at somewhat over half a million animals, an increase of 9 percent per year since the treaty came into effect. Gratifying as this increase was, biologists of the time noticed that it was less than it might have been based on the production of pups. After ruling out other sources of mortality, such as illegal sealing, disease, and starvation, the finger of blame pointed to killer whales, as no other fur seal predators were known. Dallas Hanna of the California Academy of Sciences estimated that some 300,000 seals were unaccounted for and had probably been eaten by killer whales between 1911 and 1921.[22] Certainly, killer whales were active predators of smaller marine mammals at this time. Hanna refers to a Captain Bryant who examined the stomachs of two Alaskan killers and found 18 seals in one and 24 seals in the other.

Hanna overlooked the possibility of shark predation on seals. Certainly, large sharks were far more abundant in seas of the early twentieth century than they are today, as they had yet to become significant targets for fishers. Great whites are active predators in the waters off California frequented by fur seals on their winter migrations. Even so, killer whales probably also took a large slice of the thirty thousand or so annual kill. Jim Estes and his colleagues have estimated how much redirected predation on Steller's sea lions and sea otters would have been necessary to cause the declines seen in Aleutian populations in the 1980s and 1990s.[23] Their calculations were based on the food requirements of a killer whale and the calorific value of seal lions and sea otters. The average adult killer whale would need to eat 2 or 3 Steller sea lion pups per day, or around 840 a year to get by. If they consumed adult sea lions, a single kill every two or three days would suffice. Sea otters are much less calorific, the equivalent of a snack rather than a meal. An adult female killer whale would need 3 to 5 sea otters a day, and a male 5 to 7.

Whatever way you look at the numbers, that is a lot of sea otters. If all the killer whales in the Aleutians ate nothing else, they would wipe out sea otters in three months. Clearly the four thousand or so killer whales believed to live in these seas cannot all be otter hunters, or sea lion hunters for that matter. Close observation of Aleutian killers suggests only 10 percent of them eat marine mammals; the rest feed on fish and squid. It needs only a few of these mammal eaters to switch prey from whales, however, to have caused the late twentieth century declines in sea lion and otter populations: forty killer whales in the case of sea lions, and a single pod of five in the case of otters.

What can be done about killer whales on the rampage? Steller's sea lions and sea otters are both high on the conservation agenda. To see past success in rebuilding populations slipping away is agonizing for those who have battled to bring them back from the edge of extinction. The possibility that killer whales are responsible creates the ultimate conservation dilemma: should we kill the killers? Such action seems unconscionable today. But Dallas Hanna made exactly this suggestion in 1922, arguing for a cull for more prosaic reasons.[24] By sparing thirty thousand fur seals per year, slaughtering killer whales would generate up to three million dollars for the fur industry.

If any sea on this planet remains beyond the power of human influence, surely it would be the icy, storm-savaged waters of the Bering Sea. But here our presence has long been felt. Food items preserved in ancient Aleut middens show how native people thousands of years ago shaped nearshore food webs. By hunting sea otters and reducing their control over seaweed-munching invertebrates, people facilitated the transformation of kelp forests into rocky barrens, probably hastening the demise of Steller's sea cow in the process. Today, killer whales switching prey from great whales or their slaughtered carcasses appear to be reshaping this sea in a long-term legacy of industrial whaling. The Bering Sea remains in the grip of a fleet of ghostly whalers long after their harpoon guns and winches fell silent.

The Bering Sea supports some of the most productive fisheries on the planet and, in American waters, arguably among the best managed. These waters have demonstrated the resilience of marine life, showing that species can recover after devastating population crashes. But they also show us that exploitation can have unexpected and long-lasting effects, a message that we are now reading in many different forms in the waters of other parts of the world.

# — *Chapter 14* —

# Emptying European Seas

— ❧ —

MIDWINTER IN 1967, far north of the Arctic Circle, the British trawler *Arctic Fox* has her gear down and is towing for fish. William Mitford, one of the crew, described conditions as they trawled:

> The sea was now running a heavy swell, crashing over the whaleback and down on to the foredeck in a brilliant, cruel display of force and grandeur before it ran out through the scuppers, all aquamarine and pearl. Gale force eight, freshening to strong gale nine. The wind intensified to 40 knots, filling the lungs with minute stilettos of ice and freezing the sensitive muscles each side of the mouth. Ice, too, covered the winch, froze the lifeboats solid in their davits, thickened the rigging and welded every wire into its sheave or pulley block. The waves were now sweeping in towards the vessel in a wide, lethal crescent of green sea, touching 30 ft. in height. The temperature, too, had fallen, and stood at minus 39 degrees Fahrenheit—71 degrees below freezing point. The air was now colder than the sea and the dreaded Black Frost began to rise from the surface until vitrified water hung everywhere in the freezing air like amorphous black glass. The masts were sugar candy—ice blue and strangely beautiful. Spray froze on the underside of the ship's rail into long points of ice, looking like fairy dragon's teeth in endless array.[1]

What tempted men to fish in these heartless waters? The *Arctic Fox* steamed from Grimsby on the North Sea coast of England on January 3. By the time she returned twenty days later, she had covered nearly 5,500 kilometers of sea (3,421 miles) and brought home 126 tonnes of fish. Long-distance fishing was perilous hard toil, but the rewards made it worth the risks. It had been a long time since such catches could be landed from the home grounds of the North Sea.

The nineteenth century closed with unequivocal proof, at long last, that fishers' mutterings about depletion of fish and falling catches were true. Walter Garstang's study demonstrated a halving in catch per unit of bottom trawl fishing effort for that century's last decade.[2] Early experiments with tagged fish provided further dramatic confirmation of overfishing. Between 1903 and 1916, scientists marked seventeen thousand plaice with labeled tags.[3] Analysis of tag return rates from fishers indicated that something like 70 percent of catchable fish were removed from the population every year. Figures for other species were less reliable but suggested removal rates by fishing of a quarter to a half of the fish every year.

Far from this depletion putting people off fishing, the industry prospered, benefiting from the development of ever more efficient steam engines.[4] This technological revolution made up for falling catch per unit effort by enabling boats to fish for longer, trawl faster with larger nets, and reach grounds farther from port where fish populations were in better shape. Greater towing power together with net modifications also enabled boats to penetrate into areas of rough bottom that had been impossible to fish previously. In the years leading up to World War I, fishing fleets across the world grew in size and fishing power, and the geographic footprint of the fisheries spread and pressed deeper. The herring fishery was among the fisheries transformed by steam. At the turn of the twentieth century, less than 3 percent of the nearly seven hundred herring drifters in England and Wales had steam power. By the outbreak of war, nearly 80 percent were equipped with steam.[5]

While herring fisheries enjoyed a boom, extra fishing power placed heavy pressure on already depleted bottom fish populations. Although boats caught fewer fish per haul, they made up for it with more hauls and by retaining species considered trash fish in the nine-teenth century. Countries neighboring Britain who fished in Europe's common pool faced similar pressures, and their fisheries developed in much the same way, substituting new species as populations of prime fish dwindled.[6] Throughout Edwardian Britain, for example, shops selling fried fish-and-chips were growing in popularity. Covering fish fillets with batter hid a multitude of sins, and trash fish, like monk-fish, poor cod, and coley, found a market. The extra range afforded by steam tempted some at the time to voyage to Iceland and the Barents Sea to try their luck. But they lacked freezing facilities and fish stored on ice would keep for only a few weeks, making the trips hardly worth the effort.[7]

World War I interrupted fishing in the North Sea, especially bot-tom trawling and the herring fisheries of southeast England. Fishers were in great demand as skilled seamen for the navy, and many boats were pressed into service to clear mines and hunt submarines. As the war ground on, vessels out fishing were targeted by the military on both sides. Submarines sank 156 steam trawlers in 1916 alone.[8] After that, fishing petered out almost completely in the North Sea until the end of hostilities.

After the end of the war, suspicions about the previous depleted state of fish stocks were confirmed as fishers enjoyed a catch bonanza. The respite from fishing had allowed fish populations time to rebuild. But with little in the way of regulation to control fishing, big catches were short lived, lasting only a couple of years before catch rates fell to prewar levels again. Matters grew worse with time, and by the 1930s fishing the North Sea was a luckless grind. Michael Graham, later to become the British government's chief fisheries officer, described the hardship of fishing then, contrasting it with the situation just a decade earlier in the 1920s, which by comparison seemed easy:

> In the early '20's [Danny's] trawl was lighter, without a heavy ground rope or tickler chain, so it was easier to handle. It was not necessary in the '20's to fish among boulders, and to use three-hour hauls, which, with average amount of trawl mending, reduce the period of rest to under six hours out of twenty-four, *including* meal times.
>
> This is scraping for a living—expensive, skilful and up-to-date scraping; but anxious and ill-rewarded—with every sign of being an

*Aberdeen fish market on Scotland's North Sea coast around the turn of the twentieth century. Such large fish were landed that many were sold individually. Source: Contemporary postcard.*

effort contending with some invincible force of nature and economics —as men struggle on the edge of the Dustbowl, or cling to eastern American lands when the forest is coming back.[9]

Fisheries stagnated. Landings into England and Wales from the North Sea fell from 193,000 tonnes a year between 1909 and 1913, to 93,000 tonnes between 1934 and 1937. Something had to be done. In 1933, a momentous step was taken in Britain with the passage of the Sea-Fishing Industry Act that set minimum mesh sizes and landing-size limits for some of the main species caught. It ended a period of virtual freedom from regulation that had lasted for sixty-five years since the 1868 repeal of fishing laws prompted by Thomas Huxley's first commission of inquiry. The new regulations were also embodied in a 1937 convention agreed among European nations to regulate their shared fisheries.[10] (Although similar fishery problems were recognized in New England in the 1930s, it would be 1953 before minimum mesh size restrictions were introduced there.)

The industry reacted to falling yields from the North Sea in the way that it has always done, by fishing farther afield. During the 1920s steam trawlers had increasingly been making voyages north, trying their luck in the waters around Spitsbergen and Bear Island (Svalbard). The latter is a small volcanic remnant halfway between the northernmost tip of Scandinavia and the island of Spitsbergen, from which it is separated by a trough 800 meters deep (2700 feet). Fishers found plenty to catch in the fertile and virgin polar seas. William Robinson, a Hull trawlerman of the time, claimed, for example, that in fishing around Bear Island it only took five minutes to fill a trawl.[11]

The variations by distance in catch per unit effort were striking. In the 1930s, one hundred hours of fishing around Bear Island yielded an average of 120 tonnes of fish. Icelandic waters yielded 72 tonnes for the same fishing time, while the North Sea gave up just 7 tonnes. The difference more than justified the greater expense and risk of fishing northern seas. William Mitford described catches made by the *Arctic Fox* as including cod weighing 82 kilograms (180 pounds) and a halibut of 172 kilograms (378 pounds).[12] Shipyards purpose-built larger steam-powered trawlers for the northern fisheries. Between 1906 and 1936, the average size of steam trawlers in the British fleet increased from 174 tonnes to 267 tonnes.[13] Britain returned to distant-water fishing at levels not seen since the Newfoundland cod fisheries of the sixteenth to eighteenth centuries. Other countries in Europe pursued similar ends at the same time, including Germany, France, Portugal, the Netherlands, and especially the USSR.[14]

World War II interrupted fishing once again. Much of the North Sea was placed off-limits due to minefields and military restrictions.[15] The larger boats built for long-distance fishing trips to northern waters were requisitioned for naval service, taking out much of the Arctic fishing capacity, too. In contrast to the fighting above water, peace returned below the North Sea as fish populations were for several years largely spared the hook, net, and trawl. E.S. Russell, one of the founders of fishery science, writing on fisheries during the war, urged governments across Europe to take advantage of the recovery this time, rather than renewing intensive fishing as had happened after the first war.[16] But it was not to be. The new bounty was expended as swiftly as the old after the war ended, creating a minor local fishing blip in the shift to distant waters that began between the wars.

After World War II, almost all new trawlers built on Britain's east coast were for distant-water trawling, a trend mirrored across Europe.

By the 1960s, when the *Arctic Fox* fished the pack ice–strewn waters around Svalbard, its neighboring port of Hull had switched entirely to long-distance fishing, spurning the North Sea. Catches from polar seas were ideal for the fish-and-chips market, being made up mainly of firm round fish like cod and haddock. To cut the travel costs of these long voyages, companies began to construct enormous factory freezer trawlers. By freezing fish immediately after capture, they could remain fishing for longer periods and store hundreds of tons of fish in their holds.

With these ships came other innovations. Stern ramps replaced the side-hauled trawls that forced the boat to turn beam on to wind and waves to bring the net aboard, often a dangerous maneuver in rolling Arctic seas. Factory trawlers also carried equipment to extract cod liver oil and process fish waste into meal. Eastern European nations followed the lead of western Europe, but took distant-water fishing to a new level. They built fleets of ships that serviced giant factory ships at sea. These fleets were entirely self-contained, having aboard doctors, operating rooms, and movie theaters, and they returned only occasionally to home ports to discharge fish and for maintenance. They were floating towns built for the sole purpose of processing marine life into food. These boats were joined by fishing vessels from the Far East, notably, Japan and Taiwan. By the 1970s, distant-water fleets spread fisheries across the Atlantic from pole to pole.

After being subjected to several decades of trawling in the post–World War II period, Europe's distant-water fishing grounds in the far north and along the eastern seaboard of North America began to show signs of depletion, suffering falling catch per unit effort. The Icelandic government grew worried that foreign fleets put Iceland's main source of revenue and foreign earnings at risk. In the 1950s, Britain and Germany caught roughly the same quantity of fish from Icelandic waters as did Icelanders. In 1958, Iceland declared territorial waters extending 12 nautical miles from land.[17] At the time, the international consensus was that territorial waters extended only 3 miles from the coast, although some countries claimed more based on historical precedent. Britain was incensed, and the government urged trawlers to ignore the limit, protecting them with naval frigates while they fished. It was the beginning of the cod war with Iceland, and the second in her waters since the fourteenth century. The dispute lasted until 1961 when Britain finally agreed to the 12-mile limit with a three-year phase-in period during which her trawlers could work up to 6 miles from shore.

Relations soured again a decade later. Iceland declared a 50-nautical-mile limit in 1972, provoking Britain and West Germany into a second confrontation. Icelandic patrol vessels cut trawling gear away and rammed foreign fishing boats. The following year, naval escorts were once more sent to protect Britain's distant-water interests. But the international tide was turning in Iceland's favor. At a United Nations conference called to develop the law of the sea held in New York in 1973, more than a hundred nations agreed to the creation of 200-nautical-mile Exclusive Economic Zones by 1975.[18] Iceland declared its 200-mile zone in July 1975. Since 1976, Icelandic waters have been closed to the fishing vessels of other nations.

Meanwhile, the North Sea and waters adjacent to mainland Europe were far from spent. The zenith of the British herring fishery came just before the First World War, when landings peaked at nearly 600,000 tonnes. They dropped back during the 1920s to a little under 400,000 tonnes a year, and fell again in the 1930s to around a quarter of a million tonnes. Contraction of the British herring industry was not due to falling stocks but arose from competition with Norway and Germany, whose catches were growing. Herring fisheries of these nations benefited from improvements in catching technology. Beginning in the 1930s, drift nets were replaced by purse seines and midwater trawls, made possible by greater engine power, developments the British were slow to adopt. These fishing methods were much more efficient, enabling vessels to actively target entire herring schools rather than simply set obstacles in their path in the hope that some of the school would be caught. Purse seines consist of large curtains of net buoyed up by floats at the surface and weighted at the bottom. They are generally a few tens of meters deep and are paid out around a school of fish by a small tender vessel to the main ship. The operation is completed when the tender passes the end of the net back to the ship and the net is closed at the bottom by pulling a drawstring, like a purse, trapping the fish inside. Freed of the constraint of touching bottom, nets could be greatly enlarged, able to capture hundreds of tons of fish at a haul.[19] Herring vessels increased in size and worked farther offshore, catching schools before fish came inshore to breed. By the 1950s, these vessels also targeted immature fish, as much of the herring was by then being processed into fishmeal and oil.

If a fishery is allowed to expand without sufficient check, there comes a point where the catching power of the fleet outstrips the ability of a fish population to replace itself. This point comes at different times for different species depending on their rate of population increase and behavior. In mixed-species fisheries, such as those pursued by bottom trawlers, species gradually drop out, sometimes almost unnoticed, as their populations decline. The fishery continues despite their loss because populations of other species remain viable. But where there is only a single species targeted, collapse means the end of the fishery. Fisheries for schooling fish that live in midwater usually target single species, the herring fishery being a classic case. Schooling fish remain highly catchable even as their populations decline. The remaining fish stay grouped together, enabling fishers to catch them as easily as when they were abundant, provided they can find the schools. And with the adoption of echo-sounding sonar in the 1950s, fishers no longer had to wait for schools to rise to the surface to find them. They could detect fish from the comfort of the bridge and send the nets down to them, extending the fishing season and increasing efficiency of capture.

Stock collapse, when it comes, can happen very quickly. In 1955, the first of the great herring fisheries collapsed off the East Anglia coast of England. This herring population had sustained a highly productive fishery for over a thousand years, but it could not survive the onslaught of twentieth-century industrial fishing. In 1966, the total herring catch from the North Sea reached 1.2 million tonnes. Through the late 1960s and early 1970s, herring stocks crashed one after another across Europe, and by 1975, North Sea catches came to just 200,000 tonnes. Soon after, when the final collapse came, it was estimated that fisheries extracted over 70 percent of the herring from the North Sea every year, a take that even the most resilient species cannot withstand for long. In 1977, a moratorium was called on herring fishing in the North Sea and extended to western waters of Europe in

1978. Vessels redeployed into other open-water fisheries, such as that for mackerel off western France and Britain and for Norway pout in northern waters. The herring fishery reopened in 1981, with much-reduced catch quotas (annual limits on the weight of fish that could be landed).

By 1950 Europe's sea fisheries could be said to have enjoyed a thousand years of growth, in terms of the overall size of catch, interrupted here and there by a few poor spells when people succumbed to plague or major fish stocks declined due to environmental shifts and fluctuations. From the beginning of the twentieth century, however, these fisheries ran on borrowed time. Catches were sustained only by growing fishing power, by fishing farther afield, by going deeper, and by switching to previously less favored species like dogfish and monkfish. These trends masked local decline and disappearance of once favored species. However, following the Second World War, the scale and might of fishing fleets expanded at a rate unprecedented in human history. In the 1970s, the effects of this fishing power became apparent not only with the final collapse of Europe's largest fishery, herring, but also with the collapse on the other side of the world, off the coast of Peru, of the world's most productive fishery, for anchoveta. There, intense El Niño conditions depressed the upwellings that fueled production of this schooling fish, and concentrated the remaining anchovies close to the coast where they were easy to catch. These catastrophic fishery collapses signaled a change in the relationship between people and fish. Humanity now had the means to drive fish populations to collapse, it was clear, even those sustaining the most productive fisheries. Thomas Huxley's 1883 assertion that the great sea fisheries were inexhaustible was proven wrong.

Although there was big money in distant-water fisheries, trawlers continued to scratch and scrape their way back and forth across the continental shelf around Europe. Smaller boats could still turn a profit, making short voyages to and from ports dotted all around the North Sea, Baltic, and Atlantic coasts. As catches fell, fishers responded by working harder. Trawling intensity in the northern North Sea, for example, tripled between 1960 and the mid-1990s.[20] Today, the seabed in many parts of the North Sea is hit by trawls and dredges two to three times per year, and intensively fished regions get hit tens of times per year. In defending their trawls, some nineteenth-century fishers argued that they increased the productivity of the seabed, like ploughing benefits the soil. Trawling stirred up food off the bottom and brought the fish in, they said. In the twentieth century, this argument gained a more scientific basis. By removing the accumulated biomass of bottom-living organisms, like sponges, corals, and sea fans, many of which are old and senescent, the trawl opens up the seabed for species with faster growth and high population turnover rates. The idea was borrowed from terrestrial agriculture. Grasslands are dominated by short-lived annual plants that turn over rapidly, producing biomass at high rates. By contrast, habitats dominated by slow-growing species, like oak woodlands, have lower productivity. Our ancestors found they could produce more food by converting woodlands to grassland for pasture and crops. Why shouldn't the same be true in the sea?

The answer is that it is true—but only to a point. Some species, like many flatfish, prefer open habitats made up of sand and mud rather than complex communities of coral, shell, and sponge. They do not need the shelter from predators provided by these complex habitats because they can blend into the seabed, either by changing color or burying themselves. They feed on invertebrates like worms and mollusks that live in the sediment. By removing biologically created habitats from above the seabed, trawling increases the area of feeding habitat available to flatfish. But there comes a point where even species with high population turnover rates cannot cope. A recent study suggests the North Sea has passed that point, and that populations of invertebrates living in sediments in heavily trawled areas are less productive than their counterparts in places with lower trawling frequency.[21] Intensive trawling is undermining the food webs that support commercial fish species. The sea has been put to the plough, but we do not sow—we only reap. Today, the degradation of the seabed noticed by fishers in the nineteenth century has been brought almost to its conclusion. With such frequent visitation by trawls, few animals or plants that live above the surface can survive, just as little other than a few weeds would survive ploughing the land two or three times a year.

The 1970s marked a turning point in the fortunes of Europe's bottom fisheries. Landings of fish from the North Sea had risen from under a million tonnes in 1900 to a twentieth-century peak of more than 3.5 million tonnes in 1970.[22] The collapse of herring was only the first of a wave of declines that quickly spread to species caught by the trawl. The 1970s also heralded a change in management for fisheries. A coalition of six European nations formed the European Economic Community in 1958.[23] In the early 1970s, several more countries joined up, including the United Kingdom. Management of fisheries was ceded to bureaucrats in Brussels under the new Common Fisheries Policy. Just when nations like Iceland took control of their own waters, Europeans pooled resources, guaranteeing one another the right to fish in the waters of any member state. Instead of responding to mounting evidence of overfishing by easing pressure to allow recovery, Europe's politicians sought to prop up an ailing industry with overgenerous quotas. More fish stocks declined. Like gamblers desperately seeking a change of luck, they spent from their savings with inevitable consequences—exhaustion both of luck and of fish. In 1970, only 10 percent of fish stocks in the North Sea were classified as seriously overfished. By 2000, the figure had risen to nearly 50 percent and only 18 percent of stocks were still considered healthy.

It is difficult if not impossible to reconstruct the full history of exploitation of fish populations in Europe. Fisheries stretch back hundreds of years or more in many cases, and it was only very recently that we began collecting systematic data. Decent catch data can be traced back to the early twentieth century for a few species, whereas estimates of population sizes of target species are often available only as far back as the 1950s or 1960s. To estimate population sizes in the past, we have to develop theoretical models constructed using knowledge of marine biology and of the life histories of the species involved, together with the patchy historical records that can be pieced together. The sparse fishery data available enable us to assess the performance of these models and work out refinements. Villy Christensen, a scientist from the University of British Columbia, and his colleagues examined trends in European catches and developed models to reconstruct the state of fish stocks from 1900 to 2000. They estimate that, in aggregate, today's stocks are just one-tenth of their size in 1900, and two-thirds of that decline has happened since 1950. But as I showed in Part One of this book, 1900 is far from being an unexploited baseline from which to measure change. By then, Europe's waters had already been heavily fished, with complaints of falling catches for at least forty years and the first serious steps taken to protect fish stocks in the 1890s. The year 1900, then, represents a waypoint in the downward trajectory of fish populations, rather than a pristine baseline from which to measure declines. In relation to true unexploited population sizes, we probably have today less than 5 percent of the total mass of fish that once swam in Europe's seas.

Lumping fish together in catch statistics hides important detail. Some species are more affected by fishing than others. Simon Jennings, from the Centre for Environment, Fisheries and Aquaculture Science in England, and his colleagues looked at change between the 1920s and 1990s in the composition of fish catches taken from an area of the northern North Sea between the Shetland Isles and Norway. They found that large-bodied, long-lived, late-maturing fish had declined faster than species that matured earlier in life. The big fish had low resilience and could not keep up with the mortality imposed by fishing. Some of these species have now all but disappeared from European waters, like the angel shark and common skate. The common skate, as its name implies, was once abundant and frequently caught from Iceland and Norway south to Senegal. It is a large-bodied animal that could reach 120 centimeters (4 feet) from wing tip to wing tip and weigh up to 100 kilograms (220 pounds). For a fish, it produces relatively few young, laying up to forty eggs per year. Common skates were rarely targeted directly but often caught in trawls, tangled in gill nets, and hooked on longlines. Little by little they declined, silently disappearing from former haunts. Today, they are restricted to a few small patches of rocky habitat where trawlers still cannot go.

Jennings and his colleagues estimate that in combination, today's populations of large-bodied fish species in the North Sea are only one-fiftieth the size they would be in the absence of fishing. Species like the common skate have declined more, probably as much as a thousandfold, others less. Small-bodied species with high rates of population turnover—that is, those most able to withstand high rates

*Common skate caught by an angler at Ballycotton, Ireland, in the early twentieth century. This animal, as its name implies, was once abundant but is now extinct across large parts of its former range due to overfishing by trawlers. Source: Hol-combe, F.D. (1923)* Modern Sea Angling. *Frederick Warne & Co. Ltd., London.*

of fishing mortality—have also been affected. They include animals like herring, sprat, and sardines, and together they have been reduced to about a quarter of their natural abundance. One of the large-bodied species among the disappeared is the bluefin tuna. These giants of the sea breed in the Mediterranean, but when warmer climatic conditions allowed, would venture into northern waters to feed on abundant herring and other schooling fish. In the 1920s, bluefin tuna were a nuisance to herring fishers in the Kattegat at the entrance to the Baltic because they shredded their nets.[24] They were abundant enough in the 1930s to attract big game fishers to the Yorkshire coast of England where the largest caught weighed 387 kilograms (851 pounds). Today, conditions are again warm enough for the bluefin to visit the North Sea, but there are so few left they no longer make it that far north.

The legacy of intensive fishing extends far beyond the species we have targeted and pervades every sea on the planet. Trawling has virtually eliminated entire habitats. The Wadden Sea affords a telling example of the losses wrought by centuries of fishing and human influence. This sea fringes the northern coast of mainland Europe between the Netherlands and a point two-thirds of the way up the peninsula of Denmark. It is an area of shallow seas and estuaries, partially enclosed by a string of offshore barrier islands. Reefs built over thousands of years by *Sabellaria* worms secreting stony tubes used to dot tidal channels of the Wadden and adjacent North Seas. Today, almost all these reefs have been destroyed, ground to rubble and sand by trawls.[25] Structurally complex bottom habitats including *Sabellaria* and oyster reefs, eelgrass, and seaweeds have all but disappeared due to destructive fishing and pollution. Reclamation of the Dutch Zuider Zee part of the Wadden Sea in the 1930s led to the local extinction of the bottlenose dolphin and its prey, the Zuider Zee herring. Harbor porpoises have also been virtually eliminated from the Wadden Sea and from the Bay of Biscay to the west. Today, the few sightings of these creatures occur in offshore waters, far from their coastal haunts of past centuries. The bottom-fish fisheries that the Wadden Sea once supported have all collapsed. At the turn of the twentieth century, the handline fishery for haddock alone yielded two million fish annually.[26] Today, only a handful of wild species of shellfish support commercial fisheries. Pollution problems have grown not only because of greater inputs from inland populations, but also because the capacity of marine species that remain to filter and process organic matter has been so reduced.

Elsewhere in Europe's waters, habitat destruction continues. On Britain's west coast, scallop dredges are still busy destroying some of the last maerl beds. These rich habitats were built over hundreds of years by slow-growing coralline algae. They occur in places flushed by strong tidal streams of clear water and are important nursery habitats for species like scallops. Extensive areas of maerl once occurred in Strangford Lough, a finger of the sea that points deep into Northern Ireland. Despite legislation passed to protect the beds, scallop dredgers destroyed them. Oyster reefs were once common along Europe's coasts and estuaries, but dredging, overexploitation, and siltation have destroyed most of them. So, too, have the largest and most productive mussel beds been lost to fishing and siltation. Together, all of these habitats once supported hundreds of associated species whose fates we can only guess.

It was into the scraped, pulverized, and looted North Sea that I made my first, hesitant scuba dives in the early 1980s. At the time I had no inkling of the degree to which fishing had changed what I saw. I was disappointed to find so few fish; a handful of diminutive animals darting among straggling seaweeds, or the half-imagined flicker of something large at the edge of visibility, had to keep me satisfied. Occasionally, I would find disgruntled-looking crustaceans picking over the carcass of a dead fish, but the seas were unexpectedly empty, even in places considered great diving spots by those in the know. I was unaware then of how different it once was. Today I see the ghosts of the disappeared and am saddened by what has been lost.

— *Chapter 15* —

# The Downfall of
# King Cod

— —

ULY 1, 1992, was a day of celebration, marking Canada's 125th anniversary. But John Crosbie, Canadian fisheries minister, had little to cheer him that day. Walking along the wharf front in Bay Bulls, a small coastal community in Newfoundland, he was met by a hostile crowd of cod fishers. Why was the cod fishery in such a dire state, they demanded to know, and what was he going to do about it? Crosbie lost his composure and shouted back at one of his attackers, "There's no need to abuse me. I didn't take the fish from the Goddamn water!" The next day he faced worse in St. John's, Newfoundland's capital. A mob of angry fishers tried to force its way into the hotel ballroom in which he was about to make a momentous announcement.[1] Surrounded by more than a dozen police, Crosbie hastily announced a two-year moratorium on cod fishing before being bundled to a waiting car, leaving outraged fishers to contemplate the collapse of their industry.[2]

The cod moratorium put forty thousand people out of work in five provinces and has been called the biggest layoff in history. Things turned out worse than even Crosbie had planned. His two-year moratorium was extended indefinitely in 1993 and, with a few small exceptions, remains in place as I write, fourteen years later. Worse still, the two main populations of Atlantic cod were added to Canada's list of endangered species in 2003. To the south, cod populations have also plummeted, and New Englanders have struggled throughout the last fifteen years to keep cod fishers in business, with limited success.

It is almost unimaginable that a species as prolific as cod could be brought down. Cod were not simply a part of this environment; they defined it, just as bison defined the American Plains before Buffalo Bill and the railroads. Cod were keystone predators of northern seas and once influenced every aspect of life there.

To understand why the cod fishery collapsed, we must go south to the Gulf of Maine and back to the early twentieth century, shortly before the First World War, to the time when steam trawlers were introduced on that side of the Atlantic. The trawlers met with the same distrust and hostility that had greeted them in Europe several decades earlier, but resistance soon crumbled in the face of their greater fishing power. By the 1920s trawlers were well established. At first they worked close inshore, but they soon moved seaward as catch rates fell. They headed for offshore banks like Brown's Bank and Georges Bank, which had until then been the province of sailing schooners whose crews fished with hook and line for cod and halibut.

Georges Bank is a great rolling range of sand, gravel, and boulder hills that extends 240 kilometers (150 miles) offshore northeast from Cape Cod. It is a legacy of past ice ages, marking the southernmost extent of ice sheets where they heaped up material scraped from the land into a 20,000 square kilometer (8,000 square miles) bank of terminal moraine. Most of the bank is shallow, ranging in depth between a few tens and 100 meters (60 to 330 feet). Together with Brown's and Seal Island Banks, Georges Bank separates and encloses the shallow Gulf of Maine from deep offshore waters of the Atlantic. In early summer, fingers of cool and nutrient-rich water from the icy Labrador Current turn south past Newfoundland and Nova Scotia, creeping between these banks and the mainland. Warm Gulf Stream waters flowing from the south strike the ocean side of the banks before turning east for Europe. Tidal streams slosh cold and warm

waters across the banks, combining nutrients and warmth to fuel prodigious plankton growth that in turn supports vast shoals of fish like
mackerel and herring. They in turn feed cod and a host of other predators. The Gulf of Maine and waters to the north are summer feeding
grounds of migratory humpback and right whales, swordfish, tuna,
sharks, and even turtles. It was these waters that seventeenth-century
fishers found thronged with huge cod and halibut.

About the same time as trawlers came into use in North America,
fast-freezing techniques were developed and the fish fillet was born.
In the nineteenth century, schooners fishing for halibut and cod on
the banks threw away haddock because it would not preserve well on
salt. But the advent of frozen fish fillets gave fishers of the 1920s a
ready market: haddock is a tough fish that freezes well and can be
transported to markets far inland without spoiling. Trawlers soon
discovered enormous shoals of haddock visiting the southeast part
of Georges Bank to spawn in winter[3] and swooped in. Through the
1920s hundreds of new trawlers swelled the fleet, and haddock landings soared, reaching more than 120,000 tonnes in 1929, the peak of
the boom. The following year, three hundred trawlers landed thirty-
seven million haddock into Boston,[4] but more were left dead at sea
than landed. The small-mesh nets in use were indiscriminate, catching juvenile haddock and dozens of other species of fish that were
simply thrown overboard. More than two juvenile haddock were discarded for every adult landed.[5]

American fishers quickly tasted the bitter fruits of overfishing that
had earlier afflicted European seas. Haddock landings crashed as
quickly as they peaked, falling back to 28,000 tonnes in 1934, about
one-quarter of the catch just five years earlier. They rallied again soon
after, settling at around 50,000 tonnes per year throughout the rest of
the 1930s and continuing until 1960. Fishers had adapted to reduced
haddock numbers by moving north into waters off Canada and by
seeking other local species. The next most lucrative local fish was redfish, or rosefish as it was then called.[6] This bright pink, perchlike fish
is firm fleshed and compact, reaching 45 to 50 centimeters long (18 to
20 inches). At the time it was common throughout the Gulf of Maine.
Henry Bigelow, a biologist from the Woods Hole Oceanographic
Institution on Cape Cod, described the fish in the 1950s:

This is one of the most plentiful of the commercially important fishes in all but the shoalest parts of the Gulf: on the offshore banks, in or over the deep central basin, and along shore. To list its known occurrences would be to mention practically every station where hook-and-line or otter-trawl fishing is carried on deeper than 20 fathoms. Thus considerable numbers are sometimes taken on lines or trawls in 20 to 35 fathoms or more in the Massachusetts Bay region both winter and summer, especially on or near rocky bottom.[7]

Before the haddock fishery wobbled, the few redfish caught incidentally were thrown away as trash. By the time Rachel Carson wrote her booklet describing unfamiliar fish for wartime housewives in 1943,[8] though, much of the fishing fleet had switched to catching redfish. Like haddock, redfish withstood filleting and freezing well. In 1941, New England catches hit 62,000 tonnes, outstripping those of cod and barely surpassed only by haddock.

Although Bigelow makes much of redfish in relatively shallow water, their main stronghold was deeper down. They inhabit deep rocky and muddy regions on the continental shelf and slope, to depths of more than 700 meters (2,300 feet). What would only later be discovered is that deepwater fish live rather slower lives than those of species that inhabit the shallows. The frigid waters of the deep sustain only a sluggish metabolism, and growth rates are low. Moreover, redfish live long lives, reaching ages of fifty or older. Unlike most fish, which release their eggs into the sea at spawning, redfish brood their young until the eggs hatch into larvae and so produce relatively few offspring compared to species like cod. Redfish thus could not sustain high fishing mortality for long. Catches plummeted from their mid-1940s peak to around 14,000 tonnes per year in the late 1950s. Even these catch levels were sustained only by fishers searching out new grounds, such as waters off Nova Scotia.

Flounders were another species, or, rather, group of species, to find favor with the frozen-fish trade in the 1930s and 1940s. They were virtually unknown in catches from nineteenth-century line fishers because they never took baited hooks. Trawls revealed an unexpected abundance, lifting them from the bottom by millions. Witch flounder, winter flounder, American plaice, and yellowtail flounder dominated early catches. By the late 1950s, flatfish graced tables throughout the United States and were at the heart of New England fisheries.

Events in the 1960s changed everything for fisheries in the United States and Canada. At the time, national waters extended 3 miles off-shore,[9] and the rest was open to anybody who cared to try their luck. The fertile waters of eastern North America proved irresistible to European nations whose own waters were by then yielding much-reduced catches. In the mid-1950s, the first distant-water trawlers were put into service by Britain, followed swiftly by the Soviet Union, who copied the British design.[10] The first arrived on the Grand Banks in 1956. Eastern European countries embarked on a boat-building spree that would see them join the first rank of fishing nations within a decade. Their distant-water fleets consisted of groups of trawlers supplying mother ships that processed the catch. By 1965, the Soviet Union had 106 factory trawlers and 425 smaller trawlers supplying 30 mother ships. They fished from Greenland south to Georges Bank and beyond to waters of the Carolinas. Polish and East German trawlers joined the Soviets, elbowing for space on the banks with vessels from Spain, Romania, Portugal, France, Britain, and West Germany. Charles Philbrook, a pilot for the U.S. National Marine Fisheries Service recalls encountering these flotillas in 1968:

> I remember flying surveillance out of North Carolina in the winter of '68, flat-hatting in a *Grumman Goat* 300 feet above the water. Often you could count as many as two hundred Communist-bloc trawlers within a 20-mile area off Hatteras Island. Every one of them would be wallowing—filled to the gunwales, you might say—with herring.[11]

Distant-water trawlers with their mother ships had astonishing fishing power. They could catch and process thousands of tons of fish in days, far exceeding the capacity of local fleets. William Warner describes their effect in his book *Distant Water*:

> [T]ry to imagine a mobile and completely self-contained timber-cutting machine that could smash through the roughest trails of the forest, cut down trees, mill them, and deliver consumer-ready lumber in half the time of normal logging and milling operations. This was exactly what factory trawlers did—this was exactly their effect on fish—in the forests of the deep. It could not long go unnoticed.[12]

In 1965, the Soviet catch off North America came to 872,000 tonnes to which Spain, Portugal, and France added another 600,000 tonnes. It wasn't just their size that made these fleets so lethal to fish. Eastern European boats worked cooperatively, hunting fish over wide geographic regions, free of the tethers that held smaller vessels within reach of home ports. When a boat found a large concentration of fish, it would call others in. Factory fleets were able to target aggregations of fish as never before, fishing them to exhaustion before spreading out again in search of new opportunities.

By 1974, distant-water fleets dominated fishing off eastern North America. Over a thousand Eastern and Western European vessels fished the banks, shelves, and slopes that year. Together they took over 2 million tonnes of fish, three times the Canadian catch and ten times that of New England.[13] They had scant regard for the niceties of fishing, sucking fish from the sea irrespective of whether they were juvenile or adult, and regardless of whether or not they were spawning. A dead fish was a dead fish. This was industrial fishing on a monumental scale.

Georges Bank and the Gulf of Maine suffered badly. Between 1960 and 1965, total landings of bottom fish from the Gulf of Maine went from 200,000 tonnes to more than three-quarters of a million, far exceeding sustainable catches. Haddock catches spiked at 154,000 tonnes in 1965 before collapsing spectacularly in the early 1970s. The pressures that forced Iceland to extend its coastal waters were at work in North America. In 1977, the United States and Canada declared 200-nautical-mile Exclusive Economic Zones and pushed the foreign fleets out.

Both Canada and the United States expected a bonanza from the exclusion of foreign boats and poured money into new fishing vessels to cash in. Between 1977 and 1982, the New England trawl fishing fleet nearly doubled in size from 825 to over 1,400 boats.[14] In 1975, the Canadian east coast fishing industry employed fourteen thousand people; by 1980, there were thirty-three thousand. Domestic overfishing replaced foreign overfishing, and life for fishers seemed never to get any easier. North American fishers of the time might well have felt sympathy with the plight of their predecessors as characterized by an anonymous mid-nineteenth-century poet:

*A perilous life and sad as life can be,*
*Hath the lone fisher on the lonely sea,*
*In the wild waters laboring far from home,*
*For some bleak pittance e'er compelled to roam!*[15]

By the early 1980s, fishing catches in the Gulf of Maine rose to twice the level that would have been sustainable, and fish populations nosedived. There was still enough out there to make a living, which encouraged fishers to invest in electronic fish-finding devices and better gear. By the mid-1980s, fishers killed 60 to 80 percent of all the cod, haddock, and yellowtail flounder in the Gulf of Maine every year.[16] Combined landings of these species fell from 100,000 tonnes in the early 1980s to only 40,000 tonnes by 1989.[17] By 1985, U.S. fisheries scientists foresaw impending collapse and urged the New England Fisheries Management Council to slash fishing effort. The council, whose membership was dominated by fishing industry representatives, resisted until a lawsuit from the Conservation Law Foundation forced their hand. Eventually, fish and time for procrastination ran out, and in the mid-1990s, 17,000 square kilometers (6,500 square miles) of Georges Bank were closed to fishing methods that take bottom-living species. At the same time, bottom trawling and scallop fishing efforts were cut in half outside the closed areas.

By this time, Georges Bank and the Gulf of Maine were very different from the seas fished by nineteenth-century sailing schooners. One unexpected consequence of overfishing on Georges Bank was first noticed in the 1970s and became progressively worse in the 1980s. Bottom fish like cod, haddock, and flounder had dominated these waters for thousands of years, ever since the ice sheets melted and the seawater flooded the Gulf of Maine.[18] Fishers in the 1970s began to be troubled by growing packs of dogfish that tore into nets and catches and packed their trawls. Small species of skate and stingray were also on the rise. When the tie closing the cod end of the net was slipped, instead of flatfish, haddock, and cod, a writhing mass of grey-skinned dogfish and flapping rays collapsed onto the deck, leaving fishers aghast. The removal of whitefish from New England waters had opened up a niche that these species were quick to exploit. This reversal of fortune saw dogfish and rays climb to eight to ten times the abundance of whitefish by the 1980s.

At first fishers threw these impostors overboard, often after club-bing them to death. But resistance became futile in the face of ever-renewing hordes, and a better solution was found—sell them. Sharks and rays with their tough and stringy meat are poor substitutes for succulent flaked haddock or cod. But necessity gave them a market. Their sovereignty was brief, however, and by the mid-1990s, they too were in decline from overfishing.

Bottom habitats of the Gulf of Maine and associated shallow banks also saw dramatic changes. Trawling in North America was just as destructive of seabed communities as it was in Europe. George Matteson describes hauling a trawl on Georges Bank in the 1970s, showing how trawls stripped the seabed of vegetation and other organisms:

> The head and the ground ropes wind onto the drum and then the yards and yards of netting that make up the body of the net. Where the belly of the net has been brushing against the sea bottom it is fes-tooned with dark brown seaweed. Here and there a small fish or a squid has become tangled in the mesh and is wound onto the drum, buried and crushed under succeeding layers of twine.
>
> The chain, the rings, and all of the metal on the lower lip of the net as well as the steel runners on the bottom of the doors are polished bright silver by sliding on the sea bottom. . . .
>
> The first tow has been a good one and Kaare [the captain] will tow back right through the same area. The net is back on the bottom within five minutes of the time it was hauled up the ramp. Any fisher-man knows you catch no fish while the net is on the deck.
>
> The net has left about 4,000 pounds [1.8 metric tonnes] of fish and debris piled in the middle of the deck. Included in the pile are yellow-tail flounder, cod, haddock, several other species of valuable flounder (lemon sole, gray sole, dab, winter flounder, perhaps a small halibut) plus anglerfish, scallops, a few lobster, and a butterfish or two. All of these will be kept and altogether amount to about 1,000 pounds [450 kilograms]. Everything else is thrown, shoveled, kicked, and hosed back over the side. . . .
>
> Finally there is nothing left in the middle of the deck but trash. There are many small sharks known as dog fish. There are crabs and small rays, called skate. There are sculpin—small bony fishes with long spikes from their heads so sharp they easily pierce the men's boots and

stab into their feet. It is these nasty little fish that utter the croaking sound when the net is being dumped.

There are bits of junk, scraps of metal and wood, bottles, tin cans, stones, weed and clam shell. Sometimes there are bones, the skull or vertebra of a porpoise. There may be strange fishes. Yesterday the net brought up a large sea turtle. . . .

Sometimes the net may pick up a bagful of stones or tons of weed and thick mud. Another time it may get thousands of dogfish, or a peculiar orange sponge the men call "monkey dung." Sometimes so much trash is caught that the net is impossible to bring back aboard. To be emptied it must be slit open.[19]

Heavy damage to the bottom had already been done years earlier, when trawlers first hit the Gulf of Maine in force in the 1920s. But trawling in the 1970s was more intense and more invasive than earlier fishing, employing heavier gear. With dwindling fish stocks, fishers pursued fish into places they once shunned as too risky for their gear.[20] Before the Exclusive Economic Zone was declared, foreign factory trawlers towed their oversized nets through the shallow banks and depressions of the Gulf of Maine, causing damage on an altogether new scale:

Their massive nets, the American fishermen said, were gouging the sea bottom so badly that great areas of Georges Bank were becoming lifeless deserts. Their tow wires and rigging were so strong that when the foreign ships snagged wrecks and boulders they often dragged them for miles across the bottom before they finally got free. Charts of snags became useless to fishermen who had them because the foreign ships were all the time mixing things up.[21]

Flounder fishing and scallop dragging on Georges Banks and elsewhere in the Gulf of Maine were even more invasive than otter trawling, as nets and dredges dug up the seabed as they were towed. The front end of a scallop dredge consists of a steel frame with downward-pointing teeth, rather like the steel harrows that are dragged over ploughed fields to break up the soil. The teeth excavate scallops from the bottom that are scooped up by a trailing chain-mail bag. Flounders, rather like scallops, hug the bottom, burying themselves in mud. Flounder trawls are set so the ground rope cuts beneath the mud, digging out fish.[22] The combined forces of decades of fishing by domestic and foreign trawl fishers stripped the bottom of life and rearranged the very foundations of the gulf. Trawling had become a geological force. Outsiders seldom understand how much damage bottom trawling does, but fishers themselves often recognize it. Fred Bennett started fishing in the Gulf of Maine in the 1960s. Over his long career as a fisher, he has witnessed trawlers transform the structure of the seafloor:

> One example is an area about 25 miles east-southeast of Chatham called the Peaks. When I first fished at the Peaks in the late 1960s, they were a row of hills running northwest to southeast for about a mile. I had a paper depth recorder, and on it I could watch the bottom go up and down. There were four big steep peaks whose height from bottom to top was about ten fathoms [18 meters], and there were several smaller hills as well. I would set my longline right across those peaks, because the fishing for cod was excellent. When I went back in 1987, after taking up longlining again, all I could find was a couple of little bumps in the bottom, just little hills, none higher than two to three fathoms [3.6 to 5.4 meters]. The fishing was not as good as before, though I still fish there at times. I do not know what happened to that topography, but I suspect that it was destroyed the by trawlers and scallopers that have fished there.[23]

Rich animal and plant communities were lost with the rearrangement of the seabed. Fred Bennett described another favorite fishing spot in the Gulf of Maine, called Big Mussels by fishers. Over an area of about 15 square nautical miles (50 square kilometers), the bottom consisted of rolling hills thick with mussels, crabs, anemones, tube-worms, and a panoply of invertebrate life. But in the mid-1990s, trawlers targeted the area. After the trawlers moved on, Bennett returned to find the mussel beds gone and the hills bulldozed smooth. Les Watling, a scientist from the University of Maine, recalls another place destroyed by the trawl.[24] On a research cruise in the late 1980s he discovered a boulder-strewn rough spot on the bottom of the Gulf of Maine near Jeffrey's Bank not yet reached by trawlers. It was a veritable Garden of Eden for sponges and other invertebrates, easily the richest spot he had seen in more than twenty years of research.

Hoping to find out more about this community, he organized a return expedition in 1993 with a submersible. Sadly, the trawlers had got there first with their new rock-hopping gear. For two depressing hours, Watling searched a wasteland of bare rock, mud, and silt where the sponge groves had been. He found none.

Removing a voracious, broad-spectrum predator like cod from the Gulf of Maine profoundly affected nearshore ecosystems as well as those offshore.[25] Much of the New England coast, especially in the north, is fronted by impressive rocky platforms backed by rugged cliffs. These platforms extend underwater and are generally too rough even for the most hard-pressed trawler captain. When dense shoals of cod prowled these submarine ravines and gullies, invertebrates like lobsters, sea urchins, crabs, and mollusks lived in constant fear of death. Cod kept numbers low, and wary invertebrates retreated to crevices by day and fed at night. Grazing pressure was light, and thick blankets of kelp and other seaweeds cloaked the rocks, creating swaying liquid gardens. With the cod gone, invertebrate numbers exploded. By the 1980s, sea urchins studded almost every rock up and down the New England coast. Immense numbers of these grazers cleared the seaweed forests and scraped the rocks clean.

About this time, trade was becoming increasingly global, and local markets no longer limited what fishers could sell. New Englanders quickly saw an opportunity and began urchin fisheries to supply Asia, where the roe is eaten as a delicacy. Urchins were readily accessible in the shallow, nearshore waters, and divers scooped up hundreds of thousands of them. With no regulation, enterprising fishers took as much as they could find. The inevitable population collapse soon came, helped along the way by urchin predators, like lobsters, whose populations had also been freed from the yoke of cod predation. The disappearance of urchins eased grazing pressure, giving seaweed the chance to recover. But instead of brown seaweeds like bladderwrack and kelp reestablishing dominance, a posse of alien species invaded the Gulf of Maine, spreading like weeds.[26] In 2001, while snorkelling off the Isles of Shoals in New Hampshire, I saw the change. Beneath me, waving velvety fingers of dark green *Codium fragile*, a species of green alga, blanketed the rocks. Only scattered tussocks of a native brown alga, *Desmarestia aculeata,* sprouted here and there through the green canopy. Parting the soft carpet, I could see the rocks below crusted with grey, yellow, and orange patches of an invasive sea squirt.

Many of these species had been in the Gulf of Maine for some time but had spread little while the seabed was dominated by native species. *Codium* had been there since the late 1950s, probably having hitched a ride with a boat from its native Japan, or from Europe where it had already established as an invader. New Englanders nicknamed it "oyster thief," referring to its ability to blanket and then choke out species that live on hard bottoms, like oysters.

While the Gulf of Maine suffered, Canadian cod fisheries prospered briefly after declaration of the 200-mile limit. Conditions for survival of young cod were good in the late 1970s and early 1980s. But the seeds of disaster were sown even then. Canadian government fishery scientists made an overoptimistic prediction about future cod production, basing estimates on past levels of recruitment from stocks that had been up to ten times larger. They set themselves the aim of ratcheting up catches to a target yield of 350,000 tonnes by 1985. Canadians fished with energy and enthusiasm, but they could not catch as much as the government would allow. The cod seemed not to be there.

Government predictions of the size of cod stocks had been based mainly on data on catch-per-unit-of-effort compiled by the fishing industry, since the government began its own research surveys only in 1978. The approach was badly flawed because fishers adapted their methods over time to increase catching power by using new electronics, larger nets, and boats with a greater steaming range. These changes make catch-per-unit-effort a poor index of stock size. Fish that form tight schools or shoals, as cod do when they gather to spawn, also remain highly catchable even as their overall density plummets. As long as boats can find these shoals, they can catch fish as easily as when the animals were abundant. Through the second half of the 1980s, fishers removed cod at five times the rate the stock could have sustained.

The warning signs were ignored. The government rejected pleas from inshore fishers to curb the offshore fishery and brushed aside the concerns of fishery scientists worried by the low numbers they were seeing in their stock assessments.[27] Inshore fishers saw the bottom drop out of their livelihoods before the big offshore trawlers first had trouble finding fish. Cod overwinter in deep water. Come spring, they gather in immense shoals at the edge of the continental shelf to spawn before following shoals of their prey, the capelin, inshore where they spend the summer feeding. By the late 1980s, few cod made it inshore any longer. Trawlers that worked the shelf edge were catching them all.

When gamblers start to bet future earnings, you know they are in trouble. This is exactly what happened in Canada. The government set overgenerous quotas in the expectation of production that never materialized. Like the gamblers they were, they lost big-time in the end. By 1992, it was all over for cod and the cod fishers, and has been ever since.

How many cod have been lost? George Rose of Memorial University in Newfoundland has reconstructed the population size of cod back to 1505 when Europeans first dipped their hooks and nets in North American waters.[28] We can't go back in time and count cod, so Rose created a model to estimate past populations. This model combined information on the number of fish caught with elements of cod biology. His model didn't predict recent changes in population size very well, for which we do have good estimates, until he added a measure of prevailing climatic conditions. The model then provided a quite reliable tool for estimating cod populations back through time. Data on the width of tree rings, a proxy for temperature, provided estimates of climate back to the sixteenth century enabling Rose to hindcast population size to the time of John Cabot. His best guess is that there were 7 million tonnes of cod swarming the banks and coasts of Canada in 1505, made up of several billion fish. By the time the cod moratorium was announced in 1992, there were just 22,000 tonnes left, one-third of 1 percent of the original population.

Andy Rosenberg and colleagues from the University of New Hampshire have taken a different approach to estimate the former abundance of cod in grounds further south.[29] They examined logbook records from the 1850s for boats from the port of Beverly, Massachusetts, fishing the Scotian Shelf. The records are remarkably complete for this port, with 326 logbooks available for boats fishing all or part of their time in this area. This shallow continental shelf extends 200 kilometers (125 miles) into the Atlantic from the coast of Nova Scotia. Like the Gulf of Maine, it combines warmth and high nutrient levels, making the overlying waters highly productive. Both Canadian and New England boats fished the area heavily in the nineteenth century, targeting cod and halibut with hook and line. Rosenberg's team used the detailed logbook records of catches made to estimate fishery productivity and size of the cod population. Their best guess is that there were 1.26 million tonnes of cod on the shelf. The figure is in the same range as Rose's, given that the Scotian Shelf covers a smaller area and that by the 1850s, fishing had almost certainly significantly reduced the size of stocks from their pristine levels. The estimated stock size in 2002 was just 3,000 tonnes, one-third of 1 percent of the 1850s level.

The Scotian catch data are sobering. In the 1850s, forty-three sailing schooners fishing with about twelve hundred hooks in total brought back 7,800 tonnes of cod. In 1999, the Canadian fishery (which remained open in this southerly region) landed only 7,200 tonnes from a much larger area that included the Bay of Fundy. All the cod in the water today on the Scotian Shelf, as Rosenberg points out, amount to less than half the annual catch in the 1850s.

Why have cod not made a comeback? There are many theories and few agreed-upon facts, but it seems that fishers have unwittingly brought the rule of cod to an end. Whatever the impediments to cod reasserting dominance, the seas of eastern North America are emptier than before, and rich cod fisheries live on only in the memories of people who experienced them. Today, cod catches are heavily restricted in the Gulf of Maine by limits on fishing effort and closed areas. To the north, Canadian cod catches are limited to a small, artisanal catch by nearshore fishers.

We have devastated cod by overwhelming their ecosystem. In our pursuit of fish we have transformed the leafy glades and rolling forests of the sea into endless muddy plains. We should worry a great deal about losing cod. To bring a species from a state of such plenty to the point of annihilation indicates that there is much more going wrong than the mere removal of a species from its ecosystem. It is a symptom that the ecosystem itself is at the point of ruin. Far more species than cod have disappeared. Rachel Carson recommended two of them to consumers seeking culinary adventure in the 1940s, as I mentioned earlier. Wolffish, she said, is "one of New England's underexploited fishes, a condition that will be corrected when housewives discover its excellence."[30] Carson also recommended barndoor skate. Both are now threatened species.

There is a coda to this tale. Stripped of their number-one predator, prey species like snow crab, northern prawns, lobsters, rock crab, and sea urchins prospered. Just as in the Gulf of Maine, the Canadian seabed today feels the scratch and suck of legions of invertebrate feet where fish once dominated. Fishers were quick to see opportunity in this new regime, and have switched their efforts to lucrative invertebrate fisheries. In 2003, Newfoundland's fisheries were worth Can$515 million compared to Can$170 million in 1991 just before cod collapsed.[31] But how long will these good times last? There isn't much else to catch when they are gone.

# — *Chapter 16* —

# Slow Death of an Estuary: Chesapeake Bay

$$\sim\!\!-\!\!\sim$$

C HESAPEAKE BAY in the late nineteenth century was a wild, lawless place where fortunes were won and many just as quickly lost. Four or five murders a week would not have been uncommon. Bay communities like Crisfield and Cambridge in Maryland had more in common with the West of Jesse James than with their more cultured East Coast neighbors in Philadelphia and Delaware. By night the towns were centers of hard drinking and carousing; floating brothels dotted the waters. The railways, which had only just reached the bay, jolted the Chesapeake from a network of tranquil backwaters cut by shipping lanes to and from Baltimore and Washington, D.C., to a bustling and dangerous frontier. Oysters and caviar fueled this boom.[1]

The advent of railways and plentiful ice for preserving the catch hugely expanded markets for seafood in inland America. The industrial revolution had brought unprecedented prosperity to numerous nineteenth-century Americans. The nation's growing middle classes were keen to experience delights that had previous been the purview of only the wealthy, and the Chesapeake was ready to supply them.

Oysters were much admired. As a Maryland resident observed in 1877, "Nobody tires of oysters. Raw, roasted, scalded, stewed, fried, boiled, escalloped, in pâtés, in fritters, in soup, oysters are found on every table, sometimes at every meal, and yet no entertainment is complete without them."[2]

At the height of the last ice age, Chesapeake Bay was a lush valley where the course of the great Susquehanna River joined the York, the Potomac, and the James rivers amid a host of smaller tributaries. When the glacial ice caps melted, sea levels rose by over 100 meters (330 feet), flooding the valley for 300 kilometers inland (195 miles). Today, the former course of the Susquehanna is still recognizable as a channel 10–20 meters deep (32 to 64 feet) through the middle of the bay. But most of the bay is shallow enough for oysters and seagrass to thrive, averaging only 6.5 meters deep (21 feet). When the first European colonists sailed into the Chesapeake, oysters were everywhere and reefs built from their shells extended for 150 kilometers (94 miles) into the bay. The Native American name *Chesepioc* is said to mean "Great Shellfish Bay."[3]

From around 1820 to the 1880s oyster fisheries expanded without check, and hundreds of kilometers of waterfront were peopled on the wave of this boom. By 1860, railways carried 3 million pounds (2,500 metric tons) of oysters west every year, while clipper ships plied the east coast supplying the epicures of New York and New England with hundreds of thousands of bushels (a bushel is an 8-gallon measure containing approximately seventy oysters). A decade later, 9 million bushels were shipped from the Chesapeake annually.[4] As with so many other fisheries, the advent of new technology heralded the beginning of the end for oysters.

Early fishers "tonged" oysters from the reefs using long-handled wooden poles tipped with iron. They were operated by hand in the manner of pincers to pick clumps of oysters off the bottom. Up north, New Englanders had for a long time captured oysters with dredges, a technology imported from Europe. Oyster-dredging vessels would drag steel rakes powered by hand-operated windlasses across the reefs built from shells of countless generations of oysters. The matrix of living oysters and dead shells is habitat for hundreds of others species, such as mussels and sponges. Oyster dredgers tore away the upper

*Oyster dredging in the nineteenth century. Dredges were dragged across the seabed to dislodge clumps of oysters from reefs along with many other organisms that were later discarded. Source: Whymper, F. (1883)* The Fisheries of the World. An Illustrated and Descriptive Record of the International Fisheries Exhibition, 1883. *Cassell and Company Ltd., London.*

surface of these reefs as they worked, removing living oysters and underlying dead reef material with each pass. At the peak of oyster fishing in New England in the late eighteenth century, reefs were dragged throughout the day; after the peak, they were also dragged by night. Oyster dredgers ground the reefs down strip by strip, pass after pass, until there was nothing firm left for juvenile oysters to settle on. In the 1860s, New England dredgers, having destroyed their local beds, sought new opportunities in the Chesapeake. Initially, relations with resident watermen were amicable; there were plenty of oysters for all, and the dredgers kept to deeper areas of the bay, away from grounds favored by tongers. By the early 1870s, however, a thousand dredge boats worked the bay, and incursions into shallow river waters had become frequent. Tongers complained that dredgers were destroying the beds and pressed for laws to limit where they could fish. A series of progressively more restrictive laws had little influence over the dredging fleet with so much money to be made. Dredgers gained a further edge in the late nineteenth century when backbreaking hand-operated windlasses were replaced by steam-powered ones. Before long, Chesapeake oysters were in decline.

The story of oyster fisheries is an oft-repeated one in the history of human exploitation of natural resources. Where a resource is common property, shared by all, there is a tendency for individuals to take more of that resource than is sustainable. Individuals can obtain a private gain but at a cost to the rest of society by acting selfishly. If everybody exercised restraint, and took only a sustainable share of the resource, everyone would be better off. But restraint seldom occurs without some kind of regulation, whether it be through legal or traditional means. The Maryland police chief, Hunter Davidson, told the State Oyster Commission in 1869 that the fishers were uneducated and daring men reckless of consequences. The industry was "more like a scramble for something adrift, where the object of everyone appears [to be] to get as much as he can before it is lost."[5]

Davidson was given a boat early in the 1870s to enforce the law and keep the peace. Despite his best efforts, fishers continued dredging for oysters, now doing it illegally by night. Firefights often broke out between police and pirate fishers, killing many in what are known as the "oyster wars" of Chesapeake Bay.[6] Sadly, many local people, including their elected officials, believed they had too much to lose from restraint, and by the early decades of the twentieth century, the oyster bonanza was over.

Michael Kirby of Scripps Institution of Oceanography in California has reconstructed the rise and spread of oyster fisheries around the United States.[7] He looked at catch records from twenty-one estuaries spanning east, west, and Gulf of Mexico coasts. Fisheries began close to growing urban centers, spreading away from these estuaries along the coasts as stocks were depleted. With passing time, catches in each estuary peaked rapidly and then fell as beds were exhausted and fishers moved on. Kirby found the same pattern in attempts to stem oyster declines. In the waters around New York, then a Dutch colony, there were signs of trouble as early as the mid-seventeenth

*Pirate oyster fishers working by night on the Chesapeake Bay in the 1880s to evade regulations limiting where oysters could be taken. Source:* Harper's Weekly. *March 1, 1884.*

century. A proclamation of 1658 states that "the Director General and Council of New Netherland . . . interdict and forbid all persons from continuing to dig or dredge any Oyster shells on the East River or the North River, between this City and Fresh Water."[8]

As fisheries collapsed, local authorities attempted to bolster stocks by transplanting oysters from more distant, less exploited estuaries. An article in the journal *Science* in 1891 makes it clear that such intervention had by then seemed essential if people were to continue eating oysters: "All the various persons, officials, and bodies, working at different times, in different localities, and without connection, have uniformly reported, that the natural oyster beds were either extinct or fast becoming so, and that the only remedy was to encourage cultivation by private enterprise."[9]

The earliest recorded dates of oyster cultivation signal the times at which problems had become so serious to warrant such a drastic move. Connecticut and New York, for example, began imports of oyster spat (juveniles) from Delaware Bay and Chesapeake in 1808, some seventy years before people in the Chesapeake were forced to try transplantations themselves. Problems on the Gulf of Mexico coast are more recent, dating from the mid-twentieth century. On the Pacific coast, exploitation gradually spread north from San Francisco, beginning about the time of the 1849 gold rush and reaching Washington's Puget Sound in the early twentieth century. Kirby found the same pattern of sequential oyster declines in Australian estuaries, too.

Dredging in British estuaries, like that of England's River Thames, threatened to destroy oysters there long before this tragedy of the commons played out in North America. Oyster beds were under such pressure from dredgers that parliament banned the practice from the Thames estuary in 1557.[10] History simply repeated itself from one estuary to another down the east and west coasts of North America as oyster dredgers mined the habitat on which their industry depended. Growing scarcity threatened to push up prices. The 1891 article in *Science* quoted above lamented, "It would not be surprising if oysters were soon out of the reach of most people's pockets."[11]

Price rises were avoided, however, by opening up new estuaries for exploitation and by artificial cultivation. In a fascinating study, Glen Jones and colleagues from Texas A&M University pieced together a 150-year record of changing tastes in seafood in the United States. They sifted through a collection of two hundred thousand menus compiled from the mid-nineteenth century to the present day. Around ten thousand of them showed dates and prices, enabling Jones and his team to track changing prices alongside availability. Oyster prices remained nearly constant in New York and Massachusetts at fifty cents to a dollar apiece despite the sequential, estuary-by-estuary decimation of oysters. By the early twentieth century the vast natural oyster reefs of the Chesapeake had been destroyed, and its wild oyster boom was over. Efforts shifted toward artificial propagation, and with help, the bay continued to produce oysters through the first half of the twentieth century, albeit at much lower levels. Then in the 1960s a disease called MSX was accidentally introduced to the eastern United States through Asian oysters, and native oyster stocks plunged. A price hike could no longer be avoided, and menu prices doubled, thereafter holding steady for the rest of the twentieth century. Today, the whole bay yields only 80,000 bushels a year, down from a peak of 15 million in the nineteenth century.

The economic boom based on seafood greatly increased development around the bay, attracting tens of thousands to make their homes there. Population growth precipitated a chain of events that led to a dramatic decline in water quality through the twentieth century. Chesapeake Bay drains a vast watershed of 165,000 square kilometers (64,000 square miles) in six states. That watershed has changed radically since Captain John Smith sailed up the James River in 1606. When Smith landed, it was almost completely forested. Following colonization, settlers cleared small farms, creating pockets of open space. But for the first two hundred years or so, deforestation was patchy and slow. In the nineteenth century, the scale and rate of impact picked up. Between 1830 and 1880, 80 percent of the original forest cover was cleared, largely for agriculture.[12] Cleared fields were deep-ploughed to grow crops, increasing the rate of sediment loss into the bay threefold since precolonial times.

Deforestation also changed the way in which water reached the bay. Beneath a forest canopy, rain reaches the ground by gentle drip and creeping trickle. It falls onto a heavy mulch of leaf and needle that soaks up moisture and delivers it slowly to streams and rivers. When the canopy is removed, rain strikes the ground directly with greater force. It quickly runs off into streams, carrying with it soil exposed by farming. Peaks flows are much higher from cleared land, raising the frequency and severity of floods, while minimum flows are lower, increasing the impact of dry weather. Forested watersheds are like vast sponges that soak up moisture and release it gradually over the year, benefiting species that live downstream.

Mud and silt pouring into Chesapeake choked tributaries. The Potomac at Alexandria was 13 meters deep (42 feet) in 1794 but had clogged to only 5.5 meters (18 feet) by 1974, despite frequent dredging.[13] The silting up of estuaries happened all along the coast, just as it had been widespread in medieval Europe. From the 1830s, for example, efforts to keep Delaware's St. Jones River navigable included straightening and regular dredging. They were eventually abandoned in 1925 and the river left to silt up. Today, it meanders as a trickle over mud deposits more than 4 meters deep (15 feet).[14] Although mud clogged rivers and streams, it did have some positive effects, hugely increasing the area of coastal salt marshes and mud-flats. These act as nurseries for fish and shellfish, and provide food and habitat for resident and migratory birds.[15]

Runoff entering the bay from farmlands carried elevated levels of the plant nutrients nitrogen and phosphorus. The bay was also recep-tacle for sewage from the growing population that inhabited its sprawling watershed. Sewage added further fertilizing nutrients that enriched the water and boosted plant growth. Excessive nutrients trigger prolific plant growth in a process known as eutrophication. Explosive growth of phytoplankton—microscopic plant cells floating in the water—turned the bay green. Early signs of eutrophication can be detected in sediment cores as early as 1750 and gradually worsen thereafter with the nineteenth-century clearing of the watershed. But it was the late nineteenth-century oyster boom that set the scene for a dramatic turn for the worse that came in the 1930s and 1940s.[16] Oysters filter water to feed, sifting from it plankton and suspended organic matter. Before fishing depleted them, the combined efforts of countless millions of oysters filtered all of the bay's water in just a few days.[17] Today, the few oysters left can manage to filter this volume only once a year. Jeremy Jackson of Scripps Institution of Ocean-ography likens the removal of oysters to switching off the pump in a swimming pool—it doesn't take long for the water to go bad. With oysters, Chesapeake Bay coped well with rising levels of pollution. Without them, the bay began to die.

If phytoplankton growth goes unchecked, it can cause serious problems for enclosed bodies of water like estuaries. Under normal conditions, the dead bodies of planktonic organisms sink to the bot-tom where microbes and other animals decompose them, using up oxygen in the process. But during blooms, the sheer volume of decom-posing plant matter strips oxygen from the water faster than it can be replaced, causing anoxia. The first reports of anoxia in the bay came in the 1930s[18] and worsened with time.

Leveling of oyster reefs by nineteenth-century dredgers added to problems of low oxygen. When networks of reefs spread over the bay and extended up its tributaries, the bay bottom was a complex of hills and valleys. Water churned and bubbled past the reefs with the rise and fall of the tide, mixing it from surface to bottom. Today, water flows more evenly over the flattened bottom, and stagnant pools form in hollows and troughs. Rising temperatures stratify the water in summer, creating a warm surface layer that floats over cooler, denser water beneath. When this happens, the ponded water below is rapidly deoxygenated by breakdown of organic matter, creating dead zones. Within these dead zones, the bottom is blanketed by stinking mud that belches toxic hydrogen sulfide and kills or drives away all animals that need oxygen to survive.

By the 1960s, anoxia was compounded by a further problem from eutrophication. Water darkened by phytoplankton and suspended mud shaded the bottom, causing sea grass and seaweeds to wither. Early sailors gazing through clear waters while drifting with the tide marveled at the seemingly endless meadows passing beneath. In the early seventeenth century, an estimated 240,000 hectares (590,000 acres) of the bay were cloaked with sea grass and weeds. These habitats afforded shelter, food, and nursery to hundreds of species of fish and invertebrates, in turn supporting the vibrant food web of the bay. Bottom vegetation also helped keep the bay healthy, taking up nutrients from spring floodwaters that would otherwise have promoted phytoplankton blooms. According to the U.S. Environmental Protection Agency, the original extent of submerged meadows could take up nitrogen and phosphorous equivalent to half of all present-day sewage inputs.[19] More than half of this vegetation has been lost since the 1960s, rendering the bay less diverse, less productive, and less beautiful.[20]

Eutrophication has shifted the balance in the Chesapeake from animals and plants that live on and around the bottom to ones that live in the overlying waters. It is a change repeated in many other estuaries the world over. Animals that live in the water column and feed on plankton gain an early boost from eutrophication. One of them was the Atlantic menhaden. This fish is among the preeminent species of the eastern United States. They are silver-skinned, plump, and smooth-bodied, growing to 40 or 50 centimeters long (16 to 20 inches), with blunt, toothless mouths set in a permanent frown. A migratory fish, they approach the coast from offshore regions in spring to fatten up on the seasonal plankton bloom. Hence, like oysters, they also help to filter bay waters. Many shoals penetrate estuaries like the Chesapeake where they spend the summer, drifting back and forth with the tide as they feed. The American fishery biologist George Brown Goode described them in 1884:

> The arrival of the Menhaden is announced by their appearance at the top of the water. They swim in immense schools, their heads close to the surface, packed side by side, and often tier above tier, almost as closely as sardines in a box. A gentle ripple indicates their position, and this may be seen at a distance of nearly a mile by the lookout at the masthead of a fishing vessel, and is of great assistance to the seiners in setting their nets. At the slightest alarm the school sinks towards the bottom, often escaping its pursuers. Sailing over a body of Menhaden swimming at a short distance below the surface, one may see their glittering backs beneath, and the boat seems to be gliding over a floor inlaid with blocks of silver.[21]

When Goode penned this description, menhaden shoals supported a large-scale industrial fishery that stretched from Maine to Florida. Thousands of fishers in hundreds of boats pursued the shoals along the coast. Menhaden was an all-purpose fish. Comparatively few were eaten directly, although some were canned in oil like sardines.[22] Others were caught for bait—26 million of them in 1877. But the majority were rendered down for animal feed and fertilizer. Native Americans had spread the fish on fields to fertilize crops, and the practice was adopted by early settlers. The Abnaki called them *pooka-gan* or *poghaden,* meaning "fertilizer." Toward season's end, the menhaden were fat with up to 20 percent of their body weight in oil, five times that of the average fish. Factories up and down the coast took in fish and poured forth oil. The refuse bones, scales, and flesh were turned into fertilizer that was in great demand from cotton plantations. In 1874, according to Goode, the yield of menhaden oil, at 200,000 gallons, nearly equaled that of all the whale, seal, and cod oil made in America. Menhaden oil was used in making leather and rope, lubricating machinery, and manufacturing paint and soap.[23] It was the largest fishery in the United States. Goode also recognized the linchpin role of menhaden in ocean food webs:

It is not hard to surmise the Menhaden's place in nature; swarming our waters in countless myriads, swimming in closely packed unwieldy masses, helpless as flocks of sheep, near to the surface and at the mercy of every enemy, destitute of means of defense or offense, their mission is unmistakeably to be eaten. . . . [24]

In estimating the importance of the Menhaden to the United States, it should be borne in mind that its absence from our waters would probably reduce all our other sea-fisheries to at least one-fourth their present extent.[25]

In Goode's day, seiners caught menhaden. When the season arrived, they watched the water for circling flocks of terns and the telltale splashes of predators like striped bass working the schools from below. When a school was spotted, fishers would shoot the net around it, encircling the fish. While the seining operation is much the same today, the boats are far larger, and they use planes and helicopters to guide them to the shoals. Few menhaden end up on the table. The vast majority are rendered into animal feed for chickens, pigs, and the growing aquaculture industry.[26] A surprising number also make their way into capsules of omega-3 fatty acid supplements taken by people hoping to prevent heart disease. Since this "reduction fishery" for menhaden became concentrated in the Chesapeake in 1965, stocks have plummeted. One of the bay's last productive fisheries is in trouble.

By the 1960s, signs that Chesapeake Bay was sick were obvious enough to prompt calls for action to reverse the decline. Not all were convinced, however. As late as 1971, responding to one such call for action, some scientists argued that the bay was healthy.[27] In the way that people in denial often will, they argued away evidence of the many indicators of decline seen to that date. Their arguments are full of inconsistencies. For example, in challenging the assessment that decline of oysters was due to overfishing, they pointed out that vast areas of oyster bed had been closed to fishers because of sewage pollution. They also confused cause and effect. Pointing to the fact that the Chesapeake was still one of America's richest fishing grounds, they concluded that it must be healthy.

Despite the controversy, evidence of pollution problems could no longer be ignored. By the 1970s, Chesapeake Bay suffered regular toxic plankton blooms and oxygen lows causing mass fish kills. A group of concerned citizens and scientists founded the Chesapeake Bay Foundation in 1967 to study the bay's problems and find solutions.[28] Decades of effort have seen gains made on some fronts, further retreat on others. Some kinds of pollution have been reduced significantly by better sewage treatment, for example. In some tributaries, aquatic vegetation is once more spreading over the bottom.

The story of striped bass in the bay highlights how inadequate may be our efforts to manage marine life piece by piece when only attention to the whole can yield long-term security. Striped bass is an icon for the Chesapeake, a symbol of both the resilience of nature and its fragility.[29] Bass were prized as food by Native Americans and by new colonists alike, who often called them rockfish because of their close association with oyster reefs. They are among the most nutritious fish, growing to over a meter long and, in season, fat and succulent. Tightly packed, predatory shoals of bass sometimes drove other fish ashore, like alewife and menhaden, providing a welcome food supplement for people. In the late nineteenth century they came to prominence as game fish, attracting anglers by their vigorous fight when hooked. Generations of anglers cast their lines into the Chesapeake and other estuaries through summers of the early twentieth century. However, overfishing of bass by commercial trawlers in their offshore wintering grounds caused a steep decline in the 1930s. Cooperative efforts between coastal states revived bass numbers from the 1940s to 1960s, but the population fell again through the 1970s due to the combined effects of offshore and recreational fishing, together with habitat degradation in the bay. By the early 1980s, bass had reached an all-time low, prompting drastic measures to promote recovery. In 1985, Maryland introduced a complete ban on bass fishing, followed by Virginia in 1989. The moratorium led to a remarkable comeback with a tenfold increase in the size of the spawning population by 2000.

But success helped to breed failure in the case of bass. In the mid-1990s, after the ban had been lifted for recreational fishing, anglers began catching diseased bass. Some fish had white fungus spots, others angry red sores all over their skin and lips that came from bacterial infection, and many were emaciated. Other fish looked healthy from the outside, but when cut open were in a terrible state. Jim White, a recreational fishing charter captain, described one such fish:

Last year I cleaned a fish for a customer. After I filleted it, I went to throw it away, but I said, "Let's see what she's eaten." I cut the stomach open some more. The spleen fell out. It was the most ungodly thing I'd ever seen in my entire life. Red, green, black, all kinds of sores.[30]

The recovery of striped bass went into reverse. After much testing of diseased fish and even more head scratching, local scientists realized that bass were afflicted by a variety of ills rather than victims of some new disease. The question was, why? Jim Uphoff of Maryland's Department of Natural Resources finally solved the mystery.[31] He discovered that striped bass were emaciated not because of disease but because they were starving. They succumbed to infections that well-fed bass could shrug off. The simple truth was that the expanded population of bass could not find enough of their primary prey, the menhaden. The menhaden fishery had stripped the bay of food that, as Goode recognized in the nineteenth century, was vital to sustaining the Chesapeake web of life.[32]

The Chesapeake's problems do not end with striped bass. In 1997, around the same time that bass began to sicken, fish died in their thousands around Maryland's lower Pocomoke River. Some two dozen fishers and state water quality workers exposed to the fish and water of this area developed health problems, including rashes and memory loss. The cause was traced to a harmful algal bloom. *Pfiesteria piscida,* as scientists know it, is a microorganism that blooms under high-nutrient conditions and, under certain circumstances, secretes a corrosive poison that causes lesions on fishes. Dubbed "the cell from hell," it can eat through the body wall of fishes, exposing their guts and killing them. The toxin affects the nervous system, too. People entering the water risk illness when toxic blooms flare, so in the sweltering months of summer the bay can offer little relief to worried bathers. Outbreaks of *Pfiesteria* have flared several times since 1997, and "the cell from hell" offers one more good reason to reduce pollution entering the bay, if any other was needed.

What has happened to the Chesapeake is emblematic of problems afflicting estuaries throughout the world. Since the early days of civilization, estuaries have been focal points for human impact on the sea. They tend to have the longest histories of human occupation, are often heavily modified by ports and industry, and form the place of entry to the sea for riverborne pollution. They have also been intensively fished for hundreds and sometimes thousands of years. This concentration of impacts has made them hotspots for biodiversity loss and extinction of marine species.[33] Furthermore, the pollution-driven anoxia that first emerged in estuaries is today spreading into adjacent seas. Anoxic dead zones are now permanent or seasonal features around dozens of estuaries worldwide. Many of the species described so graphically by the first European settlers no longer occur in the Chesapeake, and several are on the U.S. Endangered Species List. The New World has followed the Old in transforming its estuaries from astonishing abundance to abject poverty.

# Chapter 17

# The Collapse of Coral

ITTING ON THE edge of a rocking boat, I make the final checks to my equipment: weight belt present, air turned on, mask clear. Ahead of me, the island of Saba rises sheer from the sea. A low swell foams against the base of volcanic cliffs that glint darkly in the Caribbean sun. I twist around for a final look to check for obstacles to my entry. I can make out indistinct shapes of green and yellow that signal the presence of coral reefs far below. Among them, areas of lighter hue suggest sand patches and channels. The moment before a dive is always one of keen anticipation, a time when anything is possible. Beneath the surface, shifting light and shadows conjure in the imagination vivid scenes of giant fish and towering castles of coral. Today I feel more than the usual thrill, because this is my first dive in the inviting waters of the Caribbean.

After a second of weightlessness, I hit the water and my world turns blue. As the bubbles clear and I descend, the green shapes resolve into craggy reefs liveried in coral, anemone, and sponge. Schools of bright yellow fish the size of my finger bob and dance amid waving sea fans. More than a hundred blue surgeonfish stream over the reef, dodging the angry rushes of damselfish to plunder luxuriant seaweed in their territories. There's a flash of green as a parrot fish scuds by, pursued by another. Spreading elkhorn coral arbors shelter resting shoals of plump grunts, their striped bodies painting the reef blue and gold. Above coral and waving sea fans, thousands of tiny gray fish mingle with others of sparkling blue, picking plankton from the current. The fish seem barely to notice me, the noisy intruder, huffing clouds of bubbles.

Coral reefs are geological structures built over millennia by the creeping growth of corals and algae that secrete calcium carbonate, a stony white material. Corals are made up of hundreds to thousands of colonial polyps and come in a profusion of forms and colors. Intricate, convoluted forests and thickets of coral provide homes for more species than any other shallow-water habitat in the world. Paradoxically, they are robust but delicate, and surprisingly susceptible to human disturbance.

Now, sixteen years later, I still remember that first Caribbean dive, so different from all dives I'd made before then. Until that time, I was most familiar with reefs of the Red Sea off Saudi Arabia, where as a student I studied fish behavior. The remote Saudi reefs had changed little since early explorers sailed their waters. Large areas of the charts we used were last updated in the nineteenth century, and most of the reefs I visited were rarely fished and had never been seen by a scuba diver. Things were very different in the Caribbean, where fishing, I soon learned, had radically altered the reefs. During that first Caribbean dive I was amazed not by the profusion of life but by its scarcity. Although Saba's reefs thronged with fish, most were smaller than my hand. The lurking shadows beneath the boat were just shadows, not large groupers or gliding sharks. There were no serried ranks of toothy snappers guarding the coral on this reef, no explosions of fish fleeing attacking predators—only a docile community of plankton pickers and seaweed eaters, and the occasional larger grunt sifting invertebrates from the sand.

Before I read early accounts of the region, I misunderstood the differences I saw between the Caribbean and the Red Sea. Caribbean reefs, I reasoned, must be this way because the environment and species there are different. This sea has been separated from the Pacific Ocean for three and a half million years, since North America and South America collided, and the two regions have followed separate evolutionary paths since. The Caribbean and Pacific of today share few species in common, and their reefs look very different as a result. But I missed the most obvious explanation for the scarcity of large fish: they had been eaten!

Early travelers and settlers in the Caribbean mainly targeted food in large packages. William Dampier and his ship of pirates in the late seventeenth century dined on turtles, manatees, seals, porpoises, giant groupers, sharks, and seabirds. But as human populations on the islands grew and slaves were freed, fisheries developed on reefs and banks fringing the coast. In some heavily populated islands, such as Jamaica, reef fish have been exploited intensively for over a century. In most, fishing effort has gradually crept upward throughout the twentieth century. Visitors to the Caribbean in the early 1900s found reefs that looked much closer to those I had seen when diving in the Red Sea.

In 1908, Percy Lowe, a Cambridge University–educated naturalist, visited the Swan Islands aboard the yacht of Sir Frederic Johnstone and his wife, Laura, Countess of Wilton. The Swan Islands are mere specks of land in the western Caribbean, 175 kilometers (110 miles) north of Honduras. They were familiar to Dampier but at the time of Lowe's visit had virtually been forgotten. Sir Frederic and the countess were keen on sports—which meant they liked to kill pretty much anything that moved. The Swan Islands offered all the sport they could have desired, for the waters swarmed with big fish:

> On most days, as soon as breakfast had been comfortably disposed of, it was the custom of Lady Wilton and Sir Frederic to be towed out to the banks to spend the morning fishing. . . . The water over these banks . . . is gin-clear. There are may be, eight, nine or ten fathoms of water, that is to say, anything up to sixty feet or more [18 meters]; but a bright tropical sun lights up the fairyland below, so that you can see with ease the smallest object upon the bottom, even to those animals which by means of their mimetic colouring seek to render themselves inconspicuous upon the sand and coral mud. And among groves of sea-fans and waving zoophytes; in and out of dark mysterious grottos; and over bright stretches of white coral sand, the multicoloured procession of fish passes like a silent pageant of another world.[1]

A faded photograph in the book Lowe wrote of their adventure shows the results of "[a] morning's catch with rod and line by Lady Wilton."[2] It is a scene of slaughter, remarkable today for the size, number, and species of fish caught. At least twenty fish dangle from a makeshift line aboard the yacht, none smaller than a man's forearm, the largest a chest-high titan. All are groupers—formidable reef predators, second only to sharks. Another photograph shows a goliath grouper that must be heavier than the white-suited sailor who poses beside it. There are few places in the Caribbean today, if any, where such a throng could be found. But scenes like this were so commonplace to Lowe that he barely remarks on them in his book. Above the coral banks were larger predators:

> [M]oderate sized sharks seemed to swarm, and were a great nuisance, swimming constantly around the boat and repeatedly coming so close that it required the frequent use of an oar to keep them at arm's length. One was so friendly that the boatswain hit it across the head with the boat-stretcher; and even this greeting had to be repeated before the brute realized that its company was not enjoyed.[3]

In their annual winter jaunts around the Caribbean, Sir Frederic and Lady Wilton killed countless animals, both below and above water. With the distance of time and hindsight, their sport seems like pointless barbarity, but then it was a perfectly reasonable way to enjoy the outdoors if you were rich enough and had time on your hands. Percy Lowe dedicated his book, without apparent irony, "To Laura, Countess of Wilton, in appreciation of her wonderful powers of observation and intense sympathy with wild nature."[4]

Lowe's observations of life below water in the Swan Islands were restricted to peering through a glass-bottomed bucket held over the side of the boat. Sixteen years later, an American explorer and adventurer, William Beebe, wanted more. He mounted an expedition by the New York Zoological Society, of which he was the director, to the coral gardens of Haiti. Beebe came equipped with a heavy steel helmet fitted with a glass window at the front and supplied down a hose with air pumped from the surface. Like a space-walking astronaut tethered to the ship, Beebe's dives were limited to a small radius below the boat. There he strolled among the corals making notes about marine life on a slate. It was a rich and magical world of castles built of coral, populated by damselfish and fairy basslets:

> On one of my dives I discovered a coral castle of marvellous beauty. The simile was more than an empty phrase, for in outline, in castellated battlements, in turrets and an astonishing mimicry of a drawbridge the comparison was irresistible. Even more exciting were the tenants, for in addition to the usual demoiselles, butterfly-fish and gobies, there was a school of most exquisite beings.
>
> They were only two inches in length. Although resembling the demoiselles in general appearance, we later found that they were actually diminutive sea-basses belonging to the genus Gramma. The anterior two-thirds of the body was rhodamine purple, the head, the jaws, scales and fins being equally deep colored. Abruptly, the remaining third changed to glowing cadmium yellow. But all this detailed description is forgotten, when we see the living fish, and we feel only an inarticulate appreciation of the fairy-like beauty, as we watch the school swimming in and out of their coral castle.[5]

But life in this fairyland was cheap. Corals were abundant, and castles and their inhabitants commonplace. A page later, desperate to possess one of these fish, the collector in Beebe takes control:

> I went swiftly up my rope, and soon an innocent looking white sausage of a dynamite stick was lowered close to the great cavern of millepores. We rowed off a short distance, then down went the plunger and the explosion jarred the boat as if we had rammed a rock. . . . I descended at once and found an immense cone of impenetrable cloud where the coral had been.[6]

Beebe's expedition was based close to the capital Port-au-Prince in a bay of the same name. He found brilliant, clear water and reefs covered in coral, the largest colonies of which may have been alive at the time Columbus sighted Haiti, then called Espaniola, in 1492. Beebe again:

> [Lamentin or Sea-Cow Reef] . . . was of a barrier or shore fringing type, and lay parallel with the land, about four miles west of our schooner . . . its sea-fans and gorgonias were subordinate to its corals—massive brain mounds big as automobiles, and elkhorn forests

twelve and fifteen feet high [3.6–4.5 meters]. . . . The Isopora or branched corals, grew in a ghostly tangle of cylindrical, white thickets fathoms down, quite impenetrable. As they neared the surface the branches flattened into the moose-antlered type, and grew less closely together. I ventured, more than once, to creep down into these tangles of coral branches, testing each before I put my weight on it, and striving to keep my hose free from being jammed and perhaps torn in a crotch. In the open reef, no matter what happened, one could always lift off the helmet and swim up, but here there was a cruel, interlaced, cobweb of sharp-edged ivory overhead, and escape was possible only by slow deliberate choice of passage.[7]

What Beebe calls the *Isopora* are today known as *Acropora*. Until the 1980s they were among the most important reef-building corals in the Caribbean. He describes the classic sequence of the robust, spreading elkhorn corals (*Acropora palmata*) at the surface, giving way to a dense scrub of more delicately branching staghorn coral (*A. cervicornis*) in deeper, less wave-beaten water below.

Today, reefs in the Baie de Port-au-Prince provide a shocking contrast to what Beebe saw. The enchanted forests of *Acropora* have disappeared; only a few tumbled piles of dead elkhorn fragments remain to suggest they ever existed. Instead of clear water, white sand, and flourishing reef, divers find only scattered corals amid thick layers of mud. The slightest fin stroke lifts dense clouds of red and brown sediment, blocking light. Here and there, seaweed-fringed rock heaps mark the remains of the larger coral castles that Beebe strolled among. There are few fish to break the monotony. A speckled lizardfish stares upward from the mud while loose groups of damselfish hover over any coral they can find. But the reef, if it still deserves the name, is moribund.

Since Beebe's visit, Haiti's reefs have fallen victim to the island's overpopulation and extreme poverty. People stripped trees from the hillsides, triggering landslides and massive erosion. Millions of tons of soil have been dumped into the bay, choking the reefs. Added to this despoliation, a flotilla of fishers has picked the reefs clean of almost every larger fish, lobster, and clam.

There are two ways to document the impacts of fishing. One is to a find a place and follow it over time as fishing intensifies, recording how catches change and watching its effects on animals in the water. The second is to contrast places that are subject to different levels of fishing. The island of Bonaire in the southern Caribbean offers a telling example of both kinds. With my wife Julie, also a marine biologist, I visited Bonaire for the first time in 1993. Bonaire is low and craggy, built of the fossil skeletons of reefs that thrived in some long-ago Caribbean. They lie piled one atop another like layers of cake in a series of terraces that geologists have used to date the height of past sea levels. The oldest terraces contain reefs more than a hundred thousand years old, many of their corals still as crisp in detail as the day they were alive. At sea level, cliffs of dusty beige dip into aquamarine water and fossils yield to living coral. The reefs we found were beautiful; their crests and slopes studded with huge heads of brain coral rising over dense carpets of finger coral while feathered sea fans bent in the current. The reefs thronged with fish. Walls of gray snappers hung motionless beneath the spreading shade of elkhorn corals, surveying the reef with thoughtful yellow eyes. Bold parrot fish of midnight blue scudded overhead as they passed from shallows to the depths, defecating vapor trails of sand. Paired angelfish sailed past, pausing momentarily to browse a sponge, their blue flanks inscribed with golden lunar crescents. And in dark caves, between the flexing blades of sea fans, and above spreading stony plates of coral, were large groupers, lots of them. Fine black groupers with checkerboard flanks and vacant stares hung in the water beside fat yellowfin groupers with red backs. Occasionally, I glimpsed a tiger-barred Nassau grouper heading for the depths. Here at last were the big predators so familiar from the Red Sea but so scarce in other places we had dived in the Caribbean.

For me, Bonaire was an awakening. It had a marine park that surrounded the entire island and, compared to other places I had been to, only a few people seemed serious about fishing. I concluded that this must be what a healthy, unfished reef should look like in the Caribbean. Julie and I spent the following five years counting our way around the Caribbean to compare the state of fish populations and reefs in places experiencing different intensities of fishing. From estimates of the length of each fish seen in counts, we calculated the weight of fish present. We did this to account for differences in fish size between islands, since a few small fish are very different in weight from the same number of giants. The results shocked us. From Bonaire, the least-fished island we studied, to Jamaica, the most heavily exploited, there was a 90 percent fall in the weight of predatory fish present. More worrying though was that exactly the same was true of fish that dined on seaweed. There was only a tenth the weight of such herbivores on Jamaica's reefs as in Bonaire.

You didn't have to search hard for the reason there were so few fish in Jamaica. Lost in concentration while counting flitting shoals of small and nervous fish, I was more than once surprised to find myself looking at the sharp end of a speargun. These were brandished by lithe snorkelers whose effortless skill at depths of 15 meters (50 feet) spoke of continuous practice. From their belts they trailed strings of fish, most no larger than a hand. Strewn over the reef were so many fish traps they were hard to avoid. Jamaica has been overfished for so long that the island has a unique speciality dish developed to overcome the processing problems that attend small-bodied fish: fish "tea." Simply throw fish into a pot whole and boil for several hours. Sieve out bones, scales, and fins, and enjoy the refreshing protein broth that remains.

Julie and I also plotted changes in the weight of commercially important species present on reefs of the different islands. As fishing pressure increased, species began to disappear, dropping out one by one in sequence of body size. The largest species succumbed first under pressure, giving way to smaller species under the escalating onslaught of trap, net, hook, and spear. Bonaire's black, yellowfin, and tiger groupers yielded to graysbys and coneys, the smallest Caribbean groupers. The same pattern held for other families of fish. Mighty cubera and chunky dog snappers passed the baton to grays and then on to small schoolmasters. Midnight and rainbow parrot fish yielded to the smaller stoplight and queen, and they in turn disappeared in favor of even smaller redband and striped parrots. Many fishes once abundant are missing altogether from Caribbean reefs.

How vulnerable a species is to fishing depends on its life history as well as the intensity of the fishing. Species that live fast, reproduce early, and die small and young can withstand high fishing intensities. Chances are that enough will escape fishers for long enough to reproduce and the species can persist. The struggle for life gets harder as fish species grow larger and reproduce later in life. For them, the likelihood of avoiding capture for long enough to reproduce falls sharply as the fishing assault increases. For an audacious predator like a grouper that doesn't mature until seven years old and 40 centimeters long (16 inches), capture before maturity is almost a certainty, even at low fishing intensities. The big and the bold are the first to go as fishing pressure climbs.

I returned to Bonaire a decade after my first visit. After long study of the effects of fishing, I was eager to get back into the water to see a "healthy" reef. But the reef in front of the hotel was depressingly empty. After an hour I was rewarded by a brief glimpse of a grouper far below. That first day I snorkeled for kilometers in search of the richness I remembered. As the week passed and I dived and snorkeled more reefs, and returned to favorite haunts, I realized that Bonaire was losing its groupers. For every ten big groupers I had seen in 1993, there were perhaps one or two left. One day I got chatting with an old sea captain, Don Stewart, a longtime resident who set up one of the first scuba-diving resorts on the island. He told a tale that led me to rethink all I knew about the island's fish.

Hans Hass, the famous Austrian diver of the 1940s and 1950s, visited Bonaire in 1939 on his first-ever expedition to a coral reef, a trip he describes in his book *Diving to Adventure*.[8] He was there to shoot fish, with spear and camera, but mostly, it seems, with spear. He and two friends systematically hunted their way around Bonaire and the neighboring island of Curaçao. Little was safe. Snappers, barracuda, puffer fish, triggerfish, rays, nurse sharks, and parrot fish were poked, pierced, and nailed to the reef by their harpoons. They spent six to eight hours per day in the water, and by Hass's own account sold fish on the sly to local restaurants to fund their stay. Among the great catalog of diversity that fell to their spears, none were more favored than groupers:

. I follow [the angelfish] in the direction of shore, and it leads me to the shallow reefs, over which I swam heedlessly before, and thus to a gigantic head with pop eyes, peering out from amid the coral trees. That head must belong to a thirty-five-pound grouper. What can the fellow be doing here in shallow water? I wonder, at the same moment driving the harpoon into him. But that very instant it is in pieces. The fish snaps the iron shaft with a single motion, and breaks the line as well. Bleeding, it rushes past me, and vanishes among the reefs.

I call for Joerg and Alfred, and we hunt together. We do not find the individual we are looking for, but we do find a number of other groupers, likewise very large. One tries to flee into the depths, but Joerg is right after him, and he is the first to pay the penalty.[9]

Reading his book, I realize that Hass's experience of Bonaire's reefs was completely different from my own. The abundance of large groupers I found on my first visit was relative only to islands that had less. When Hass was there, the reefs held groupers at every turn. Even the largest Caribbean grouper, the goliath, was present, and Hass took a particular interest in killing these giants:

[In deep water] I met a sea bass that was obviously too big for me to bring up alone. I don't know what induced me to harpoon him just the same; at all events he was so strong that he snapped the iron head of the harpoon right in two before my eyes, and then dragged me downward like child's play by the short line. With an odd sort of resignation, I recalled the similar situation near Drammond, when the big grouper was towing me, but I did not let go; I fought back against the pull, hopeless as it was. Not until I felt myself fainting did I finally draw my knife and cut the line.[10]

Hans Hass also found that predators larger than groupers were plentiful:

Leafing through my diary of the Curaçao expedition after the first ten days, you will find encounters with sharks mentioned on almost every page. First described in detail, then only fleetingly noticed—but sharks were always there. They passed by in the distance or circled around us or popped up unexpectedly among the reefs.[11]

By contrast, during a month of diving in Bonaire in 1993, counting fish almost continuously, I glimpsed sharks only twice.

Don Stewart blamed Hass for single-handedly exterminating Bonaire's goliath groupers. As much of a killer as Hass was, it would be unfair to blame him alone for their demise. Bonaire's loss, like that of reefs on other islands, has been death by a thousand cuts. Since World War II, the islanders and tourists have been steadily completing Hass's work. By the early 1970s, formerly plentiful Nassau groupers had gone, and by the 1980s the slightly smaller marbled groupers followed. The groupers that became scarce between my first and second visits were just the latest in a string of losses. Bonaire's groupers were victims of sequential overfishing. The largest, most vulnerable and valuable species are targeted first. As they become scarce, the target shifts to the next most desirable on offer, and then the next, until eventually only the most resilient species will be left. Taken to its extreme, sequential overfishing leaves only the small, low-value ingredients of Jamaica's fish tea.

Today, throughout much of the Caribbean, what remain are ghost reefs. The physical structures may be crumbling but in most places

*A day's catch of fish caught on the charter boat* Gulf Stream *near Key West, Florida, circa 1950. Several of the goliath groupers weigh 140 to 230 kilograms (300 to 500 pounds). Source: Contemporary postcard.*

their outlines are still there. But the big fish, turtles, manatees, and monk seals that once thronged in these habitats have all but disappeared. Of course, if you look hard enough, you can still find goliath groupers or manatee, but largely their ranges have dwindled to a handful of pockets scattered across the region. In a few places you can still imagine yourself in the Caribbean of old: parts of the Caymans, Turks and Caicos, and Bahamas, for example. But they are exceptions to the rule of poverty. Loss of this megafauna has had far-reaching effects on the reefs themselves. For example, green turtles were once major grazers of sea grasses, and when there were tens of millions of them munching their way through leafy submarine pastures, the grass was close cropped. Dampier describes sea grasses in his *New Voyage Round the World* of 1697: "Green Turtle live on Grass, which grows in the sea, in 3, 4, 5, or 6 Fathom Water. . . . This Grass is different from Manatee-grass, for that is a small blade; but this is a quarter of an inch broad, and six Inches long." [12]

Both manatee and turtle grasses are today much more luxuriant than Dampier reports, because they are hardly grazed at all. Instead of fields of close-cropped blades, sea grasses straggle in thick vegetative tangles. The buildup of grass leads to blades rotting at their ends and becoming susceptible to fungal disease. Huge areas of sea grass, such as that in the bay between south Florida and the Keys, have succumbed to disease epidemics, aided by pollutants like sewage that encourage pathogens.

Pollution problems on coral reefs have escalated worldwide due to land being cleared for agriculture and development. When Columbus first sighted the islands of the Caribbean, they were covered in deep forest. "All are most beautiful, of a thousand shapes," he wrote, "and all are accessible and filled with trees of a thousand kinds and tall, and they seem to touch the sky." [13]

Over the ensuing centuries the islands were cleared first for planting sugarcane used in making rum, then for planting bananas, then for tourism. Across the region today's reefs, like those of Haiti, are being smothered and stressed by clouds of sediment that block the sun and choke coral polyps. Sewage and fertilizers in runoff promote diseases and seaweed growth at the expense of coral. It is not just sea grasses that suffer disease problems. Corals and other organisms are being leveled by disease after disease sweeping the Caribbean. The thick banks of staghorn and elkhorn corals that Beebe clambered over in Haiti succumbed to disease epidemics in the 1980s. In just a few years, their coverage fell by over 95 percent. In many places, the few remaining pockets of coral are dying slowly, unable to regain ground. Scientists looking at the composition of fossil reefs, like those of Bonaire, and drilling through the deposits below living reefs have found that the dominance of these corals on Caribbean reefs has not been challenged for a hundred thousand years. Today's population collapses are unprecedented. These two species of coral, once so abundant, have been added to America's endangered species list.

A little before staghorn and elkhorn corals were stricken, another of the Caribbean's signature animals was felled by disease. In the mid-1980s disease wiped out 99 percent of the abundant black-spined sea urchin (*Diadema antillarum*). Under normal circumstances slow-growing corals dominate on reefs because fast-growing seaweeds are cropped short by fish and other herbivores that are like these urchins. With the urchins gone, fish were left to control seaweed growth but were unable to keep pace, especially in places that were heavily fished. Since then, algae have gradually been taking over the Caribbean, with explosive shifts in some places following mass coral destruction by hurricanes. Throughout the region, living coral now covers an average of just 10 percent of the reef surface, compared to 50 or 60 percent as recently as the 1970s. Along Jamaica's north coast and in Haiti's bays, seaweed-covered mounds rise where once stood coral. The "coral" reefs of today would be unrecognizable to the pioneers of scuba diving.

The first skin divers and scuba enthusiasts to venture into Caribbean waters were there to kill—including Hans Hass and Jacques Cousteau who later became ardent conservationists. Perhaps the abundance of life they found seemed as inexhaustible as it did to scientists like Huxley, contemplating prolific fisheries in the nineteenth century. Their views shifted when confronted by the withering of life in the places they loved. It is no coincidence that among the first people to notice the profound impact of fishing in the sea were those working on coral reefs. For most of human history, fishers have plied their trade from above water. Their only guide to what was going on below was what they did or did not catch. When catches declined, it was often blamed on fish moving elsewhere, not to overfishing. With the advent of scuba diving, today's scientists have been able to witness directly the depopulation of their study sites. The conclusion that fishing bears much of the responsibility for the deterioration of ocean life can no longer be avoided.

# ⟶ Chapter 18 ⟶

# Shifting Baselines

⟶ ⟶

ANE GREY's tales of frontier life in nineteenth-century America were hugely popular in the early twentieth century, firing the imagination of a nation whose recollections of the hardship and rough justice of the Old West had become more romantic with the separation of time. By the 1920s, Grey was a wealthy man with leisure to indulge his passion for fishing. In 1925, he visited the Gulf of California, often called the Sea of Cortés, where few had yet tried their luck in big game fishing, a sport then in its infancy. In a jaunt around the eastern Pacific in his yacht *Fisherman*, taking in Cocos Island, the Galápagos, Mexico's mainland coast, and the southern Gulf of California, he and his companions enjoyed a fishing bonanza unlike any he had previously experienced (and Grey was a man reputed to have fished up to three hundred days a year). The waters seethed with giant fish. In a three-month frenzy of bloodshed that would have made Grey's most lurid Western tales seem tame, they racked up a huge body count of marlin, swordfish, sailfish, giant tunas, wahoo, dolphin, grouper, and seemingly countless other species. Grey recounted his adventures in his *Tales of Fishing Virgin Seas*.[1] Like previous visitors to the region, sharks plagued his efforts to fish, snapping animals from the hook before they could be boarded, and taking baits meant for more sporting quarry:

Some time later I was out of bait, tarporenos, spoons, feathered jigs, but I had no fish. The great tackle, however, had accounted for more sharks than I cared to count. I had hooked tuna, albacore, dolphin, yellowtail, and other fish I could not name. There had been several harrowing moments when it seemed I might outwit the sharks and catch a fish. But always when I labored strenuously and gazed with distended eyes down into the clear water [off Cocos Island], to see my fish with the other fish, and all surrounded by the pale gray-green shadows of monsters, varying, fading, coming clear, darting down and sheering away, the same inevitable tragedy happened. This virgin sea was alive with fish, and on this day, few that I saw weighed under a hundred pounds [45 kilograms]. The dolphin and yellowtail were the largest I had ever seen, larger than I had ever imagined they could grow. How perfectly at home all these fish![2]

Grey had a great love of nature and sketches the beauty and grandeur of the region in vivid prose. He admired the fish he sought no less than the scenery. Here he describes a giant tuna that he has just fought from the sea:

The tuna weighed a little over a hundred pounds, and as it lay on the deck I doubted if I had ever seen a more beautiful fish. Gold, silver, purple predominated over many other hues. As in the others we had caught, I marked particularly the large beautiful black eyes. They reminded me somewhat of the eyes of a Florida ladyfish. Another striking feature was the mottled bronze of the body along the sides toward the tail. It seemed almost that the fish was checkered with iridescent spots and bars, quivering, changing, coalescing, fading.[3]

Like many "sportsmen" of the time, Grey's appreciation of the beauty of wildlife was inseparable from a compulsion to catch and kill what he saw. This hunting fever even extended to animals that he and his fellow travelers could neither handle with the equipment available nor use if they succeeded in catching them. Off Cabo San Lucas at the southern tip of Baja California, Grey came upon a large group of whales, probably false killer whales:[4]

One afternoon a vast school of blackfish, scattered all over the ocean, came down on us from the west. As far as we could see in every direction the big black snub noses and black hooked fins clove the blue water. At first we contented ourselves with chasing them to take pictures. But when it dawned on us that they in turn were chasing tuna, we remembered what wolves of the sea they were, and according to ichthyologists should be exterminated, and we got out the rifles. . . . I wasted a good deal of ammunition without doing them any harm. It was hard to shoot accurately from a bobbing boat. But at last I hit a huge ugly brute, and instantly wished I had missed him, for he heaved up, showing twenty feet of black bulk, and lunged in our direction. It did not matter whether this was accident or intent. Assuredly he was a fierce monster. He could have stove in our boat with his battering-ram of a head or smashed us with his wide flukes. I shot him twice in quick succession, hearing the impact of both bullets. Then he leaped. What a fearful creature![5]

Later on, near where he had seen the whales, Grey and his party came across a whale shark that measured between 15 and 18 meters long (50–60 feet), lazily swimming at the surface and feeding on plankton. Again, the urge to kill overwhelmed common sense, and before reason prevailed, they had a gaff hook in the creature's tail. After a fruitless day being dragged around by a shark that barely seemed to notice their presence, the giant escaped with the gaff and 500 meters (1,700 feet) of rope as it sounded on a deep dive.

Zane Grey was not alone in robbing the Pacific coast of some of its larger inhabitants in the name of sport. About the same time, another "fearless" big game fisherman, Mitchell Hedges, accompanied a wealthy British lady around the region, describing their exploits in a book titled *Battles with Giant Fish*. Like Percy Lowe, Hedges dedicated the book to his patroness, Lady Richmond Brown: "A 'Damned Good Sportsman,' without whose inspiration and help [and money, no doubt] these battles would yet be unfought." He then added, "The best or worst of any individual comes out in the primitive wilds."[6] Hedges was the incarnation of British Empire derring-do. In the introduction to his book, he shows his mettle:

Big game hunting has of late years lost much of its attraction, largely owing to the fact that modern arms have been conducive to indiscriminate slaughter, and that the sport has to-day become confined to those who are fortunate enough to have a well-lined purse. Big game fishing and the hunting of beasts in their marine home is still in its infancy. There is a thrill and danger attached to it which will be welcomed by all true sportsmen; and one need have no compunction in ridding the ocean of certain species, for nothing living to-day on land can compare with the savagery and ruthlessness of—as an example— the tiger shark.[7]

Hedges certainly took the job seriously. On page after page of photographs there he is, pipe between gritted teeth, clutching giant stingrays, dragging huge snappers from the water, holding open sharks' jaws, gutting sawfish, and winching porpoise onto the yacht. Nothing was safe, so long as it was big, and big animals were plentiful. Eagle rays wider than a man is tall and weighing 200 kilograms (440 pounds) dangle from trees; a mute row of crocodiles pose in death, their jaws propped agape with sticks; a pile of sharks sprawls over the beach, their combined weight recorded as 6,490 pounds (nearly 3 metric tons). Doubtless though, the largest individual fish caught was the sawfish taken in Panama Bay and pictured with Lady Brown. The beast was 9.5 meters long (31 feet) and weighed 2,590 kilograms (5,700 pounds). On cutting it open, Hedges discovered thirty-six

*F.A. Mitchell Hedges and Lady Brown with a big catch of sharks taken off Taboguilla Island on the Pacific coast of Panama around 1920. That day they landed 6,490 pounds of sharks (nearly three tonnes) between three anglers. Source: Hedges, F.A.M. (1923) Battles with Giant Fish. Duckworth, London.*

fetal sawfish, each brandishing a tiny saw in perfect replica of its mother. Despite his bravado, Hedges himself was scared of fish in the water:

> I have never bathed in these waters, for what with the barracoudas, sharks, rays, stinging seaweed, and other life which dwells therein, I always felt discretion was the better part of valour, though many times the beautiful limpid clearness of the water was an almost irresistible temptation.[8]

There is something wonderfully amusing about the thought of a hot and very bothered fisherman, surrounded by refreshing water but too afraid to bathe!

Zane Grey's experiences and books encouraged other adventurers to visit the Gulf of California to hunt the colossal fish that lurked there. The Gulf of California is a 1,000-kilometer-long (625 miles) finger of the Pacific Ocean that splits mainland desert from desert peninsula on the west coast of Mexico. Peninsular Baja California was settled in the seventeenth century by Jesuits and was a frequent haunt of pirates, including William Dampier. In the eighteenth and nineteenth centuries, whales were pursued in and around the peninsula, but fish were largely left alone. The inhospitable deserts surrounding the Gulf of California could support only small communities of people who had little impact on fish stocks. When the whales were fished out in the late nineteenth century, Baja became a dusty backwater, not revived until the late 1920s and 1930s.

Another among the sportsmen attracted by the extraordinary tales of Baja fish was Griffing Bancroft, who wrote in 1932,

> In unimaginable numbers, from one edge to the other, [groupers] haunt the rocky ledges of coast and islands. If a jigger is trolled at a speed of about four miles an hour over the proper bottom there is no question of catching something, the only gamble is in species and size. The slogan "a ton an hour" can often be bettered.[9]

Another keen sportfisher was Ray Cannon, a onetime actor in silent movies and later a Hollywood director. In his fifties, he gave up the pressure of Hollywood to freelance as correspondent for *Western Outdoor News*. One of his first assignments took him to Baja California. It was the beginning of a love affair with the region that would last the rest of his life.

One of the first fish to attract Ray Cannon's attention was the totoaba, often spelled totuava. This is a species of croaker, so called because males make drumming or grunting noises, especially at spawning times, by twitching sonic muscles that resonate their gas-filled swim bladders. They spawn in shallow coastal areas, many entering estuaries to reproduce. Totoaba were remarkable for their size and numbers. Big fish topped 2 meters in length (7 feet) and weighed over 150 kilograms (330 pounds). Even if these animals had been loners, they would have commanded attention. But there were thousands of them. In winter, totoaba inhabited the central Gulf of California. In spring, drawn by some ancient urge, they banded together and made for the coast. Immense shoals swam north on both shores of the gulf, making for the Colorado River delta where mass spawning took place.

Totoaba supported the first large-scale commercial finfish fishery in the Gulf of California, beginning in the 1920s. So thick were the shoals as they passed along the coast that people could wade into the sea and drag fish out by hand or with pitchforks. Ray Cannon described a spawning run he witnessed in 1956:

> [A] school of totuava—a host, an army—no, you'd have to count 'em by the thousand of tons. We were heading back to port at Punta Peñasco from a fishing trip to Tiburon Island, when "it" happened. An experience that will provide us with enough daydream material to last us for the rest of our lives. The Sea of Cortez was dead calm until we suddenly found ourselves in a five-mile stretch of water being churned as if in an active volcano's crater. It could have been just that, since most of that mountainous region was molded by volcanic upheavals. The thoughts, "earthquake and tidal bore and other phenomena" were soon erased when we saw foot-long tail exposures. Then clear outlines of fathom long fish [~ 1.8 meters]. The native Mexican skipper of our converted tuna clipper threw her into reverse so fast the cook skidded out of the galley and clear onto the stern rail, still holding on to a basket of shrimp he was peeling.[10]

Ironically, the only part of the totoaba used in the 1920s and 1930s was its swim bladder, sent to California and Asia as a thickener for Chinese soups. The bodies were piled high and left to rot or used as fertilizer. In the 1940s and 1950s, roads began to snake into the Baja peninsula from California as tourism increased. Enterprising Americans soon carried in ice from the north and trucked out totoaba to be sold as "sea bass" in California. The fishery prospered.

Ray Cannon's articles brought the fish popularity with anglers. It couldn't last long. Totoaba were highly vulnerable because they hugged the coast on their migrations. Commercial fishers took advantage of this behavior, in the 1960s setting gill nets across migration routes. In 1965, Cannon spoke out against the netters:

> The once enormous migrating schools have now been reduced to a scattered few, which because of their peculiar spawning habit, may now be too depleted to reproduce a sustaining number. This great croaker which once drew as many as 10,000 people for an Easter weekend to San Felipe, will cease to attract any visiting anglers unless drastic action is taken to halt gill netting.[11]

But no action was taken, and the fishery collapsed the following decade. By the 1980s, totoaba were so rare the species had to be declared endangered. The few seen today are mainly juveniles; 10-kilogram dwarfs to the titans of yesteryear.

Totoaba succumbed quickly, not just because of the fishery but also due to massive loss of their spawning and nursery areas in the Colorado delta. The Colorado River once entered the Gulf of California as a mighty torrent following Rocky Mountain snowmelt. The environmental writer Aldo Leopold described its unsullied beauty:

> It is the part of wisdom never to revisit a wilderness, for the more golden the lily, the more certain that someone has gilded it. To return not only spoils a trip, but tarnishes a memory. It is only in the mind that shining adventure remains forever bright. For this reason, I have never gone back to the Delta of the Colorado since my brother and I explored it, by canoe, in 1922. . . .
>
> When the sun peeped over the Sierra Madre, it slanted across a hundred miles of lovely desolation, a vast flat bowl of wilderness rimmed by jagged peaks. On the map the Delta was bisected by the river, but in fact the river was nowhere and everywhere, for he could not decide which of a hundred green lagoons offered the most pleasant and least speedy path to the Gulf. So he traveled them all, and so did we. He divided and rejoined, he twisted and turned, he meandered in awesome jungles, he all but ran in circles, he dallied with lovely

groves, he got lost and was glad of it, and so were we. For the last word in procrastination, go travel with a river reluctant to lose his freedom in the sea. . . .

The still waters were of a deep emerald hue, colored by algae, I suppose, but no less green for all that. A verdant wall of mesquite and willow separated the channel from the thorny desert beyond. At each bend we saw egrets standing in the pools ahead, each white statue matched by its white reflection. Fleets of cormorants drove their black prows in quest of skittering mullets; avocets, willets, and yellowlegs dozed one-legged on the bars; mallards, widgeons, and teal sprang skyward in alarm. As the birds took the air, they accumulated in a small cloud ahead, there to settle, or to break back to our rear. When a troop of egrets settled on a far green willow, they looked like a premature snowstorm.[12]

Leopold described the delta as a "milk-and-honey wilderness." But paradise withered as, from the 1930s on, a series of dams blocked the floods and irrigation siphoned water to crops in the drylands of Arizona and New Mexico. Two of the largest dams, the Hoover and the Glen Canyon, were completed in 1936 and 1963, respectively. Robbed of life-giving freshwater, the delta turned salty. The green lagoons Leopold marveled at either dried up or were poisoned by salt that crusted shores with blinding crystalline hoar. The muddy channels of the delta once supported immeasurable numbers of clams, and river discharges fertilized the sea over thousands of square kilometers. Today, few clams survive, and drifts of empty shells serve as silent testimony of a richer past. Scientists comparing shell populations in delta sediments over the last thousand years estimate that present-day production by larger mollusks is less than 6 percent of what it was before the dams.[13] Migratory birds were once so abundant in the delta that flocks taking wing blocked out the sun. They have disappeared with the river.

Dozens of species of fish and shellfish, like the totoaba, seek out the Colorado estuary to spawn. Today, they release their eggs not into a fertile and protected environment where the young gain a head start but into a desolate cul-de-sac of the northern gulf. The delta today is known as a "reverse estuary" because it becomes more saline rather than less with distance traveled inland.[14] Species that breed in the estuary and the few totoaba that are spawned today must also escape the trawl if they are to survive to adulthood. A fleet of industrial shrimp trawlers rakes over their nursery areas as it scours the shallow muddy floor of the northern Gulf of California. Their fine-mesh nets give young fish little chance. John Steinbeck described the depredations of shrimp trawlers in *The Log from the Sea of Cortez,* his account of a 1940 cruise there with marine biologist Ed Ricketts:

> There were twelve boats in the combined fleet including the mother ship, and they were doing a very systematic job, not only of taking every shrimp from the bottom, but every other living thing as well. They cruised slowly along in echelon with overlapping dredges, literally scraping the bottom clean. Any animal which escaped must have been very fast indeed, for not even the sharks got away. . . . The big scraper closed like a sack as it came up, and finally it deposited many tons of animals on the deck—tons of shrimps, but also tons of fish of many varieties: sierras; pompano of several species; of the sharks, smooth-hounds and hammerheads; eagle rays and butterfly rays; small tuna; catfish; *puerco*—tons of them. And there were bottom-samples with anemones and grass-like gorgonians. . . . Fish were thrown overboard immediately, and only the shrimps kept. The sea was littered with dead fish, and the gulls swarmed about eating them. Nearly all the fish were in a dying condition, and only a few recovered. The waste of this good food supply was appalling.[15]

The totoaba will never recover while the intensive gill net fishery continues. Gill nets are still set in northern waters today to catch other fish, such as the corvina. These nets also snare and drown vaquita, a diminutive species of porpoise that is today found only in the most northerly part of the gulf. With only a few hundred individuals left, fishing has made it the world's most threatened marine mammal.

Marine life in the Gulf of California was incredibly prolific. One of the most remarkable places Ray Cannon found was what he called the "Midriff," about two-thirds the way up the gulf where the sea narrows. There, two large islands, Isla Tiburón (Shark Island) and Isla Ángel de la Guarda (Island of the Guardian Angel), further constrict the seaway. Tidal range increases in the gulf from south to north, and tides in the Midriff can be very large, topping 5 meters (16 feet).[16] As tides rise and fall, they push huge masses of water through the narrow

*A native of the Gulf of California in the eighteenth century with what appears to be a vaquita, today the most endangered species of porpoise in the world with only a few hundred individuals left. Source: Shelvocke, G. (1726)* A Voyage Round the World. *Cassell and Company Ltd, London, 1928.*

passes between islands and coasts, causing whirlpools on the down-current side and upwellings in up-current areas. During spring tides, the energy released is immense, and upwellings occur almost with explosive power, rising in boils 1 to 3 meters (3 to 10 feet) above the surrounding sea level.

Tidal water movements act as a kind of rhythmic pump. They suck cool, nutrient-rich water from deep-sea basins close to the islands and fertilize the roiling surface layers, fueling rampant plankton growth that draws fish from hundreds, sometimes thousands of kilometers away to feed and spawn. Cannon writes,

> The words "schools" or "shoals" fall far short of describing the mass movements of fish populations in and around these islands. They must be visualized as hosts, armies or clouds when seen churning the surface from horizon to horizon in all directions.
>
> Enormous and awesome "fish pileups" occur each spring along the south rim of the Midriff. They are triggered when up-to-ten-mile-long schools of migrating yellowtail first hit the line of cool water, boiling up from the deep channels. The herring-like fishes, such as sardine and anchovies, preferring the cool temperature and the massive food supply, build up water-saturating populations. The hungry yellowtail, suddenly running into such a flourishing meadow, forget their manners and start grazing like a powered lawn mower. They become so hoggishly competitive they gorge themselves then disgorge and start over again.
>
> Thousands of sea birds that have been following overhead, join the fiesta. Their squawking broadcasts from roost to rookery bring more thousands winging in from near and distant islands. Sea lions get the message and relay it as they come barrelling in. All of the fish-eating carnivores of the deep use their own telegraphic methods of inviting all and sundry to get in on the bacchanal binge. They come and run amuck, devouring whatever is smaller than themselves, and disembowel or behead the larger, even of their own kind, in their slaughtering frenzy.[17]

Dozens of species of large oceanic fish came to the Gulf of California to breed. Cannon several times described immense numbers of billfish (sailfish, swordfish, and marlin) in the Midriff area of the gulf. At one time, near the mainland town of Guaymas, he claimed to have seen four of these fish for every 100 square feet (30 x 30 meters) in a region 20 miles in diameter (32 kilometers)—this would equal nearly nine hundred thousand billfish. The anglers who visited in the 1920s and 1930s, like Ray Cannon and Zane Grey, did not have these waters to themselves for long. Purse seiners moved south from the Pacific coast when the California sardine fishery collapsed in the 1940s. Longliners followed, targeting swordfish and marlin and more recently the sharks whose abundance so impressed early travelers. The onslaught of industrial fishing has stripped the gulf of its most magnificent wildlife spectacles. Fishers seeking to sustain dwindling catches have even targeted manta rays in recent years, once simply admired for their impressive size and effortless grace below water. The megafauna that brought fame to the gulf are disappearing, and the waters of the Midriff region no longer pulse with the colossal throngs of fish seen by Cannon and others between the two world wars.

In coastal regions, artisanal fishers working from small canoes and pangas[18] have seen their own fortunes decline with passing decades. Where once they landed giant fish, few can be found any more. Andrea Saenz-Arroyo and colleagues from a Mexican conservation organization[19] interviewed over a hundred coastal fishers from three generations in the central Gulf of California to find out how their experiences of fishing had changed with time.[20] She asked them to name species and fishing sites that had once been productive but that they knew to have been depleted. Fishers older than age fifty-five named four times as many depleted sites and five times as many species lost as fishers younger than thirty. There was also an intergenerational shift in where people fished. The older generation initially fished literally on their doorsteps. Over time, fishers had had to search farther afield to sustain catches. Today, fishers concentrate on offshore seamounts and inaccessible places far from ports. It is an experience that has been repeated around the gulf.[21]

Saenz-Arroyo also asked fishers to name their best-ever day's catch of a large species of grouper, the gulf grouper.[22] Gulf Groupers are found only in the Gulf of California and on the Pacific coast of Baja up to southern California. They can reach 2 meters long (7 feet) and weigh over 150 kilograms (330 pounds), the same size as large totoaba. They were abundant in the seas fished by Griffing Bancroft and Ray

*Big game fisher Ray Cannon with an 81-kilogram gulf grouper (178 pounds) in the Gulf of California, 1961. Reproduced with kind permission of Carla Laemmle.*

Cannon, once accounting for nearly half the total finfish catch, but have declined with time to less than 1 percent of today's landings. In the 1940s and 1950s, fishers caught twenty to twenty-five on their best days. This fell to ten or twelve by the 1960s and 1970s. Since 1990, no fisher had caught more than four in a day, and fewer than half the fishers under age thirty had ever caught this species. The size of the biggest gulf grouper that fishers said they had ever caught also declined with time, from an average of 84 kilograms (185 pounds) caught by older fishers to 63 kilograms (139 pounds) caught by the younger fishers.[23]

Older men began fishing when the sea abounded with large predators such as bull and hammerhead sharks, enormous groupers and snappers, green turtles, and large edible invertebrates such as rock oysters and conch. They testified how these animals had been depleted during their working lives. Middle-aged fishers showed less appreciation of this past abundance, and most young fishers seemed unaware that these species had ever been common. Saenz-Arroyo herself sought out places where old fishers told her that thousands of gulf groupers once gathered to spawn. In more than thirty dives over four years, she never encountered more than three gulf groupers at one time.

Ironically, fisheries policy in Mexico encourages further depletion of groupers. That nation's fishery statistics lump together sixteen different species of grouper, and the combined catches of this group have increased in recent years as people switch to fishing smaller species. The rise in catches misled officials into thinking that grouper stocks are healthy, and they consequently allowed fishing effort to increase. Catches of small species mask the virtual disappearance of the giants: goliath and gulf groupers, and black sea bass. The few that survive continue to be caught in the multispecies fishery, pushing them toward extinction. Gulf grouper has already been added to the World Conservation Union's red list of endangered species.

Decline in the marine megafauna has come comparatively recently to the Gulf of California. Times of plenty are still remembered by the oldest fishermen, whereas younger generations are already beginning to view the depleted environment as normal. In the terms of fishery scientist Daniel Pauly, their "environmental baselines" are shifting.[24] When baselines shift, each new generation subconsciously views as "natural" the environment they remember from their youth. They compare subsequent changes against this "baseline," masking the true extent of environmental degradation, even to the degree that they no longer believe anecdotes of past abundance or size of species. What is a young fisher to make of tales of mountainous schools of totoaba migrating north to spawn, or sailfish fins dotting the sea from horizon to horizon? Today's generations have never experienced the pre-dam milk-and-honey wilderness of the Colorado delta seen by Aldo Leopold. For them, the searing, salt-crusted banks and biological poverty of the region can seem natural.

The idea of shifting baselines is familiar to us all and does not relate only to the natural environment. It helps explain why people tolerate the slow crawl of urban sprawl and loss of green space, why they fail to notice increasing noise pollution, and why they put up with longer and longer commutes to work. Changes creep up on us, unnoticed by younger generations who have never known anything different. The young write off old people who rue the losses they have witnessed as either backward or dewy-eyed romantics. But what about the losses that none alive today have seen? In most parts of the world, human impacts on the sea extend back for hundreds of years, sometimes more than a thousand. Nobody alive today has seen the heyday of cod or herring. No one has watched sporting groups of sperm whales five hundred strong or seen alewife run so thick up rivers there seemed more fish than water. The greater part of the decline of many exploited populations happened before the birth of anyone living today.

In Chesapeake Bay groups of leaping sturgeon no longer break the calm of evening and threaten boaters with water-splitting crashes. Walrus rookeries off Nova Scotia have fallen silent, and snowy beluga whales no longer enliven the Gulf of Maine. Man-eating sharks have gone from the North Sea, and the Caribbean monk seal breathes no more. Today, a few turtles puff their way ashore onto beaches that over a season once felt the scrape and clatter of hundreds of thousands of shells. Where human impacts on the sea's populations extend far back in time, it is easy for us to view the diminished productivity of today's seas as normal. We have known nothing different. Scientists have made it their business to understand how these ecosystems work, not realizing they were describing places far removed from the naturalness they assumed. In many places, conservationists have developed elaborate management plans to maintain ecosystems in their present condition, little understanding that they are ghosts of their once plenteous condition. What these ecosystems really need is relief from fishing pressure so that they can recover.

With passing time and declining opportunities for catching big fish, the exploits of Zane Grey, Ray Cannon, and others have acquired an almost mythical status. The seas they described tumbled, roiled, and thrashed with fish in such immense numbers that today they seem the stuff of fiction, not reportage. But the destruction of life that has happened since is far from mythical. The most alarming thing about Saenz-Arroyo's findings is that the intergenerational shifts in perception of the Gulf of California environment happened so quickly. You might expect baselines to shift rapidly in today's urban societies where people have little contact with the natural world. But the fishers interviewed are people whose occupations bring them into daily contact with the sea and marine life. Many of the younger fishers still lived or worked with parents who also fished. Their knowledge and experience does not seem to have been passed to their children, or perhaps their tales were not believed. Whatever the reasons, if people forget what the seas were once like, and consider today's waters as something approaching natural, then we could end up trying to maintain marine ecosystems in their present degraded states. We have to do better than that.

# — *Chapter 19* —

# Ghost Habitats

— ❦ —

I GREATLY ADMIRE the white abalone shell displayed on the top shelf of my bookcase. It is humpbacked and shaped like a scoop, open on one side with a line of knobbed perforations around the outer edge. In life, the animal sucked oxygen-rich water under the shell to bathe its gills while stuck fast to some rocky reef, and exhaled through these holes. The shell was given to me by someone who caught it when he was a graduate student in California. He ate it, of course, as abalones are delicious fare, and graduate students always appreciate free food. An abalone this size, 20 centimeters (8 inches) from edge to edge, would provide a good meal.

From the outside, the shell is a rugged swirl of pink glossy ridges radiating from a flat coil at one end. Deeper elliptical lines cross the ridges at right angles and mark the passing years of this animal's life. Two repaired breaks show it survived attack from some crustacean when it was five years old. This animal carried quite a community: burnished white patches of coralline algae crust the shell; netted skeins of bryozoans follow the rise and fall of ridges; purple casts of worms coil over it; empty barnacle turrets and cup corals rise like calcareous warts; and tiny holes show the homes of boring sponges and mollusks. The greatest beauty of the shell is revealed only in death when the animal is removed and the underside exposed. Beneath the velvet fringed muscular foot, the shell is lined with lustrous nacre. As I turn it in the sunlight, it shimmers with swirls of opalescent green, yellow, pink, and pale purple that melt and merge. I wonder whether future generations will stare at this shell in some museum, just as our generation contemplates the desiccated remains of dodos. For the white abalone is today one of the world's rarest mollusks and could soon be gone forever. It was not always so. The tale of abalones on the California coast is a story of serial depletion, with one species removed after another as fisheries for them blossomed and then died as populations collapsed. California's kelp forests, a favored home to abalone, also offer a telling example of the creation of ghost habitats. The kelp is still there, but many of the species that once inhabited these forests have disappeared. For nearshore habitats in many parts of the world, like kelp forests, commercial fishers are not the sole cause of declines. Recreational anglers and sport divers share this responsibility.

Abalones inhabit wave-swept temperate coasts across the world and have long been prized for their meat and shells. Coastal middens show people in the California Channel Islands ate abalone as many as ten thousand years ago.[1] Abalones themselves eat kelp and drift algae, trapping fronds under the edge of their shells and grazing them with rasping mouthparts. A few species dine on smaller seaweeds found in shallow regions. Eight species occur in California, each staking out its preferred turf in rocky regions from the tide line to depths of 60 meters or so (130 feet).[2] Most are named after the color of their shell, although all look much the same underwater when covered by a crust of seaweeds and animals.

Commercial fishing for California abalones began in the 1850s as immigrant Chinese brought in to labor in the gold rush caught red, green, and black abalones from shallow intertidal regions. They were dried and eaten locally as well as exported to China. By the late nineteenth century, abalone collecting was intense, and the fishery had spread south to Baja California. Nearly 2,000 tonnes were removed from California to Baja in 1879 alone,[3] and abalones grew scarce enough that efforts were made to curb the fishery. In 1900, abalone fishing was banned in shallow waters of California,[4] and the Chinese were forced out of the fishery, only to be replaced by Japanese hard-hat divers pursuing abalone into their kelp forest strongholds, where they were most plentiful. Adventurous Americans soon joined them.

Hard-hat divers wore cumbersome suits weighed down with leaden boots. They were tethered to a boat above by a rope and the hose that fed them air. Long slippery blades of kelp wrapped around limbs and hoses to further restrict their movements. Despite these impediments, early divers were incredibly successful, often collecting five or six hundred abalones per person per day. When divers moved north to California's Mendocino area, they found even greater abundances. There a single diver working underwater for six hours could average twenty-three hundred abalones a day. There were so many that divers found them stacked one upon another in piles five to twelve animals deep. An observer of this fishery in 1913 said,

> I have seen the diver send the net up, filled with about fifty green and corrugated [pink] abalones, every six or seven minutes. During his [five- to six-hour] shift below the diver gathers from thirty to forty basketfuls, each containing one hundred pounds of meat and shell [45 kilograms], or altogether one and one-half to two tons.[5]

Southern California's abalone fisheries could not withstand such unfettered fishing pressure and ran into difficulty before the 1930s. As the animals grew harder to find, California's Department of Fish and Game began to place restrictions on the minimum size and the number of animals that could be taken per day, where you could fish, and what fishing methods you could use. No-take reserves were introduced in southern California as early as 1907 to provide refuges for spawning abalone, bolstering the effect of the shallow-water collecting ban of 1900.

Regulating the commercial fishery was challenge enough, but by the 1920s these fishers were joined by throngs of amateurs. A fisheries official commented in 1931 that "many hundreds of tourists and ranchers can be seen going over every accessible reef and ledge with a fine-toothed comb. State and county authorities are hard-pressed to enforce laws on limits and minimum size which are so easily broken by thoughtless people."[6]

The sheer numbers of recreational fishers hunting abalone denuded the shallows in all but the most inaccessible places, since recreational fishing was not affected by the ban on commercial collection from shallow water. At this time, recreational collecting was limited to depths of a few meters and overlapped little with areas fished by hard-hat divers. During World War II, many of the no-take reserves established to protect stocks were reopened to supply demand for protein. Despite growing scarcity of abalones, the dive fishery continued to expand and was given a boost after World War II by an influx of military-trained divers. In 1960, more than five hundred commercial permits were issued by the California Department of Fish and Game. Even as stocks dwindled, the abalone industry prospered because of rising prices.

Restaurant menus show that prices gained a "rarity premium." In San Francisco, a plate of abalone cost seven dollars in 1930 (converted to 2004 equivalent value) according to Glen Jones of Texas A&M University.[7] Prices rose faster than inflation in the late 1930s as abalones were overfished, and rose again in the 1950s. The latter rise has continued to this day at seven to ten times the rate of inflation, and now abalone is a luxury food for the wealthy. In 2006, an abalone meal cost over eighty dollars in the United States; the irony is that most of the abalones served are imported from Australia and New Zealand.

The fishery was also sustained for a time in an era of crashing abalone populations by expanding northward into Oregon, Washington, and Canada, and by widening the abalone species considered desirable. There was a distinct preference order based on size and accessibility. In the nineteenth century, the species targeted were the largest available to people wading in the shallows, including red, green, and black. When divers started fishing deeper, they first targeted reds, and this was the main species taken until the 1940s.[8] Red abalone is the largest species, reaching 30 centimeters across (12 inches). As each preferred species in the ensuing years became rare, the industry moved to the next best. Pinks are the second largest at a maximum span of 25 centimeters (10 inches). After World War II, total landings rose quickly, at first based mainly on pinks because reds had already been depleted in the more accessible sites. Pinks are slow growing, and removals quickly outstripped natural replenishment. Pink landings began a long decline in the early 1950s, but overall abalone catches held up because divers switched to reds in more distant, less-fished locales. Catches of reds peaked in the early 1960s before a precipitous decline began in the late 1960s. Green, black, and white abalones reach 20 to 25 centimeters in span (8 to 10 inches). When reds faltered, the fishery switched to green, with a massive rise in catches spiking between 1970 and 1973 before collapsing.

White abalones live deeper, 25 to 60 meters down (80 to 200 feet). They became serious targets only in the early 1970s, with catches peaking the same decade before collapsing in 1977. Threaded abalone, an uncommon southern subspecies of the small pinto abalone, were also targeted at this time, but the population was quickly exhausted. At this point, fishers were forced back into the intertidal region where the fishery began in the nineteenth century. Black abalones live from the tide line to depths around 8 meters (26 feet) and had enjoyed a period of little commercial exploitation since 1900. They sustained landings through the early 1980s until an epidemic disease called withering syndrome struck in 1985 and populations collapsed. Even then abalones got no respite, as divers switched to target the abundant red sea urchins that pockmarked almost every reef, collecting abalones whenever they found them.

Further measures were taken to protect abalones through the 1960s to 1980s, but they were too little and too late to save the fishery. By continually expanding the range of fishing and switching species, the industry appeared healthy. While catches held up, regulators were reluctant to impose more than cosmetic restrictions on take. With hindsight, it is clear that the industry was on a path to self-destruction from 1900 on. By the 1960s, it ran out of new fishing grounds; in the 1980s, it ran out of abalones. In 1997, the commercial fishery was officially closed, although it had already been moribund for a decade. Abalone had succumbed, species by species, to serial overfishing.

Over a century and a half, abalone fisheries removed hundreds of millions of animals from the reefs and intertidal zones of California. Today, several species are extinct or nearly so in southern California. One estimate suggests pink abalone, with densities in the 1940s of thousands of animals per hectare of rocky bottom, languish at less than one-hundredth of 1 percent of their former abundance. Red abalone are rare throughout the region and have been eliminated from most accessible places. On offshore islands, divers are lucky to find a handful of individuals per hour of searching.

White abalones, on the U.S. Endangered Species List since 2001, occur only in southern California and northern Baja in Mexico. California populations were estimated to total between a third of a million and a million before exploitation.[9] In 1996, scientists took to the sea in submarines to search for the last animals. They found only a few widely scattered individuals, mostly at depths below 33 meters (100 feet). Based on the total area of available habitat, they estimated there were just sixteen hundred to three thousand left throughout the species' range.

It has long been believed that fishing for a species will cease well before it is reduced to such low numbers that it is threatened with extinction. The reasoning is that returns from the fishery will fall to uneconomic levels before animals become this rare. Thomas Huxley said as much in 1883: "Any tendency to overfishing will meet with its natural check in the diminution of the supply, . . . this check will always come into operation long before anything like permanent exhaustion has occurred."[10]

Huxley, whose thoughts were filled with herring and cod, never imagined a fishery like that for abalones. Two factors acting together meant that abalone could be removed almost to the last animal. Rising prices meant that it remained economic to fish abalones even as densities fell. Today, abalones command US$200 to US$300 apiece, making it worthwhile to hunt them even when very rare. The second factor is that because the fishery targeted several species together, as populations of the preferred animals fell, they continued to be collected whenever they were encountered. So long as some species were present in commercial quantities, others continued to be fished down to extremely low densities.

White abalone is today in extinction's waiting room. Even though there are still animals around, the way they are distributed condemns them to almost certain extinction unless active restoration efforts are made.[11] Abalones reproduce by males and females shimmying up to each other and then simultaneously releasing eggs and sperm, which fertilize in open water as they mix. Fertilization is successful only if the animals are very close to each other. But to reproduce at all, they first have to find each other. Abalones are no sprinters. At a fast clip they might cover a meter (about a yard) per minute. When abalones were abundant, finding mates was never hard. But the remaining whites are widely scattered over hundreds of kilometers of coast, and only a few tens are thought to be within reach of one another. Most of them are in deep water that is too cold for the eggs to develop properly. White abalones have produced hardly any offspring since the late 1960s. Red abalone populations in southern California are suffering a similar fate. They have continued to decline in all areas except San Miguel Island, despite the fishing ban. There are just too few left to reproduce successfully.

Abalones were not the only animals living around kelp forests to attract fishers. Recreational fishing was on the rise in California in the 1920s, and amateur abalone hunters were joined by a growing number of anglers. In the 1930s, they took to the water with spear and goggles in search of pretty much anything large enough to eat (and much in the way of trophies that wasn't very palatable). California was developing its sun, sea, and surf lifestyle, and magazines like *National Geographic* celebrated the exploits of early spearfishers, encouraging thousands to follow their lead. A 1949 article featured the Bottom Scratchers club of San Diego and typified the gung-ho attitudes of the time.[12] Membership was restricted to people who had brought up three abalone from a single, breath-hold dive to 9 meters (30 feet), a spiny lobster from a dive to 6 meters (20 feet), and two sharks from 6 meters. The sharks had to be caught by hand, by their tails (one at a time, at least!). Unsurprisingly, the club had only fifteen members. These people hauled California halibut, giant groupers, black sea bass, and wrasse from the surf, along with sackloads of abalones.

Early spearfishers like the Bottom Scratchers were rewarded with large, sometimes titanic, catches. Jack Prodanovitch recalls one of the giant black sea bass that used to lurk among the kelp blades:

> About four years ago, Wally Potts and I took our wives out fishing near the La Jolla caves. We were swimming "battle formation," about 50 feet apart, and I held the inside position nearest the cliffs. From experience, I knew we would swim over a channel where we usually found good fish. Suddenly I spotted a reef I knew didn't exist. The "reef"

moved, and I backed water and yelled for Wally. Together we peeked into the depths and spotted a monster—a black sea bass, or jewfish,[13] that must have weighed 500 pounds.[14]

Needless to say, they took a whack at him with their spears. Although this fish survived their attack that day, it may have been less fortunate next time. These large animals had only limited home ranges within the kelp forests and probably restricted their movements to areas no bigger than a few hectares.[15] Time and again, fishers would target the same animals until one finally got lucky. Five fishhooks, a meter of line, leaders, and a 170-gram sinker were found in the stomach of one giant black sea bass caught around the same time that Prodano-vitch and Potts spotted their monster. Catching fish weighing 50 to 100 kilos (110 to 220 pounds) and upward was made more certain with the development of powerful spearguns from the 1950s onward. That same decade, the range of spearfishers was much extended with the growing availability of scuba equipment. Sharks and rays were favorite targets for sport rather than taste, and spiny lobsters were quarry for commercial and recreational fishers alike. Numbers of all target species thinned rapidly, and, with time, the most vulnerable disappeared.

If the Bottom Scratchers could have turned back the clock fifty years, they would have found giant black sea bass everywhere in and around the kelp. The species is found from southern California to Baja and in the Gulf of California. It was fished commercially with hook and line from around 1870 and has been sportfished since 1895.[16] The peak in California catches came in 1931 with 115 tonnes of fish and in Mexico three years later with 367 tonnes. Like most big fish, black sea bass lived long lives. A 198-kilogram (435-pound) fish was aged at seventy-five years old, suggesting that 250- to 270-kilogram titans (550 to 600 pounds) are ninety to one hundred years old.

Black sea bass, like many fish species, aggregate to spawn at tradi-tional sites at the same time every year. Once these aggregations were discovered, divers and anglers would return day after day until the last few fish were taken. Once an aggregation has been lost, experience from other parts of the world shows that it may never recover. As California's sea bass populations declined, anglers began to travel to

*Giant black sea bass landed at Santa Catalina Island, California, around 1907. The fish weigh 57, 100, and 146 kilograms (126, 219, and 321 pounds). Source: Holder, C.F. (1909)* Big Game at Sea. *Hodder and Stoughton, London.*

Mexico on "black sea bass specials" in which they could catch fifty to a hundred bass per trip, among dozens of other species. Ray Cannon described fishing a Mexican spawning aggregation in the Gulf of California in 1956, before the population plunged:

> Black sea bass in such vast numbers I have never seen before. . . . We hit the black sea bass concentration a half mile off the south cove, over rock bottom in 60 to 75 feet of water. . . . A small hand-lining commercial had caught three tons of black sea bass and was trying to make it five tons. We landed nine and farmed a like number [hooked and lost]. The largest one decked weighed about 250 pounds [113 kilograms].[17]

The toll taken by spearfishing was not restricted to California and Mexico.[18] All over the world, armies of skin divers took to the sea armed to the teeth. Jacques Cousteau described the effects in the Mediterranean in the 1930s to the 1950s:

> Undersea hunting raged, with arbalests, spears, spring guns, cartridge-propelled arrows, and the elegant technique of the American writer, Guy Gilpatric, who impaled fish with fencing lunges. The fad resulted in almost emptying the littoral of fish and arousing the commercial fishermen to bitter anger. They claimed we drove away the fish, damaged nets, looted their seines, and caused mistrals[19] with our schnorkels. . . .
>
> In the goggle-diving era Dumas made a lighthearted bet at Le Brusq that he could spear two hundred and twenty pounds of fish [100 kilograms] in two hours. He made five dives within the time limit, to depths of forty-five to sixty feet [14 to 18 meters]. On each dive he speared and fought a mammoth fish in the short period he could hold his breath. He brought up four groupers and an eighty-pound liche [a kind of jack[20]]. Their total weight was two hundred and eighty pounds [127 kilograms].[21]

In Australia, spearfishing flourished in the late 1950s and beyond. John Ottaway, now with the Western Australia Department of the Environment, described his experience of the impact of spearfishing:

> I have no doubt that the popularity of spearfishing in the 1960s, and no controls (when scuba gear became readily available) on spearfishing on scuba in the mid to late 1960s, was the major factor in the staggering

decline in the near-shore fish populations along the South Australian coastline, starting with the reef areas near Adelaide, and then radiating away from Adelaide as the nearer reefs became depleted.

There were many reefs along the Hallett Cove to Port Stanvac area where during the early 1960s I always saw many hundreds of fish, and commonly saw reef and pelagic specimens that would have been 5 kg plus [11 pounds] and occasionally 10 kg plus [22 pounds]. We left those big fish alone because the smaller fish were abundant, better eating, and we thought the big fish were probably important breeding stock. We also saw sharks reasonably often, ranging from 60 cm [2 feet] wobbegongs (frequently) to 4 to 5 meter [13 to 17 feet] white pointers (rarely).

In 1978, I went back to that same area on several occasions to have a look around, and was shocked to find the whole area where I used to spearfish was now a "wasteland" with not a single fish over a couple of hundred grams to be seen. Even the big schools of pelagics were absent.[22]

Recreational divers and anglers don't carry all the blame for the depletion of nearshore animals. Commercial fishers diversified into nearshore fish about the same time, moving from species that had been depleted, such as abalone and sardines. At first they used hook and line, but added gill nets to their armory in the 1960s and 1970s, setting them along the fringes of the kelp. Paul Dayton and colleagues from the Scripps Institution of Oceanography have documented the decline of kelp forest animals at La Jolla since the 1970s. What Dayton found when he first dived there in the 1970s was already very different from what the Bottom Scratchers encountered. The Bottom Scratchers, in turn, were too late to see the forests in their unexpurgated magnificence. There were no sea otters left when they dove, and fur seals and sea lions were much reduced in numbers. Anglers and commercial fishers had by then profoundly reduced populations of some species, such as the white sea bass. This handsome fish is a species of croaker with a slender, muscular body, steel blue on the back fading to silver-white belly.[23] It once reached over a meter in length (39 inches) and weighed more than 30 kilograms (66 pounds). Dayton reports that divers in the 1950s might expect to see schools of hundreds around the margins of kelp forests, mixed with yellowtail, a kind of jack.[24] Ray Cannon visited the La Jolla kelp beds in 1955 and found the abundance and variety of fish (and fishing boats!) still remarkable:

> The enormous number of fish caught in the small area off La Jolla is astonishing. Just about all species of game fishes of Southern California waters seem to collect in and around the relatively small kelp field that lies between Scripps Institute of Oceanography and Point Loma.
>
> On a trip there last week I counted 150 boats fishing the area at one time. Included were 12 party boats [commercial boats each carrying tens of paying anglers] and 16 large private boats. The balance were outboard skiffs. This was not an unusual occurrence. It happens most every weekend and just about everyone aboard, with any degree of know-how, gets fish.
>
> The official counts at the end of our day's fishing as posted at the H&M and Point Loma Sport Fish Landings: yellowtail, 18; barracuda, 865; albacore, 3; white seabass, 62; bonito, 375; marlin, 1 (weighing 406 pounds [185 kilograms]); black sea bass, 1 (weighing 640 pounds [291 kilograms]); miscellaneous fishes, 640. Also a world record (for skin divers) of a 48-pound yellowtail [22 kilograms]. Among the miscellaneous were shallow water rockfish, kelp bass, sheephead, Pacific mackerel, halibut, sharks, cabezon, and numerous other species.[25]

Nearshore regions were clearly subjected to extremes of recreational fishing pressure in the 1950s. Even so, it wasn't until the early 1960s that commercial catches of white sea bass dived as gillnetting took hold, falling to a few tens of tons by 1980 and remaining there ever since.[26] But to find the heyday for white sea bass you have to go back to the beginning of the twentieth century and earlier. Catches were initially much higher but collapsed in 1922, over a decade before Dayton's earliest catch data.[27] What tremendous schools must have once swirled around the heads of the first hard-hat abalone divers!

Those divers must also have seen thousands of rockfish inside and out of the kelp forests. Rockfish attracted commercial interest early on and would soon suffer a fate similar to that of the abalones. This is the same group of spiny, perchlike fish to which the Atlantic redfish belongs. All are members of the genus *Sebastes,* part of the scorpion fish family. Rockfish are wonderfully diverse on North America's Pacific coast, with ninety-six species between Mexico and Alaska.[28] At the northern and southern fringes of their distribution, in the Bering Sea and Gulf of California, respectively, there are only a handful of species. But California's coast has over fifty species. In shape, all of these species are variations on a perch theme—some long and slim, some squat, some barrel-chested, others dainty. Their colors range from drab gray to gaudy carmine. The tiger rockfish, for example, is marked with brilliant red stripes on a cream body, whereas the china rockfish is black slashed through by a yellow stripe and speckled with a blizzard of yellow spots. All the species have large, beautiful eyes of blue or green rimmed with gold or silver. Underwater, many rockfish allow divers to approach closely, holding their gaze with these alluring eyes. Rockfishes inhabit reefs, rock piles, and canyons to depths of 1,000 meters (3,300 feet) and more, each species occupying its own specific depth range.

Commercial fishing for rockfish began around the same time as that for abalones, primarily to feed the people of San Francisco. Early fishers worked from small boats in twos or threes using handlines and setting short longlines studded with baited hooks. This technology prevailed until the twentieth century when bottom trawls were added in regions where the seabed was relatively free of obstructions, such as Puget Sound in Washington State.

Like the Atlantic redfish, Pacific rockfish flesh freezes and transports well as fillets. However, it took time for people to get a taste for most species. Trawl catches were a very mixed bag, and while more familiar fish were still common, most rockfish caught in Oregon and Washington State were ground up and sold as food for mink in fur farms during the 1950s and 1960s. Other people were less fastidious in their tastes. Offshore in the North Pacific, Japanese and Soviet distant-water fishing fleets began catching Pacific Ocean perch and several other rockfishes using midwater and bottom trawls in the 1960s, taking over half a million tonnes from the Gulf of Alaska in 1965.[29]

The growing popularity of rockfish with anglers helped them gain markets in the United States and Canada in the 1970s. In the late 1970s, an Oregon fisherman discovered that widow rockfish rise off the bottom at night and could be caught over rough ground using trawls towed above the seabed.[30] This led to a brief boom with annual catches of the species rising to over 20,000 tonnes. When widow rockfish numbers thinned, fishers turned to trawling for other species. The proliferation of gillnet fishing in the 1960s and 1970s added further pressure.

Like so many other species, larger rockfish have been reduced to bare survival numbers today, or have been lost from places that are intensively fished. Milton Love studied for a doctorate on rockfishes in Santa Barbara during the 1970s. On heavily fished reefs near the town, he saw only two mature olive rockfish in two years of weekly dives. A clear indication of the loss of fish can be gleaned from the fishing patterns of recreational anglers. Pleasure boats carrying anglers saw catch rates plunge from 3,000 rockfish per thousand hours fishing in 1980 to only 345 in 1996.[31] Overall catches fell, too. Bocaccio were down 98.7 percent, blue by 95.2 percent, olive by 83 percent, and chillipepper could hardly be caught any longer. The animals landed in 1996 were mainly small species or juveniles, compared to the big fish common decades earlier. By 2000, recreational fishing boats traveled over 160 kilometers offshore (100 miles) to find good fishing.

Fisheries data collected on the main commercial species tell us that today many species of rockfish are in deep trouble, having fallen to a few percent of their numbers in the 1960s. When you consider that the 1960s does not represent anything like natural abundance levels, the declines have probably been greater. Today's numbers are likely below 1 percent of unfished levels for many species, and some are threatened with extinction.[32] Graham Gillespie, of Canada's Department of Fisheries and Oceans has said of the fishery, "Rockfish fishery management is like a Greek tragedy. Everyone dies at the end."[33]

The emptying of the Pacific coast continues today. In the late 1970s, fishers began catching live fish in British Columbia to supply Asian restaurants in Vancouver. Asian diners esteem fresh fish, and nothing can be fresher than a live fish chosen from a restaurant aquarium and killed to order. The fishery quickly spread south, and by the late 1980s, Californians were fishing for live animals using hook-and-line and traps. They target a broad range of species hardy enough to survive capture and transport to the restaurants, but the most desirable are highly colored, like the china and black-and-yellow rockfishes. Others taken include species that play important roles in structuring biological communities in kelp forests and other habitats. The cabezon, for example, is a burly scorpion fish that seems to be all mouth and eats abalones, octopus, and other invertebrates. The California sheephead, also a favorite with spearfishers, is a kelp forest wrasse with powerful jaws and teeth built for grinding up grazing sea urchins. After the elimination of sea otters, these species prevented the loss of kelp forests due to overgrazing by urchins in southern California. As fish populations collapsed, the role of keystone urchin predator shifted to people, and the red sea urchin fishery assured a future for kelp. Like most new fisheries, the live food fish industry has yet to see its activities curtailed. As of 2006, the California Department of Fish and Game admits that catches can only be guessed at and they have no idea of the impact of the fishery on target species or their habitats.

Today, kelp forests and many other nearshore habitats across the world are ghosts of what they once were. I dived a kelp forest in the California Channel Islands a few years ago. Small fish flitted through the canopy, and occasionally I would spot something larger lurking among the waving stems of kelp plants. The scene was pretty, but commercial and sport fishing have long since removed the giants of the past, robbing it of grandeur. The scientist Paul Dayton shares this sense of loss. To study today's kelp communities is to investigate something that is debased and incomplete:

> It would be similar to studying the Serengeti after all the large grazers and carnivores were eliminated; one could still appreciate termites and other small grazers, but one's expectations of nature pale beside what it used to be. Here, we may understand the kelps; however, they are but a beautiful gossamer veil, undulating peacefully in the ocean, offering no hints of the marvellous species that should live there but for human greed.[34]

— *Chapter 20* —

# Hunting on the High Plains of the Open Sea

— ❧ —

> *Day after day, day after day,*
> *We stuck, nor breath nor motion;*
> *As idle as a painted ship*
> *Upon a painted ocean.*
>
> *Water, water, everywhere,*
> *And all the boards did shrink;*
> *Water, water, everywhere,*
> *Nor any drop to drink.*[1]

ECALMED in the doldrums far from land, Coleridge's ancient mariner captures well the awful monotony of the open sea. For centuries the boundless empty plains of the high seas were feared. Striking out from the security of coastal waters, early mariners knew that many would never see land again. Ships fell victim to sudden typhoons, or drifted in windless uncharted waters while crews died of thirst, taunted as was the ancient mariner by the beckoning salty lake surrounding them. It was in the terrible vastness of the open ocean that the grip of scurvy tightened, draining energy, then hope, then life. It is easy to understand how seamen could feel, like Coleridge's sailor:

> *Alone, alone, all, all alone,*
> *Alone on a wide wide sea!*
> *And never a saint took pity on*
> *My soul in agony.*[2]

The open oceans were places to cross as quickly and directly as possible, not to tarry. Only the salt-crusted, oil-grimed whalers were at home on the high seas, constantly seeking fertile hunting grounds. In more recent years, faster and more reliable ships, detailed charts, and daily weather forecasts have taken much of the uncertainty out of ocean passages. The open sea is no longer dreaded, although it still commands respect.

For most of history, fishers have shunned the high seas as too remote, too unproductive, too dangerous, and too expensive to fish. Only whales were sufficiently valuable to lure men far beyond the horizon, braving extremes of pack ice and oppressive equatorial heat, sometimes on the same voyage. Besides, while coastal fish were plentiful, there was little point in venturing far offshore, particularly when, in the absence of ice, methods of preserving fish for the long voyage home were limited. In any case, the deep water of the open sea had far less to offer fishers. Compared to the fertile, shallow seas that bathed the continental shelves, the high seas were deserts.

Only 8 percent of seas and oceans cover the shallow shelves that are underwater extensions of the continents, but these waters account for 75 percent of global fish catches.[3] Continental shelves are gently sloping seascapes of rolling hills, valleys, and open plains that give way, at depth of around 200 meters (660 feet), to continental slopes that descend steeply into the abyss. They vary in width from hundreds or thousands of kilometers, such as off eastern Canada and northern Europe, to being nonexistent, as off the mid-Atlantic islands of the Azores. Continental shelf waters receive the nutrient-laden runoff from rivers. Their shallow bottoms lie within reach of storms and tidal currents that lift fertile deposits and mix them throughout the water column. Plentifully supplied with nutrients, plankton grows prolifically in the sun-drenched surface layers, making continental shelves among the most productive places in the sea.

Compared to coastal waters, most of the high seas are barren, overlying very deep water. Eighty-seven percent of the area of the sea is over 1,000 meters deep (3,300 feet). In these areas, nutrients in the sunlit surface layers where plant growth is possible are continuously lost to the deep, sinking beyond the reach of storm waves and tidal currents. Far from terrestrial river runoff, the high seas are starved of nutrients, including vital trace elements like iron that are needed for plankton growth. The vivid blue waters of the high seas fascinate sailors who pass an idle moment on deck. The ginlike clarity of the water draws the gaze far into the depths, robbing objects of scale. The 4-meter (13-foot) oceanic whitetip shark gliding below appears little more than the size of a bonito, its attendant consort of pilot fish a darting shoal of minnows. The 2-meter (7-foot) loggerhead turtle is reduced to pie-plate dimensions amid playing shafts of light that fade toward the indigo deep. The open sea owes its startling clarity to lack of plankton and suspended material. With so little to eat, large animals are relatively scarce.

Early navigators on ocean crossings had to carry their full store of provisions with them because they could not rely on fishing. Captain Cook sailed across a barren stretch of ocean in his passage from Hawaii to North America shortly before discovering Nootka Sound and its richly clad sea otters in 1778, writing in his log, "[I]f we had not known that the continent of America was not far distant, from the few signs we had met with of the vicinity of land we might have concluded that there was none within some thousand leagues of us, for we had hardly seen a bird or any other Oceanic animal sence we left Sandwich islands."[4]

La Pérouse hit a dry patch sailing south from Kamchatka across the central Pacific in 1787: "[T]he birds had totally disappeared and we were very strained by a heavy easterly swell which, like the western one in the Atlantic Ocean, dominates this vast sea in which we saw neither bonito nor dorado and merely a few flying fish, our supplies of fresh food were totally exhausted and we had counted rather too much on finding fish to soften the austerity of our diet."[5]

Not all of the open sea, however, is so devoid of life. Just as on land, where fertile river valleys may cut through deserts, there are places that brim with life alongside the swathes of scarcity. These places are favored by quirks of geology and oceanography that bring nutrients to the surface and concentrate wildlife. Upwelling currents, for example, carry nutrient-rich bottom water from the deep sea to the surface. In some places upwellings are driven by offshore winds pushing surface waters away from land to be replaced by water from below. Along central latitudes of the Pacific, prevailing winds blow from east to west in non-El Niño years. Planetary spin gives them a northward rotation north of the equator and a southerly rotation to the south. This parting sea brings up water from below. In his 1787 voyage, La Pérouse's fortunes changed about four degrees south of the equator. Although there was no land in sight, he then entered a region where gentle upwelling fertilizes the central Pacific, and scattered coral islets afford seabirds a tenuous foothold amid the watery plains. The sudden appearance of seabirds afforded welcome relief for their hunger. White and sooty terns in particular "flew in such numbers around our ships, especially during the night, that we were deafened by their noise and it was difficult to hold a conversation on the upper deck, so that our fairly successful hunts provided us with some revenge for their screeching, as well as a bearable meal."[6] But this rich spot in the ocean was limited, and after sailing two degrees farther south the birds disappeared.

Upwellings support some of the world's great fisheries, like that for Peruvian anchoveta off the coast of northern South America. James Colnett, who criss-crossed the eastern Pacific in the 1790s in search of sperm whales, vividly describes life in the Peru upwelling:

> The fish common to this coast, are dolphins [dorado], and all those which inhabit tropical Latitudes; and in calm nights, there are seen large shoals of small fish which have the appearance of breakers [from the phosphorescence]. Of turtle, we saw none till we were North of Lima, they were of the kind called the loggerhead, and North of the Equator we found the hump-backed species on the surface of the water in great numbers [leatherback turtle]. We frequently took out of the seals and porpoises large quantities of squid, which is the food of the spermaceti whales, and at times saw many devil-fish [manta rays]

and sunfish, the latter of which proved an agreeable and wholesome addition to our daily fare. . . . In our passage . . . we passed great quantities of herring [probably anchoveta], turtle, porpoises, black-fish [pilot, bottle-nosed, or false killer whales], devil-fish, and fin-back whale, but the number of birds appeared to be greatly diminished since we left the coast: for at that time there were innumerable flocks of boobies, which were so tame, as not only to perch on the different parts of the ship, but even on our boats, and the oars while they were actually employed in rowing. When the appearance of the weather foretold a squall, or on the approach of night, the turtle generally afforded a place of rest for one of these birds on his back; and though this curious perch was usually an object of contest, the turtle appears to be perfectly at ease and unmoved upon the occasion. The victorious bird generally eased the turtle of the sucking fish and maggots that adhere to and troubled him. We now saw dolphins and porpoises in abundance, and took many of the latter, which we mixed with salt pork, and made excellent sausages, indeed they became our ordinary food. Sea snakes were also in great plenty, and many of the crew made a pleasant and nutritious meal of them.[7]

The Peruvian upwelling is driven by offshore winds from South America. They turn the Humboldt Current, a great stream of cold water that pours north from the southern ocean, offshore from Peru toward the Galápagos. Like the upwelling itself, the Humboldt is tremendously fertile. The boundaries between these great ocean currents and other water masses—especially where cool water contacts warm—also concentrate life in the open sea. Colnett rode the Humboldt Current from South America to the Galápagos:

[A]n innumerable flight of birds accompanied us, and we had turtles in great plenty, but they soon grew scarce; though we continued to take bonnettas, dolphins, porpoises and black fish in great abundance. The weather then changed to rain with thunder and lightning; and we every day remarked our passing through strong ripplings and veins of currents. . . . In the course of our passage, we fell in frequently with streams of current, at least a mile in breadth, and of which there was no apparent termination. They frequently, changed the ship's course, against her helm, half the compass, although running, at the rate of three miles and an half an hour. I never experienced a similar current but on the coast of Norway. The froth, and boil, of these streams, appear, at a very small distance, like heavy breakers; we sounded in several of them, and found no bottom with two hundred fathoms of line. I also tried the rate, and course of the stream, which was, South West by West, two miles and an half an hour. These streams are very partial, and we avoided them, whenever it was in our power. Birds, fish, turtles, seals, sun-fish and other marine animals kept constantly on the edge of them, and they were often seen, to contain large beds of cream-coloured blubber [jellyfish and other gelatinous plankton], of the same kind as those of a red hue, which are observable on the coast of Peru.[8]

Some production hotspots of the open ocean can be seen from space. Astronauts flying the space shuttle in 1992 spotted a line drawn in the sea across the mid-Pacific. Oceanographers in the region were called in to investigate. The line marked the convergence of the North and South Equatorial Currents, concentrating plankton in a streak 10 kilometers (6 miles) wide and several hundreds long. It was visible from the ship as a region of breaking, turbulent waves and bright green water rich in diatoms. William Beebe, the explorer and naturalist of the early twentieth century, described crossing such a convergence zone in the Pacific in his book *The Arcturus Adventure*:

> At seven-thirty, after sounding, temperatures, and breakfast, I went on the bridge and saw a very distinct line in the water to the north. The captain said we had been steaming parallel to it since dawn. I had the *Arcturus* turned toward it at once, and found the Sargasso Sea of the Pacific, only in this instance it was a wall of water, against which all the floating jetsam for miles and miles was drifted and held. . . .
>
> When I approached within the possibility of more accurate examination, I saw that the line, which stretched from horizon to horizon, extended in a northeast and southwest direction. On our side, the south, the water showed dark and rough, but much lighter and smoother to the north. When the *Arcturus* was at last actually astraddle of the rip, I saw it as a narrow line of foam, zigzagging across the placid sea, with spouting white-caps shooting up through the froth that marked the meeting place of the great ocean currents.[9]

Creatures of passage connect hotspots of oceanic production like this, migrating from place to place, their movements tuned by nature. Tuna are the ultimate high-seas wanderers, the migrations of some species spanning oceans. Pacific albacore tuna each year undertake a 9,000-kilometer (5,600-mile) migration from the seas off Japan to waters of the eastern Pacific. They time their appearance on either side of the ocean to the bloom of plankton and attendant flush of prey fish like anchovies and sardines. The migrations of Atlantic bluefin tuna into the Mediterranean through the Strait of Gibraltar and then onward into the Black Sea were known to the ancients and described in detail by Aristotle and Pliny the Elder. In places like the Mediterranean, large animals of the high seas pass close to coasts on their migrations, especially where deep water hugs the land and ocean currents press the shores. They sometimes remain in the vicinity of land for weeks or months to feed or breed. The warm Kuroshio Current bathes the coast of Japan and to the north mixes with cold currents from the seas of Okhotsk and Bering. These waters are Grand Central for whales and fish, like tuna, that converge from across the Pacific to feed in the prolific waters. Gray whales, seals, and salmon skirt the North American coast on their passage from the Baja peninsula, California, and countless rivers northward to the Bering Sea. Along the coasts of Mexico and California, giant pelagic fish—including swordfish, sailfish, and marlin—move inshore seasonally to hunt and harry huge shoals of sardines, anchovies, and squid.

In the early twentieth century, interest grew in fishing for high-seas fish where large animals like tuna and swordfish dipped into coastal waters. The largest species were initially targets mainly for recreational fishers, the meat being considered inferior to other species readily available. One of the world's most valuable fish today is the Atlantic bluefin tuna. In the western Atlantic, spring sees these fish migrate north from winter spawning grounds in the Gulf of Mexico to their summer feeding grounds off the Gulf of Maine and Nova Scotia. They ride the warm Gulf Stream to where this current collides with the southward-flowing cold, nutrient-rich waters of the Labrador Current. Where southern and northern seas coalesce, their vernal union begets copious plankton growth, greening the waters and filling them with fish.

Tuna epitomize what it is to be a fish. Their sleek muscle-bound bodies cut through water with effortless mastery, driven by high crescent tails beating side to side in rapid staccato. Pectoral fins shaped like hydroplanes flick and twist on the unseen marine breeze, lending remarkable agility to such stiff-bodied creatures.

Bluefin tuna are the giants of the tuna tribe. I once spent a week at White Point Lodge on the south shore of Nova Scotia. Surveying the lounge from above a roaring log fire was a magnificent moosehead whose antlers seemed to span the room. According to an inscription, when this giant commanded the woods of Nova Scotia it weighed in at over 450 kilograms (1,000 pounds). Below the head were faded photographs of big-game fishers of the 1930s and 1940s. Giant bluefin suspended from dockside gantries dwarfed exhausted, grinning anglers. These fish weighed up to 700 kilograms (1,500 pounds) and reached over 4 meters long (13 to 14 feet), humbling the mighty moose.

Prime bluefin tuna fetch over US$100,000 per fish at auction and realize double the price in restaurants. Almost all bluefin today are flash frozen and flown to Japan for immediate sale at Tsukiji, the great Tokyo fish market. In the dark of early dawn, buyers pick their way among bodies that lie in stiff rows, inspecting each fish for color and fat content. Fat fish are the most valuable, and buyers judge the best by rubbing a piece of meat between finger and thumb. Only a day before, these fish may have felt the rush of the cool Atlantic on their flanks as they rode the billows of the Gulf Stream, springing shoals of herring from the water with lethal dashes. In the 1920s and 1930s when the anglers of White Point Resort were charming bluefin tuna from Nova Scotia seas, the fish could be sold only for pet food! However, development of canning technology and the discovery that tinned tuna preserves wonderfully well created a product for which there was a ready market. Tuna fisheries developed first off the west coast of North America, targeting the large, white-fleshed albacore. Soon after, commercial fishers began to try their gear on east coast bluefin. One famous big game angler of the day, Kip Farrington, lamented in 1942,

> Easterners also like to harpoon giant tuna, even though they are harder to strike than swordfish. I hold no brief for this so-called sport; and, as these grand fish bring but three or four cents a pound, there is even less reason for harpooning them than there is in sticking swordfish.[10]

The distinctions between the sport fish and commercial fish of Farrington's world were at that time being turned upside down. The giant fish, top predators of the sea, were now prey for a growing cadre of commercial fishers. By the early 1940s Americans had developed a taste for big fish. New Englanders then landed about 3 million pounds (over 1,300 metric tons) of swordfish a year, but a further 4 million pounds (1,800 metric tons) were imported from Canada and Japan.[11] Up to the Second World War, it was still too expensive to pursue these species far offshore. Like bluefin tuna, swordfish are seasonal visitors to New England waters, arriving to work the glittering seam of fish that separates Gulf Stream from Labrador Current. They could be caught close to shore, within sight of Long Island, Cape Cod, and Nova Scotia. But the entire face of high-seas fishing changed after the end of hostilities.

Both Japan and the Soviet Union were desperate for food and possessed large fleets of ships in need of peacetime occupation. For Japan, fishing was already a way of life. In the 1930s, Japan became the world's largest fishing nation, with twice the landings of the United States, for example.[12] The Japanese fished for crab in the Bering Sea, for whales in Antarctica, and for croakers and bream in the South China and Yellow Seas. Japan's sizeable distant-water fishing fleet had been pressed into war service and now was released to begin fishing anew. For the first few years postwar, Japanese fisheries concentrated on waters close to the islands, stocks benefiting from the respite in fishing caused by the war, just as did fish stocks in Europe. Fishing technology advanced rapidly, including onboard freezers that gave fishing boats greater reach, and larger nets that enabled them to fish more economically. The era of high-seas fishing had begun.

At first, high-seas fishing fleets worked relatively close to home. But as time passed, captains found they could get better catches by pushing farther afield. Repeating the pattern seen in shallow coastal seas, over the ensuing decades high-seas fishing fleets spread ever farther into virgin seas where fish remained large and abundant. As the years passed, other countries joined the fishing fleet, drawn by the promise of large rewards. Data collected by the Japanese longline fishing fleet between the 1950s and the end of the twentieth century enable us to see the evolution of this fishery in unprecedented detail.

The late Ransom Myers, Boris Worm, and colleagues from Dalhousie University in Canada have sifted through the records, reconstructing the growth and spread of fishing effort and the effects it had on ocean fish.

By the mid-1950s the Japanese fleet fished the entire western Pacific, from the Sea of Japan to the Australian coast, east to Hawaii and French Polynesia. By 1960, they had crossed the Indian Ocean and penetrated the Atlantic, fishing a swathe of equatorial water from Brazil to West Africa. By 1970 they fished the entire globe, spanning the Pacific from west to east, the Indian Ocean, and the Atlantic from Newfoundland to the Falkland Islands. The size of the high-seas fleet was augmented when countries declared 200-nautical-mile Exclusive Economic Zones, pushing boats from coastal areas into international waters. But by the mid-1970s there is the beginning of a change. The blanket coverage of the fleet begins to develop holes as some grounds are abandoned. More years pass, and these holes grow and shift, new ones develop, and others are patched as some grounds get fished again.

Looking deeper into the catch records, Myers and Worm found a common pattern that was repeated in every new fishing ground exploited. Catches at first were tremendous, with fleets hauling fat tuna, swordfish, marlin, and sailfish as fast as they cast their longlines. But early success soon waned. Averaged across nine high-seas fishing regions they examined, in the first fifteen years following the onset of fishing in virgin grounds, catch rates fell by 80 percent.[13] No wonder captains took their vessels ever farther from port in the search for fish. To sustain their catches, fishers also adopted the age-old ploy of increasing fishing effort. Today's high-seas longliners set lines up to 100 kilometers long (62 miles) and bristling with thirty thousand hooks. They drape the oceans north to south and east to west in a lethal web.

Alongside the valued target species, longliners also caught sharks by the millions. Sharks represent the epitome of wild nature and have always inspired fear and awe. In 1899, William McIntosh chose the blue shark as the frontispiece to his book *The Resources of the Sea*, calling it "the type of a group that often ruins man's nets and hooks, and defies his influence." Many people still think of sharks in this way, but times have changed. In McIntosh's day, the seas were alive with sharks pursuing the giant shoals of herring, mackerel, and capelin that crowded the shores. Explorers, merchants, and adventurers of earlier centuries repeatedly remarked on the abundance and enormous size of sharks following their boats. But the late twentieth century signaled a shift for sharks from being the predators and competitors of our fishing endeavors to becoming the target of them.

Sharks used to be a nuisance bycatch on longlines. They were cut free and thrown back by fishers in the 1950s, or clubbed to death before being tossed over the side. Today, globalization and growing wealth in Asian countries, where shark fins are prized, has given them value in their own right. Sharks are now hunted across the high seas, with devastating effects. In a fisheries research cruise through the eastern Pacific, the conservationist Stuart Pimm was astonished to learn that almost every shark caught already had one or more hooks lodged in its jaws. These were the lucky ones—they had escaped before. Others were less lucky. Pinned to the deck of some longliner, their fins would be hacked off before the still-living fish was pitched into the depths to suffer a lingering death.

Using data from longline fisheries, Myers and his colleagues also documented declines in shark abundance. More than 90 percent of sharks have been lost from massive expanses of the world oceans. Some species have been hit particularly hard, such as the large oceanic whitetip. This onetime scourge of naval seamen whose ships were sunk in battle has experienced a 150-fold decline in the Gulf of Mexico, and likely a similar decline in many other places for which there are no data. Not long ago, this was probably the most common large animal in the world.

Like other species in high-seas fisheries, sharks also got smaller with time. This is because fishing preferentially removes older, larger fish, leaving populations dominated by young animals. Between the 1950s and 1990s, the size of oceanic whitetips in the Gulf of Mexico fell by a third and mako sharks by a half, dusky sharks were 60 percent smaller, and silky sharks a staggering 83 percent smaller.[14] In the Pacific, the blue shark of MacIntosh's book halved in size.[15] These declines in average size have greatly reduced reproduction by populations, since big animals are more fecund than small.

Target species like tuna are not the only animals affected by high-seas fishing operations. Although drift nets, some reaching 90 kilometers (56 miles) long and dubbed "walls of death" for their indiscriminate massacre, were banned by the United Nations in 1992, the giant longlines that have largely replaced them also exact colossal mortality on nontarget species: loggerhead, leatherback, and olive ridley turtles are being slaughtered in the thousands, as were albatross of all varieties until new methods for setting lines were adopted to keep the bait away from hungry birds.[16] For the leatherback turtle in the Pacific, extinction may be a few breaths away. The leatherback is the largest living reptile, reaching over 700 kilograms (1,540 pounds) and 2.5 meters in length (over 8 feet). These harmless jellyfish feeders do not take hooks, but instead blunder into longlines where they get tangled and drown. Numbers of leatherbacks returning to Pacific beaches to nest—the best means we have of estimating their populations—fell from over ninety thousand to less than five thousand between 1980 and the present. Some rookeries have been lost altogether.

Worm and Myers used longline catch data to look at the effects of fishing on the open sea in another way. They calculated the number of different types of fish from the tuna and swordfish families caught per fifty hooks, and mapped patterns across the global oceans. The study revealed rich and predictable congregations of life where ocean predators gather, with a dearth of species in others. Areas of exceptional diversity represent oceanic crossroads and productivity hotspots such as places where warm and cold-water currents meet. They include the mid-Atlantic east of Florida where the Gulf Stream leaves the Caribbean on its journey north; northeastern Australia in the Coral Sea; the central eastern Pacific; and the seas bordering Japan's Kuroshio Current. These congregations have also drawn the attention of the world's fishing industry, to the detriment of the animals that live in them. Worryingly, depending on the area considered, there were declines of between 10 percent and 50 percent in species diversity between the 1950s and the 1990s. Fishing is impoverishing the global oceans. After the study was published in 2005, Worm described his feelings on making this discovery. Finding these oceanic oases was like solving a giant puzzle and seeing the night sky in constellations for the first time—even as the stars are blinking out. It's beautiful and tragic at the same time. . . . Everywhere you go, in every ocean basin, our "hotspots" today are only relics of what was once there.[17]

Fishing is transforming the high seas. Giant predatory fish are today following the fate of the great whales, disappearing place by place, species by species. Bycatch is killing other titans of the waves: the leatherback turtle, dolphins, porpoises, whale sharks, albatross . . . the list is long. The leatherback has a 100-million-year evolutionary history. Today we are on the point of ending it all for the leatherback because of our unbridled desire for tuna, swordfish, and marlin.

Some effects of fishing are unexpected. Tuna hunt by driving schools of their prey fish toward the surface where there is no escape. Seabirds home in on these fish boils to take advantage of easy prey pressed into the shallows from below. With the decline of tuna, prey fish boils have become sparse, and birds find it harder to catch prey. Some species now subsist on offal discarded from fishing boats while others go hungry. Yet other species have benefited from gaps opening in food webs as competitors are removed, but overall the trends, like those in coastal seas, are of loss. We can only guess where this will end if high-seas fisheries continue unfettered.

When nations of the world declared 200-nautical-mile Exclusive Economic Zones through the 1970s and 1980s, a third of the ocean was brought under national control for the first time. In these waters, the cherished principle of freedom of the seas was restrained as countries sought to limit access to their fisheries and other resources like oil and gas. In waters beyond, freedom of the seas prevails almost unchanged since the seventeenth century. High-seas waters are governed today by international fishing agreements operated under the United Nations Law of the Sea by regional fishery management organizations. These bodies supposedly control catches from the high seas and are responsible for conserving fish stocks. Most, like the International Commission for the Conservation of Atlantic Tunas, are ineffective. And, just as in the sixteenth and seventeenth centuries, there are still pirates at large on the high seas. Pirate fishing vessels—working beyond law and regulation—are estimated to account for up to half of the global catch from the high seas, drawn by the large profits that can still be made. They sail under flags of convenience bought from nations that have not signed up to conventions whose aim is to protect the high seas. They land their catches in clandestine operations at least as lucrative as international drug smuggling, often with the tacit blessing of national authorities who care little for what goes on beyond their national limits. Until they are brought under control, there is little hope for rational fishery management on the high seas.

If Kip Farrington were alive today, how he would rue the loss of his beloved game fish. The waters of New England and eastern Canada no longer throng with giant bluefin and swordfish. It is hard to know just exactly how scarce bluefin are today compared with the interwar heyday of game fishing. Since records began to be kept in the 1970s by the misnamed International Commission for the Conservation of Atlantic Tuna, bluefin have declined by over 90 percent. But this was not the beginning of their decline. The fishery commenced over forty years earlier. Using Ransom Myers and Boris Worm's estimate of 80 percent decline in stocks in the first fifteen years of the fishery as a conservative lower bound for pre-1970 decline, there is probably only one bluefin left for every fifty present in 1940. The last of these regal fish are today pursued more relentlessly than ever by the descendents of the harpooners that Farrington railed against. The fish are now so valuable that it pays to employ planes and helicopters to scan the ocean, guiding boats in for the kill when fish are spotted. This isn't fishing any more—it is the extermination of a species.

# ~ Chapter 21 ~

# Violating the Last
# Great Wilderness

~━━ ━━~

*I*LEARNED TO fish in 1967. It was a heavenly summer for a five-year-old, and I spent hours on my belly by the grassy edge of a pond not far from home in the highlands of Scotland. Gazing into the shallows, I became one with the creatures below water, tracing their minute lives among mud and weed. I tracked creeping caddis larvae dragging their pebble and stick cases through leaf mold cave and canyon. I watched angular larvae haul themselves up reeds and as dragonflies break free from their aquatic lives. But most arresting were the dancing sticklebacks, my quarry. Males with vivid red bellies tempted female sticklebacks and small boys alike. By day's end, success was measured by the number of angry faces in my jam jar.

Far from the borders of my pond, the Beatles were at the height of their fame and the Cold War gripped the world. The Soviet fishing fleet was at large on the high seas looking for new stocks to exploit. While America reached for the moon, the Soviets probed the endless night of the planet's final wilderness frontier, pioneering fishing in waters more than 1,000 meters deep. Their efforts marked the beginning of the third and final trawling revolution. The first revolution, discussed earlier in this book, was heralded by the invention of the trawl in the fourteenth century, while the second came with the addition of steam power to trawlers in the late nineteenth century.

The first Soviet deepwater trawlers were simple adaptations of those already in use over the continental shelves, with longer, thicker cables and larger winches. Through the mid-1960s, Soviet, Polish, and East German fishery research vessels systematically searched the Atlantic and the Pacific oceans, sweeping the flanks of continents with echo sounder and trawl. In the near-freezing waters of the deep Atlantic, beyond the reach of shallow-water trawlers, they discovered huge stocks of exotic species like Greenland halibut and roundnose grenadier. Trawls plunging through these untouched shoals could take 15 to 30 tonnes of prime fish per hour, giving twentieth-century fishers a taste of the success their nineteenth-century forebears once enjoyed in shallower seas. Greenland halibut look like a dark, more slender version of the halibut fished over continental shelves, and it found a ready market. The grenadier, with its blunt head, goggle eyes, and tapering whiptail, was less familiar. But in taste it compared favorably to the old staples, fishery scientists describing the flesh as "tasty, less fibrous and more tender than that of cod."[1] The fish were large and the meat firm. Consumers waiting patiently in the endless cues of the communist Soviet Union were not about to complain.

Encouraged by early success, soon there was a fleet of trawlers at work on the high seas, supplying cavernous factory ships that processed catches. Initially, they fished the muddy slopes where continental shelves fell away into the abyss of the deep ocean. But trawlers were troubled by net-shredding "rough ground." The Russian fishery scientists Pechenik and Troyanovskii, who took part in early surveys, described the kinds of seabed they encountered around the northern rim of the Atlantic: "Everywhere along the edge of the shelf and the upper part of the continental slope to a depth of 800 to 1000m there are patches of gravel, pebbles, or large stones. Sponges are almost everywhere; in places there are corals."[2] And, "Numerous large stones, corals and sponges, combined with the complex relief of the bottom, make work with fishing gear very difficult on the continental slope to the south of Iceland: fouling and tearing of the trawl frequently occur here. . . . In some sections [of the Labrador slope] trawls are greatly endangered by corals which occur at depths of 800 to 850m."[3]

Something had to be done. Before long, nets were adapted by replacing the small bobbins and tickler chains found on the footrope of shallow-water gears with hefty steel-and-rubber rollers and heavy chains. Trawl nets could now penetrate rugged areas by "hopping" across the rocks and any other obstructions—such as corals and sponges—that lay in the path of the net. Rockhopper gears, as they are called, opened up the flanks and pinnacles of underwater seamounts to fishing, and a far more rewarding fishing ground was discovered.

The deep sea is less productive even than the high seas. Most animals that live in the abyss rely almost entirely for food on organic matter originating in shallow water where sunlight fuels plant growth. They depend on a lightly falling snow of dead animals and plants sinking into the darkness from the well-lit surface layers. Some animals search more actively for food, migrating from the deep to shallow layers by night to feed. But the nutrient-poor waters of the high seas produce little, and food is sparse. Nonetheless, they provide an important link in the ocean food web, carrying food from the surface to the waiting mouths of deep sea predators lurking below.

Muddy plains as large as continents cover much of the deep ocean floor. But where mountains elbow their flanks above the monotonous prospect and thrust their peaks into overlying waters, they create pockets of higher productivity. Currents draw nutrients upward from the seabed where they mix with water circulating from the surface in giant pirouetting loops around the submerged mountains. By bringing nutrients to the surface, seamounts generate oases of higher production that attract wildlife. For species like tuna, they are refueling stops and waypoints on transoceanic migrations. Albacore from Japan stop by on Hawaiian seamounts, spending a few days bounce-diving between warm surface waters and cold mountain slopes to feed, before moving on. Albatross fly thousands of miles to catch fish and squid in waters swirling around the slopes of hidden summits, then carry them to waiting chicks perched on distant islets.

The currents flowing over seamounts carry food, bringing the production of huge areas of open ocean on a ceaseless conveyor to the animals that live on and around them. This enables seamounts to support large concentrations of fish. In the late 1960s, Soviet fishers discovered magnificent aggregations of pelagic armourhead fish around Hawaiian seamounts, for example.[4] Pelagic armourhead look much like tropical snappers, high-backed and plump, with dark staring eyes. Their silver-gray bodies merge like ghosts in the gray-blue twilight of deep water. Packed schools of armourhead could be scooped up with ease by trawlers. The Soviets discovered a gold mine in the deep, and the fishery exploded as Soviet and Japanese boats cashed in on the bounty, removing tens of thousands of tonnes of fish a year. But the bonanza lasted only a decade before the crash came. Between 1976 and 1977, catches collapsed from 30,000 tonnes to just 3,500 tonnes and have never recovered. Fishers were unperturbed. With an estimated eighty thousand or more seamounts spread over the world oceans, they could afford to be optimistic.

Seamounts are of prime interest to fishers. Most fish encountered over muddy continental slopes are unsuitable for human consumption. In the trickling currents of the deep, they have little need for powerful muscles. In any case they could not sustain an energetic life on the meager fare available, and the watery flesh of these animals tastes appalling. Nor is it much use for animal feed, having low oil content. By comparison, seamount fish are desirable, with muscles toned by more vigorous currents and nourished by wholesome food.

The next bonanza came from New Zealand waters. Soviet ships fishing in depths of 800 to 1,000 meters (2,600 to 3,300 feet) over the Chatham Rise chanced upon commercially viable concentrations of a vivid orange fish. These deep-bodied animals had robust, armour-plated heads with staring owl eyes and a downward-curving mouth. Although they reached just 70 centimeters long (28 inches), they were thickset and muscular.[5] New Zealanders soon joined Soviet boats in pursuit if this fish, pushing offshore to explore the underwater canyons and mountain ranges that surround their country.

The first task in marketing this exotic animal was to change the fish's name. *Hoplostethus atlanticus,* as scientists know it, is a member of the slimehead family. Filleted slimehead, no matter how beautifully packaged, would probably not find its way under that name into many shopping carts. But as "orange roughy" the fish had consumer appeal. Their firm porcelain flesh looked good on the shelf. More over, it could withstand several cycles of freezing and thawing without spoiling, making it an ideal substitute for shallow-water fish like cod. There is nothing very special about the taste of orange roughy, however, and much was sold processed into breaded fillets, fish cakes, and fish fingers (fish sticks).

The Chatham Rise is an underwater mountain range that stretches east of New Zealand's South Island and covers an area as large as the island itself. The tallest peaks in the range reach to around 500 meters (1,650 feet) below the surface, well within reach of deepwater trawlers. Fishers rushed to gear up for deep-sea fishing, and catches soared, reaching 50,000 tonnes a year by the mid-1980s. Success in New Zealand tempted Australian fishers to try their luck off Tasmania as well. Alan Barnett was one of the first fishers to catch orange roughy there. He struck gold, fishing a seamount called St. Helen's Hill off the edge of the eastern Tasmanian continental shelf in 1989. St. Helen's Hill is a conical, extinct volcano that rises 600 meters (2,000 feet) from a seabed deeper than a kilometer (about 0.6 mile). Orange roughy, like many other commercially valuable species from the deep sea, gather around seamounts to spawn. St. Helen's was a melee of mating fish. Fishing boats would use sonar to find the tightly packed shoals and then run their trawls through them. If they got it right, they could for a few minutes' work take 50 or 60 tonnes. One fisher said that in the early days of fishing the Hill, the fish were so easy to catch you could take them by towing a chaff bag through the water.[6] In the first year, St. Helen's Hill yielded an astonishing 17,000 tonnes of orange roughy. So many fish were landed that they swamped freezing facilities, and truckloads had to be dumped in landfill sites.

It was all too much too quickly. In the early days, fishery managers had no information on orange roughy and no experience with regulating deepwater fishing. Feeling a need for some restraint, New Zealand fishery managers set catch quotas based on what they knew of the biology of similar-sized fish from shallow seas. They assumed that deep-sea fish were the same as those in shallow water in every respect except depth. But life in the deep proved very different, and the roughy a strange beast. Catches soon plummeted as fish were removed from seamount after seamount. It turned out that the animals being caught were old—very old indeed. Although seamounts are productivity hotspots, this is relative only to other parts of the deep sea. The pace of life in the dark and cold is glacial. Scientists were initially misled by estimating the age of orange roughy based on counts of rings on their scales. In shallow-water fish, variation in growth rate during the year produces characteristic annual rings. But rings on orange roughy scales turned out to be laid down much less frequently. Measuring the decay of radioisotopes sealed into the ear bones of the fish as the animal grew gave more accurate estimates, revealing that orange roughy could live to be at least 150 years old. The animals on the fishmonger's slab were geriatric by human standards! Moreover, fish didn't reach reproductive maturity until between ages 22 and 40 years.

A combination of long life and late maturity, as shown on other occasions, makes animals extremely vulnerable to overfishing. The population growth rates for such species are low. For a fishery to be sustainable over the long term, it must keep to the principle that fish are not removed faster than they can replace themselves. Given the sedate growth of orange roughy, sustainable rates of extraction would amount to only 1 or 2 percent of the population taken each year. Their tendency to gather around seamounts make them easy to find and catch, adding to the risk of overfishing. To cap these problems, they were caught on their spawning grounds. In shallow seas, the heightened vulnerability of species when they gather to spawn has long been recognized. Herring in temperate seas and groupers in the tropics, for example, are often protected by seasonal or spatial fishing bans at spawning times. One of the ironies of deep-sea fishing is that fishers have to target spawning aggregations to get sufficiently high catch rates to turn a profit.

Deep-sea fisheries removed animals at rates far beyond sustainability, and collapse was inevitable. Within a decade, Australian and New Zealand fisheries blundered into difficulties, and catches began to nosedive. Managers struggled to stem declines, imposing ever more ruthless quotas. By the late 1990s, the Australian roughy boom was over, and boats brought in only a few hundred metric tons a year. New Zealand's fishery was more robust, but only because its deepwater fishing grounds were far more extensive. Catches fell through the 1990s, stabilizing at around 15,000 tonnes per year. But this stability came not through management control but by a process of discovery and serial overfishing of new grounds. The New Zealand orange roughy fishery will go the way of Australia's when the new grounds have all been found and fished.

Unperturbed by problems down under, deep-sea fishing boomed across the world through the 1980s and 1990s. Declining stocks and more restrictive regulation of shallow-water fisheries drove fishers from the continental shelves, especially in Europe. For ambitious young skippers with no quota, the deep sea was a place where a living, and perhaps a fortune, could still be made. For investment bankers, it offered attractive returns for less risk than traditional fishing ventures. A new fleet of giant supertrawlers set sail, each costing millions of dollars and equipped with highly sophisticated gadgetry to locate and catch fish.

In the North Atlantic, these supertrawlers have relentlessly worked the seams opened by Russian and Eastern European fleets. Roundnose grenadier, so promising in the 1960s, have been stripped from the Atlantic. Many fishery scientists fear the species has been driven below the point of recovery. Orange roughy, rarer in the Atlantic than around Australia and New Zealand, boomed and bust in just five years. For three decades now, species have been coming and going from deep-sea fisheries in a fast-forward replay of earlier serial overexploitation of shallow-water fish stocks. The difference is that there is much less certainty deep-sea fish will recover, even if we were to stop fishing them today. Their leisurely growth and sporadic reproductive success, and the lasting damage to their habitats by trawls, undermine the little ability they have to bounce back after depletion.

Complaints over the destructive effects of trawling on fish and their habitats fell silent early in the twentieth century. The rumbling progress of trawls across the world's shallow continental shelves perhaps seemed so irresistible that fishers saw little point in further argument. But perhaps they stopped protesting because evidence of damage also declined over time. The first trawlers that broke into virgin grounds tore up bottom life that had taken decades or centuries to establish. In the first few years of dragging, corals, sponges, sea fans, and anemones gave way to mud, gravel, starfish, and worms. While later on trawlers continued to catch many undersized fish, the worst devastation was already complete, for the most vulnerable animals had been removed and so were no longer caught in any great numbers. In the late twentieth century, deep-sea fishing—by violating a pristine realm—rekindled the controversy over bottom trawling.

The most lucrative deep-sea fisheries target areas of great biological significance, including seamounts, canyons, and ridges. Most deep-sea habitats are blanketed in mud, but in these places currents are strong enough to sweep away sediment. The currents bring food that supports fish aggregations, and they sustain a rich fauna of suspension-feeding animals, including corals, sponges, sea fans, hydroids, and myriad other fragile species. The dry prose of Soviet fishery scientists recorded these animals only as obstacles to fishing in the 1960s.[7] But more recently, picked out in the floodlit beam of submarine lights, the slopes of seamounts have been revealed as opulent gardens resplendent with invertebrates. Passing over the flanks of an Alaskan seamount in their submersible in the mid-1990s, U.S. scientists encountered coral groves of irresistible beauty. Brilliant orange hydroids hung their delicate fronds over billowing waves of yellow

*A rich fauna of corals, seafans, sponges, and myriad other invertebrate species cloaks the underwater slopes of Adale Island in the Aleutian Islands of Alaska. This scene was taken through the window of a submersible and shows an area that has never been hit by bottom trawls. ©Alberto Lindner/NOAA.*

ochre sponge; rockbound gorgonians stretched red fans upward, their maze of stinging polyps sifting plankton from the liquid breeze; here a dark cherry basket starfish clasped a branching coral of light shell pink, folding its labyrinthine arms quickly in the sudden glare; there a spindly crab tiptoed across heaped folds of encrusting lavender sea squirts. Amid the glades, startled fish froze momentarily in the spot-light before flicking spangled tails and diving for darkness.

It is strange to think, faced with such a vibrant scene, that people in the eighteenth century believed the deep sea was devoid of life. Noth-ing, argued the sage men of the day, could withstand the crushing pressure, permanent darkness, and arctic chill of the abyss. In *Natural History of European Seas,* the naturalist Edward Forbes plumbed the depths with net and dredge, probing to 2,000 feet (615 meters). Forbes, a native of the Isle of Man in the British Isles, summed up what was known in the early 1850s:

> Last and lowest of our regions of submarine existence is that of the deep-sea corals, so named on account of the great stony zoophytes characteristic of it in the oceanic seas of Europe. In its depths the number of peculiar creatures is few, yet sufficient to give a marked character to it. . . . As we descend deeper and deeper in this region its inhabitants become more and more modified, and fewer and fewer, indicating an approach towards an abyss where life is either extin-guished, or exhibits but a few sparks to mark its lingering presence. Its confines are yet undetermined, and it is in the exploration of this vast deep sea region that the finest field for submarine discovery yet remains.[8]

Forbes did not live to take further part in that discovery, dying in 1854 at age thirty-nine as he was about to take up a professorship at Edinburgh University. Had he survived, he would surely have partici-pated in the first great exploration of the deep—the *Challenger* Expedition. HMS *Challenger* sailed from Portsmouth, England, in 1872 and was at sea for over three years. The ship circled the planet, painstakingly lowering steel-jawed grabs into the void and winding them back hundreds of times. They hauled back evidence of life from every place visited and even the deepest depths.

Deep-sea biology was finally recognized, and from then on many countries joined in exploring the depths. These expeditions led to a gradual cataloging of deep-sea life and a new appreciation of the enormous depths of the ocean. It was soon evident that most of the living space on the planet was in the deep sea. Ninety-five percent of the volume of the biosphere—the part of the planet that supports life—is in the deep. Frustratingly, most of the time animals were brought to the surface lifeless and often horribly distorted by the release of pressure. Nobody had ever seen living deepwater animals in their natural element, until the American adventurer William Beebe and his companion Otis Barton decided to experience life in the deep sea firsthand. In the early 1930s, they developed the bathysphere to take them far into the deep sea. The sphere was cast from 1.5-inch-thick steel (4 centimeters) and was large enough for two uncomfortable men. Crouched within, they could observe life of the abyss through two tiny portholes of 3-inch fused quartz as they were lowered from a ship at the end of a steel cable. In 1934, off the coast of Bermuda, the bathysphere was successfully lowered half a mile (800 meters) into the Atlantic. As they descended, Beebe recorded the experience:

> The twilight . . . deepened, but we still spoke of its brilliance. It seemed to me that it must be like the last terrific upflare of a flame before it is quenched. I found we were both expecting at any moment to have it blown out, and to enter a zone of absolute darkness. But only by shutting my eyes and opening them again could I realise the terrible slowness of the change from dark blue to blacker blue. On the earth at night in full moonlight I can always imagine the yellow of sunshine, the scarlet of invisible blossoms, but here, when the searchlight was off, yellow and orange and red were unthinkable. The blue which filled all space admitted no thought of other colours.[9]

Descending farther, they encountered water layers thick with life: long translucent strings of gelatinous salps—animals like sea squirts —hung like ribbons, scudding shrimps, fish petrified in the lamp glare, inquisitive squid, and countless tiny copepods and other microscopic plankton. When they switched off the lights, they discovered that the darkness was lit by living constellations of fish and plankton, communicating through the void in a pulsing silent semaphore of blue, mauve, pink, and pure white light. Beebe continues,

At times there were flashes from unknown organisms so bright that my vision was confused for several seconds. Often the abundance of lights was so great that the comparison was unavoidable with the major stars on a clear, moonless night. The constant movement tended to confuse direct, concentrated vision, but by continual effort I managed to follow definite, related groups of lights, and in many cases could ultimately make out the outline of the fish.[10]

Beebe and Barton initiated the era of manned exploration of the deep sea. Over the following decades, explorers and scientists visited seamounts and canyons, rode the Gulf Stream at depth, and in 1960 touched bottom on the deepest part of the ocean—the Challenger Deep in the Mariana Trench near the Pacific Mariana Islands. At 10,920 meters deep (35,827 feet), the trench could easily hold Mount Everest with plenty of space to spare. Even at the very bottom of the world there was life. When resting on the bottom, the pilots of the 1960 voyage, Jacques Piccard and Don Walsh, saw a fish, a shrimp, and the tracks of sea cucumbers, finally putting to rest the notion that life cannot exist in the deepest corners of the ocean.

By the 1970s, deep-sea scientists had developed cheaper methods to reach the sea floor, building remotely operated vehicles (ROVs) that are tethered to a mother ship and controlled by a shipboard team. At that time, biologists had sampled only a millionth of the deep-sea floor. There was much still to learn, and people joked, accurately, that we had better maps of the dark side of the moon than of the deep sea. Remote systems greatly increased the rate of exploration and, in combination with manned submersibles, exciting discoveries piled one on another. In 1977, oceanographers cruising at depths of 2,000 to 3,000 meters (6,600 to 10,000 feet) in the submersible *Alvin* off the Galápagos Islands, discovered hydrothermal vents. These hot springs belched forth black, sulfur-rich water, superheated to nearly 300 degrees Celsius (570 Fahrenheit). The high pressure prevented the water from boiling as it would have done from a land-based hot spring. Bathed in the hot, mineral-laden water was a profusion of animals that turned deep-sea biology on its head: blood red tube worms, huge white clams, red shrimps, pale lobsters, crusts of tightly packed brown mussels, and much more. It was a mystery how they survived, until a Harvard biologist worked out that they harbored symbiotic bacteria that could break down sulfur-based compounds to produce energy and food without sunlight. Hydrothermal vents are now known from every ocean.

It is only in the last decade or so that we have realized there are remarkable coral reef communities in the deep cold waters of the North Atlantic. Edward Forbes was well aware of deepwater corals in the mid-nineteenth century, but he had no idea they formed reefs. Early trawler captains knew there was significant coral growth deep down because corals tore their nets. In the 1920s, the French scientist M.L. Joubin published a paper entitled "Deep Sea Corals: A Nuisance to Trawlers," in which he mapped out the distribution of corals along the fringes of Europe's continental shelf to enable fishers to avoid high-risk areas.

> The considerable increase in tonnage and power of fishing vessels employed by French ship-owners has allowed them, in the last few years, to manoeuver their trawls at increasingly great depths which they have never before reached.
>
> While operating in these deep waters they meet, starting from approximately 200 meters, branching corals which are located in this cold and dark water. These corals are made up of extremely hard lime-stone, with an aspect and consistency of porcelain, that produce white and cutting fractures; the nets tear there and can remain hung on the corals; the least evil which happens to them is to fill with broken branches, preventing trawls from working. The trawl of the *Tanche* retrieved, one day, from 5 to 6 tons in only one tow.[11]

It was not until the 1980s, when North Sea oil companies were scouring the sea floor with ROVs to map routes for pipelines, that the magnificence of these reefs was revealed. Some extended for tens of kilometers and were built over thousands of years by corals growing at a few millimeters a year on gravel ridges. These reefs support over a thousand species and are home to many commercially important fish as well as less familiar creatures.

Amid the chill ethereal beauty of these reefs, Norwegian scientists found disturbing evidence that others had been there before them. Skirting the edge of a reef with their ROV, living coral would suddenly give way to rubble and sand. In places, huge blocks of coral meters across appeared to have been dragged and rolled over living reef. Deep gouges scythed across the bottom through glades of sea fan and sponge. It didn't take long to discover the culprit—trawling. Ripped trawl nets wrapped around coral heads gave that away, as did the grooves cut by heavy steel trawl doors dragged across the reefs. Counting up the damage, they estimated that between 30 percent and 50 percent of Norway's deepwater coral reefs had been seriously damaged or destroyed by trawling by the late twentieth century. Damage to some of the shallower reefs may have been done before the present wave of deep-sea trawling, as Joubin's paper attests. Norwegian fishers working over "rough ground" once fished in pairs, first towing a chain suspended between two boats to level the obstructions, and then returning to scoop fish from amid the wreckage.

Today's commercial trawlers reach depths of 2,000 meters, over a mile below the surface. These ships have reached more than twice the depth of William Beebe's early descents. Everywhere that scientists look they find evidence of the devastating impact of the trawl. For decades now deepwater trawlers have roamed the high seas, destroying habitats of incalculable biological significance; places that would be treasured in national parks if they were on land. We are losing life in the deep sea before it has even been described by science. Today's oceanographers know the frustration of Egyptologists, who on discovering a new tomb find it was ransacked long ago. Touching down in their submersibles on a newly charted seamount, scientists flick on the lights to find only the broken remains of past lives. Les Watling from the University of Maine had this experience when he visited seamounts in the northwest Atlantic in 2005:

> We went to the Corner Rise seamounts to study deep sea corals and seafans. Even though they were about as far away from any North Atlantic landmass as you can get, the Russians fished them for about 20 years from the 1970s to 1990s. The first we called Lyman Seamount after a famous American brittle star taxonomist (not knowing then that Russians called it Yakutat). After doing a thoroughly modern mapping job, we picked several dive sites, and prepared the ROV. There is always great anticipation when the ROV descends through more than a thousand metres of water. Everyone in the control room is asking questions: what kind of a bottom we will land on, how many

and what kinds of corals will we find, what will be the scientific implications, and on and on for the two hours or so of the descent. Still, at
Lyman, we weren't prepared for what came into view. We were
amazed and confused. Amazed because it looked like the upper layers
of the seamount had been torn up, crushed and crumbled. It had evidently been covered in a crust of some sort that had been slashed by
deep gouges which were everywhere. And confused because we didn't
think fishing gear could wreak such havoc. We asked the ROV pilots
to drive this way and that, with each new view producing the same
battered landscape. Many ideas were voiced, each trying to explain the
heavy damage. Or was it damage? Could this be the result of some
natural process? But we knew people had fished here, so the questions
turned to what kind of gear, or what part of the gear, could have done
this. It seems that the heavy trawl doors of the Russian fishing gear
were repeatedly hauled over the summit of this mid ocean peak, with
the result that almost nothing lives there now. With the surface being
nothing but rubble, it is unlikely that any corals will recolonize for a
very long time.[12]

The same destructive force has been visited on other places. Bizarre
and beautiful fields of glass sponges have been trawled to oblivion
along North America's eastern seaboard. Seamounts of the Southern
Ocean that once supported lush forests of invertebrates have been
stripped to bare rock by a few decades of orange roughy trawling. One
study of coral "bycatch" taken by boats fishing for orange roughy
south of Australia in the early days of the fishery found that a metric
ton of coral was dragged to the surface for every 2.25 tonnes of roughy
caught.[13] How much was destroyed and left on the bottom we can
only speculate. But when Australian scientists compared seamounts
that had been trawled with those that had not, the contrast could not
have been more extreme. Untrawled seamounts were carpeted with a
near complete cover of corals and other invertebrates. Trawled seamounts were shocking in their sterility: exposed stark vistas of bare
rock, criss-crossed with the scars of repeated trawl passes.

The damage being wrought by deep-sea trawlers will last for generations, if indeed it can ever be repaired. Many of the largest corals
took hundreds or thousands of years to reach their present size. The
environmental organization Greenpeace in New Zealand used the
Freedom of Information Act there to force the release of photographs

taken onboard deepwater trawlers by fishery observers. They showed giant corals taller than a man and weighing hundreds of kilos being winched back into the sea by crane after coming up in the net.

Deep-sea fishing is more akin to mining than harvesting, and deep-sea fish, like coal or oil, are being extracted like nonrenewable resources. The huge vessels that fish the deep sea cost thousands of dollars a day to run. They have to fish at unsustainable rates simply to break even. There is no such thing as an industrial-scale deep-sea fishery that is economically viable *and* sustainable. If stocks were fished at sustainable rates, people would go broke. But the madness of deep-sea fishing goes beyond the mining of target fish stocks. Countless unmarketable species also fall victim to hook and net. Like the target species, they are highly susceptible to overfishing because they live life in the slow lane: prickly sharks with humped backs and glowing eyes; goblin sharks with strange unicorn horns; gulper eels that can swallow prey larger than themselves; giant single-celled protozoans—xenophyophores—large as footballs; jawless hagfishes

*Coral brought up by a New Zealand bottom trawler from around 1,000 meters deep (3,300 feet). This huge colony is certainly hundreds, perhaps more than a thousand years old. Photographed by Greenpeace activists protesting against the destruction of deep-sea habitats by trawlers. © Greenpeace/Malcolm Pullman.*

dripping with slime; tripod fish that stand on their fins. Many are disappearing unnoticed, their tenure on this planet soon to end without obituary or epitaph.

Since the 1970s, the world's seamount fisheries have been ruthlessly exploited for fast profits. The Soviet fleet cleaned out most Atlantic seamounts before any other country noticed what they were up to. For deepwater trawlers, as for eighteenth-century sealing captains who hunted the seas for undiscovered haul-outs, it pays to be first because the discoverer of the resource is also its destroyer. Not many years ago, the deep sea seemed more remote and less known than the moon. It is still the planet's last frontier for human expansion and appropriation, yet in these abyssal waters, we continue to play out our long-established pattern, eliminating the megafauna and ruining their habitats. Once again, and for the final time, trawlers are violating virgin wilderness in the sea, tearing up unseen forests and leveling unknown Yellowstone Parks. Giving evidence to the British Commission of Inquiry into the effects of trawling in 1883, Robert Smyth of Dunbar in Scotland said, "If the public in general knew more of the destruction [trawling] is likely to do if continued they would denounce it to be an evil system of catching fish."[14] His words are as true today as they were then.

*Part Three*

## The Once and Future Ocean

## — *Chapter 22* —

# No Place Left to Hide

S OMEWHERE OFF the West African coast, in a sea that is empty from horizon to horizon, a floating log bobs up and down with the passing waves. From above it is the only object in an endless spread of water, adrift and isolated. From beneath it is landmark and focus in the lives of countless fish and other animals. Shoals of tiny baitfish hang beneath the log, darting back and forth in nervous shimmering masses as it shifts with the waves. Jellyfish pulse in the gentle current, trailing curtains of tentacles among which juvenile fish shelter, looking like silver baubles. A school of skipjack tuna circles languidly in the water around the log, while shadowy forms of blue sharks lurk in the distance. A loggerhead turtle breaks the surface nearby to breathe and with ancient dewy eyes surveys the log for a moment. Unknown to the turtle, the log carries a satellite beacon that will guide a purseseine boat to this spot a few days later.

Nobody knows exactly why fish gather around floating objects in the open sea. It cannot be because the objects provide protection for the schools of baitfish that gather around them, for how much protection can a log or a mat of floating vegetation provide? Perhaps it is simply because they provide some reference point, however slight, in this boundless, seemingly featureless liquid world. Purse-seine boats

have long sought out floating logs and other objects around which to
set their nets, knowing that catches will be good.

It would not be long before somebody thought of putting their
own logs into the sea, but how to find them again in the trackless
waters of the high seas? Those far-sighted fishery scientists of the
1960s mentioned earlier, whose imaginations concocted the idea of
using submerged nuclear reactors to create upwellings, thought of a
way.[1] In 1964, just seven years after the first artificial satellite, *Sputnik
1*, was launched, they suggested attaching satellite positioning bea-
cons to logs that would float for a week or two concentrating fish
before the purse seiners returned for the bounty. In today's electronic
age, the technology they imagined is reality. Purse-seine boats now
seed the ocean with veritable forests of floating decoy logs and other
fish-aggregating devices to bring together scattered shoals of fish.
When they return, they scoop up the fish with ruthless efficiency, taking with them turtles, sharks, and dolphins—whatever happens to be
there. For some reason, logs preferentially attract juvenile tuna, so
their take even of the target species is wasteful. By catching young
tuna before they reach adulthood, purse seiners forgo much higher
catches for themselves later, and they are also denying these tuna the
chance to reproduce, putting future catches at risk. Where once the
vast canvas of the sea was great enough for fish to lose themselves in,
escaping capture, today even the high seas afford little refuge. New
technology has given old fishing methods a far more lethal edge.

The fishing industry has been lent a hand in the search for fish
from some surprising quarters. Sonar depth sensors and fish finders
were first introduced in the 1930s, but were much improved during
the Second World War. They work by beaming pulses of sound into
the water below the boat and recording the echoes from the seabed
and any shoals of fish in between. Sonar was further developed during
the Cold War when submarines skulked in foreign waters. The fishing industry gained an unexpected dividend when East–West relations improved and military technologies were declassified. Apart
from enhanced fish detection capability, sonar is now used to create
visual images of the structure of the bottom. Modern multibeam
side-scan sonar equipment can map the seafloor in exquisite detail.
In just a few weeks, a ship fitted out with this equipment can map

hundreds of square kilometers of the bottom, revealing every crease, wrinkle, and boulder. Geologists have adopted the technology with great enthusiasm, embarking on a mapping spree not seen since the nineteenth and the early twentieth centuries when cartographers systematically mapped the contours of land. In the United States, for example, the U.S. Geological Survey is publishing maps that give fishers a new look at familiar terrain, allowing them to pick out previously unsuspected seamounts and canyons. Coupled with high-precision global positioning systems (GPS), another part of the peace dividend from the end of the Cold War, fishers can now land hooks or drag nets through places that were much too risky to fish in the past, penetrating deep into the ocean's last refuges from fishing. Where previously nets were almost invariably lost, catches can be taken in relative safety. The large catches yielded from these former de facto fishing refuges make it worth the residual risk. A Gulf of Maine fisherman describes the benefits new technology brought him:

> This stuff has turned the ocean into a glass table. The stuff's so good you can find [some pinnacle], which would be completely surrounded by cod—cod just about clinging to it—and which before you would have steered clear of for fear you'd lose your net, and you can fish it so closely, going around and around, that you can pick virtually every last fish off the thing.[2]

Not surprisingly, the fishing industry is impatient, wanting seabed maps faster than government agencies can produce them. Private companies are weighing in, selling the secrets of the seabed for profit. For a price, they will map the seabed wherever a captain desires. Most fishing vessels carry their own bottom-imaging devices these days, albeit less sophisticated ones than advanced side-scan sonar. The bridge of a modern fishing vessel more closely resembles the cockpit of a jumbo jet than that of a boat. Sonar systems onboard show the shape and texture of the seabed in real time, allowing fishers to choose the best fishing sites and avoid obstructions. New computer software allows captains to "fly" trawl nets, with net-based sensors beaming up data on the spread of the net, its fullness, and what lies ahead of it. Some nets are equipped with powered units to adjust gape and trim. Skilled captains can steer their nets toward shoals of fish they can "see" as if they were riding on the net itself.

Longline fisheries have also evolved rapidly in the last half century. The nineteenth-century longliners who worked the Grand Banks and fought to keep trawlers off their lines used tarred hemp twine. Their response to declining catches was to set longer lines with more hooks. But after the Second World War, their gear experienced the first major technological revolution in over two hundred years. In 1958 the DuPont Corporation invented monofilament fishing line. Monofilament is made from a chemical polymer and was much stronger and more durable than traditional materials, as well as being translucent and thus harder for fish to see. The new lines triggered a phase shift in fishing, enabling fishers to set longer, more lethal lines than ever before. High-seas fishing fleets swiftly adopted the gear, hastening the decline of newly discovered fish populations.

More recently, longliners have benefited from the same high-technology electronics revolution that has transformed trawl fishing. Lynda Greenlaw, a swordfish boat captain who worked the high seas off eastern North America, describes in *The Hungry Ocean* the changes she saw as new technology was adopted:

> Finding a piece of water, and swordfishing in general, has changed considerably since I first started with Alden aboard the *Walter Leeman* the summer following my freshman year of college. Technological progress manifesting itself in marine electronics is responsible for what has amounted to a revolution in the industry. The *Walter Leeman* had no GPS, no down temp bird [temperature sensor], no Doppler, no color sounder, no video plotter, and no beeper buoys. We had no monofilament fishing line; instead, we were equipped with a twisted, three strand, tarred type of mainline. Snaps and hooks were secured to leaders by knots; we had no need for crimps. Alden Leeman had a sixth sense when it came to finding fish, and needed only minimal electronics. He could smell fish, and often set out in a piece of water simply because it "felt right." As much time as I spent with Alden learning how to catch swordfish, the most important lesson could not be taught. Alden's fish savvy never rubbed off on me.
>
> The most successful fishermen of my generation are pseudo-scientists, fishing gear engineers, and electronics wizards. Rather than flying by the seat of our pants, as Alden did, we study data and base decisions on statistics. We rely heavily on technology and are perfectionists about bait and tackle. I couldn't "feel" my way out of a paper

bag, but with all of the *Hannah Boden*'s state-of-the-art equipment, I am always confident of exceeding even the best of what Alden accomplished in his many years of longlining.[3]

Swordfish fishing as practiced by Greenlaw is sophisticated indeed. These animals, like other large predators, seek out the most productive places in the oceans to feed. Off the east coast of North America, they migrate in spring to the convergence zone between the warm Gulf Stream current flowing from the south and the cold Labrador Current coming from the north. If you can find the places where warm and cold currents wrap around each other, where high nutrient levels in the cold water combine with warm conditions to stimulate rampant plankton growth and that in turn feeds swarms of tiny baitfish, you will find the fish. Old-time fishers like Alden Leeman read the signs from the water to decide where to set their gear. They watched for circling birds and feeding dolphins, scrutinized the color of the sea, judged the height and set of the waves, and felt for subtle changes in air temperature and wind. Today's fleet relies on a daily fax or e-mail from the U.S. National Oceanic and Atmospheric Administration showing satellite images of sea surface temperature. Captains use GPS to navigate to places with the steepest gradients in temperature, and when there they tow depth sensors to measure the temperature of different water layers to identify the perfect depth to set their gear. In this they are also guided by other onboard electronics, described by Greenlaw:

> The Doppler is the most advanced piece of electronics aboard the *Hannah Boden* . . . . The Doppler is used to detect and define thermoclines, layers of water, certain layers being more abundant than others in fish. The layers are quite distinct; imagine blankets of varying thickness heaped over a bed. But now imagine the blankets in motion. Each separate layer has its own temperature and current; once the fisherman determines which layer is most productive, the Doppler is used to keep track of it.[4]

Greenlaw's swordfish bait also used technology once not even dreamed of. To each leader, the sideline that carries a hook, she attaches a chemical lightstick. In the dark of night, their cool unearthly glow attracts the fish. They also attract loggerhead turtles to the hooks. But for boat captains struggling to make a living, anything that gives you an edge seems worth using. Radio beepers attached to the longlines signal their position, so there is less gear loss than in the past when simple floats were used. They also allow more gear to be fished because of reduced time spent looking for sets.

With the assistance of her constellation of electronics, Greenlaw was a highly successful swordfish boat captain, outfishing most of her rivals. But even with the latest gadgetry, catching fish was still hit-and-miss:

> The electronics are not always foolproof but can help me avoid some disastrous sets. The most frustrating sets are the ones that look perfect: a tight break on the surface and below, deep tide, blue water, birds and bait fish—but no swordfish on the haulback. No matter what electronics a captain has and how much know-how, you can't catch 'em if they're not there. And the only way to know whether the fish are at home or not is to put the gear in the water. I guess that's why what I do is called "fishing." If it was easy, we would refer to it as "catching," and there would be a lot more people doing it. Then, perhaps, there would be reason for the conservationists and swordfish rights activists to advocate putting an end to commercial fishing. Alden once told me that he believed fishermen using only hooks and harpoons could never wipe out any species of fish that reproduce by spawning, such as swordfish. And in seventeen years of swordfishing, I have seen no evidence of depletion.[5]

Greenlaw failed to see evidence of depletion only because her ever-growing battery of instruments took her direct to the last concentrations of swordfish. Her catch rates remained high, like those of Canadian cod fishers on the Grand Banks before the collapse, because she could chase the fish into their last strongholds. In the 1930s and 1940s, swordfish abounded south to Long Island and beyond. But as fishers worked these regions, the fish thinned and their range shifted north. Ecologists now recognize a contraction in geographic range of a species as one of the effects of severe population reduction. Animals or plants at the periphery of a species' range struggle harder to make a living than those at the center where conditions are most favorable. When times get tough, they are the first to disappear. Greenlaw also overlooked another change in the fishery. The average weight of fish she caught was around 45 kilograms (100 pounds). In the 1960s, it was over 100 kilograms (220 pounds). New fishing technologies mask declines in target species, often blinding people to the consequences of their actions.

Many supposedly traditional fishing technologies have also changed with time, making them more deadly and fish ever more vulnerable, even in areas that are meant to offer fish some protection. In 1962, the sea around the Caribbean island of St. John in the U.S. Virgin Islands was added to the Virgin Islands National Park, which encompassed half of the island's land area. At the time, nobody saw any reason to restrict fishing using traditional methods like fish traps, although spearfishing was banned. Antillean fish traps are Z-shaped mesh pots with one or two mesh funnels set in the sides through which fish can enter. They are often baited with fish, shellfish, coconuts, or bread. Fish investigating the trap from the outside follow the mesh as it curves into the funnel and soon find themselves inside. Although some fish do escape, most are unable to find their way out again. The design of this trap was probably imported from Africa with slaves, since they closely resemble traps in use there. Traditionally, traps were constructed from a framework of mangrove roots and branches lashed together with twine made from plant fibers. Over this, fishers wove a mesh from palm fronds, creating a lattice with a mesh size of 2 to 4 centimeters (0.8 to 1.6 inches). Small traps are generally set for a period of a few hours before being lifted on the same fishing trip, but large traps are typically left for several days to a week before checking.

The expanded park around St. John was renamed the Virgin Islands National Park and Biosphere Reserve. A basic feature of biosphere reserves is that they are parks designed to include people and the constructive uses they make of the environment, rather than exclude them. At the time the park was created, only a few families fished the reefs around St. John. They used traditional traps, although by this time mangrove roots and palm fronds were giving way to chicken wire stretched over a welded steel frame.

Over the years, the island economy developed, and there was a creeping shift in the fishery. Fishers moved from catching to feed themselves to catching for the tourist market. They bought larger boats equipped with outboard engines and set increasing numbers of traps to keep pace with demand. By the 1990s, families who set ten traps when the park was established now set hundreds. Not only did fishing intensity rise, but so did problems of ghost fishing—which occurs when fishing gear is lost but continues to catch and kill fish. When modern traps are lost, as they often are, they continue fishing for much longer than traps made of palm fronds, killing fish for months. Fish traps are surprisingly good catching devices. Like large-scale industrial gears, they reduce populations of large-bodied, predatory fish that are the most valuable and the most vulnerable. At high fishing intensities, they eliminate species like Nassau and goliath groupers. Since traps are unselective, catching upward of a hundred species in the Caribbean, their impacts are apparent in virtually every family of fish inhabiting the reef. By the late 1990s, park staff realized the reefs were in trouble. In a frank assessment, they concluded that fish communities in the park were no better than in unprotected waters nearby. For all the appearance of protection over the nearly forty years it had been in place, the park had offered no refuge at all from the impacts of fishing.[6]

In the Pacific, there have been similar modern adaptations of old fishing methods that have extended the reach of fishers and diminished refuges for fish. Bumphead parrot fish are the largest of all parrot fish, growing up to 1.3 meters long (52 inches) and weighing as much as 46 kilograms (101 pounds). Large individuals have prominent bulging foreheads that give them their name. They are one of the few fish on reefs that eat living coral, biting off branches and excavating deep gouges in coral heads with their parrotlike beaks. The coral then gets passed through a grinding mill in the fish's pharynx, where it is crushed to pieces prior to digestion of the tissue layer. Bumpheads move across the reef in loose groups. A diver lucky enough to have encountered this animal will never forget the sight of a bumphead shoal hoving into view, a muscular mass of green-brown flesh charging across the reef. All at once, as on some unseen signal, they descend onto a beautiful coral patch and with clashing and grinding beaks smash it to pieces.

Bumpheads are wary animals by day, never taking the hook and never letting divers get close enough to spear them. But at night, they retreat to shallow, sandy lagoons where they rest in groups on the seabed. Fishers in the island of Samoa discovered their nighttime vulnerability and set forth after dark with torches, snorkel gear, and spears. Soon they adopted scuba gear, giving the fish no chance. Chuck Birkeland, a University of Hawaii professor, after having witnessed bumpheads slaughtered in Samoa, commented, "Spear-guns and nightlights are as lethal to bumphead parrot fish today as rifles and railroads were for American Plains bison in the nineteenth century."[7]

Bumpheads in other parts of the Pacific are suffering, too, now that the new catching technology has spread. In Fiji, for example, bump-heads are almost extinct. Like other large-bodied species, they are especially vulnerable to depletion by fishing because their rate of pop-ulation growth is too slow to compensate for any but the lightest fish-ing intensities.

Even recreational anglers are beating up the high-technology trail, with further devastating consequences. A day spent angling is no longer the easy jaunt into the countryside that it was in Isaak Walton's day. I was an enthusiastic angler when I was a boy. Packing lunch, a rod, and a few home-tied flies, I would hike into the hills to some shady pool or river bend to try my luck and while away time. I was probably the most unsuccessful angler ever, catching only a single rainbow trout in three years, and that was hooked in the gill as I reeled in for another cast. Perhaps I would have benefited from some of the technological aids employed by today's anglers. Walking the banks of the River Ouse in my home city of York, I see them struggle to reach their fishing spots, dragging giant coolers stuffed with gear. Too heavy to carry, anglers wheel their kit on trolleys while bent under the weight of bags containing at least ten different rods. Like commercial fishing, recreational angling is an escalating conflict between people and fish.

Many recreational fishers now employ sophisticated technology in the pursuit of fish. New high-strength fluorocarbon lines are thinner than monofilament and have the same refractive index as water, mak-ing them virtually invisible to fish. Carbon fiber rods are more sensi-tive to movements at the end of the line. Even poor anglers can cast modern lightweight lines as far as the best of thirty years ago, reach-ing those once inaccessible spots. Computer modeling software has enabled the development of lures that behave in the water almost like real fish, sculling up and down, nodding or bending, and even emitting pops and crackles as they go. The latest employ holograms to make them appear more three-dimensional and "alive" than traditional lures.

For anglers who fish from boats, there is even more technological support. Walleye fishers in the Great Lakes, for example, use GPS, sonar fish finders, depth sensors, and aerial imagery to build a picture of where the fish are. Some even have onboard video cameras that can be lowered over the side to relay pictures of fish and habitat to a screen on the boat. This is no longer "sport" fishing, for the fish have little chance against such uneven odds.

These technological marvels are the result of a process that characterizes nearly every fishery. As stocks are depleted, and catches fall, ingenious fishers arm themselves with ever-better equipment to catch fish. Steam trawlers vastly increased catching power in the late nineteenth century but became victims of their own success by the mid-1920s. Catch per unit of fishing effort declined by 24 percent between 1906 and 1937, despite a short-lived boom after the First World War.[8] Faced with falling catches, fishers made a key modification to trawl nets in the 1920s that increased catching power by 25 percent. They moved the trawl doors that keep the net open off the net itself, placing them closer to the boat on lengthened wire bridles (the cables that towed the trawl). In their new location, the doors held the net open better, helped herd fish into it, and allowed the use of bigger nets. Fishers also made another change. They added steel-and-rubber discs to the ground rope that is dragged over the seabed. With these rollers, or bobbins, the net could ride over obstructions allowing boats to tow in areas of bottom that were formerly too rough to fish.

The prominent British fisheries scientist Michael Graham described in 1943 the process of technological creep in fisheries:

> In the North Sea in 1909–1913 the average yield of all fish, other than herring, caught by fishermen of every nationality, was 434,000 tons. By 1928–32 it was 428,000 tons—a little less than before. . . . These figures show that all the skill and anxiety of the modern North Sea trawler crew only yields the world what could be taken before with much less trouble. . . .

Indeed one of the strangest and most sardonic effects is on the position of the inventor. His invention is first hailed as just what is required, to remedy the fallen catch per ship with the old gear. The novelty produces excellent trips of fish at first. Those who use it say, "You must be up to date". But soon everyone has it; and then, in a year or two, it reduces the stock to a new low level. The yield goes back to no more than before, perhaps less; but the fisherman must still use the new gear. He was better off without it; but owing to the depleted stock, he could not manage without it now. He needs the additional fishing power that it gives, in order merely to stay where he was before it came in, so he has to accept the expense.[9]

Technological advance goes hand in hand with the spread and expansion of fishing grounds. The bobbins described by Graham were small discs up to about 20 centimeters diameter (8 inches). Behind the ground rope, "tickler chains" scared fish off the bottom and into the net. Together they allowed fishers to penetrate areas of rough seabed formerly avoided. Before the introduction of bobbins, rough areas were refuges from exploitation where adult fish could live with little risk of capture. They supported large and highly fecund animals. Areas of rough bottom were also recognized as nurseries for juvenile fish of many species, including cod, halibut, ling, and rockfish. Once these were opened to fishing, they hastened the decline of populations. The opening up of new grounds continues today in the deep sea using nets fronted by steel balls 60 to 80 centimeters across (2 feet to 2 feet 8 inches). These bloated descendants of early bobbins allow nets to penetrate rocky, coral-filled canyons, and thunder across the reefs and ridges of the deep. Trawls are towed by boats whose 10,000-horsepower engines can drag rocks (or reefs) 3 meters in diameter (10 feet). The nets are held open by trawl doors that weigh 5 metric tonnes and are aptly named "Canyonbusters" by the manufacturers.

The twentieth century was a time of technological revolution for fisheries—faster boats, bigger nets, stronger materials, better weather forecasts, visuals beamed from the sea floor. But for all their science and gadgetry, today's fishing captains are no more successful than their nineteenth-century forebears. They are chasing resources in decline, and each new technology presses nature harder, ratcheting down populations to new lows. Every advance into previously unfished terrain shrinks the last refuges for fish. The battle between people and fish has become very sophisticated and extremely uneven. We have left no place for fish to hide. Left unchecked, this arms race will have no winners. Fishers will put themselves out of business when their target species run out. The beauty and plenitude of the oceans that has inspired countless generations of humanity will have been ruined.

But it doesn't have to end like that.

# Chapter 23

# Barbequed Jellyfish or
# Swordfish Steak?

———

SIGNIFICANT moment in the history of world fisheries came in 1988, but at the time it passed unnoticed. For all of human history, excepting a few blips due to war and pestilence, the global fish catch has expanded. The rocketing growth in fish catch of the last two centuries leveled off in the 1980s. Since then total landings remained roughly constant, or so people thought, bringing sparse relief amid burgeoning evidence of trouble. Even if some stocks had declined or collapsed, at least the overall fish supply was being maintained, it seemed. In 2001, even this comfort evaporated when scientists from the University of British Columbia discovered that Chinese catches were being systematically overreported by officials keen to meet national production targets.[1] They noticed that catches reported from the South China Sea could not be supported by the biological productivity there. When the figures were corrected to the true, lower catch levels, they revealed that global fish landings went into reverse in 1988, despite undiminished growth in catching power. Since then overall landings have declined by over half a million tonnes per year.[2]

Extrapolating the current downward trend suggests that availability of fish will fall to around 70 percent of today's level by 2050. At a time when people more than ever appreciate the health benefits of eating fish, supply is dwindling. Nutritionists from the World Health Organization recommend we eat 200 to 300 grams (7 to 11 ounces) of fish per week. Today's world fish landings only barely meet this need for people alive today, although in reality much of the fish caught is fed to livestock and many people are denied fish protein. However, if world landings continue to decline as predicted, and taking into account projected human population growth from six billion to around ten billion people by 2050, there will be enough fish to meet this need for only half of all people.

Aggregate catch figures, as gloomy as they appear, conceal the full scale of carnage in the sea. The pageants of local losses played out in previous chapters can be sketched as generalities on the world stage. Fisheries first target large and high-value species—generally predators—moving to other areas or switching to the next most profitable species as stocks decline. Fishers respond to falling catches by escalating fishing power, developing ever better ways of finding fish and extracting them from their dwindling refuges. Rising fish prices and government subsidies prop up ailing fisheries as stocks fall. The effects are loss of predators and a shift toward catching species we once shunned, termed "fishing down the food web." Ecosystems where once legions of sharks, porpoises, and seabirds pursued unimaginable numbers of smaller fish have been stripped of their predators, and the smaller animals have become our prey. Daniel Pauly, of the University of British Columbia, who first described the phenomenon, memorably said that we are eating today what our grandparents used as bait.[3] The prime fish of their day dined on the flesh of other fish, while many of the animals we eat now have fed on plankton or scratch a living sifting "dirt" on the seabed. Today we pursue prawns, crab, and lobster where once hungry cod held sway. We vacuum sand eels, capelin, and squid from the sea, bypassing the animals that once consumed them and were in turn eaten by people. Pauly warned that in due course we will end up consuming plankton directly, drawn from seas without fish.

*Illustration of the process of fishing down marine food webs. The arrow shows the trajectory of passing time. In the past (to the left), ecosystems supported many predatory fish living in rich and complex habitats. At present (middle), predator populations are much depleted and complex bottom habitats have been replaced in many places by sand and mud. If present trends continue (to the right), we may end up eating jellyfish, because there will be few large fish left. Courtesy of Daniel Pauly.*

Pauly and his colleagues have reconstructed the path of compression of food webs worldwide since 1950. They used catch statistics reported by countries to the United Nations Food and Agriculture Organization. Based on what it eats, they assigned each species caught a value for its trophic level, that is, the level in the food web from which a species derives its nourishment. Plants—seaweeds and tiny drifting phytoplankton—are the first trophic level, scoring 1. Herbivores are the next level, scoring 2, and they are eaten by carnivores, making up trophic levels 3, 4, and 5 (because big carnivores eat smaller carnivores in trophic levels below them). The top predators of the sea, scoring 5 or close to it, are animals like swordfish, killer whales, great white sharks, and people. Most animals take food from a variety of trophic levels. We are omnivores, for example, eating plants as well as animals from all other trophic levels. The score assigned to each species or group of species (where catch statistics were aggregated) reflects this diversity of diet. Pauly then multiplied values for trophic level by the proportion of the total catch each species or group made up. This gave a single figure that showed the average trophic level of species in the catch for a given year and region.

Since 1950 the average trophic level of fish in landings has fallen, in the North Atlantic, for example, dropping from around 3.5 to 2.8 by the late 1990s. Perhaps not coincidentally, the average trophic level of catches was lower at the outset in the Mediterranean than anywhere else, starting around 3.1. The length of food chains—that is, the number of links between plants and the top predators that are present— varies between seas according to their productivity. Energy is lost at each trophic level due to respiration and reproduction. Only around 10 percent of energy consumed by one level is passed to the next when those organisms are in turn eaten, so more productive ecosystems can support more trophic levels. The Mediterranean is not highly productive, but it has also been commercially fished for longer than any other sea, and probably experienced fishing down the food web earlier than other regions. Roman, Greek, Egyptian, Assyrian, and Jewish fishers plied their trade there more than two thousand years ago.[4]

From the perspective of fisheries production, smaller populations of fish are not necessarily bad; on the contrary. A central tenet of fisheries science states that reducing the size of fish populations will enhance productivity. Fishery scientists worked out in the 1930s that thinning fish populations could boost population growth by easing competition for food and space, processes that restrict growth at high population densities. A Danish fishery scientist, C.G.J. Petersen, is credited with originating the idea.[5] He noticed that plaice catches in the Kattegat region of the Baltic Sea had much improved between the 1870s and 1890s. Fishers told him that when they began catching plaice in the 1870s, there were many large, lean, and unpalatable fish around. By the mid-1890s, catches were dominated by small plaice, and big fish had become scarce. The old and tired gave way to lithe and succulent young fish. Lower fish densities and supplanting of old by young boost population growth in two ways. First, at lower densities, there is more food around per fish. Second, almost all fisheries preferentially remove large animals. Over time the average size of fish diminishes, and young fish grow faster than hoary old-timers. A population dominated by young, vigorously growing animals will be more productive than one where big, old, fat fish prevail. E.S. Russell described the effect with Petersen's plaice and other fish in 1942:

> [U]p to a certain point, fishing is good for the stock. It clears out the accumulated stock of old slow-growing fish, enables the remainder to grow more quickly, and makes room for the oncoming broods so that they can survive in greater numbers and grow more rapidly. A stock under the influence of fishing utilises the available food more efficiently, through increased rate of growth, and renews itself more rapidly.[6]

Fishery scientists called this population growth spurt caused by fishing the "surplus yield." The relationship between surplus yield and fishing pressure is humpbacked: it rises with fishing effort, but there

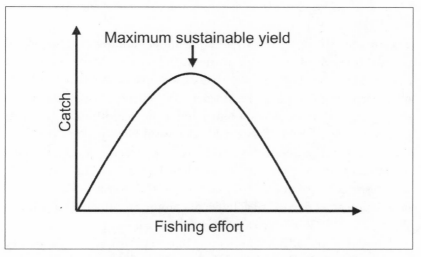

*The typical relationship between the size of the catch and the level of fishing effort expended. The maximum yield that is sustainable over the long term is usually assumed to be achieved when the exploited population has been reduced to half of its unfished size.*

comes a point when more intensive fishing meets with falling catches. The greatest surplus yield, termed maximum sustainable yield, could be obtained, according to the fishery models, by reducing a population to half of its unexploited size. This idea soon became the guiding principle of fisheries management, and maximum sustainable yield its emblem. If we could only match fishing pressure to the level that would produce the maximum sustainable yield, fisheries would thrive. Since then, the concept has exerted a hegemonic grip over fisheries science that is proving extremely difficult to loosen, despite serious shortcomings.

Experience has a bitter taste in fisheries management. The goal of sustaining yield over the long-term has proven elusive and is too often sacrificed for short-term gain. For most species, fisheries have pushed population sizes far below target levels for maximum sustainable yield, greatly diminishing production. E.W.L. Holt correctly perceived the problem as early as 1894:

> There is a consensus of experience that trawling at first improves the quality of plaice, but that this process may be carried out with such hearty good-will that the fish incur the danger of being improved off the face of this earth, is an axiom that does not find such universal acceptance.[7]

Recent research has given us a better understanding of unexploited population sizes, which often turn out to be much higher than were assumed by fisheries scientists. Historical impacts on fish populations have been far greater than most scientists believed. Today, many fish stocks languish at between a tenth and a thousandth of their unexploited numbers. Even Thomas Huxley would be forced to conclude that the great fisheries of the world have not just come under the heel of humanity, they have nearly been crushed by it. This systematic underestimation of pristine populations has led to estimates of target population sizes needed to achieve maximum sustainable yield being set too low, thus leading to a greater risk of population collapses.

There is an old adage that doctors bury their mistakes. But fishery managers and politicians have long taken comfort from the idea that mistakes in fisheries are simple to reverse. Ease back on fishing pressure, the surplus yield curve says, and populations will rebound and catches rise once more. In some fisheries this has proven true. The

overfished Pacific halibut, for example, recovered in the early twentieth century when an international agreement was reached to scale
back fishing effort. Northern populations of herring bounced back
after the 1970s moratorium in Europe. Peruvian anchoveta struggled
back after a spectacular collapse in the early 1970s and again in the
mid-1980s. Striped bass rallied in eastern North America in the 1980s.
But for every case of recovery, there are several counterexamples. The
Baltic Scanian herring disappeared hundreds of years ago and has
never come back. North Atlantic halibut, once a mainstay of line fishers, crashed in the nineteenth century and has been a bit player ever
since. Nassau grouper once held sway on Caribbean reefs, but in most
countries are scarcely seen today. The days when Gulf of California
waters boiled with spawning runs of totoaba are over, and the majestic
bluefin tuna has lost its crown in the Atlantic.

Jeff Hutchings, from Canada's Dalhousie University, looked for
evidence of recovery in ninety different commercially exploited fish
populations after they had declined by between 13 and 90 percent.[8]
Only a handful made a full recovery when fishing was reduced. He
looked at long-term recovery success for twenty-five populations for
which there were at least fifteen years of postdecline data available.
Only 12 percent made a full recovery, all of them small, open-water
species from the herring family. Forty percent showed no recovery
at all.

The most notorious example of nonrecovery is that of cod on the
Grand Banks, which was reduced to less than 1 percent of its unexploited population size. All kinds of theories have been advanced to
explain why cod did not rebound after the fishing moratorium was
declared in 1992. Some argue that the conversion of capelin shoals
into fishmeal prevents recovery because capelin are a staple food of
cod. But the offshore capelin fishery was closed in 1991, and nearshore
catches have been reduced in recent years. On the other hand, some
scientists point to the fact that capelin are predators of cod larvae, so
too many capelin may hold back recovery. Fishing them could be
good for cod. Others, notably seal hunters, say there are too many
harp seals and they are eating young cod. Their views have fueled calls
for increased culls of seal pups. Certainly, research surveys suggest
that mortality of the few juvenile cod around is extremely high, but

nobody is sure why. One reason, perhaps, is that cod are still being caught and killed by other fisheries on the Grand Banks. It is impossible to avoid catching all cod unless you stop fishing altogether. Scallopers, crab fishers, and prawn trawlers still work the banks, as do others. And then, of course, there is that old standby when all other explanations fail: the weather was wrong for cod.

Fishing seems to have changed the rules of the game on the Grand Banks, transforming cod from a force of nature to mere fish. The structure of the ecosystem has shifted, and it is not clear whether the past can be created anew. John Steinbeck understood this when he saw shrimp fishers scraping bottom in the Gulf of California in 1940: "[I]t is not true that a species thus attacked comes back. The disturbed balance often gives a new species ascendancy and destroys forever the old relationships."[9]

Bottom trawling in all its forms has done untold damage to seabed habitats. It has ripped up complex habitats built by slow-growing invertebrates over millennia. It has rearranged geology, grinding down rocky shelves, smoothing sand waves, planing mounds, and obliterating reefs. In smoothing out three-dimensional relief and removing upright animals, trawling has rendered the bottom a more hostile environment for species that depend on complexity. The transformation of the bottom by trawlers may be one reason Atlantic halibut has failed to recover, and it contributes to the high mortality of young cod on the Grand Banks.

We are belatedly realizing that fishing has effects on populations of target species that may be hard to reverse. Before cod stocks collapsed, George Rose of Newfoundland's Memorial University used sonar equipment to study shoals of cod massing to spawn at the edge of Newfoundland's continental shelf.[10] Pulses of sound bounced off fish allowed Rose to see details of the size and shape of shoals and even to resolve individual fish. Fish massed at the edge of the shelf in shoals tens of kilometers wide and consisting of hundreds of millions of fish. Fish rose in columns from the main body of these shoals to spawn, with paired males and females releasing eggs and sperm together. When spawning was complete, the fish headed across the shelf in mixed bodies of adult and immature cod. They followed deep channels cut through the shelf, keeping to fingers of warm oceanic water sitting below the colder overlying sea. Large, old fish led the shoals inshore. Fishing wiped out these scouts, as Rose called them. Perhaps recovery of cod is held back, then, because young fish can no longer find their way to spawning sites. This could certainly be true of the Nassau grouper in the Caribbean. Every year these animals gathered to spawn at traditional mating sites, some traveling tens to more than a hundred kilometers to reach the sites. Aggregations numbered tens of thousands of fish. In a pattern repeated across the region, when fishers discovered a site, it was fished to exhaustion in only a few years. Nobody knows how Nassau groupers found spawning sites. Once lost, though, there is little evidence that spawning aggregations can recover. With the experienced fish gone, the few young around may never find these places.

In the Gulf of Maine, testimony from old fishers suggests that cod once spawned in traditional, nearshore spawning aggregations.[11] Almost every significant bay along the New England coast had its own cod that would arrive to spawn at predicable times. Ipswich Bay in Massachusetts once played host to vast shoals of cod that arrived in late winter. The American fishery scientist Henry Bigelow wrote of it in 1953:

> The Ipswich Bay region, where large schools of ripe cod gather in winter and spring, is probably the most important center of production for the inner part of the Gulf of Maine north of Cape Ann, but this ground, like the Massachusetts Bay spawning ground, is limited to a rather small and well defined area. . . . [Here] the cod congregate . . . at the spawning season, in great numbers. During the spring of 1879, for example, when fishing was less intensive than it is at present, and when the cod may have been correspondingly more plentiful, more than 11,000,000 pounds of cod [5,000 metric tons], mostly spawning fish, were taken on the Ipswich Bay ground alone by local fishermen.[12]

Old-time fishers recalled how local spawning aggregations of cod failed one after another, bay by bay, along the coast during the 1930s to the 1950s, suggesting that these had been local populations homing to their own bays. Study of genetic differences among bay populations of Canadian cod support this view, suggesting that what was once seen as a single, amorphous cod stock is actually a mosaic of more local populations.[13] Many local populations have been eliminated by overfishing, and prospects for their recovery are poor. In the North Sea, for example, study of preserved remains of cod caught in the 1950s from near Flamborough Head on the Yorkshire coast indicate a distinct population that has since disappeared.[14]

It isn't just the relentless intensity of fishing today that is harming the oceans, it is the destructive and wasteful way in which we fish. In landing 80 million tonnes or so of wild fish a year, fishers throw away another 16 to 40 million tonnes. The uncertainty over the exact amount discarded is because few countries consider it important enough to warrant the expense of collecting accurate figures. The best guess that scientists have come up with is that a quarter to a third of all animals caught are simply tossed back into the sea, most of them dead or dying. If statistics on discards are hard to find, estimates of how much is killed below water but never brought on deck are even more difficult to come by. Videos of bottom trawls in action, and study of the seabed after the passage of trawls, show that many animals that escape capture are injured or killed. Ghost fishing by lost gear can also be severe. Michael Dwyer joined a hellish deep-sea gill-netting trip to northern Labrador in 1998. He wrote of his experience in *Sea of Heartbreak,* the most chilling account of destructive fishing I have ever read. His descriptions both reveal the indiscriminate waste of fish killed as bycatch and highlight just how much fishing gear is lost, to continue killing fish unseen at the bottom of the sea:

> The past four days and nights offshore had not been profitable. We had spent endless marrow-freezing hours on the lurching bridge searching for buoys in the foulest of conditions. And yet more hours toiling to pull gear that yielded little number one turbot but seemed full to bursting with other sea creatures, including a dozen ground sharks and what appeared to me to be squadrons of manta rays.
>
> To add salt to the wounds, one fleet [of nets] had broken free after we had battled back twenty nets. We lost fifty nets and we spent the rest of the day in a futile attempt to find the southern end.
>
> Another fleet parted on the very next haul. Wayne knew the webbing was snagged on the bottom. The wheel spun around another ragged end and suddenly fifty nets were gone.
>
> The fishing gear is designed, made and set in a deadly efficient way. Set like a fence across the bottom, the webbing eventually fills with sea creatures and "lies down". Crabs, the scrubbing action from contact

with the seafloor and time serve eventually to consume and break down the sea creatures. When this happens the nets rise up again and fish indiscriminately. They fill up and lie down, over and over, forever. Stories have been told of draggers finding old, lost gear and the nets are filled with skeletons of every kind. As horrible as it is, it's legal and it's a common form of commercial fishing.[15]

Dwyer describes the horror of pulling in a net that had been left out too long:

> I tried not to let the smell of rotting fish and sea sponges make me too sick. Often the floodgates clogged with the dead. The picking table piled high with tangled webbing. Production was at a snail's pace. We had rock crabs by the hundreds, chimère [chimaera[16]] by the score. Parts of the rocky bottom came round the wheel with the nets—hard coral fragments in all their colors, shades, shapes and sizes. Every piece had to be picked out because even a small fragment could tangle up three or four nets as they were being set. It was a sea of heartbreak.[17]

At the end of the trip, the fishers simply threw all their used gillnets into the sea. While this practice was illegal, it was unwittingly encouraged by Canadian government subsidies that gave fishers nets almost for free. A recent study of deep-sea fishing in the North Atlantic for sharks and monkfish suggests that some 5,800 to 8,700 kilometers (3,600 to 5,400 miles) of gillnet are in constant contact with the bottom there.[18] Over 1,250 kilometers (780 miles) of nets are lost or discarded every year—nets left to fish on and on, unknown and unattended.

Modern fishing materials are highly durable. Monofilament and plastics will take centuries to degrade. Like the *Flying Dutchman*, condemned to sail the sea forever, rafts of lost and discarded nets and ropes drift on the high seas for decades. They accumulate in the same oceanic zones where currents converge and attract pelagic megafauna to feed. Guided to such convergence zones by satellite data on currents, observers from the United States National Oceanic and Atmospheric Administration have found gyres that are mass graveyards for fishing gear, including drift nets lost or abandoned before the 1992 United Nations ban on this gear. Some of these nets remain lethal, entangling turtles, whales, birds, and fish.

There is a troubling twist in the tale of the depletion of fisheries.

With their domestic fisheries in steep decline, rather than address problems at home, many developed nations have sought new fishing grounds farther afield. The spread of fisheries to new places over time as stocks are depleted is a familiar pattern. But with nowhere else to go in their own waters, countries have looked for new grounds in the national waters of developing nations. West African countries were particularly appealing targets, as the waters of many are enriched by seasonal upwelling. Their domestic fleets are too small and unsophisticated to fully exploit their resources. The European Union and several other nations, including Japan, Taiwan, and South Korea, have vigorously pursued "access agreements" with developing nations in the Atlantic, the Indian, and the Pacific oceans. For a fee, these agreements give paying nations the right to fish in another country's waters.

In theory, access agreements are good for everybody. If developing nations lack the capacity to catch fish in their own waters, it may make sense to let others do so if some of the proceeds accrue to the host country. Managed well, fish stocks are renewable resources, and the benefits of fishing will accrue year after year. To a pragmatist interested in the short term, unexploited fish stocks are wasted opportunities, and access agreements can bring developing countries much-needed hard currency. The problem is that access agreements are generally deeply unfair. The terms currently offered by the European Union value fish far too cheaply, as judged by prices paid to vessels for the catch, for example, so nations are being cheated of the real value of their resources. Sadly, developing countries sign up to iniquitous agreements partly because they desperately need hard currency to service foreign debts, but also because corrupt politicians welcome kickbacks from the deals.

If this were all that was wrong with access agreements, it would be too much, but there is more. Many place no limits on the size of the catches that can be taken but only on the number of boats that can fish. This has had the perverse effect of creating a construction boom for giant fishing vessels. The *Atlantic Dawn,* for example, is an Irish vessel that at the time of its construction in 2000 was the largest fishing boat in the world. It was fêted in its home country as a symbol of a rejuvenated national fishing industry. The *Atlantic Dawn* weighs over

14,000 tonnes and is 144 meters long (473 feet). Its purse seines can gulp giant schools of fish within their 1-kilometer circumference and 150-meter depth span (3,300 x 500 feet).

This is a ship that should never have been built, however. In an era of severe overfishing and dramatically reduced stocks, we should be scaling back fishing capacity, not creating a new generation of fish-guzzling monsters. Unfortunately, the crude economic calculus of fishing access agreements says it makes sense. If no catch limits are specified, then the biggest boats will win the lion's share of the fish and the profit to be gained from them. The captains of these vessels must turn fish into money as quickly as possible to pay back investors. The *Atlantic Dawn*, for example, cost US$95 million in cash and government subsidies. Like the sealing boats of two centuries ago, these vast ships must chase dwindling stocks from place to place in pursuit of profit. For the new wave of giant fishing vessels, sustainability is not an issue—rather, it is the pursuit of swift profit to repay investment. The larger the catch and the faster it can be taken, the better. The waters of developing countries are being pillaged today in a rerun of the years of colonial exploitation of their terrestrial wealth. For example, by 2003, Mauritania had over 250 foreign-owned factory fishing vessels vacuuming its waters. The Pacific Nation of Kiribati is paid just 5 percent of the landed value of the catch for tuna caught in its waters by Japan. Guinea-Bissau in West Africa hosted 76 EU tuna boats and a gross registered tonnage of over 12,000 metric tons of EU trawlers in 2006. In aggregate, over 800 EU boats targeted West African fish in the early years of the twenty-first century.

Fishing under access agreements has had further unanticipated—and unfortunate—consequences in West Africa. With local catches dwindling, people have taken to hunting wild animals in the forests to supply their protein needs.[19] The burgeoning bush-meat trade is stripping forests of their wildlife and has brought people into close contact with animals like chimpanzees that can transmit exotic diseases such as HIV and Ebola to humans.

The serial depletion of the world's fish stocks is nearing an end, because there will soon be nowhere else to go. Boris Worm, of Dalhousie University in Canada, and his colleagues have estimated that

29 percent of the fish populations exploited in 2005 were collapsed, and 65 percent of all fisheries exploited since 1950 have collapsed (the latter figure is higher since it takes into account species that have been so depleted since then we no longer fish them). On the current trajectory of decline, fisheries for all of the fish and shellfish species we exploit today will have collapsed by 2048.[20] Even the deep sea, covering more than twice the area of the world's landmass, is finite and will soon to be exhausted. The only areas worth fishing are less than 3,000 meters (10,000 feet) deep because only they support fish in sufficient numbers. Sharks and rays, for example, are virtually absent below this depth.[21] Just over 3 percent of the total area of the high seas—that is, waters outside national jurisdiction in the global commons—lies between 800 and 3,000 meters deep (2,600 to 10,000 feet). It is in this small region that the 300-strong, deep-sea bottom-trawling fleet concentrates its effort on the high seas. Together they hit around 1,500 square kilometers (580 square miles) of seabed every day. This is equivalent to the area of two and a half soccer pitches or nearly four American football pitches destroyed every second, faster than the rate of loss of the world's tropical rain forests. For every breath we take, an area covering ten soccer pitches has been stripped of its fish and invertebrates. Every year, the fleet clears an area the size of France. If these trawl passes did not overlap, it would take only sixteen years to hit the entire area of vulnerable deep-sea habitat once, and thus destroy it all. Fortunately, trawlers concentrate their efforts in the same place for a time before moving on, so there is still much that has not yet been hit. These figures refer only to fishing on the high seas, however. Trawlers fishing within national waters more than double the area that is hit every year. Time is fast running out for this fragile environment.

We are today seeing new ecological states emerging in the sea as a result of fishing that are entirely unfamiliar. One widespread change has been the shift from finfish to invertebrate dominance. The switch from cod to crab, lobster, and prawns in Canada; the flip from groundfish to lobster and urchins in the Gulf of Maine; the rise of *Nephrops* prawns in northern Europe as their fish predators diminish. This invertebrate ascendancy is welcomed by fishers, for their flesh is valuable, sometimes more so than the fish they replaced. But there is grave risk in our uncontrolled experiment with nature. On land, we know that monocultures are unstable. Crops must be treated with elaborate cocktails of chemicals to maintain their vigor and purity in the face of pests, weeds, and diseases. We can do this in aquaculture facilities, but we have no such recourse in the sea. Already there are worrying signs of trouble. Off the west coast of Scotland, for example, fishers have experienced massive increases in infestation of *Nephrops* by a parasite called *Haematodinium*. This is a microscopic dinoflagellate that invades the body of its victim and converts organs into parasite. When the process is complete, the free-swimming stage of the parasite erupts from every aperture and joint, giving the prawn the appearance of smoking (hence the common name: smoking crab disease). Infected prawns slow down well before they become moribund, and they spend more time outside their burrows. When cod and other predatory fish were common in these waters, infected prawns were picked off quickly, limiting spread of the parasite. Today there is no such control. If *Nephrops* succumbs, fishers have little else to turn to.

The frequency of disease and parasite outbreaks in the sea, like smoking crab disease, is rising. By disrupting food webs we have unwittingly removed some of the natural controls on these organisms. Rising pollution levels also favor microbes and heaps of discarded fish rotting on the seabed perhaps act as reservoirs of infection. But ecosystem simplification and instability are also rendering them vulnerable to the establishment of exotic species, brought in with ships' ballast water or introduced with aquaculture. Disturbed and stressed ecosystems appear to be more susceptible to such invasions. It isn't just diseases and parasites that invade. In the Black Sea, for example, overfishing and pollution have been implicated in the establishment and explosive spread of a comb jellyfish, *Mnemiopsis*.[22] In the Gulf of Maine, overfishing led to the outbreak of sea urchins that decimated native seaweeds, and when people switched to fishing urchins, the seaweeds that recolonized were largely invaders.

Today we are seeing the first seas without fish. Estuaries, coasts, and enclosed seas like the Baltic are suffering severe deoxygenation as a combined effect of our removing animals that consume plankton and overloading these regions with nutrients from terrestrial industry and agriculture. At the mouth of the Mississippi River, a dead zone forms every year that covers over 20,000 square kilometers (7,700 square miles) of the Gulf of Mexico.[23] There are more than fifty other seasonal or permanent anoxic dead zones throughout the world.[24] In the Adriatic Sea, "mucilage events"—colossal mats of gelatinous microbes—can shut tourist beaches for weeks in the summer. Microbes rise in columns from the seafloor giving the appearance of "snot volcanoes." It seems that the Adriatic is blowing its nose on a titanic scale. Jeremy Jackson, of Scripps Institution of Oceanography, describes these regions as playing back the evolutionary history of the sea in reverse. Unwittingly, we are recreating seas that resemble the heyday of microbes in the Precambrian era, before the rise of multi-cellular life.

When species become rare in the sea, fishery managers often cast them aside to concentrate on more viable fisheries. Just when we should be investing more time and effort in the species to help them recover, they are deemed not worth the trouble. After only five years of intensive fishing in the 1970s, southern California's white abalone had become so rare that fishery managers dropped their requirement to report catches.[25] Imagine removing protection for the last snow leopards because there weren't enough left to bother with.

Rarity brings problems for wildlife that fishery agencies hardly acknowledge. For some reason, humans value rarity. Throughout history, gold and jewels have enticed thousands to endure appalling risks and commit atrocities for a few baubles. So it is with animals. Mafiosi gangs in Eastern Europe are stripping the Caspian of its last sturgeon. In China, fishers pursue the last of the fish known as bahaba with undiminished vigor.[26] The bahaba is a relative of Mexico's toto-aba and reaches a similar size of up to 2 meters long (7 feet). Like the totoaba, these huge fish gathered to spawn in estuaries of southern China from the Yangtze River to Hong Kong. Spawning aggregations were targeted by trawlers from the 1930s, and populations soon collapsed. Today the last few bahaba are so valuable they are called "soft gold." Their swim bladders fetch seven times their weight in gold. For too long marine species have been looked on only as commodities. Our attitudes to ocean life must change fast if we are to prevent species being lost forever.

I suspect mining executives are pained by the exhaustion of a pipe of prime diamond-bearing kimberlite in the African hills. Perhaps geologists feel saddened by the loss of some remarkable gypsum formation rendered to dust for plasterboard. I don't know. But I certainly feel anguish on seeing coral glades leveled. It hurts to know we are losing species whose forms have never been described and perhaps have never been seen by people. They have shared our planet for countless millennia, living undisturbed lives deep in the sea. Extinction, the irrevocable loss of a species, causes pain that can never find relief. It is an ache that will pass from generation to generation for the rest of human history.

It is too late today to throw up protected areas to prevent the disappearance of Madagascar's elephant birds. They live on only in the magical description of the Roc, a vast bird that carried Sinbad off a desert island in the Arabian Nights.[27] The giant tortoises that once plodded ancient trackways through the undergrowth of Mauritius are gone, too. So are the dodos that shared their island. Nobody will ever know what strange calls they uttered as creeping dawn spread over the Indian Ocean. All that survive are a few mute skeletons and bleached shell fragments. But the giants of the sea are still with us. We have the chance to prevent them disappearing if only we will take it. Future generations need never stand wondering in front of the resin cast of a sailfish, trying to imagine what it would have looked like leaping amid the whitecaps of the Humboldt Current, and how the sunlight reflected blues and pinks from its taut, muscled flanks. For sailfish would still exist—to be wondered at in the wild.

There are bright notes in this sea of gloom. In recent decades, many countries have made good progress to reduce coastal and ocean pollution. Sewage is treated to higher standards before release than it was in the past, and there are international agreements to greatly restrict release and dumping of wastes at sea. Although local losses are legion, very few species have yet been driven to global extinction as a consequence of our mismanagement of the oceans. Remarkably, we can count recent extinctions of marine species of which we are certain on the fingers of two hands, whereas our list of known terrestrial extinctions runs to thousands. The sea is less well known than the land and many of its organisms are small and inconspicuous, so we may have overlooked some disappearances. But it is reasonable to think that the extinction wave has yet to break in the sea. Which means there is still the possibility of recovery and time to shift course. But to avert irreparable disaster, we need nothing less than a complete reinvention of fishery management.

# — *Chapter 24* —

# Reinventing Fishery Management

—◆—

ISHERIES SCIENCE—the determination of how many fish there are in the water and how many can be taken—is only part of fisheries management. To understand why fisheries are in trouble throughout the world, we need to look at how scientific recommendations are translated into controls on fishing. Serious deficiencies in this process are as much to blame for the decline of fish populations as weakness in the science itself. European fisheries management provides a classic example of how regulators fail both fishers and fish.

Much of Europe's fisheries have been managed under the Common Fisheries Policy since 1983.[1] This policy grew out of a hastily drawn up agreement made among the original six European Union member states—France, West Germany, Italy, Netherlands, Belgium, and Luxembourg—none of which could be considered major fishing nations at that time. But they evidently had ambitions, as these countries enshrined in the Common Fisheries Policy the principle of "equality of access" to the waters and resources of all member nations.

With fisheries treated as shared resources, they had to be managed centrally by agreement among all members. In simple terms, all member nations contribute expertise in fisheries science, making assessments of the size and composition of different populations of commercially important species in each of fifty different statistical areas.[2] Scientists pool their expertise once a year under the umbrella of the International Council for the Exploration of the Sea (ICES), and their advice goes to the Directorate of Fisheries in Brussels where bureaucrats convert it into recommended fish catches. These are put to an annual meeting of the Council of Fishery Ministers drawn from all the member states. Ministers negotiate final decisions about how much can be caught from each area by vessels from each country.

I mentioned earlier that the track record of fisheries management in Europe has been disastrous. The number of fish stocks classified as seriously overfished rose from 10 percent in 1970 to nearly 50 percent by 2000. With so much expertise, how did things go so badly wrong? The underlying causes of failure in Europe explain much of the inadequacy of fisheries management in the world generally, even if the administrative particulars differ.

The pioneers of fisheries management working in the 1930s and 1940s imagined a world in which levels of fishing mortality could be adjusted to the amount each fish population could cope with. Because there are high levels of natural variability in the size of fish populations, brought on ultimately by environmental fluctuations, levels of fishing mortality should be modified from year to year in tune with changes in population size. To the bureaucrats of Europe, making such adjustments has meant setting quotas on landings of fish. When fisheries ministers meet in Brussels, they agree on a Total Allowable Catch (TAC) for each species in each statistical region of Europe's seas, and then determine how it is to be subdivided between member states.[3] It is a system of competitive bargaining in which every fishery minister competes to get the best deal possible for his or her country's fishing industry. I often wondered why the meetings were held just before Christmas every year and once asked Britain's fishery minister when I met him at a conference in London. He explained that there was no other way to reach agreement without the looming deadline of the last flight home for the holiday!

Together with colleagues at the University of York, I have looked at the decision-making record of fisheries ministers in Europe over the last fifteen years. On average, they implemented landings quotas that were 25 to 35 percent greater than those recommended to them by bureaucrats in the Directorate of Fisheries. In turn, the figures passed to the politicians had often already been increased over scientific recommendations to make them more politically expedient. The excessive quotas set by politicians are thus often not matched by fish in the sea. When fishers fail to fill quotas, as did the Canadians in the last days of cod on the Grand Banks, you know that fish are in trouble. In Europe we can see an often repeated pattern of decline in which politicians every year set quotas bigger than are caught. Rather than reducing fishing by enough to bring the fishery under control, these quotas offer no protection at all, and population collapse soon becomes inevitable. Leaving decisions on specific fish catches to politicians is the first fundamental flaw of fisheries management, but political decisions on catches are the norm rather than the exception worldwide. It contributed to the collapse of cod in eastern Canada, too, for example. But there are other flaws in fisheries management equally as bad.

Landings quotas are a bureaucratic convenience. They allow statisticians to gather information on the amount of fish landed into ports without ever having to get seasick aboard a fishing vessel. But they do not measure the amount of fish that are caught and killed at sea. This is because not all fish caught are landed. Only a handful of fisheries are able to catch their target species in isolation from others.[4] For the rest, fishing gear is relatively unselective and catch a mixed bag of species. Trawl fisheries are notoriously unselective. In the North Sea they take dozens of species of varying degrees of commercial importance, while tropical trawl fisheries can include hundreds of different species. Separate landings quotas are set in Europe for different species that are caught by the same fishing method. When vessels have used up their quota for one species, they fill up on others, but the first species is still caught. Only now, they are discarded over the side dead rather than being brought into port. (At least, that is the theory. Many countries struggle to control illegal landings of overquota fish.) Fishing vessels often have quotas for only one or a few species and must discard all others caught, even if they are perfectly good for eating. One particularly abhorrent but widespread discarding practice is "high grading." Not all fish are worth the same. Some species are worth more than others, in some species larger individuals are worth more than small, in others the opposite. When fish are plentiful, fishers fill the hold with the most valuable and throw away the rest. It makes economic sense to the fisher but is harmful to the fishery and the environment.

Regardless of the reasons for throwing them away, discarded fish are not recorded in fishery statistics. But they are just as dead as those landed. Ignoring them makes a mockery of the idea of adjusting fishing mortality according to the size of each fish population. In reality, fishing mortality levels of most stocks exceed, sometimes grossly so, the targets set by scientists based on estimates of population size. Over the last forty years, the average annual landings of North Sea haddock came to 130,000 tonnes, while the estimated tonnage discarded averaged 87,000 tonnes.[5] What a waste. Landings quotas are a tool for allocating shares of the catch to different fishers, not for protecting populations of species in the sea.

Bycatch is another problem. Unselective fishing gear catches many species that are not commercially valuable, or for which fishers do not have quotas. Over the last forty years, 31,000 tonnes of haddock a year were swallowed up in the North Sea as bycatch by industrial fishmeal fisheries. A few resilient species caught as bycatch, like starfish, live to see another day, but most animals are thrown over the side dead or dying. Shrimp and prawn trawl fisheries have the worst bycatch problems in the world, as John Steinbeck recognized, bringing up 5 to 15 kilograms (12 to 33 pounds) of assorted marine life for every kilogram (pound) of prawns. Deep-sea fisheries are also highly damaging. Most deepwater species are not marketable because their flesh is too watery, and nearly all bycatch is killed by the huge pressure difference they are exposed to on being hauled to the surface.

Frank Buckland in the 1860s was one of the earliest fisheries biologists to recognize the problems of another form of bycatch, the capture of juvenile fish and shellfish, which undermines future productivity of the species. But concern over juvenile bycatch was already widespread among fishers at the time due to expansion of trawling.

Over time, the fraction of bycatch species in fisheries tends to fall. This is because more species find commercial outlets as preferred animals are depleted, and because fishing depletes bycatch species themselves.

In addition to bycatch, there is also bykill, the hidden destruction of species and habitats that never get brought to the surface. Fish, shellfish, corals, and sponges get smashed, gashed, and pulverized in situ by some of the most destructive fishing gear but are left in the water. The thousands of kilometers of nets, longlines, and other fishing gear lost every year contribute to this carnage, ghost fishing for animals that will never contribute to human well-being, but killing them nonetheless.

Fisheries managers gave little consideration to bycatch in the past, unless the species involved were commercially important. It was seen simply as necessary collateral damage in the pursuit of protein. Nontarget species and habitats meant nothing to a science whose focus was on single species. To the pipe-smoking, tweed-jacketed fathers of fisheries science, each species of fish was a separate entity, to be managed in isolation from others. They represented fisheries through a handful of simple equations. To make advances in their science, they were forced to sacrifice the complexities of life in the sea for the heuristic simplicity of single-species models. Those models represented fish populations, one species at a time, in terms of birth, growth, and death rates, and for the most part ignored the environment that fish lived in. The equations represented fish as particles moving at random in homogenous seas and fished at random by unthinking fishers. The role of habitat was implicit because it was simply assumed there was enough habitat of a sufficient quality to support growth of the species under consideration. Likewise, food availability was implicit in the models. Even if the species considered preyed on the target species in another fishery, that fishery was not included in the model despite the fact it might limit food availability. Such single-species thinking pervades fishery management to this day even though the models in use have grown in complexity. Each species, or in some cases groups of species, is typically considered by different committees within ICES, for example.[6]

Disregarding the ecosystems in which target fish species live is perhaps the most egregious failure of fisheries management. Early scientists ignored habitats because they did not understand that fishing was changing them in ways that profoundly affected target species. Their mathematics was not up to the task of considering predators and prey simultaneously. Today, computers facilitate far more complex calculations, but there are still limits to the ability of models to help us manage fisheries.

Even the most complex models used in fishery management are cartoons of reality. They boil down hundreds of links in food webs to a handful and are very poor at representing processes operating over space. Many of their assumptions are just as flawed today as the simplest models of the past. Fish "stocks," for one, are still assumed to be populations of a species that are isolated from one another. Yet we know that many populations mix at their edges and some even migrate through areas occupied by others. Furthermore, the more complex of today's models suffer from a "crisis of complexity" where more is really less. Adding layers of detail to a model, each carrying its own set of assumptions, leads to instability in the results. The behavior of the model becomes erratic, and conclusions drawn from the results can be downright misleading.

Ecology and economics have much in common here. They both involve highly complex systems whose behavior is affected by countless different forces. This is why economists are no better at predicting the future than fisheries managers. Treasury forecasts of a country's economic performance are rarely accurate for more than a few months ahead. There are just too many unknowns. Putting terms into the models for all these unknowns doesn't help much if you can't predict or accurately measure the values plugged into the model. Fund managers understand the limitations of these models, which is why financial management is as much art as science. A few inspirational (or brave) managers trust their intuition. Some win handsomely while others lose their shirts. Most develop portfolios that spread risk widely so that they never place too much faith in one economic sector or company.

Fishery managers have only recently begun to adopt less risky management methods. Between the 1950s and the 1990s, the prime objective was to adjust fishing mortality to the level that was thought to produce the maximum yield sustainable over the long term. The notion that there is such a thing as a maximum sustainable yield is one of the products of single-species fishery models. These models assume that equilibrium can be reached between the amount of fishing mortality and the growth rate of a fish population. If only we can match fishing effort to that target, say the models, there will be fish in perpetuity. In the real world, there is no such thing as a fixed maximum sustainable yield to target. Populations are forever on the move, pushed and pulled by forces of nature as well as fishing. Add in the unrecorded complexities of bycatch and discards by other fisheries and the target is rendered meaningless.

To a layperson, one assumption made by the maximum sustainable yield model seems absurd: that replenishment of the population is independent of the size of the parent stock. In other words, how many offspring grow up to enter the fishery is unaffected by how many mothers there are. Environmental fluctuations cause major swings in population size of fish so that the relationship between reproductive output and survival of offspring is loose at best, however, so this assumption isn't as far-fetched as it may first appear. But there is one point in the relationship that we can be absolutely sure of. If there are no mothers, there will be no offspring and no fishery. Below some level of adult population size there is a rapid decline in reproductive success. To fishery scientists a population that falls below this level is said to be "recruitment overfished," because there are not enough adults producing young to replace losses to fishing and natural mortality.

In recent years, managers have gradually been dropping maximum sustainable yield targets in favor of keeping populations above recruitment overfishing thresholds. This is seen as a more risk-averse target, although, paradoxically, these levels of population size are lower than those that would produce maximum sustainable yield. For the average species, it means maintaining population size above one-third of the size it would be if there was no fishing. For comparison, the maximum sustainable yield level is typically defined as half the unexploited population size. There is still the difficulty, of course, of deciding how big a fish population would be in the absence of fishing. The historical perspective in this book shows how badly we have underestimated unexploited population sizes in many cases, putting fish stocks at greater risk of collapse because overfishing thresholds are set lower than they should be.

Even with their new and worthy goals of avoiding population collapse, fishery managers are still fixated by single species. One reason for their reluctance to reform their art is a belief that it is not the science at fault but its application. They complain that if only politicians would implement their recommendations, fisheries would not be in decline. It is certainly true, as pointed out earlier, that scientific advice is nearly always watered down or even ignored by politicians. It is also the case that the tools used to regulate fisheries, mainly controls on catching technology and what can be landed, are too blunt to deliver sustainability on their own. But the science itself is also flawed. The theory and models that underpin fisheries management still fail in most cases to acknowledge the importance of healthy, intact ecosystems to fish production.

To recover the world's fisheries we must change the way we think about and manage the oceans. For much of the last hundred years, fisheries management has been conducted as an arms race between fishers and regulators. Regulators make laws to restrain fishing; fishers think up ways around them. In most places, fishers have kept one step ahead of regulators, and fish populations have fallen. Ultimately, if fishers win the race with regulators, their industry will self-destruct. The best that managers can claim in most places is that they are slowing the pace of suicide. Fisheries will become sustainable only when we set more modest catch targets and fish in ways that have less impact on fish habitats and other marine species.

The needed reforms do not involve complicated science, and people do not need degrees from learned institutions to understand them. They are straightforward, commonsense reforms that can be summarized in seven points: (1) reduce present fishing capacity; (2) eliminate risk-prone decision making; (3) eliminate catch quotas and instead implement controls on the amount of fishing; (4) require people to keep what they catch; (5) require fishers to use gear modified to reduce bycatch; (6) ban or restrict the most damaging catching methods; and (7) implement extensive networks of marine reserves that are off-limits to fishing.[7]

## 1. *Reduce the amount of fishing.*

The first reform needed is to fish less intensively. One of the early advances in fisheries science was based on observations of the evolution of fisheries over time. Michael Graham summed it up in his 1948 book *Rational Fishing of the Cod of the North Sea*:

> It is commonly thought that some improvement in the industry could be made by better arrangements of one kind or another on the market or in distribution. It seems, however, that the properties of an over-fished stock are such that all attempts at improvement will be unsuccessful so long as there is not some limitation of the total fishing power expended per annum, involving fishing by all nations. For if any of these measures, including even regulation of mesh, promise an increase in profit, the rate of fishing tends to rise. Ships that were laid up are put to sea again; owners are more willing to replace ships and gear; the prospect of better profits probably even has an effect on the zeal of the crews. As we have seen, however, an increase in the rate of fishing on an overfished stock necessarily drives the stock down to a less profitable level. In consequence, the profit promised by any of these measures will not last very long, if indeed it is realised at all.[8]

Graham's observation is now accepted as a fundamental economic principle. Where there is no restriction on access, people will pile into the fishing industry as long as there is profit to be made. They only stop when the profit made by the average fisher is nil. Today, most industrial fisheries have limited access based on licensing and quota allocations.[9] But fishing capacity can rise to excessive levels through technical innovations, even without the addition of new boats or people. This means that fishing capacity in almost all fisheries, even where entry is regulated, is greater than necessary or desirable to secure sustainable levels of catch. With fewer boats, you could catch the same amount for less effort, and crews would all make a better living. Cutting the amount of fishing is the first reform needed to fisheries management.

In 2002, it was estimated that fishing capacity in the North Sea was 40 percent greater than that needed. One of the main planks of Europe's Common Fisheries Policy is to reduce fishing effort by decommissioning vessels, paying fishers to scrap their boats.[10] This

approach can be traced back to the 1930s when the British government bought out vessels from their ailing herring fishery.[11] Decommissioning is not a perfect solution to overcapacity, though. The first
to sell up are the worst fishers and those with the oldest, least sea-
worthy boats. Furthermore, today companies often own and operate
fleets of many boats. By decommissioning their oldest vessels, they
can reinvest the money and upgrade the remainder with new gear and
electronics. Reducing fishing effort, although an important step, will
not solve all problems.

## 2. *Eliminate risky decisions.*

The second reform needed is to eliminate risk-prone decision making. This means cutting politicians out of the decision-making process on allowable catches and making choices based on the best
available science. The timescales of politics and fishery management
are very different. Fishery ministers are a here-today-gone-tomorrow
bunch. Few see their brief as any more than a pit stop on the way to
greater things, the trade and industry secretary or foreign minister,
for example. Decisions they make while in office are taken mainly to
please their constituents in the short term. Any adverse consequences
those decisions might have will be left for the next minister or the one
after to answer for. By contrast, fisheries sustainability is by definition
a long-term endeavor. Forgoing catches today may yield benefits only
in five or ten years from now, far beyond the horizon of politicians.

Much the same difference between political and societal timescales exists in economics. Many countries have realized, following
roller-coaster swings of their economies, that setting bank interest
rates should be given to an independent group of experts who do not
stand to gain or lose personally from the decisions they take. Politicians seeking long-term economic stability have passed the task to
central bank committees. In the same way, fisheries management
decisions need to be made by independent organizations that take
scientific advice for what it is: the best judgment of a group of experts
about how much of a fish population it is safe to catch and that allows
the species to maintain its role in the ecosystem. Decisions on catches
that exceed those judgments should be made only in the most unusual
circumstances.

In some countries, there have been moves toward decentralizing management responsibility for fisheries. The United States, for example, has eight Fishery Management Councils, each covering a different region of the country. Council members are drawn from science, industry, conservation bodies, and the public, but they are dominated by people from the fishing industry, who make up half the total membership.[12] Putting fishers in charge of management decisions has been likened to having the fox in charge of the henhouse. Short-term economic arguments weigh heavily on their minds, such as where the next loan repayment on the boat is going to come from. It comes as no surprise that Fishery Management Councils have been roundly criticized for not making the tough decisions needed to ensure long-term sustainability. Independent decision making does not mean decision making by industry. That will neither secure the future for fisheries nor adequately address fishery problems that assail nontarget species and their habitats.

### 3. *Eliminate catch quotas.*

The third reform is to eliminate catch quotas and replace them with limits on fishing effort. Landings quotas, as I explained earlier, do not stop fish being killed, only from being landed (legally at least). Quotas must be abandoned in favor of limits on where, how long, and with what gear a vessel can fish. Only by limiting fishing effort can we prevent fish from being killed, giving them a chance to grow larger and produce more young. In the United States, limits on fishing effort have been in use for a long time in many fisheries, but the idea has been slow to take off in Europe. However, European fishery managers are now experimenting with regulations that limit the number of days boats can spend at sea. Of course, limits on fishing power will still have to be adjusted over time to account for technological advances.

### 4. *Require fishers to keep what they catch.*

The fourth plank in the reform package is to require people to keep what they catch. Discarding target fish is universally regarded as a tragic waste. After all, the fish are dead anyway, so putting them back into the sea isn't going to help much. Regulators insist on throwing away overquota fish, because if vessels could keep them, overfishing would be rewarded. Paradoxically, insisting that boats keep what they catch could be a powerful conservation measure, provided limits on fishing effort are enforced. Some countries, such as Norway, have already put the idea into practice.

This idea works because fish are worth different amounts depending on size and species. Requiring fishers to keep all they catch means that crews that are able to fish most selectively for the target species will make the most money. Others will be forced to carry back low-value bycatch species, which in Norway are bought by the government at a low price and turned into fishmeal. There are many ways to fish more selectively, by modifying fishing gear and choosing fishing grounds more carefully, for example. This reform gives fishers an economic incentive to adopt the best fishing practices.

### 5. *Use the best available fishing technology to reduce bycatch.*

This measure, requiring that fishers use gear designed to reduce bycatch, complements measure number 4. For years, government fisheries laboratories across the world have been experimenting with gear modifications that reduce bycatch. In only a handful of cases have their inventions ever been adopted by the industry. One notable example is the incorporation of turtle excluder devices into shrimp trawls. An angled plastic grid is set in the neck of the trawl net that guides the turtle to a flap through which it can escape. Before these devices were installed, the U.S. and Mexican shrimp fleets operating in the Gulf of Mexico drowned thousands of turtles every year and put some species on a fast track to extinction. Sadly, most bycatch species lack the charisma of turtles and don't have the legal backup afforded to endangered species to force the fishing industry to reform. And even those that do, like the harbor porpoises killed by pair trawling for sea bass in the English Channel, where a net is towed between two boats, suffer from legislative inertia or indifference by fishery managers.[13]

Experience shows that fishers are reluctant to use gear designed to reduce bycatch because it would cost them money to change gear and might reduce their total catch. Hence it is unrealistic to expect fishers to voluntarily adopt best fishing practices. Gear that reduces bycatch often reduces catch of target species as well. This is sometimes offset by gains from quicker processing, such as in shrimp fisheries where animals have to be sorted by hand from the copious bycatch. However, the gain is rarely sufficient to tempt fishers to accept the expense of changing gear, which in turn makes manufacturers unwilling to supply them. If all of the bycatch reduction devices gathering dust in fisheries research institutes were put into the sea tomorrow, fishing would become a more benign activity overnight. The only way the industry will accept this gear is when legislation forces everyone to use it.

### 6. *Ban or restrict the most damaging fishing gear.*

Some fishing gear is highly destructive and modifications cannot go far enough to make much difference to the damage it does. For example, bottom-trawl nets will always crush and sever bottom-living species like corals. The only solution for this gear is to ban it completely, or greatly restrict where it can be used.

From the fourteenth century on, the destructive tendencies of bottom trawling have generated passionate and sometimes violent complaint. Yet the method has spread to every sea on the planet. Some areas have been closed to trawling, notably close to coasts, especially in places considered to be spawning or nursery grounds for commercially important species. But for the most part, trawling grounds are defined simply as any place a fisher is willing to put down a trawl. The deep sea is a place bottom trawls should never touch. Gear used to penetrate the deep is heavier and more destructive than that used in shallow seas. The heavy steel rollers on the ground rope and the 5-tonne plates that hold the net open are incompatible with the fragile world a thousand meters beneath the surface. Anywhere trawled in the deep sea suffers immense, perhaps irreparable damage.

There are many reasons to restrict where fishing gear can be used. Trawling for pollock is already banned in a 20-nautical-mile (37 kilometer) radius of Steller's sea lion haul-outs in the Aleutian Islands of the North Pacific to protect the sea lions' food. It is inappropriate to use surface-set gill nets near seabird colonies, because diving birds tangle in them and drown. Pair trawls should not be fished in places where marine mammals are put at risk. Spearguns should not be used on coral reefs because they take the largest, most reproductively valuable fish as well as rarities. Poisons and dynamite are too destructive to be acceptable under any circumstances, although they are still widely used throughout much of the tropics to kill fish en masse.

Trawling has come in for much criticism in this book. But banning bottom trawling everywhere is not necessary. Large expanses of shallow-water continental shelf habitat are dominated by gravel, sand, and mud—perfect for trawling. Repeated trawling of these places over long historical timescales has favored communities of animals and plants that are resilient to its effects. The trawl is a highly effective means of catching fish at low cost. From a fisheries perspective, many places would produce more fish with less trawling, but that is not the same as insisting upon a halt to trawling altogether. Vast tracts of land are put to the plough every year to grow crops. There is no reason why some parts of the ocean should not be put to the plough for fish. But not everywhere.

The seas will remain impoverished and their wildlife will continue to disappear unless we put some places beyond harm. In regions that are now mud, sand, and gravel, there was so much more before the advent of the trawl. The only way to see these rich seascapes again is to protect them. The bottom-living communities will not recover by reducing fishing effort alone, even by draconian amounts. Changing the frequency with which trawls hit the bottom from once a year to once every other year will make little difference to long-lived species like corals and sponges. It is only the difference between some passes of the trawl and none that will lead to full habitat recovery. And it isn't just life on the seabed that needs respite from fishing. The thousands of species we know have been depleted and the thousands more that we don't know about need refuges, too. What may come as a surprise is that areas protected from fishing can benefit fisheries as well. Setting up marine reserves, the seventh reform to fisheries management, is the subject of chapter 25.

— *Chapter 25* —

# The Return
# of Abundance

—————

M Y FIRST DIVE into Belize's Hol Chan Marine
Reserve was a revelation. The reserve straddled
a channel through the barrier reef, connecting
lagoon with open Caribbean. Thick schools of snappers and
grunts swirled below as I descended toward the channel. Three
barrel-chested groupers, each over a meter long, split off from the reef
to lose themselves in the sea-grass carpet of the lagoon. Resting
groups of fish packed every ledge, cave, and overhang, and drifted
back and forth over coral heads with the passing swells. Moray eels 2
meters long and thicker than my thigh snaked across the sandy channel bottom. It seemed impossible, but as I swam into the channel, the
density of fish grew. Before long there were more fish than reef, and
the cliffs appeared as living flesh, a moving scaled mosaic of every
hue. A group of discus-shaped batfish hove into view above my head,
silhouetted against the light. Streamlined barracuda hung beneath
the ceiling of the surface, almost disappearing into the background as
their mirror scales assumed its flickering blue. Thick-lipped black
grunts jostled for position where the channel opened to the outer reef.

In the deepening blue beyond, a patrolling shark passed in silence, its eye fixed upon me.

It was 1991, and I was a year into a new research project studying the effects of marine reserves on life in the sea. Marine reserves are places that are protected from all fishing. Finding study sites had been hard because there were few such reserves in the world at that time and many of them existed only on paper, their protection never enforced. At Hol Chan park wardens had closely guarded the reserve for four years by the time I dived there. Compared with other Caribbean reefs I had seen, this bubbled over with life. The reserve occupied a section of reef 1,600 meters square (1 square mile). In the channel, fish densities were six to ten times greater than in areas outside the reserve, and were among the highest documented for any coral reef. Numbers thinned toward the reserve's edges, but remained 50 percent higher than found on nearby unprotected reefs.[1] It set me thinking that if fishing could so reduce the abundance of fish, it was a powerful force indeed. But just as important, this reserve demonstrated that protection could soon breathe life back into a reef.

When I published my first paper on marine reserves, studies describing the effects of marine reserves could be counted on the fingers of two hands. Fifteen years later, there are over a thousand papers, dozens of reviews, and several books. From their modest beginnings, marine reserves have spread to tens of countries and hundreds of sites, encompassing many different habitats and climes. It is easy therefore to think of them as something new.

But the idea of creating refuges from fishing has a long pedigree. Across the Pacific, from Papua New Guinea to Hawaii, islanders traditionally placed some areas of reef off limits to fishing. In most places these were "rested" for a time before being fished again to supply some feast, rather than given permanent protection. But the penalties applied for taking fish could be severe. In Hawaii, offenders were clubbed to death for violating such *kapu* areas.

In Europe, the idea surfaced in late eighteenth-century France and was picked up again a century later when experiments were made on the effects of closing areas to bottom trawling. In France, some areas were protected from all fishing as long ago as the early nineteenth century. The intent of these protected areas was not to save

*Marine reserves that are protected from all fishing, like this one at Hol Chan in Belize, soon develop dense populations of large fish when fishing stops. Photo by Callum Roberts.*

pretty fish from the hook and trawl but to benefit fisheries. For example, trawling was prohibited near Marseilles between 1793 and 1830. When the area was reopened to fishing, the catches were said to be almost miraculous, with as much as 7 tonnes caught per tow, and the landings dominated by fat dories and hake.[2] Marcel Hérubel, a French fishery scientist, described the theory behind such marine reserves in 1912:

> The idea of controlling the colossal shoals of herrings or sardines is laughable. But the fish that feed on the floor of the sea, whose habits are sedentary, invite a prudential treatment. Once the fry and the young fish are safely sheltered it is easy to extend the principle of protection to certain adult individuals, and thus to institute them guardians of the race.
>
> For this purpose choose a locality which is both a spawning-ground and a place where such fish as live on the bottom naturally congregate; delimit this area and make its position precisely known, then decree that all fishing shall be prohibited within its limits, and you will have a preserve wherein fish will multiply and grow, a "stock" of utilisable

animal material, or, to use the word employed in France, a *canton-nement*. The utility of such reservations is proved by experience. . . .

In explaining the theory of reserves I have hinted at the two meth-ods of reservation. Should they be temporary or permanent? It is obvi-ous that the ideal reservation, regarded as a stock of animal material, is by definition an inviolable asylum where life is assured to the repro-ductive adults as well as to the young; a gigantic mixed nursery, an effective centre of production whence the surplusage of individuals, driven by competition, would radiate in all directions. . . . Let us have plenty of reserves—permanent when the thing is possible, and in all other cases temporary.[3]

Herubel's account set out the essence of our theory of marine reserves seventy years before the first paper written on reserves by a modern author. His work long forgotten, today's scientists invented the prin-ciples anew. This theory says that marine reserves contribute to fish-eries in two important ways. They protect fish from capture, which allows them to live longer and grow larger. Big fish produce many times more offspring than small, so populations in well-protected reserves spawn far more young than those in fishing grounds. Fish lay their eggs on the seabed or release them into the water column. Either way, larvae hatched from these eggs spend a period of a few days to months in the plankton before they metamorphose into juvenile fish. By this time, many have moved well beyond the boundaries of the reserve, and so the young fish contribute to replenishing fishing grounds. A second fishery benefit that Herubel predicted occurs as fish populations build up in reserves. When densities rise, some fish will seek less-crowded conditions and in doing so will move from reserves to fishing grounds. Finally, Herubel's suggestion that to work well reserves should be established in networks distributed along all coasts and seas is a foundation of modern reserve theory.

The evidence in support of marine reserves in France at the end of the nineteenth century was sufficient to convince regulators, as Herubel recounts:

The "Consultation Committee of Sea Fisheries," in 1899, expressed the desire that the Department of the Marine, using the powers con-ferred upon it by the law of January 5, 1852, should make the creation of reserves general; it even went so far to state that if the reserves were absolutely respected the trawl might be authorised in free territorial waters [trawling had been banned up to 3 miles (~ 5 km) from the coast since 1862]. In 1901 it advised the maintenance and at need the establishment of new reserves in the coastal regions where the fishers are numerous but not congested.[4]

Marcel Herubel was a visionary scientist. Had his recommendations been adopted, I believe fisheries would never have reached the dire state we see them in today. In addition to setting up marine reserves, he was adamant that the most destructive fishing gears, such as shrimp trawls, should be banned outright. We are coming around to his ideas again a century late, with so much less in the sea than there was in his day. Herubel may not have been surprised that it's taking so long. As he wryly observed, "[T]he exigencies of theory often accord ill with corporate interests, and the multiplication of coastal reserves would quickly arouse the anger of fishers."[5]

Reserves were dealt a blow by William McIntosh's flawed experiments with areas closed to trawling in Scottish bays during the 1880s and 1890s. McIntosh was the Scottish fishery scientist charged by the British government to investigate the impacts of trawling. To determine whether trawling depleted fish, several bays and estuaries were closed to the gear. For over a decade, McIntosh surveyed them using experimental trawls to see whether fish populations showed any recovery. However, hook-and-line and trap fishers continued to use these areas throughout. As McIntosh observed in 1892,

> The local benefits of the closure to the fishing community are undoubtedly great. They are enabled to place their lines anywhere within the enclosed waters, and leave them for hours without risk (from incursions of trawlers). The high prices obtained for plaice in winter must materially conduce to their comfort, though, it is said the greater abundance of money is not without disadvantages.[6]

While line fishers benefited from a place they could fish undisturbed, this intensification of exploitation prevented the recovery that might have taken place had the areas been fully protected. Trawl closures were falsely discredited even though they protected bottom habitats from damage and would have reduced premature capture of young fish. Around the same time, fishers themselves proposed that to limit damage to juvenile fish, a quarter of the North Sea off the Danish,

German, and Dutch coasts should be closed to trawling.[7] This was rejected as "too visionary" by the likes of McIntosh, whose views held considerable sway with the British government.

Today's generations rediscovered the benefits of protecting areas from fishing almost by accident. During the 1970s, in Chile, the Philippines, and New Zealand, scientists established small areas protected from fishing near to their research stations. It was the blossoming of experimental ecology, and scientists began to fill sea and shore with wire cages and other bits of equipment to exclude this animal or include that one in their efforts to discover what roles species played in their ecosystems. They wanted reserves, not to conserve marine life, but to protect their experiments from damage by fishing operations! In New Zealand, along a rugged, rocky coast close to Auckland, Bill Ballantine fought for years to get the Leigh Marine Reserve established in front of his laboratory. There was no law available to create marine reserves, and government bureaucrats of the time were hostile or, at best, indifferent to the idea. Unperturbed, Ballantine worked tirelessly to build public support and to convince fishers that they could afford to lose a mere 5 square kilometers (2 square miles) of fishing grounds. In 1977, twelve years after the idea was first raised, protection was implemented for a reserve.[8]

After a few years, Ballantine and his colleagues noticed some unexpected changes in the reserve. Densities and sizes of commercially important animals, such as spiny lobsters, began to increase rapidly. The population size of lobsters, for example, grew by 10 percent for every year of protection. Their body size also increased as animals spared the trap lived longer.[9] Fish were slow to respond at first, and after six years only one of six species of commercial fish, the red moki, had increased in abundance.[10] That soon changed. After twelve years of protection, snappers, red moki, and blue cod[11] were all significantly more common in the reserve than in fished areas beyond. Snappers, dusky gray and firm-fleshed fish much in demand with consumers, continued to build up with time, by the late 1990s reaching nearly six times greater abundance inside the reserve compared to outside.[12] Their size also increased as protected animals aged. The average size in reserves reached 32 centimeters (~ 13 inches), compared to 19 centimeters (~ 8 inches) on unprotected reefs.

Experience at Leigh supported Marcel Herubel's prediction that reserves act as centers of production that radiate outward to surrounding fishing grounds. Lobster fishers in particular noticed the change and began setting traps close to reserve boundaries to take advantage of spillover as lobsters strayed out. Ballantine recalls how a visitor he showed around the reserve complimented him on how well the boundary was marked by buoys. He replied that they weren't boundary markers but the buoys of lobster traps set around the edge of the reserve. After ten years of protection, local attitudes changed. Having experienced firsthand the effects of protection, four out of five commercial fishers said they would like more reserves.[13] The same proportion said they would actively prevent poaching in the reserve. Far from seeing their catches decline, two in five thought catches had improved since the reserve was set up.

By the late 1990s, the habitat at Leigh had also changed from surrounding areas where fishing continued. When the reserve was first set up, the reefs were largely bare but for squadrons of sea urchins that munched their way methodically back and forth across the rock cropping algae. Only a few scattered clumps of seaweed broke the monotony. After twenty years of protection, the reserve came to support luxuriant kelp forests, and urchin barrens had been reduced to a few patches here and there.[14] The kelp canopy now shelters a bevy of urchin predators, such as snappers and spiny lobsters. Old snappers in the reserve have thick lips speckled with black, the telltale scars of dozens of sea urchin spines. Experiments show that predation rates on urchins in the reserve are seven times higher than in fished areas, keeping numbers low and giving kelp a chance to grow. The regrowth of kelp forest has provided habitat for many other species.

Juan Carlos-Castilla saw equally dramatic changes when he fenced off the rocky shore in front of the Las Cruces Research Station on the coast of Chile. He wanted to exclude the shore pickers who worked the rocky coasts looking for edible mollusks and other animals. Again, his motivation wasn't conservation but a desire to prevent his experiments being disturbed. The effect was as dramatic as it was unexpected. Within a few years, rocky shores in the fenced reserve grew a thick, shaggy coat of brown seaweeds, in stark contrast to the bare rock beyond. Castilla found that one of the animals shore pickers targeted was *Concholepas,* a predatory snail that fed on other herbivorous snails.[15] In the absence of human predation, snail predators recovered in the reserve and brought herbivore populations under control. This allowed seaweeds to flourish once more.

Reserves provide living proof of the resilience of marine life and give us hope that the seas can recover from the impacts of overfishing. In places where people have set up reserves and have looked after them well, the results are spectacular. I have been lucky enough to witness such a transformation in St. Lucia, one of the Windward Isles of the eastern Caribbean. Soufrière is a vibrant community of ten thousand people, nestled among mountains in the southwest part of the island. The seafront is lined with brightly painted wooden fishing boats hauled out on the beach and bobbing in the water. They carry names like *More Fire, My Money, Lord Help Me,* and *Not Much.* When *Not Much* was named, Soufrière's reefs were in a terrible state. I first visited in 1994, and the fishing was dreadful. Many boats lacked engines, and fishers rowed for hours to get to their grounds, often against currents that ran swift as rivers. They labored in baking sun and torrential rain to haul basket traps, only to be rewarded at day's end with a bucket of tiny fish. Some traps I watched come to the surface were empty, others had only enough fish to fill a sandwich. The fish were mostly undesirable species, like squirrelfish and soldier fish, more spine and scale than flesh.

Underwater, the reefs were gorgeous, crusted with corals, sea fans, and sponges of marvelous color and shape. As I swam among these glades, great schools of tiny fish parted ahead of me. On any sudden move, they flashed and swerved in unison, seeming to merge almost into some huge animal hovering above the reef. The spreading branches of elkhorn coral[16] sheltered groups of yellow-striped goatfish and golden grunts, none much larger than my hand. A few small groupers darted for shelter as I approached, turning to stare at this clumsy intruder. Peering into caves, I found dense shoals of carmine soldier fish. Their huge eyes gave away their nocturnal habits, winking like mirrors as the fish turned. Occasionally, a flash of silver and sudden rush of small fish announced the passage of a jack hunting along the reef edge, but other than that, the place almost completely lacked any big animals. Nothing was much larger than 30 centimeters long (1 foot), and most were under 20 centimeters (8 inches). No wonder fishing was such a struggle.

Problems erupted in the early 1990s when fishers came to blows with the growing tourist industry. Increasingly, boatloads of divers interrupted their fishing, and fishers blamed them for falling catches. Dive centers accused fishers of stripping the reefs of the big fish that many of their clients wanted to see. After two years of negotiation, together they hatched a plan to create a management area that encompassed 11 kilometers (7 miles) of coast around Soufrière. A network of four reserve zones protected from fishing, but permitting scuba diving, lay at the heart of this plan. They included 35 percent of the area of coral reefs of this coast. Tourist operators hoped these zones would protect fish, making for better diving, while keeping scuba divers out of the way of fishers. Fishers hoped that reserves would regenerate their ailing fishery. Creation of the management area was realized in 1995, a year after my first visit.

Together with a team of keen students and other scientists, I returned to St. Lucia every year for the next seven years to take the pulse on how the reefs were doing. At each visit, we dived dozens of locations inside and outside marine reserves. We counted fish and corals until our heads spun and our eyes bulged in our masks. By about the third week of each visit, I started counting fish in my dreams, and by the fifth, found myself counting mouthfuls of food as I ate breakfast. By the eighth week, I reached a level of tranquillity attained by Tibetan monks. It was worth it all because the figures gave us a fascinating insight into recovery of reefs from overfishing.

We calculated the weight of every fish seen from five families of commercially important fish: groupers, snappers, grunts, surgeonfish, and parrot fish. In seven years, the combined weight of these species leaped fivefold inside marine reserves. More important to the fishers, it had trebled in fishing grounds, benefiting from spillover from reserves. Five years into the study, by which time populations had increased threefold in reserves and doubled in fishing grounds, we examined fish catches to see if they had improved. Despite giving up a third of their fishing grounds as marine reserves, the trap fishery prospered. Catches using large baited traps had jumped by 46 percent, while catches with small traps nearly doubled. Fishers caught more for less time spent fishing. They also caught bigger and better fish. Their traps still contained plenty of small fish, but now also included fat snappers and grunts large enough to feed a family. St. Lucian fishers, despite their willingness to give reserves a chance, had at first been sceptical about them. With the benefit of experience they became vocal supporters.

It didn't require reams of data and graphs to tell us the reefs were changing—we could see it underwater. With the passing years, we watched what seemed like a miracle unfold in slow motion. We saw groupers and snappers grow from winsome juveniles into sturdy adults. Yellowtail snappers appeared above the reef, first in ones and twos, then in small groups. By the end of the study, shoals had formed made up of fine fish 20 to 80 centimeters long (8 to 32 inches). New fish settling from the plankton added to the throngs. Grunts, some of impressive size, began to pack under overhangs; gaudy parrot fish with bellies full of seaweed raced here and there, defending their territories; and mysterious eyes peered from holes where once there were none. In the afternoon, parrot fish would pass me on their way to group spawning sites as I counted fish. In the early years, there would be one every five or ten minutes; in later years, ten or twelve often streamed by in closely spaced columns. Seven years of protection worked wonders, giving fish the time and space to grow. Glinting schools of small fish still thronged around me like clouds of aquatic butterflies, but bigger animals now joined them. Fish I rarely saw in 1995 became frequent friends, and fish that were common became abundant. The reefs were filling up.

St. Lucia's reefs have been exploited for centuries, and it will take more than seven years' protection for them to recover fully. In my hundreds of dives there, I didn't see a single reef shark and only came across a handful of the large grouper species present in places like Bonaire and the Hol Chan Marine Reserve. If fishing has eliminated species locally, recovery will depend on recolonization from distant sources and may take time.

The Merritt Island National Wildlife Refuge in Florida demonstrates the value of patience in reserve recovery. Merritt Island includes 40 square kilometers (16 square miles) of coastal lagoon in eastern Florida and is the best-defended marine reserve in America.

It was established in 1962 to protect rockets, not fish, as it incorporates the Kennedy Space Center at Cape Canaveral. In 2000, Jim Bohnsack, an expert on marine reserves with the National Marine Fisheries Service in Florida, was intrigued when he discovered an anomalous hotspot in world-record game-fish catches around the refuge.

The International Game Fish Association keeps account of all world-record angling catches. There are many records available for any given fish species, based mainly on the strength of fishing line used and sex of the angler. Bohnsack plotted the locations and dates of record catches of black drum, red drum, and spotted sea trout[17] from 1960 to 1999. Looking at world-record-sized fish caught in Florida, 62 percent of black drum, 54 percent of red drum, and 50 percent of spotted sea trout records were landed within 100 kilometers (63 miles) to the north or south of the reserve. This cluster was striking because the region accounts for only 13 percent of the Florida coast, and there is good habitat for these species all around the state.

The timing of record catches reveals much about the long-term effects of marine reserves. Before the reserve was established, this was one of the most intensively fished sections of the Florida coast. Between 1957 and 1962, 2,700 metric tons of fish were landed annually from the vicinity of Merritt Island by more than six hundred commercial fishers.[18] Three quarters of a million sport fishers added an average of nearly 1,500 metric tons more every year. For the three species I have just mentioned, few record fish were caught in the vicinity of the reserve in the early years after protection was instigated. However, after this pause, there was a burst of record catches for all of them. Spotted sea trout, the shortest-lived species, was first to take off, after nine years' protection. Next up was red drum after a wait of twenty-seven years, and finally black drum started to produce records after thirty-one years. The pattern is easy to explain. Record fish can be caught only when some animals have grown larger than the size of the existing records. They don't pass this threshold until they are quite old. If fishing is intensive, no fish lasts long enough to get that big, so there are no records. Spotted sea trout live to age fifteen years, red drum thirty-five years, and black drum make it to seventy. Records leveled off for spotted sea trout around 1990, but there is no sign yet of any slowdown for black and red drum. Black drum, especially, will continue to grow for decades yet. Today, black drum of 40–50 kilograms are taken (88–110 pounds), giving today's generations a glimpse of the giant fish that were seen by early European settlers. Anglers have the chance to catch these behemoths because of spillover of fish from the Merritt reserve.

Most of the reserves I have described are small, but their effects do scale up. On Georges Bank, the New England Fisheries Management Council introduced large trawl closures in 1994 to help ground-fish populations recover after severe overfishing. Three closed areas straddle the Bank, covering 17,000 square kilometers of fishing grounds (~ 6,500 square miles). Although they are not proper marine reserves, since they allow some trap, longline, and other forms of fishing, all fishing gear that affects the seabed were banned, including trawls and scallop dredges. The closures give useful insights as to how marine reserves might work on temperate continental shelves. Scallop populations were first to rebound. Five years after the closures were implemented, legal-size scallops were fourteen times more abundant inside protected areas compared to outside.[19] To police the closures, boats were fitted with satellite tracking devices. Satellite data show that scallop fishers soon began to hug the edge of the closed areas, benefiting from export of young scallops by breeding populations inside. Scallopers have seen their industry rejuvenated.

Groundfish populations have also begun to respond to protection. Haddock and yellowtail flounder have mounted a strong recovery. Cod populations are still much depleted, but recent data suggests a slight improvement. Fish habitats inside the closed areas are also changing, with an increase in abundance of large invertebrates and plants living on top of the seabed. Progress is slow. Reversing nearly a century of trawling damage cannot be achieved with a decade of protection, but these early signs are promising. Recent research surveys in the closed areas have caught a few juveniles of the threatened barn-door skate. Refuges from trawling like those on Georges Bank offer the only hope of recovery for a species that is so easily depleted by this form of fishing.

Experience with marine reserves has built quickly as they have proliferated across coasts and seas. Gathering together this experience from across the world enables some general conclusions about their effectiveness.[20] The total quantity of commercially exploited fish inside a reserve can double or even quadruple within a few years of protection. Sustained protection brings larger gains. The Apo Island Reserve in the Philippines, for example, has seen a seventeenfold increase in biomass of large predatory fish in eighteen years of protection.[21] Local fishers there have experienced increased catches, just like those in St. Lucia.[22]

One of the underpinnings of fisheries science is that reducing the size of fish stocks and eliminating large, older fish will increase productivity by boosting growth of the fish that remain. But this same effect can drastically reduce egg production by a population, putting at risk the replenishment of the species and future fish catches. Marine reserves help safeguard reproduction by allowing big, old, fat fish to survive and reproduce. Fishing reduces egg production because it decreases both population size and average body size. Small fish are much less fecund than large. For example, a grouper of 10 kilograms (22 pounds) produces ninety-three times as many eggs as one weighing half a kilogram (about a pound). The large fish produces four and a half times as many eggs per gram of body weight as the small fish.

Unlike humans, the value of fish as reproducers increases with age. This is why, after sustained protection, reserves typically outperform fished areas by ten- to a hundredfold, area for area, in terms of egg production. If egg production by fish is twenty times greater in a 5-kilometer reserve like Leigh, for example, the reserve could supply the same number of offspring as 100 kilometers of unprotected coast. Reserves also enhance biodiversity by giving depleted species a chance to recover and by providing highly vulnerable species with refuges from fishing. Over time, they develop richer, more varied communities of species and promote recovery of animals that create three-dimensional habitat structures, like corals, seaweeds, and mollusks. The key to reserve success is resolute enforcement of its boundaries. Reserves have been successful from the tropics to temperate and polar regions; they work in shallow water and deep; near shore, on continental shelf, and offshore; they work in hard-bottom habitats like rocky and coral reefs as well as soft bottoms like mudflats, mangroves, and sea-grass beds. They work well regardless of whether the fishery is industrial-scale trawling, like that on Georges Bank, or artisanal trap fishing, like that in Soufrière.

Pioneering efforts with marine reserves have proved how effective protection from fishing can be. At the same time they have awakened understanding of the profound effects that fishing has on the sea. Although scattered and mostly small, today's marine reserves offer us a window on the past. They allow us to marvel again at the strangeness, splendor, abundance, and sheer exuberance of marine life.

# Chapter 26

# The Future of Fish

⚊⚊

*I* AM STANDING in the National Portrait Gallery in London, contemplating the picture of William Dampier. He stares back impassively, the curl of lip and heavy-lidded eyes suggest a man of purpose and determination. In his right hand is a copy of *Dampier's Voyages*. I look into his eyes, as the artist once did, and wonder about the world he lived in. We can no longer see with Dampier's eyes. The pages of his books stand stiff and mute, refusing further access to his world. All we can see is what he and others thought to set down. The rest is lost. But it need not be lost forever.

Our seas and oceans are not devoid of life. Children still find wonders in rock pools; anglers still catch fish from breakwaters; the diminutive scuttling lives of countless invertebrates continue across the gritty basement of the sea. But fishing has spread poverty where once there was plenty. Camera crews filming ocean wildlife must travel thousands of kilometers to witness spectacles that were ordinary and familiar to people in Dampier's day. Since then we have overwhelmed the mighty armies of herring, capelin, and sardines along with their ravening consorts of whale, dolphin, shark, and tuna. The oceans of today are filled with ghost habitats, stripped of their larger inhabitants. A few people might share the views of the early twentieth-century game fisherman Mitchell Hedges that ridding the seas of fierce carnivores is no bad thing. But our dismantling of marine ecosystems is having destructive and unpredictable consequences.

With species loss and food web collapse comes dangerous instability. The seas are undergoing ecological meltdown. Fishing is undermining itself by purging the oceans of species on which it depends. But its influence is far more menacing than simply the regrettable self-destruction of an industry. The wholesale removal of marine life and obliteration of their habitats is stripping resilience from ocean ecosystems. Moreover, it is undermining the ability of the oceans to support human needs. Overfishing is destabilizing the marine environment, contributing to the spread of anoxic dead zones and the increasing prevalence of toxic algal blooms, for example. Nature's power to bounce back after catastrophes or absorb the battery of stresses humanity is subjecting it to is being eroded, collapsed fishery after collapsed fishery, species by species, place by place. It is easy to point fingers and say this is the fault of greedy corporations with their factory ships, or faint-hearted politicians overeager to please the fishing industry, or the great masses of poor people reduced to bombing and poisoning their seas to extract the last few fish. But blaming others is unhelpful. Every fish and meat eater[1] shares responsibility for the losses, and only by working together can we restore the seas' bounty.

The face of the ocean has changed completely since the first commercial fishers cast their nets and hooks over a thousand years ago. Fisheries intensified over the centuries, but by the nineteenth century it was still felt, justifiably, that the plenty of the sea was for the most part beyond the reach of fishing and so there was little need to restrict fishing or create protected areas. The twentieth century heralded an escalation in fishing intensity that is unprecedented in the history of the oceans, and modern fishing technologies leave fish no place to hide. Today, the only refuges from fishing are those we deliberately create. Unhappily, the sea trails far behind the land in terms of area and quality of protection given.

For centuries, as fishing and commerce have expanded, we have held onto the notion that the sea is different from land. We still view it as a place where people and nations should be free to come and go at will, as well as somewhere that should be free for us to exploit. Perhaps this is why we have been so reluctant to protect the sea. On land, protected areas have proliferated as human populations have grown. Here, compared to the sea, we have made greater headway in our struggle to maintain the richness and variety of wildlife and landscape. Twelve percent of the world's land is now contained in protected areas, whereas the corresponding figure for the sea is but three-fifths of 1 percent. Worse still, most marine protected areas allow fishing to continue. Areas off-limits to all exploitation cover something like one five-thousandth of the total area of the world's seas.

Today we are belatedly coming to realize that "natural refuges" from fishing have played a critical role in sustaining fisheries and maintaining healthy and diverse marine ecosystems. This does not mean that marine reserves can rebuild fisheries on their own—other management measures I have described are also required for that. Places that are off-limits to fishing constitute the last and most important part of our package of reform for fisheries management. They underpin and enhance all our other efforts. There are limits to protection though. Reserves cannot bring back what has died out. We can never resurrect globally extinct species, and restoring locally extinct animals may require reintroductions from elsewhere, if natural dispersal from remaining populations is insufficient. We are also seeing, in cases such as northern cod in Canada, that fishing can shift marine ecosystems into different states where different mixes of species prevail. In many cases these are less desirable, since the prime fishing targets have gone or are much reduced in numbers, and changes may be difficult to reverse, even with a complete moratorium on fishing. The Mediterranean sailed by Ulysses supported abundant monk seals, loggerhead turtles, and porpoises. Their disappearance through hunting and overfishing has totally restructured food webs, and recovery is likely to be much more difficult. This means that the sooner we act to protect marine life, the more certain will be our success.

To some people, creating marine reserves is an admission of failure. According to their logic, reserves should not be necessary if we have done our work properly in managing the uses we make of the sea. Many fisheries managers are still wedded to the idea that one day their models will work and politicians will listen to their advice. Just give the approach time, and success will be theirs. How much time have we got? This approach has been tried and refined for the last fifty years. There have been few successes with which to feather the managers' caps, but a growing litany of failure. The Common Fisheries Policy in Europe exemplifies the worst pitfalls: flawed models, flawed advice, watered-down recommendations from government bureaucrats, and then the disregard of much of this advice by politicians. When it all went wrong, as it inevitably had to, Europe sent its boats to developing countries in order to ransack other people's fish for far less than they are worth.

We are squandering the wealth of oceans. If we don't break out of this cycle of failure, humanity will lose a key source of protein, and much more besides. Disrupting ecosystem processes, such as water purification, nutrient cycling, and carbon storage, could have ramifications for human life itself. We can go a long way to avoiding this catastrophic mistake with simple commonsense management. Marine reserves lie at the heart of the reform. But they will not be sufficient if they are implemented here and there to shore up the crumbling edifice of "rational fisheries management" envisioned by scientists in the 1940s and 1950s. They have to be placed center stage as a fundamental underpinning for everything we do in the oceans. Reserves are a first resort, not a final resort when all else fails.

Marine reserves can benefit fisheries in more ways than Marcel Herubel foresaw in the early twentieth century. A pervasive effect of fishing is to compress the life histories of exploited animals. Species that once lived long lives in which they reproduced many times are forced to live fast and die young. Often they have time to produce only one or two broods before falling victim to hook, net, or trawl. Species that cannot adapt disappear, while those that can adapt end up growing more slowly and maturing at smaller sizes. This is because fishing favors animals that remain small and reproduce early in life. They avoid capture for longer and so produce some young before being killed. The small-bodied fish that dominate today's depleted fish populations produce few eggs, undermining their ability to renew themselves. Compared to populations with plenty of big, old egg producers, they lack resilience to fluctuating environmental conditions and the long-term shifts expected with climate change. By providing refuges from fishing, reserves raise baseline population sizes and allow the development of more natural age structures. Egg production is increased and can be sustained through periods of unfavorable conditions for the survival of young. This restores resilience. Without marine reserves, the runs of bad years that inevitably strike industries dependent on the environment could cause population and fishery collapse, as indeed they have done. It is because the way we fish today destroys resilience that depleted populations find it so hard to struggle back, even after fishing is reduced or stopped altogether.

Fishery regulations can be wiped out by the stroke of an official's pen. Marine reserves are more enduring because permanence is a cornerstone of the idea of protection, making it much harder to remove them on a legislative whim. They should provide, as Herubel described, inviolable asylums for marine life. If management goes wrong outside reserves, and populations are overfished, there will still be protected animals left to kick-start recovery. Reserves provide insurance against management failure.

Reserves do not just promote resilience of the species we catch to eat, but will also restore it in their habitats. Putting areas off-limits to fishing allows recovery of species, such as corals, sponges, sea squirts, and mollusks, that create complex bottom structures that bind the seabed and perform countless other vital roles, like filtering the water. This is important, because through its mechanical destruction, fishing has depleted populations of these animals, too. With time, after reserves have become established, such "bioengineers" will also begin to experience higher and more stable reproduction. In turn, the recovery of habitats that have been damaged by fishing will aid the productivity of commercially valuable species.

By integrating marine reserves into fishery management, we can overcome an enduring dilemma that arises in managing multispecies fisheries. Fish species all differ in how much fishing they can sustain. If many species are caught using the same gear, a compromise must be struck between the needs of vulnerable and resilient species. Should you fish at a level that can be sustained by the most vulnerable species and so maintain populations of all, or should you fish harder to catch more of the resilient species? In nearly all cases, the dilemma has been resolved, either consciously or by default, by sacrificing larger, more vulnerable species. These species are the "weakest link" in fisheries.[2]

We can get bigger catches from other species if we fish harder, but we risk eliminating weaker links if we do so. Marine reserves offer a way out of this dilemma. Vulnerable species gain a refuge within reserves, while fishing grounds can be exploited more intensively to produce bigger catches.

How much of the sea do we need to protect in marine reserves to restore what has been lost, head off extinctions, and achieve the sustainability that flits through fishery managers' dreams but evades them in daily life? Small reserves, like the network in St. Lucia, can provide local fishery benefits. With a few exceptions, like Australia's Great Barrier Reef and the Northwest Hawaiian Islands National Monument in the United States, present-day reserves are small and scattered. In order to have any significant impact at national and global scales, our existing marine reserves would need to be scaled up by adding networks of new reserves.

Some insight into the coverage that is needed can be gained from the population models used by fisheries managers. Recall that managers today aim to avoid recruitment overfishing—that is, the reduction of a population to such low levels that it cannot replace itself. According to fishery models, recruitment overfishing can be averted for most species by sustaining populations above one-third of their unexploited size. For many species, there is much rehabilitation to do before they approach these levels of abundance, especially given new historical perspectives that suggest populations are often below 10 percent of unexploited population sizes and sometimes much lower. Success in recovering populations will likely be far greater if marine reserves are part of the rebuilding package. Managers of the Georges Bank fisheries have seen promising recovery of scallops and groundfish because they complemented reduced fishing effort with areas closed to trawling and dredging. Within six years there were five times more haddock, fourteen times more scallops, and cod were up 50 percent, and benefits are spilling into surrounding fisheries. Those closures would have been even more effective if they were real marine reserves and had prohibited all forms of fishing.

You can do a back-of-the-envelope calculation about how much protection is needed to boost reproduction by depleted fish populations to sustainable levels. Populations of many fish species have been depressed to less than 10 percent of natural abundance; we've seen this in bluefin tuna, Nassau grouper, cod, Atlantic turbot, and halibut, among others. Let's assume for simplicity the figure is 10 percent. Marine reserves, for the sake of this exercise, raise reproductive output to ten times the level, area for area, of that in fishing grounds. To lift overall population reproductive output to sustainable levels, summed across reserves and fishing grounds, roughly 30 percent of the sea will need to be covered with reserves. This calculation assumes business as usual outside reserves. If other management measures were put in place to reduce the impact of fishing in nonreserve areas, they might be expected to double reproduction by animals in fishing grounds. In this case, we would need about 20 percent coverage of marine reserves to meet the sustainability target.

Other scientists have used more sophisticated approaches to estimate how much of the sea we should protect. Their answers have a great deal of consistency despite the variety of methods used to make the calculations. They suggest we need to protect between 20 percent and 40 percent of the sea from all fishing.[3] Doing this will maximize returns to the fishing industry, provide adequate refuges for vulnerable species, sustain genetic variability in populations, and afford protection to the full spectrum of biodiversity. This answer makes intuitive sense. If you have no marine reserves, there can be no fishery or conservation benefit. If you have 100 percent coverage, there will be maximum conservation benefit but no fisheries. Fishery benefits peak somewhere in the middle, between 20 and 40 percent reserve coverage, according to the models. Some of the best-performing marine reserves and partially protected areas support these predictions. Reserve zones in St. Lucia's Soufrière Marine Management Area cover 35 percent of coral reef habitat. Merritt Island National Wildlife Refuge includes 22 percent of the area of northern Florida's lagoons. The trawl closures on Georges Bank cover around 25 percent of groundfish habitat and about 40 percent of scallop habitat. These are not trivial numbers. This is the degree of scaling up of protection that is necessary to achieve a turnaround in world fisheries.

Because all species are different, not all will benefit to the same degree from reserves. Marcel Herubel scoffed at the idea of protecting sardines or herring, regarding them as too mobile to gain any benefit. Certainly, highly mobile species will gain less protection from marine reserves than species like rockfish, or striped bass, that spend most of their lives rooted to some reef or rock pile. But strategically placed reserves can benefit mobile species, too. The Caribbean Nassau groupers that migrated tens of kilometers to reach mass spawning sites would not be in such trouble today had those aggregations been protected in reserves. Belatedly, such protection is being extended to other species that reproduce at spawning aggregations. In the U.S. Virgin Islands, another grouper, the red hind, has shown a swift increase in average fish size on the heels of protection of their spawning aggregations.[4] There has also been a rise in the number of large males in this hermaphroditic fish, which should promote greater spawning success. Tunas on their ocean passages use seamounts and convergence zones as way stations and refueling stops. At present, we target them in these vulnerable places where they concentrate to feed. Protecting some of these places in particular could significantly increase tuna survival. Juveniles of migratory species like cod survive better in complex, biologically rich bottom habitats that have not been hit by trawls, and so these animals too will benefit from reserves. However, migratory species, like all exploited marine life, also need some protection outside of reserves. There is no point in having a network of protected areas but scorched-earth fishing everywhere else. This is why other measures such as I have set out are also essential.

We have much to do to realize a vision of the world where the oceans and seas are spangled with mosaics of marine reserves. With just three-fifths of 1 percent of the ocean currently protected, we need fifty times more reserve areas to do the job well, spread across the waters of coastal nations and the high seas. This is far more than many politicians, fishery managers, and even some people in conservation agencies are willing to countenance. I have spoken to hundreds of them in my career. Their worldview has yet to incorporate the new evidence of the scale of human impact in the oceans I describe in this book. Even in unguarded moments, the most that many are willing to concede is that a few percent of the sea should be protected as reserves. The rest would either continue to be used as it is now or would be zoned to exclude certain kinds of activities, like dredging for aggregate or drilling for oil.

If we stick to that management paradigm, I am convinced that marine life will continue its long slide toward jellyfish and slime. A handful of special places protected by reserves might remind tourists of what has been lost. But these scattered reserves could sustain only a fraction of the species that live in the sea because in the long term they will not be sufficient to maintain viable populations of the largest, most vulnerable and mobile species. Diving in them would be like looking at a Roman fresco where great patches of plaster have crumbled away. Do we really want to have to imagine what has been lost?

I believe that we need to flip this paradigm on its head. Rather than thinking that marine reserve protection should be afforded to only a few special or out-of-the-way places, we need to view reserves as the foundation and underpinning for all other management. According to this view, reserves would cover some 30 percent of the sea, perhaps more in some places. They would be complemented by other kinds of marine protected areas that allow a range of low-impact activities such as certain kinds of fishing. Added to this would be areas zoned for other uses, such as bottom trawling. The aim would be to contain the impacts of more invasive activities and keep them away from sensitive areas. Places that are given no protection would make up a small minority of the sea, not the large majority that they constitute now.

Opinion surveys show that the public is ready for such a change in thinking. For example, when Americans were polled on their attitudes to the oceans a few years ago, they were surprised to find so little protection given to the sea. On average, they thought that 22 percent of the sea was already fully protected from all fishing in marine reserves and were upset and angry to discover that most national marine sanctuaries allowed fishing. The name "sanctuary" was a sham. At a conference in 2003, I picked up a leaflet put out by the U.S. Fish and Wildlife Service that proclaimed, *"Discover Nature's Best Hunting and Fishing: The National Wildlife Refuge System."* Clearly, even some conservationists have trouble with the concept of "refuge." One of my students has also polled public opinion in Britain. On average, people thought that 16 percent of Britain's seas were already protected in marine reserves (at the time of the survey the correct answer was 0.0004 percent). When asked how much of

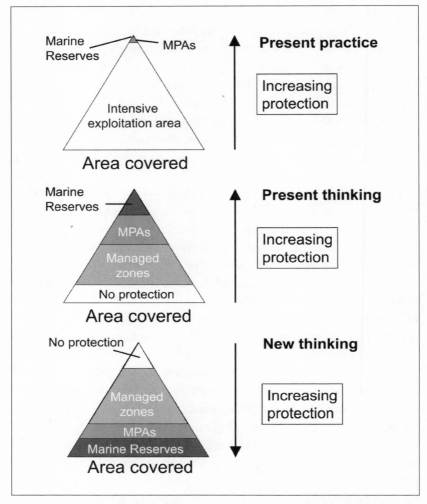

*At present, marine reserves that are protected from all fishing cover a tiny fraction of the sea (top figure), while marine protected areas in general cover just 0.6 percent of the area of the oceans. Most governments now accept that we need to increase protection (middle figure), but the majority still see marine reserves as the pinnacle of protection to be applied to only 5 percent or 10 percent of the sea, with lesser amounts of protection given to the rest. Emerging scientific understanding of human impacts on the oceans suggests we need to flip this management paradigm around. According to this view, marine reserves must be extensive, covering between 20 and 40 percent of the sea, in order to sustain ecological processes and services—like fisheries—that are vital to humanity. Source: Callum Roberts.*

Britain's seas they thought should be protected this way, the average answer given was 54 percent. Ninety-five percent of people thought more than 20 percent should be marine reserves.[5]

People love the sea. Some of our most cherished early memories are of trips to the seaside, gathering shells, paddling, fencing with seaweeds, and gazing into rock pools. The sea inspires and soothes us; it can rouse us to rapture and terror. It is in constant motion but never seems to change. The whisper of rising tide over sand is the same today as it was when Dampier and his companions rocked at anchor in some Caribbean bay. The radiant blue of the Mediterranean dazzles in the same way as it did when Hannibal set forth with his fleet to conquer Rome. But many of the animals that sported around their ships are rare today or already in deep trouble and need our help to make a comeback.

A starting gun has been fired to change all of this. In 2000, President Bill Clinton issued an executive order, later endorsed by the Bush administration, charging government agencies to create a national network of marine protected areas. At the World Summit on Sustainable Development in 2002, coastal nations of the world pledged to create national networks of marine protected areas by 2012. Meanwhile, European nations had already committed to create a Europe-wide network by 2010. However, these pledges remain vague on targets for numbers or size of protected areas and how they should be managed. Marine protected areas must offer genuine refuges. The World Conservation Union's World Parks Congress of 2003 recommended that at least 20 to 30 percent of every marine habitat should be protected from all fishing, and that marine protected area networks should straddle the high seas as well as national waters. Moves are afoot at the United Nations to develop a mechanism that would allow the establishment of marine reserves in this global commons, for which there appears to be widespread support.

Several countries have made good progress. South Africa has committed to protect 20 percent of its waters. Eighteen percent of its territorial waters are already reserves and the network is being expanded offshore. In Australia, a third of the Great Barrier Reef Marine Park, more than 100,000 square kilometers (40,000 square miles) of reef, sea grass, and swamp, was protected from fishing in 2004. This network of reserve zones is representative of all the different habitats in the park and sets a shining example for others to follow. Britain's Royal Commission on Environmental Pollution recommended in 2004 that 30 percent of the country's waters should become marine reserves. We are on the path to a global network of marine reserves that could restore the oceans to much of their former glory. But we have to be bold and move rapidly if we are to achieve success.

Can the world afford to protect the oceans? One estimate, made in 2004, put the cost at US$12 to 14 billion per year to run a worldwide network of marine reserves covering 30 percent of all oceans and seas.[6] Initial onetime set-up costs would be about five times this amount. These sums seem like a lot but are put in perspective when we consider they are less than the US$15 to 30 billion we currently spend on harmful subsidies that encourage excess fishing capacity and prop up overexploitation. Most countries offer fishers tax breaks on fuel, for example, or free nets, and many countries pay for access to fish in another country's waters. Compared to global defence spending, estimated at US$900 billion in 2004,[7] the sums needed to keep our oceans

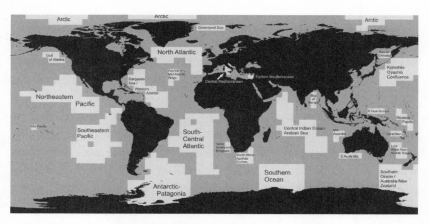

*A Greenpeace proposal for a global network of marine reserves that would cover 40 percent of the area of the high seas—places beyond the limits of national jurisdiction. The high seas remain the least protected place on the planet, and we must think big to reverse the adverse effects of centuries of overexploitation. Source: Roberts, C.M., L. Mason and J.P. Hawkins (2006)* Roadmap to Recovery: A Global Network of Marine Reserves. *Greenpeace International, Amsterdam.*

healthy are trivial. The costs are also less than the US$31 billion that Europeans and Americans collectively spend on ice cream, and roughly equate to the US$15 billion we spend on perfumes or US$14 billion on ocean cruises. In addition, this reserve network would create more than a million permanent jobs for managers, wardens, and administrators. Much of the running costs of coastal reserves could be recouped from visitors. Some reserves, like the Saba and Bonaire marine parks in the Caribbean are already self-funding, based on modest payments made by visitors. The costs could also be offset by the very large contribution reserve networks can be expected to make to fisheries. It would take only a 10 percent uplift in fishery productivity in Britain's Irish Sea and 2 to 3 percent in the North Sea for reserves there to cover all their management costs.[8] The world can certainly afford marine reserves. What it can't afford is to be without them any longer.

In southern Belize, 50 kilometers (30 miles) offshore, is a place called Gladden Spit where an elbow in the barrier reef forms a sheer underwater promontory. Here the reef plunges to depths of more than 1,000 meters (3,300 feet) as it falls away into the Cayman Trench. The sun has dipped below the horizon, staining the sky red and purple. A stiff breeze has kicked up the waves and rattles cables on the boat. I roll into the water with three companions, pausing briefly to check my equipment before beginning my descent. It is a relief to leave the violently heaving boat and enter this tranquil world. I peer downward looking for the reef, but the bottom is too far below to see. Shafts of light pick out flecks of plankton like dust motes suspended in deep indigo. In this watery cathedral, I feel very small. Dropping deeper, I see vague movements and a flash of silver flank, then another and another as fish wheel and turn below. When I get close, I realize they are sleek dog snappers; there must be hundreds of them. As I descend into their midst, the group parts and engulfs me in a moving wall of bodies. Countless eyes watch impassively as fish swirl past, every cheek marked with a pale teardrop shape. Glowing silver bodies tinged with pink press in upon me in the revolving mass as the dog snappers abandon themselves to the primal urge that drew them here. I revise my estimate upward. There must be five thousand of them, maybe more. They lull me into a reverie that is broken only when the fish start to thin and then leave. But it is the current that has moved me. The fish remain in the same place as if held by an invisible force.

From a distance, I can see the whole group. They form a spinning column that rises above the reef. Where the column contacts the reef, fish fan out, giving the appearance of a plinth. Fish spiral up from this base and into the column, while animals near the top turn and head downward in continuous renewal. Many appear fat, their swollen bellies heavy with eggs. They have gathered here to spawn, many having traveled long distances, and the time has arrived. In the gathering gloom, a small group of fish makes an excited upward rush, their bodies pressed together in shivering embrace. A few meters below the surface, they release a white cloud of eggs and sperm in an explosive burst before turning to dash for the bottom. Other groups break off in similar rushes like spurting jets from a fountain. Then the fountain itself thrusts upward as a further great mass of fish follows, saturating the water with their seed before spilling down into the depths.

I drift suspended amid billowing clouds of eggs and sperm, surrounded by a frenzied but unseen struggle as new lives are forged. Out of the corner of one eye I see a dark, moving shadow in the gloom. At first it seems small and formless, but as it approaches, I make out the rhythmic sickle tail beat that signals the approach of a shark. A gaping black grin fills the width of its broad, flat head. Huge pectoral fins spread like hydroplanes from the sides of a giant body painted with a constellation of white spots. It is a whale shark, the largest fish in the sea. The leviathan ploughs into the egg cloud and toward me, opening its mouth in a giant gape to sieve eggs from the water. It barely registers my presence, betraying no flicker of alarm or recognition. Muscled flanks glide by like a submarine as I backpaddle to avoid being bowled over. Then another shark appears from behind me, this one even bigger than the first. For the next half hour the sharks crisscross the area, feasting on the dispersing caviar cloud as darkness falls. With perfect timing, as if called by some aquatic dinner gong, whale sharks come to Gladden Spit when the fish congregate to spawn, and then leave when the spawning is over.[9]

There are still places in the world, like Gladden Spit, where it is possible to find something of the miraculous in nature. In Alaskan estuaries, salmon still gather in impenetrable throngs as they prepare for their spawning ascents upriver. They attract packs of toothy salmon sharks, seals, otters, and killer whales to feed on them. Great shoals of hammerhead sharks still circle Galápagos seamounts. Mighty boils of tuna still erupt from the Humboldt Current, thrashing their way into dense balls of anchovies. Great white sharks still thrill as they burst clear of South African seas, twisting in midair with seals grasped in their jaws. Such scenes are remnants of the seas of long ago. They offer us windows to past worlds, letting us see the oceans as they must have looked to travelers and fishers of centuries past. They also give us hope that today's oceans can yet recover. But even these places are critically threatened, and we are running out of time to save them.[10] I am an optimist. I cherish the hope that a hundred years from now, a family might find a copy of this book in a dusty secondhand bookshop and, on reading it, shake their heads in amazement at how close we came to destroying the seas' riches. Instead of wishing the world had taken action to protect the oceans, as I did when I read Marcel Herubel's call for marine reserves in the early twentieth century, this future family of readers will feel thankful that sense prevailed in time. They will think back to their recent summer vacation and the amazing reserves they dived in; how they were filled with dense shoals of fish and ranks of beady-eyed crab and lobster, and thronged with large predatory beasts. When these vacationers sat down to dinner on some sunshine coast, the paella they enjoyed contained only seafood caught from sustainable fisheries.[11] (See note 11 on page 421 for advice on how to choose sustainably caught seafood today.)

We can restore the life and habitats of the sea because it is in everyone's interest that we do so. The same large-scale networks of marine reserves, complemented by other measures of fish and habitat protection, best serve the interests of both commerce and conservation. You can have exploitation with protection, because reserves help sustain catches in surrounding fishing grounds. But you cannot have exploitation without protection, not in the long term.

# Notes

### Preface
1. Fanning, E. (1833) *Voyages Around the World; with Selected Sketches of Voyages to the South Seas, North and South Pacific Oceans, China etc.* Collins & Hannay, New York.

### Chapter 1: The End of Innocence
1. Waxell, S. (ca. 1745) *The American Expedition.* Translated by M.A. Michael. William Hodge and Company Ltd., London, 1952. Waxell's account of the expedition went unpublished at the time. The manuscript disappeared for two hundred years before its discovery in a St. Petersburg bookseller's window in 1938, when it was acquired for the state.
2. Bell, M.E. (1960) *Touched with Fire: Alaska's George William Steller.* William Morrow and Company, New York.
3. Steller, G.W. (1988) *Journal of a Voyage with Bering, 1741–1742.* Translated by M.A. Engel and O.W. Frost. Stanford University Press, Stanford, California.
4. Ibid.
5. Ibid.
6. Ibid.
7. Ibid.
8. Ibid.
9. Waxell (ca. 1745) *The American Expedition.*
10. Steller (1988) *Journal of a Voyage with Bering.*
11. Golder, F.A. (1925) *Bering's Voyages. An Account of the Efforts of the Russians to Determine the Relation of Asia and America.* Volume II. Translated by L. Stejneger. American Geographical Society Research Series No. 2.
12. Steller estimated the weight of the largest sea cows at around 8,000 pounds, or over 3.5 tons. Steller, G.W. (1751) *De Bestiis Marinis.* Translated as *The Beasts of the Sea* by W. Miller and J.E. Miller in *The Fur Seals and Fur-Seal Islands of the North Pacific Ocean,* part 3. Government Printing Office, Washington, DC, 1899.
13. Steller (1988) *Journal of a Voyage with Bering.*
14. Ibid.
15. Ibid.
16. Ibid.
17. Krasheninnikov, S.P. (1754) *The History of Kamtschatka and the Kurilski*

*Islands, with the Countries Adjacent.* Translated by J. Grieve. Quadrangle Books, Chicago, 1962.

18. Goode, G.B. (1884) *The Fisheries and Fishery Industries of the United States. Section I. Natural History of Useful Aquatic Animals.* Government Printing Office, Washington, DC.

19. Ibid.

### Chapter 2: The Origins of Intensive Fishing

1. Barrett, J.H., A.M. Locker, and C.M. Roberts (2004) The origins of intensive marine fishing in medieval Europe: The English evidence. *Proceedings of the Royal Society B* 271: 2417–2421. Barrett, J.H., A.M. Locker, and C.M. Roberts (2004) Dark Age economics revisited: The English fish bone evidence AD 600–1600. *Antiquity* 78: 618–636.

2. Hoffmann, R.C. (1997) *Fishers' Craft and Lettered Art: Tracts on Fishing from the End of the Middle Ages.* University of Toronto Press, Toronto.

3. Radcliffe, W. (1921) *Fishing from Earliest Times.* John Murray, London. Currency conversions are to 2005 values.

4. Hoffmann, R.C. (1999) Fish and man: Changing relations in medieval central Europe. *Beiträge zur Mittelalterarchäologie in Österreich* 15: S187–S195.

5. Barrett et al. (2004) The origins of intensive marine fishing.

6. Ibid.

7. Barrett, J.H. (1999) Archaeo-ichthyological evidence for long-term socio-economic trends in northern Scotland: 3500 BC to AD 1500. *Journal of Archaeological Science* 26: 353–388.

8. Ibid.

9. Roberts, N. (1989) *The Holocene: An Environmental History.* Blackwell, Oxford.

10. Bitel, L.M. (2002) *Women in Early Medieval Europe, 400–1100.* Cambridge University Press, Cambridge.

11. Hoffmann, R.C. (1996) Economic development and aquatic ecosystems in medieval Europe. *The American Historical Review* 101: 630–669.

12. Pliny the Elder (AD 23/24–79). *Natural History: A Selection.* Translated by J.F. Healy. Penguin Books, London, 1991.

13. Hoffmann (1996) Economic development and aquatic ecosystems.

14. Reynolds, T. (1983) *Stronger Than a Hundred Men: A History of the Vertical Water Wheel.* Johns Hopkins University Press, Baltimore.

15. Hoffmann (1996) Economic development and aquatic ecosystems.

16. Ibid.

17. Ibid.

18. Hoffmann, R.C. (1995) Environmental change and the culture of common carp in medieval Europe. *Guelph Ichthyology Reviews* 3: 57–85.

19. Ibid.

20. Hoffmann, R. (2000) Medieval fishing. Pages 331–392 in P. Squatriti (ed.) *Working with Water in Medieval Europe*. Brill, Leiden. The dissolution of the monasteries in England in the 1530s also led to the wholesale collapse of aquaculture there.

21. Ibid.

22. Barrett et al. (2004) The origins of intensive marine fishing.

23. Barrett (1999) Archaeo-ichthyological evidence.

24. Gade, J.A. (1951) *The Hanseatic Control of Norwegian Commerce During the Late Middle Ages*. E.J. Brill, Leiden.

25. Urbańczyk, P. (1992) *Medieval Arctic Norway*. Institute of the History of Material Culture, Polish Academy of Sciences, Warsaw, Poland.

26. Ibid.

27. Hoffmann, R.C. (2001) Frontier foods for late medieval consumers: Culture, economy, ecology. *Environment and History* 7: 131–167.

28. Magnus, O. (1555) *Historia de Gentibus Septentrionalibus. Description of the Northern Peoples*. Volume 1. Translated by P. Fisher and H. Higgens. Hakluyt Society, London, 1996.

29. Nilsson, L. (1947) Fishing in the Lofotens. *The National Geographic Magazine* 91: 377–388.

30. Gade (1951) *The Hanseatic Control of Norwegian Commerce*.

31. Hoffmann (2000) Medieval fishing.

32. Starkey, D.J., C. Reid, and N. Ashcroft (eds.) (2000) *England's Sea Fisheries: The Commercial Sea Fisheries of England and Wales Since 1300*. Chatham Publishing, London.

33. Ibid.

34. Myers, R.A., and B. Worm (2003) Rapid worldwide depletion of predatory fish communities. *Nature* 423: 280–283.

35. In 1415, English fishers blamed failure of fisheries in home waters for their need to make long-distance voyages to Iceland. Hoffmann, R.C. (2002) Carp, cods, connections: New fisheries in the medieval European economy and environment. Pages 3–55 in M.J. Henninger-Voss (ed.) *Animals in Human Histories: The Mirror of Nature and Culture*. University of Rochester Press, New York.

### Chapter 3: Newfound Lands

1. Williamson, J.A. (1962) *The Cabot Voyages and Bristol Discovery under Henry VII*. Hakluyt Society, Cambridge University Press, Cambridge.

2. Pope, P.E. (1997) *The Many Landfalls of John Cabot*. University of Toronto Press, Toronto.

3. De Soncino's letter to the Duke of Milan, 18 December 1497. Quoted in J.A. Williamson (1962) *The Cabot Voyages and Bristol Discovery under Henry VII*. Hakluyt Society, Cambridge University Press, Cambridge.

4. Peter Martyr's first account of Sebastian Cabot's voyage, 1516. Quoted in

J.A. Williamson (1962) *The Cabot Voyages and Bristol Discovery under Henry VII.* Hakluyt Society, Cambridge University Press, Cambridge. "Bacalao" was the southern European name for cod, deriving from the Flemish word for cod, *bakkeljaw,* which itself came from the Germanic word *kabeljaw.* This has led some people to speculate that the people of eastern Canada had contact with Basque sailors before the Cabot voyages.

5. Sabine, L. (1853) *Report on the Principal Fisheries of the American Seas.* Robert Armstrong, Printer, Washington, DC.

6. Cell, G.T. (ed.) (1982) *Newfoundland Discovered: English Attempts at Colonisation, 1610–1630.* Hakluyt Society, London. The first (unsuccessful) attempt at colonization was by Sir Humphrey Gilbert in 1583.

7. Currency conversions are to 2005 values.

8. Mason, J. (1620) *A Brief Discourse of the New-Found-Land.* Andro Hart, Edinburgh. Reprinted in G.T. Cell (ed.) (1982) *Newfoundland Discovered: English Attempts at Colonisation, 1610–1630.* Hakluyt Society, London.

9. John Davis, for example, exploring the coast of Labrador in 1586: "wee saw an incredible number of birds; having diverse fishermen aboord our barke, they all concluded there was a great skull of fish; we, being unprovided of fishing furniture, with a long spike nayle made a hooke and fastened the same to one of our sounding lines. Before the baite was changed we took more than fortie great cods, the fish swimming so abundantly thick about our barke as is incredible." Davis, J. (1595) *The Worldes Hydrographical Discription.* Thomas Dawson, London.

10. De Charlevoix, P. (1744) *Journal of a Voyage to North America.* Reprinted by University Microfilms Inc., Ann Arbor, Michigan, 1966.

11. Briere, J.-F. (1997) The French fishery in North America in the 18th century. Pages 47–64 in J.E. Candow and C. Corbin (eds.) *How Deep Is the Ocean? Historical Essays on Canada's Atlantic Fishery.* University College of Cape Breton Press, Sydney.

12. Tulloch, J. (1997) The New England Fishery and Trade at Canso, 1720–1744. Pages 65–74 in J.E. Candow and C. Corbin (eds.) *How Deep Is the Ocean? Historical Essays on Canada's Atlantic Fishery.* University College of Cape Breton Press, Sydney.

13. Gabriel Archer's account of Captain Gosnold's Voyage to "North Virginia" in 1602. Reprinted in D.B. Quinn and A.M. Quinn (eds.) (1983) *The English New England Voyages 1602–1608.* Hakluyt Society, London.

14. Brereton, J. (1602) *A Briefe and True Relation of the Discoverie of the North Part of Virginia.* Reprinted in D.B. Quinn and A.M. Quinn (eds.) (1983) *The English New England Voyages 1602–1608.* Hakluyt Society, London.

15. Ibid.

16. Rosier, J. (1605) *A True Relation of the Most Prosperous Voyage Made in this Present Yeere 1605, by Captaine George Waymouth, in the Discoverie of the Land of Virginia.* George Bishop, London. Reprinted in D.B. Quinn and

A.M. Quinn (eds.) (1983) *The English New England Voyages 1602–1608.* Hakluyt Society, London.

17. Davies, R. (1607) *The Relation of a Voyage, Unto New-England, Began from the Lizard, y$^e$ First of June 1607. By Captain Popham in y$^e$ Ship y$^e$ Gift, & Captain Gilbert in y$^e$ Mary and John.* Reprinted in D.B. Quinn and A.M. Quinn (eds.) (1983) *The English New England Voyages 1602–1608.* Hakluyt Society, London.

18. Pring, M. (1603) *A Voyage Set Out from the Citie of Bristoll at the Charge of the Chiefest Merchants and Inhabitants of the said Citie with a Small Ship and Barke for the Discoverie of the North Part of Virginia, in the Yeere 1603. Under the Command of me Martin Pring.* Reprinted in D.B. Quinn and A.M. Quinn (eds.) (1983) *The English New England Voyages 1602–1608.* Hakluyt Society, London.

19. The lands were also blanketed with old-growth forest, providing ample habitat for game animals as well as a valuable commodity for local use and export. De Charlevoix described forests along the coast of the Gulf of St. Lawrence in 1719: "We are here surrounded with the vastest woods in the whole world; in all appearance, they are as ancient as the world itself, and were never planted by the hand of man. Nothing can present a nobler or more magnificent prospect to the eyes, the trees hide their tops in the clouds, and the variety of different species of them is so prodigious." De Charlevoix (1744) *Journal of a Voyage to North America.* Farther south in the Carolinas, early eighteenth-century traveler John Lawson was similarly impressed: "Chestnut-Oak, is a very lofty Tree, clear of Boughs and Limbs, for fifty or 60 foot. They bear sometimes four or five Foot through all clear Timber; and are the largest Oaks we have, yielding the fairest Plank. They grow chiefly in low Land that is stiff and rich. I have seen them so high, that a good Gun could not reach a Turkey, tho' loaded with Swan-Shot." Lawson, J. (1709) *A New Voyage to Carolina.* Reprinted by University Microfilms Inc., Ann Arbor, Michigan, 1966.

20. Lindholt, P.J. (ed.) (1988). *John Josselyn, Colonial Traveller: A Critical Edition of Two Voyages to New-England.* University Press of New England, Hanover, New Hampshire.

21. Bad luck also played a part in the failure of colonies. Sir Walter Raleigh's ill-fated attempt to colonize North Carolina coincided with the worst years of the worst drought for eight hundred years. Stahle, D.W., M.K. Cleaveland, D.B. Blanton, M.D. Therrell, and D.A. Gay (1998) The lost colony and Jamestown droughts. *Science* 280: 564–567.

22. Wood, W. (1634) *New England's Prospect.* Edited with an introduction by A.T. Vaughan. University of Massachusetts Press, Amherst, 1993.

23. Brereton (1602) *A Briefe and True Relation of the Discoverie of the North Part of Virginia.*

24. De Charlevoix (1744) *Journal of a Voyage to North America.*

25. Gaskell, J. (2000) *Who Killed the Great Auk?* Oxford University Press, Oxford.
26. Today's Gulf of St. Lawrence Beluga whale population numbers approximately five hundred. In the middle of the nineteenth century there were more than fifty thousand, with perhaps more at the time of first European contact.
27. Gaskell (2000) *Who Killed the Great Auk?*
28. Black guillemots now breed only in the high Arctic. Ehrlich, P.R., D.S. Dobkin, and D. Wheye (1988) *The Birders Handbook.* Simon & Schuster Inc., New York.
29. Gaskell (2000) *Who Killed the Great Auk?*
30. De Charlevoix (1744) *Journal of a Voyage to North America.*
31. Cartwright, G. (1792) *Journal of Transactions and Events during a Residence of Nearly Sixteen Years on the Coast of Labrador.* Reprinted in C.W. Townsend (ed.) (1911) *Captain Cartwright and his Labrador Journal.* Dana Estes & Company, Boston.
32. Ibid.

*Chapter 4: More Fish than Water*

1. Smith, J. (1612) *A Map of Virginia with a Description of the Country, the Commodities, People, Government and Religion.* Joseph Barnes, Oxford. Reprinted in P.L. Barbour (ed.) *The Jamestown Voyages Under the First Charter 1606–1609.* Volume II. Hakluyt Society, Cambridge University Press, Cambridge, 1969.
2. Letter from the Council in Virginia, 22 June 1607. Reprinted in P.L. Barbour (ed.) *The Jamestown Voyages Under the First Charter 1606–1609.* Volume I. Hakluyt Society, Cambridge University Press, Cambridge, 1969.
3. These first impressions were later countered by bitter experience in the early years of colonization. The Chesapeake's fish and game was seasonal, as was its climate. Not knowing the pattern of arrival and departure of fish and game, and lacking sufficient salt and barrels to store food for the winter, the colonists failed to provide sufficiently for themselves. Many suffered severe hunger, and a disease epidemic in 1608 cut deeply into the skilled labor force, compromising their ability to acquire sufficient food. Bad planning was met with ill luck with a severe winter frost in 1609 that froze the James River. Local Native Americans, although sometimes hostile, provided vital supplies of game and corn to help the colonists survive. Of five hundred settlers in 1609, only sixty were alive by the time relief ships arrived from England in 1610.
4. Tilp, F. (1978) *This Was Potomac River.* 2nd edition. Frederick Tilp, Alexandria, Virginia.
5. Ibid.
6. Studley, T., A. Todkill, W. Russell, N. Powell, W. Phettyplace, R. Wyffin,

and T. Abbay (1612) *The Proceedings of the English Colonie in Virginia.* Reprinted in P.L. Barbour (ed.) *The Jamestown Voyages Under the First Charter 1606–1609.* Volume I. Hakluyt Society, Cambridge University Press, Cambridge, 1969.

7. Captain Smith nearly paid dearly for his sport, being stung in the arm by a stingray he had speared. His companions, fearing him about to die, began preparing a grave. Fortunately, he recovered and dined well that evening on the fish that stung him!

8. Archer, G. (1607) *The Description of the Now Discovered River and Country of Virginia.* Reprinted in P.L. Barbour (ed.) *The Jamestown Voyages Under the First Charter 1606–1609.* Volume I. Hakluyt Society, Cambridge University Press, Cambridge, 1969.

9. Wharton, J. (1957) *The Bounty of the Chesapeake: Fishing in Colonial Virginia.* Virginia 350th Anniversary Celebration Corporation, Williamsburg.

10. Both pilot whales (*Globicephala melas*) and killer whales (*Orcinus orca*), together with some other members of the dolphin family (Delphinidae), such as Risso's dolphin (*Grampus griseus*), were referred to as "grampus" by writers up to the early twentieth century. The word is a corruption of the French *grand pisces*, or "big fish." It is not clear which species is referred to in Smith's description, possibly more than one. Killer whales were also often called "threshers" by early writers, and there are descriptions of them off the coast near the Jamestown colony around this time. See, for example, Lawson, J. (1709) *A New Voyage to Carolina.* Reprinted by University Microfilms Inc., Ann Arbor, Michigan, 1966.

11. Wharton (1957) *The Bounty of the Chesapeake.*

12. Wharton (1957) *The Bounty of the Chesapeake.*

13. Lawson (1709) *A New Voyage to Carolina.* John Lawson arrived in the Carolinas in 1700 and spent eight years there, much of that time traveling around the country in the company of Native Americans. He visited England briefly to oversee the publication of his account in 1709, then returned to the Carolinas. His descriptions of the indigenous people are important records of their customs and culture at this time. While most of the Native Americans he encountered were friendly, while traveling in the backcountry, he was taken by a tribe who believed he wanted to rob them of their land, and they tortured him to death.

14. Anonymous (1965) *The Watercolor Drawings of John White.* National Gallery of Art, Smithsonian Institution, Washington, DC.

15. Lawson (1709) *A New Voyage to Carolina.*

16. Wharton (1957) *The Bounty of the Chesapeake.*

17. Ralph Hamor described the fishing in 1614: "For fish, the rivers are plentifully stored with sturgeon, porpoise, bass, rockfish carp, shad, herring, eel, catfish, perch, flat-fish, trout, sheepshead, drummers, jewfish, crevises,

crabs, oysters and divers other kinds. Of all which myself has seen great quantity taken, especially the last summer at Smith's Island, at one haul a frigate's lading of sturgeon, bass and other great fish in Captain Argall's seine. . . . If we had been furnished with salt to have saved it, we might have taken as much fish as would have served us that whole year." Wharton (1957) *The Bounty of the Chesapeake.*

18. Wharton (1957) *The Bounty of the Chesapeake.* Robert Beverley said in his *History and Present State of Virginia* in 1705, "In spring of the year, herrings come up in such abundance into their brooks and fords to spawn that it is almost impossible to ride through without treading on them." Beverley, R. (1705) *The History and Present State of Virginia.* Edited by Louis B. Wright. Published for the Institute of Early American History and Culture by the University of North Carolina Press, North Carolina, 1947.

19. Wharton (1957) *The Bounty of the Chesapeake.*

20. Tilp (1978) *This Was Potomac River.*

21. Ibid.

22. Wood, W. (1634) *New England's Prospect. A True, Lively, and Experimental Description of that Part of America, Commonly Called New England: Discovering the State of that Countrie, Both as it Stands to our New-come English Planters; and to the Old Native Inhabitants.* Edited with an introduction by A.T. Vaughan. University of Massachusetts Press, Amherst, 1993.

23. Ibid.

24. Ibid.

25. Cartwright, G. (1792) *Journal of Transactions and Events During a Residence of Nearly Sixteen Years on the Coast of Labrador.* Reprinted in C.W. Townsend (ed.) *Captain Cartwright and his Labrador Journal.* Dana Estes & Company, Boston, 1911.

26. De Charlevoix, P. (1744) *Journal of a Voyage to North America.* Reprinted by University Microfilms Inc., Ann Arbor, Michigan, 1966. The Province of New France (Quebec) had approximately seven thousand inhabitants at this time.

27. Wood, W. (1634) *New England's Prospect. A True, Lively, and Experimental Description of that Part of America, Commonly Called New England: Discovering the State of that Countrie, Both as it Stands to our New-come English Planters; and to the Old Native Inhabitants.* Edited with an introduction by A.T. Vaughan. University of Massachusetts, Amherst, 1993.

28. Wharton, J. (1957) *The Bounty of the Chesapeake.*

29. The story of Judge Cooper and his fish weir is beautifully told by David Grettler's (2001) The nature of capitalism: Environmental change and conflict over commercial fishing in nineteenth-century Delaware. *Environmental History* 6: 451–473.

30. Wharton (1957) *The Bounty of the Chesapeake.*

31. Grettler (2001) The nature of capitalism.

32. Buckley, B., and S.W. Nixon (2001) *An Historical Assessment of Anadro-*

*mous Fish in the Blackstone River.* University of Rhode Island Graduate School of Oceanography, Narragansett.

33. Sabine, L. (1853) *Report on the Principal Fisheries of the American Seas.* Robert Armstrong, Printer, Washington, DC.

34. Sabine likewise blamed dams for the decline of alewife in rivers from Maine to the Carolinas, writing, "And that the practice [of fishing] was continued, substantially, without interruption, until the waters resorted to by the herring [alewife] for the deposite of its spawn were obstructed by dams and mills, is hardly to be doubted. It is certainly true that, on some of the rivers, where the fishery is now nearly extinct, the supply at the revolutionary era was considered inexhaustible."

35. Lawson (1709) *A New Voyage to Carolina.*

36. Wharton (1957) *The Bounty of the Chesapeake.*

37. Tilp (1978) *This Was Potomac River.*

38. Lawson (1709) *A New Voyage to Carolina.*

*Chapter 5: Plunder of the Caribbean*

1. Dampier, W. (1697) *A New Voyage Round the World.* Dover Publications Inc., New York, 1968.

2. Esquemeling, J. (1684) *The Buccaneers of America.* Dover Publications Inc., New York, 1967.

3. Basil Ringrose's account is included as part 4 of Esquemeling's book. See note 2.

4. Parry, J.H. (1963) *The Age of Reconnaissance. Discovery, Exploration and Settlement. 1450–1650.* Phoenix Press, London, 2000.

5. *The Voyages and Travels of Sir John Maundeville, K$^t$* (1905) Cassell and Company Ltd., London.

6. Walker, D.J.R. (1992) *Columbus and the Golden World of the Arawaks: The Story of the First Americans and their Caribbean Environment.* Ian Randle Publishers, Kingston. Nobody who reads any firsthand accounts of the conquest and subjugation of Native American peoples can doubt the capacity of their conquerors for extreme cruelty. Indeed, instances of great brutality and torture are common from both sides and make chilling reading. But the silent killer of disease played the biggest role in depopulating the New World of its native peoples. See Jared Diamond's (1998) *Guns, Germs and Steel* (W.W. Norton and Company, New York) for a fascinating discussion of the effects of disease and technology in the establishment of European overseas empires.

7. Dampier (1697) *A New Voyage.*

8. Ibid.

9. Long, E. (1774) *The History of Jamaica,* London. Reprinted by Ian Randle Publishers, Kingston, 2003.

10. Jane, C. (ed.) (1930) *Select Documents Illustrating the Four Voyages of Columbus.* Volumes I and II. Hakluyt Society, London.

11. Ibid.
12. Drake, Sir Francis (1586) *Sir Francis Drake's West Indian Voyage 1585–86.* Edited by M.F. Keeler. Hakluyt Society, London, 1981.
13. Ibid.
14. Quoted in A. Carr, (1967) *So Excellente a Fishe.* Charles Scribner's Sons, New York.
15. Long (1774) *The History of Jamaica.*
16. World Conservation Union www.iucn-mtsg.org/red_list/
17. Jackson's talk was published two years later in the journal *Coral Reefs.* Jackson, J.B.C. (1997) Reefs Since Columbus. *Coral Reefs* 16: S23–S32.
18. Sauer, C.O. (1966) *The Early Spanish Main.* University of California Press, Berkeley and Los Angeles.
19. McClenachan, L. (2006) Conservation implications of historic sea turtle nesting beach loss. *Frontiers of Ecology and Environment* 4: 290–296.
20. Esquemeling (1684) *The Buccaneers of America.*
21. Jane (1930) *Select Documents.*
22. Esquemeling (1684) *The Buccaneers of America.*
23. Goliath groupers were formerly known as jewfish.
24. Walker (1992) *Columbus and the Golden World of the Arawaks.*
25. Wing, E.S. (2001) The sustainability of resources used by Native Americans on five Caribbean Islands. *International Journal of Osteoarchaeology* 11: 112–126.

### Chapter 6: The Age of Merchant Adventurers

1. Dampier, W. (1697) *A New Voyage Round the World.* Dover Publications Inc., New York, 1968.
2. Ibid.
3. Rogers, Captain W. (1712) *A Cruising Voyage Round the World.* Dover Publications Inc., New York, 1970.
4. Ibid.
5. Ibid.
6. One died of scurvy, nine of fever, six were killed in acts of piracy, and one was poisoned after eating a seal liver.
7. Colnett, J. (1798) *A Voyage to the South Atlantic and Around Cape Horn into the Pacific Ocean for the Purpose of Extending the Spermaceti Whale Fisheries and Other Objects of Commerce.* N. Israel, Amsterdam, and Da Capo Press, New York, 1968. The place described in this quotation is Cocos Island. Colnett also said, "Fish were in great abundance, but would not take the bait, which we attributed to the great number of sharks off this island. Some of them followed the boat until the water left them almost dry: those we caught, were full of squid and cray-fish, as were the porpoises which we struck. These were innumerable, and we took them whenever we pleased."

8. Lamb, W.K. (ed.) (1984) *A Voyage of Discovery to the North Pacific Ocean and Round the World 1791–1795.* Volumes I–IV. By George Vancouver. Hakluyt Society, London. Vancouver's description of sharks is from Cocos Island in the eastern Pacific.

9. Originally, giant tortoises of the genus *Dipsochelys* occurred on all the islands in the western Indian Ocean. They were present on the smaller islands, including Mauritius, La Reunion, Rodrigues, and Seychelles into the eighteenth century, but were exterminated by hunting from all but the remote Aldabra. J. Gerlach and K.L. Canning (1997) Evolution and history of the giant tortoises of the Aldabra Island group. Phelsumania. www.phelsumania.com/public/articles/fauna_dipsochelys_1.html

10. Rogers (1712) *A Cruising Voyage.*

11. About the time of Darwin's visit, a fleet of sixty or seventy American whaling ships frequented the Galápagos every year. Logbooks from seventy-nine ships between 1831 and 1868 indicate over thirteen thousand tortoises taken. In total, some seven hundred whaling ships visited the islands during this period, many of them repeatedly. Four island races of tortoises were driven to extinction and others much depleted by the slaughter. Townsend, C.H. (1925) The Galápagos tortoises in their relation to the whaling industry: A study of old logbooks. *Zoologica*, New York Zoological Society. www.du.edu/~ttyler/ploughboy/townsendgaltort.htm

12. The map of the known world in Dampier's day petered out around the peninsula of Baja California off Mexico's west coast. There was much controversy in the charts as to whether Baja was actually an island or joined to the coast. Rogers argued for a peninsula, but none could be sure because it had been so long since anyone had sailed far enough north to tell. In fact, Baja was established as a peninsula as early as 1540, when Hernando Cortés, after whom the sea it encloses was named, dispatched Francisco de Ulloa north to explore the coast of New Spain. Two years later, Juan Cabrillo made it as far as San Francisco Bay. Baja appears as a peninsula on maps published soon afterward. Sir Francis Drake called in California in 1579; Juan de Fuca claimed to have found a large inlet farther north in 1594; and another Spaniard, Sebastián Vizcaíno, made it as far north as Cape Mendocino in 1602. (The results of Vizcaíno's survey were not published until 1802 when Spain made them public for the first time to counter claims being made that Cook and Vancouver discovered the lands of the northwest coast of America. See note 8, above.) After that, nobody bothered exploring north of Baja until, spurred by Bering's discovery of Alaska in 1741, the Spanish decided in 1773 to colonize today's California. Commenting on this peculiar state of disinterest in the seventeenth century, Rogers puts it down to the Spanish having more in the way of colonies than they could manage already. Lands and coasts of western North America thus appeared mysteriously (and inaccurately) on maps as

"Terrae Incognitae" well into the eighteenth century. Hayes, D. (2001) *Historical Atlas of the North Pacific Ocean*. Sasquatch Books, Seattle.

Spanish colonization of California was slow to begin with. In 1792, the Spaniard José Mariano Moziño called in on the colony of New California and was captivated by its natural riches, as have been so many others since. He wrote, "Throughout most of New California, the landscape is very beautiful, the soil fertile, the mountains wooded, and the climate benign. There is no European product that could not be successfully grown there. There is pasturage for all kinds of livestock. These have multiplied so prodigiously that between the Presidio of Monterey and the Mission of Carmel are counted more than ten thousand head of cattle and a considerable number of horses and sheep. In the sea that bathes its coasts, fish swarm and whales, sea otters, and sea lions abound. In short, God is generously offering an immensity of wealth which we are not enjoying for lack of people. Five hundred leagues of territory do not have as inhabitants even two thousand persons who can be regarded as vassals of our monarchy, and of these, not even five hundred, including women and children, can be called civilized people." Moziño, J.M. (1792) *Noticias de Nutka. An Account of Nootka Sound in 1792*. Translated and edited by I.H. Wilson. McClelland and Stewart Ltd., Toronto and Montreal, 1970.

13. Cook, J. (1999) *The Journals of Captain Cook*. Edited by Philip Edwards. Penguin Classics, London.

14. Gough, B.M. (1992) *The Northwest Coast: British Navigation, Trade, and Discoveries to 1812*. University of British Columbia Press, Vancouver.

15. Steller, G.W. *Journal of a Voyage with Bering, 1741–1742*. Translated by M.A. Engel and O.W. Frost. Stanford University Press, Stanford, California, 1988.

16. Gough (1992) *The Northwest Coast*.

17. Cook never made it back to England. He was bludgeoned to death in Hawaii during an altercation with the natives.

18. Ogden, A. (1941) *The California Sea Otter Trade: 1784–1848*. University of California Press, Berkeley and Los Angeles.

19. Jackman, S.W. (ed.) (1978) *The Journal of William Sturgis*. Sono Nis Press, Victoria, Canada. Sturgis notes that in addition to muskets, cloth, molasses, rice, and greatcoats were in high demand for barter. He deplored the trading of rum, which was soon to become the downfall of many tribes.

20. Ibid.

21. Ogden (1941) *The California Sea Otter Trade*.

22. Ibid.

23. Ibid.

24. By 1998 the Canadian population had grown to around 2,500 otters, and there are around 2,200 on the California coast today.

25. Lamb (1984) *A Voyage of Discovery*.

26.  *The First and Second Discovery of the Gulf of California, and the Sea-coast on the Northwest or Back Side of America by M. John Baptista Ramusio.* In volume XI of R. Hakluyt. *The Principal Navigations Voyages Traffiques & Discoveries of the English Nation.* James MacLehose and Sons, Glasgow.

27.  Clavigero, F.J. (1786) *The History of [Lower] California.* Translated from the Italian by S.E. Lake. Edited by A.A. Gray. Manessier Publishing Company, Riverside, California, 1971.

28.  Only two species of abalone range north to Vancouver Island, the pinto (*Haliotis kamtschatkana kamtschatkana*) and flat abalone (*H. walallensis*). Both are smaller than several of the common intertidal species that occur in California and Mexico, such as the black, red, and pink abalone (*H. cracherodii, H. rufescens,* and *H. corrugata*).

29.  Ogden (1941) *The California Sea Otter Trade.*

30.  Farther south, in California, the kelp forests did not disappear with the sea otters because local species of fish, crab, and lobster kept sea urchin numbers under control.

31.  Darwin later had ample opportunity to taste Galápagos tortoise cooked for him by local guides as he explored the islands, and also aboard ship. The *Beagle* carried away more than thirty tortoises, using the Galápagos for provisions, like thousands of other ships before. Chambers, P. (2004) *A Sheltered Life: The Unexpected History of the Giant Tortoise.* John Murray, London.

32.  Rogers (1712) *A Cruising Voyage.*

### Chapter 7: Whaling: The First Global Industry

1.  Lund, N. (ed.) (1984) *Two Voyagers at the Court of King Alfred.* William Sessions Limited, York.

2.  Lee, S.-M., and D. Robineau. (2004) The cetaceans of the Neolithic rock carvings of Bangu-dae (South Korea) and the beginning of whaling in the North-West Pacific. *L'anthropologie* 108: 137–151.

3.  Gardiner, M. (1997) The exploitation of sea-mammals in medieval England: Bones in their social context. *Archaeological Journal* 154: 173–195.

4.  Jenkins, J.T. (1921) *A History of the Whale Fisheries.* Kennikat Press, Port Washington, New York, 1971.

5.  Drive hunting of whales and smaller cetaceans continues to be practiced in the Faroe Islands, that lie between the United Kingdom and Iceland, and Japan.

6.  Gardiner (1997) The exploitation of sea-mammals.

7.  Wolff, W.J. (2000) The south-eastern North Sea: Losses of vertebrate fauna during the past 2000 years. *Biological Conservation* 95: 209–217.

8.  Jenkins (1921) *A History of the Whale Fisheries.*

9.  Cartier, J. (1535) *A Shorte and Briefe Narration of the Navigation Made by the Commandment of the King of France, to the Islands of Canada.* In volume

VIII of R. Hakluyt (1904) *The Principal Navigations Voyages Traffiques & Discoveries of the English Nation.* James MacLehose and Sons, Glasgow.

10. Ibid.

11. Major, K. (2001) *As Near to Heaven by Sea: A History of Newfoundland and Labrador.* Penguin Books, Toronto.

12. Ibid.

13. *The First Voyage Made by Master Anthonie Jenkinson from the Citie of London Toward the Land of Russia, Begun the Twelfth of May in the Yeere 1557.* In volume II of R. Hakluyt (*1904*) *The Principal Navigations Voyages Traffiques & Discoveries of the English Nation.* James MacLehose and Sons, Glasgow.

14. Magnus, O. (1555) *Historia de Gentibus Septentrionalibus.* Volume III. Edited by P. Foote. Hakluyt Society, London, 1998.

15. Ibid.

16. Best, G. *A True Discourse of the Three Voyages of Discoverie, for the Finding of a Passage to Cathaya, by the Northwest, under the Conduct of Martin Frobisher Generall.* In J. McDermott (ed.) (2001) *The Third Voyage of Martin Frobisher to Baffin Island: 1578.* Hakluyt Society, London.

17. Biscayan whalers were already fishing in waters to the south of Greenland. On John Davis's 1587 voyage in search of a northwest passage, they saw a boat whaling: "The 17. we met a ship at sea, and as farre as we could judge it was a Biskaine: we thought she went a fishing for whales; for in 52 degrees [°N, to the south of Greenland] or thereabout we saw very many." Pages 414-422 in M. John Janes Marchant, *The Third Voyage Northwestward, Made by M. John Davis Gentleman, as Chiefe Captaine & Pilot Generall, for the Discovery of a Passage to the Isles of the Moluccas or the Coast of China, in the Yeere 1587.* In volume VII of R. Hakluyt (1904) *The Principal Navigations Voyages Traffiques & Discoveries of the English Nation.* James MacLehose and Sons, Glasgow.

18. Credland, A.G. (1995) *The Hull Whaling Trade: An Arctic Enterprise.* Hutton Press, Yorkshire.

19. Barron, W. (1895) *Old Whaling Days.* Conway Maritime Press, London, 1996.

20. Dykes, J. (1980) *Yorkshire's Whaling Days.* Dalesman Books, Yorkshire.

21. Hartwig, G. (1892) *The Sea and its Living Wonders.* Longmans, Green, and Co., London.

22. Mr. Richard Mather, *Journal to New England, 1635.* www.newengland-ancestors.org/libraries/manuscripts/images_nehgs_mather_intro_656_61801.asp

23. Ibid.

24. Jenkins (1921) *A History of the Whale Fisheries.*

25. Shelvocke, G. (1726) *A Voyage Round the World.* Cassell and Company Ltd., London, 1928.

26. Other writers encountering concentrations of whales were also appalled by the stink of whale breath. J.R. Forster, scientist on Captain Cook's voyage of discovery in 1772–1775, wrote, "We were scarce gone near the *Tierra del Fuego*-shore, when we found ourselves surrounded by at least 20 or 30 whales & hundreds of Seals. When the Whales blew to windward, we found the Effluvia of their breath stinking in a most infecting manner, & poisoning all the air with a cadaverous Smell for 2 or 3 minutes." Page 702 in M.E. Hoare (ed.) *The Resolution Journal of Johann Reinhold Forster 1772–1775.* Volume IV. Hakluyt Society, London, 1982.

27. Dunmore, J. (ed. and trans.) (1994) *The Journal of Jean-François de Galaup de la Pérouse: 1785–1788.* Volume I. Hakluyt Society, London.

28. Ibid.

29. Gosse, P.H. (1845) *The Ocean.* Society for Promoting Christian Knowledge, London.

30. Beale, T. (1835) *A Few Observations on the Natural History of the Sperm Whale, With an Account of the Rise and Progress of the Fishery, and of the Modes of Pursuing, Killing, and "Cutting In" that Animal, with a List of its Favorite Places of Resort.* Effingham Wilson, Royal Exchange, London.

31. Dunmore (1994) *The Journal of Jean-François de Galaup de la Pérouse.* One of the earliest explorers of California, Francisco de Ulloa, had a similar encounter in Monterey Bay in 1539: "above 500 whales came athwart of us in 2 or 3 skulles within one houres space, which were so huge it was wonderfull, and some of them came so neere unto the ship, that they swum under the same from one side to another, whereupon we were in great feare, lest they should doe us some hurt." *The First and Second Discovery of the Gulf of California, and the Sea-coast on the Northwest or Back Side of America by M. John Baptista Ramusio.* In volume IX of R. Hakluyt, (1904) *The Principal Navigations Voyages Traffiques & Discoveries of the English Nation.* James MacLehose and Sons, Glasgow.

32. Lamb, W.K. (ed.) (1984) *A Voyage of Discovery to the North Pacific Ocean and Round the World 1791–1795.* Volumes I–IV. By George Vancouver. Hakluyt Society, London.

33. Scammon, C. M. (1874) *The Marine Mammals of the North-western Coast of North America.* Dover Publications Inc., New York, 1968.

34. Ibid.

35. Bullen, F.T. (1904) *The Cruise of the "Cachalot": Round the World After Sperm Whales.* MacMillan and Co., London.

36. Melville, H. (1930) *Moby Dick.* Random House, New York. Pages 663-664.

37. Barron, W. (1895) *Old Whaling Days.* Conway Maritime Press, London, 1996.

38. Roman, J., and S.R. Palumbi (2003) Whales before whaling in the North Atlantic. *Science* 301: 508–510.

*Chapter 8: To the Ends of the Earth for Seals*

1. William Dane Phelps (1871), quoted in B.C. Busch, (1985) *The War Against the Seals: A History of the North American Seal Fishery.* McGill-Queen's University Press, Kingston and Montreal.

2. Cooke, G.A. (1807) *Modern and Authentic System of Geography.* C. Cooke, London.

3. Lund, N. (ed.) (1984) *Two Voyagers at the Court of King Alfred.* William Sessions Ltd., York.

4. Magnus, O. (1555) *Historia de Gentibus Septentrionalibus.* Volume III. Edited by P. Foote. Hakluyt Society, London, 1998.

5. Busch (1985) *The War Against the Seals.*

6. I am indebted to Dr. James Barrett of the University of York Archaeology Department for this suggestion.

7. Jacques Cartier found several large walrus rookeries on his exploration of the Gulf of St. Lawrence. See Cartier, J. (1531) *Certaine Voyages Containing the Discoverie of the Gulfe of Sainct Laurence to the West of Newfoundland* . . . Pages 183-271 in volume VIII of R. Hakluyt (1904), *The Principal Navigations Voyages Traffiques & Discoveries of the English Nation.* James MacLehose and Sons, Glasgow.

8. A letter sent to the right Honorable Sir William Cecill Lord Burghley, Lord high Treasurer of England &c, from M. Thomas James of Bristoll, concerning the discoverie of the Isle of Ramea, dated the 14th of September 1591.

9. De Charlevoix, P. (1744) *Journal of a Voyage to North America.* Reprinted by University Microfilms Inc., Ann Arbor, Michigan, 1966.

10. Hacquebord, L. (2001) Three centuries of whaling and walrus hunting in Svalbard and its impact on the Arctic ecosystem. *Environment and History* 7: 169–185.

11. Micco, H.M. (trans.) (1971) *King Island and the Sealing Trade 1802.* A translation of chapters XXII and XXIII of the narrative by François Péron, published in the *Official Account of the Voyage of Discovery to the Southern Lands.* Roebuck Society, Canberra.

12. *The First Voyage of M. John Davis, Undertaken in June 1585 for the Discoverie of the Northwest Passage, Written by M. John Janes Marchant, Sometimes Servant to the Worshipfull Master William Sanderson.* Pages 381–392 in volume VII of R. Hakluyt (1904), *The Principal Navigations Voyages Traffiques & Discoveries of the English Nation,* James MacLehose and Sons, Glasgow.

13. While walrus hide was valued for its strength, the animals did not carry fur.

14. Amasa Delano, quoted in Busch (1985) *The War Against the Seals.*

15. Micco (1971) *King Island and the Sealing Trade 1802.*

16. Hardin, G. (1968) The tragedy of the commons. *Science* 162: 1243–1248.

17. Hamilton, R. (1839) *Jardine's Naturalist's Library. Mammalia Volume VIII.*

*Amphibious Carnivora Including Walrus and Seals, Also of the Herbivorous Cetacea, &c.* W.H. Lizars, Edinburgh.

18. Campbell, R.J. (2000) *The Discovery of the South Shetland Islands.* Hakluyt Society, London.
19. Stackpole, E. (1955) *The Voyage of the Huron and the Huntress: The American Sealers and the Discovery of the Continent of Antarctica.* Marine Historical Association, Mystic, Connecticut.
20. Credland, A.G. (1995) *The Hull Whaling Trade: An Arctic Enterprise.* Hutton Press, Yorkshire.
21. Busch (1985) *The War Against the Seals.*
22. Ibid.
23. MacDonald, D. (ed.) (2001) *The New Encyclopedia of Mammals.* Oxford University Press, Oxford.
24. Busch (1985) *The War Against the Seals.*
25. *Reports of Agents, Officers, and Persons, Acting Under the Authority of the Secretary of the Treasury, in Relation to the Condition of Seal Life on the Rookeries of the Pribilof Islands, and to Pelagic Sealing in Bering Sea and the North Pacific Ocean, in the Years 1893–1895,* part 1 (1896). Government Printing Office, Washington, DC.
26. Busch (1985) *The War Against the Seals.*
27. Cairncross, F. (2004) What makes environmental treaties work? *Conservation Biology in Practice* 5: 12–19.
28. Barron, W. (1895) *Old Whaling Days.* Conway Maritime Press, London, 1996.
29. Hacquebord (2001) Three centuries of whaling and walrus hunting in Svalbard.

#### Chapter 9: The Great Fisheries of Europe

1. The herring (*Clupea harengus*), sprat (*Sprattus sprattus*), and sardines and pilchards (*Sardina pilchardus*).
2. Wood, W. (1911) *North Sea Fishers and Fighters.* Kegan Paul, Trench, Trübner & Co. Ltd., London.
3. Bertram, J.G. (1873) *The Harvest of the Sea.* John Murray, London.
4. Ibid.
5. Moray McLaren, in his book *Return to Scotland* (1930), describing the herring fishing on the island of Barra in the Hebrides, quoted in C. Hall (ca. 1940) *The Sea and Its Wonders.* Blackie & Son Ltd., London and Glasgow.
6. Bertram (1873) *The Harvest of the Sea.*
7. Thomas Pennant is mistaken in this. Chesapeake Bay is the southern limit of herring (*Clupea harengus*), and the species is less abundant than this at its range limit. He is probably referring to the menhaden or alewife, both of which were then extraordinarily abundant in the Chesapeake.
8. Goldsmith, O. (1776) *An History of the Earth and Animated Nature.* Volume VI. James Williams, Dublin.

9. Herubel, M. (1912) *Sea Fisheries: Their Treasures and Toilers.* T. Fisher Unwin, London.

10. Goldsmith (1776) *An History of the Earth and Animated Nature.*

11. Smylie, M. (2004) *Herring: A History of the Silver Darlings.* Tempus Publishing, Stroud.

12. Buckland, F. (1873) *Familiar History of British Fishes.* Society for Promoting Christian Knowledge, London.

13. Holdsworth, E.W.H. (1877) *Sea Fisheries.* Edward Stanford, London.

14. Sir John Boroughs (1633), quoted in H. Schultes, (1813) A dissertation on the public fisheries of Great Britain, explaining the rise, progress, and art of the Dutch fishery, &c. &c. *The Quarterly Review* IX(XVIII): 265–304.

15. It is to the historical importance of fishers as a reservoir for naval seamen that could be called on in times of war, that we can attribute the disproportionately high level of political influence enjoyed by the fishing industry in many countries today. In the United Kingdom, for example, the fishing industry is only about the size of the cucumber-growing or lawn-mower industries. Yet there is a Minister for Fisheries, but none for cucumbers or lawnmowers!

16. Hartwig, G. (1892) *The Sea and its Living Wonders.* Longmans, Green and Company, London and New York.

17. J. Knox. (1784) *View of the Highlands,* quoted in H. Schultes, (1813) A dissertation on the public fisheries of Great Britain, explaining the rise, progress, and art of the Dutch fishery, &c. &c. *The Quarterly Review* IX(XVIII): 265–304.

18. Wilkie Collins, quoted in L. Figuier (1891) *The Ocean World: Being a Description of the Sea and Some of its Inhabitants.* Cassell and Company Limited, London, Paris and Melbourne.

19. Buckland (1873) *Familiar History of British Fishes.*

20. Noall, C. (1972) *Cornish Seines and Seiners: A History of the Pilchard Fishing Industry.* Bradford Barton, Truro.

21. Goldsmith (1776) *An History of the Earth and Animated Nature.*

22. Magnus, O. (1555) *Historia de Gentibus Septentrionalibus. Description of the Northern Peoples.* Translated by P. Fisher and H. Higgens. Hakluyt Society, London, 1996.

23. Pauly, D. (1995) Anecdotes and the shifting baseline syndrome of fisheries. *Trends in Ecology and Evolution* 10: 430. Scott, J. (1936) *Game Fish Records.* H. F. & G. Witherby Ltd., London.

24. The Reverend J.G. Wood in his book *Common Objects of the Sea Shore,* published in 1857 (George Routledge and Sons, London and New York) gives a description on page 16 of the porpoise, which he ends with an apology: "The porpesse is rather a sociable animal, being generally seen in shoals, or schools, as the sailors call them. I should hardly have said so

much about so common a creature, were it not for the purpose of pointing out these remarkable facts in its structure and habits."

Sailors often fell in with huge pods of porpoises, like that encountered in 1585 by John Davis shortly after leaving England on his voyage in search of a northwest passage to the Far East: "The first of July [three days sail north from the Scilly Isles off southern England] wee sawe great store of Porposes. The Master called for an harping yron, and shot twise or thrise: sometimes he missed, and at last shot one and stroke him in the side, and wound him into the ship . . . The 3. wee had more in sight, and the Master went to shoote at them, but they were so great, that they burst our yrons, and we lost both fish, yrons, pastime and all." *The First Voyage of M. John Davis, Undertaken in June 1585 for the Discoverie of the Northwest Passage, Written by M. John Janes Marchant, Sometimes Servant to the Worshipfull Master William Sanderson.* Pages 381–392 in volume VII of R. Hakluyt (1904) *The Principal Navigations Voyages Traffiques & Discoveries of the English Nation.* James MacLehose and Sons, Glasgow.

25. De Buffon, Goldsmith, and others (1810) *A History of Earth and Animated Nature.* Volume II. Apollo Press, Alnwick.
26. Goldsmith (1776) *An History of the Earth and Animated Nature.*
27. Marine mammals very rarely enter the Thames today. When a bottlenose whale swam to the Houses of Parliament in 2005, half of London lined the banks of the river to watch it. It was the first whale seen there since the early twentieth century.
28. Compagno, L., M. Dando, and S. Fowler (2005) *A Field Guide to Sharks of the World.* Collins, London.
29. Buckland (1873) *Familiar History of British Fishes.*
30. Goldsmith (1776) *An History of the Earth and Animated Nature.*
31. Alheit, J., and E. Hagen (1997) Long-term climate forcing of European herring and sardine populations. *Fisheries Oceanography* 6: 130–139.
32. Hoffmann, R.C. (2002) Carp, cods, connections: New fisheries in the medieval European economy and environment. Pages 3–55 in M.J. Henninger-Voss (ed.) *Animals in Human Histories: The Mirror of Nature and Culture.* University of Rochester Press, New York.
33. Magnus (1555) *Historia de Gentibus Septentrionalibus.*
34. Wood (1911) *North Sea Fishers and Fighters.*

*Chapter 10: The First Trawling Revolution*

1. Alward, G.L. (1932) *The Sea Fisheries of Great Britain and Ireland.* Albert Gait, Grimsby.
2. Ibid.
3. Robinson, R. (1996) *Trawling: The Rise and Fall of the British Trawl Fishery.* University of Exeter Press, Exeter.

4. Anonymous (March 19, 1921) The history of trawling: Its rise and development from the earliest times to the present day. *Fishing Trades Gazette and Poultry, Game and Rabbit Trades Chronicle* 38(1974): 21–71.

5. Alward (1932) *The Sea Fisheries of Great Britain and Ireland.*

6. Ibid.

7. Holdsworth, E.W.H. (1877) *Sea Fisheries.* Edward Stanford, London.

8. Buckland, F. (1891) *Natural History of British Fishes.* Society for Promoting Christian Knowledge, London.

9. *The National Cyclopaedia of Useful Knowledge* (1851). Charles Knight, London.

10. *Report of the Commissioners Appointed to Inquire into the Sea Fisheries of the United Kingdom,* volume 1 (1866). Her Majesty's Stationery Office, London.

11. Collins, J.W. (1889) *The Beam Trawl Fishery of Great Britain with Notes on Beam Trawling in Other European Countries.* Government Printing Office, Washington, DC.

12. Wood, W. (1911) *North Sea Fishers and Fighters.* Kegan Paul, Trench, Trübner & Co. Ltd., London.

13. Gosse, P.H. (1845) *The Ocean.* Society for Promoting Christian Knowledge, London.

14. Wood (1911) *North Sea Fishers and Fighters.*

15. At the time, dogfish were eaten in Italy, France, and Spain, and Londoners had recently begun eating them fried. Ironically, the picked dogfish, *Squalus acanthias,* the main species caught around Britain, is now one of the most highly valued on the world market for shark meat, fetching US$10–$15 per kilogram.

16. Anonymous (1880) *The Great Fisheries of the World.* T. Nelson and Sons, London.

17. Barron, W. (1895) *Old Whaling Days.* Conway Maritime Press, London (1996).

18. Goldsmith, O. (1776) *An History of the Earth and Animated Nature.* Volume VI. James Williams, Dublin.

19. *Report of the Commissioners* (1866).

20. Collins (1889) *The Beam Trawl Fishery.*

21. *Report of the Commissioners* (1866).

22. Ibid.

23. Ibid.

24. Ibid.

*Chapter 11: The Dawn of Industrial Fishing*

1. *Report of the Commissioners Appointed to Inquire and Report Upon the Complaints That Have Been Made by Line and Drift Net Fishermen of Injuries Sustained by Them in Their Calling Owing to the Use of the Trawl*

*Net and Beam Trawl in the Territorial Waters of the United Kingdom* 1885. Eyre and Spottiswoode, London.

2. Ibid.
3. Ibid.
4. Desmond, A. (1997) *Huxley: Evolution's High Priest.* Michael Joseph, London.
5. Holdsworth, E.W.H. (1877) *Sea Fisheries.* Edward Stanford, London.
6. There are earlier records of steam trawling from France where it began in 1865, but the practice did not catch on widely until about the same time as in England, the late 1870s to early 1880s. Hérubel, M.A. (1912) *Sea Fisheries, Their Treasures and Toilers.* T. Fisher Unwin, London.
7. Wood, W. (1911) *North Sea Fishers and Fighters.* Kegan Paul, Trench, Trübner & Co. Ltd., London.
8. Holdsworth (1877) *Sea Fisheries.*
9. Ibid.
10. Collins, J.W. (1889) *The Beam Trawl Fishery of Great Britain with Notes on Beam Trawling in Other European Countries.* Government Printing Office, Washington, DC.
11. *Report of the Commissioners* (1885).
12. Ibid.
13. Ibid.
14. Ibid.
15. Ibid.
16. Ibid.
17. Ibid.
18. Wood (1911) *North Sea Fishers and Fighters.*
19. Olsen, O.T. (1883) *The Piscatorial Atlas of the North Sea, English and St. George's Channels.* Taylor and Francis, London.
20. *Report of the Commissioners Appointed to Inquire into the Sea Fisheries of the United Kingdom,* volume 1 (1866). Her Majesty's Stationery Office, London.
21. "These areas [the Yorkshire and Lincolnshire coasts]," said J.T. Cunningham in his 1896 book on marketable fishes, "produce an extraordinary quantity of 'scruff,' of which the most abundant constituent is a form known to the fishermen as 'curly cabbage,' a fixed compound gelatinous organism (*Alcyonidium gelatinosum*). Hydroids [feathery invertebrates like little bushes] (chiefly *Sertularia* and *Hydrallmannia*) are also abundant." Page 366 in J.T. Cunningham, (1896) *A Natural History of the Marketable Marine Fishes of the British Islands.* Macmillan and Co. Ltd., London.
22. *Report of the Commissioners* (1885).
23. Ibid.
24. Like many other witnesses, when Swinney said "spawn," he was probably

referring to the spawn of invertebrates, like whelks or cuttlefish, laid on the seabed, or possibly to other invertebrates like sponges and ascidians (sea squirts) that looked something like spawn.

25. *Report of the Commissioners* (1885).
26. Ibid.
27. Ibid.
28. Ibid.
29. Collins (1889) *The Beam Trawl Fishery.*
30. *Report of the Commissioners* (1885).
31. Ibid.
32. A similar story has been recounted to me by staff at the Port Erin Marine Laboratory on the Isle of Man in the Irish Sea, the sea that separates mainland Britain from Ireland. Oyster reefs were once extensive around the island, but the last living oysters were trawled up in the 1970s by scallop dredgers.
33. *Report of the Commissioners* (1885).
34. Ibid.
35. "A Correspondent" (1899) *Reply to the So-called Criticism and Analysis of Professor M'Intosh on Trawling and Trawling Investigations.* Rosemount Press, Aberdeen.
36. "Whelks, or 'buckies,' as they are called in Scotland, are exclusively employed as bait on the long-lines in these smacks. They are not only attractive to the cod, but from their toughness they give a good hold to the hook. The collection of whelk bait is a regular trade in which many small craft . . . are constantly employed; yet great difficulty is sometimes found in procuring a sufficient quantity for the purpose, the demand for whelks, in the London market especially, as an article of food among the poorer classes, interfering considerably with the supply of these shell-fish for the purpose of bait. . . . Some idea of the number of whelks required in the North Sea cod fishery may be gathered from the fact, that a smack takes with her on each 'voyage' during the regular long-line season, as many as forty wash of whelks; the 'wash' being a stamped measure capable of holding twenty one quarts and a pint of water." Page 78 in Holdsworth, (1877) *Sea Fisheries.*
37. *Report of the Commissioners* (1885).
38. Wood (1911) *North Sea Fishers and Fighters.*
39. McIntosh, W.C. (1899) *The Resources of the Sea as Shown in the Scientific Experiments to Test the Effects of Trawling and of the Closure of Certain Areas off the Scottish Shores.* C.J. Clay and Sons, London.
40. The trawl was introduced to America in 1905, to eastern Canada in 1908, to Australia in 1907 (after some early unsuccessful experiments), and to New Zealand in 1900. Matteson, G. (1979) *Draggermen: Fishing on Georges Bank.* Four Winds Press, New York. Roughly, T.C. (1951) *Fish and Fisheries of Australia,* Angus and Robertson, Sydney. Commission of

Conservation, Canada (1912) *Sea-Fisheries of Eastern Canada.* Mortimer Co., Ottawa.

41.  Collins (1889) *The Beam Trawl Fishery.*
42.  Hérubel (1912) *Sea Fisheries. Their Treasures and Toilers.*
43.  Quoted in D. Pauly (2004) Much rowing for fish. *Nature* 432: 813–814.

## Chapter 12: The Inexhaustible Sea

1.  Schultes, H. (1813) A dissertation on the public fisheries of Great Britain, explaining the rise, progress, and art of the Dutch fishery, &c. &c. *The Quarterly Review* IX(XVIII): 265–304. Schultes continues, "We now know that travellers do not exaggerate, when they tell us of swarms of locusts obscuring the light of the sun; of flights of white ants filling the whole horizon like a snow shower; of herds of antelopes scouring the plains in thousands; neither are fishermen disbelieved when they speak of shoals of herrings, occupying, in close array, many millions of acres near the surface of the sea; nor when they tell us that, on the coast of Norway, in passing through narrow inlets, they move in such deep columns, that they are known by the name of herring mountains. The cod, hake, ling, mackerel, pilchard, and salmon, though not quite so numerous as the herring, are all of them gregarious, and probably migrating animals. In thus ordaining that the most numerous of the finny tribe should be those which afford the most wholesome food for man, we acknowledge the benevolent intentions of an all-wise and good Providence."

2.  *Report of the Commissioners Appointed to Inquire into the Sea Fisheries of the United Kingdom,* volume 1 (1866). Her Majesty's Stationery Office, London. Apart from the error in assigning the production of the fish entirely to the area of seabed in which the fish were caught, the commissioners also appear to have significantly underestimated the area of bottom swept. With a 10-meter beam trawl, a size typical for the time, towing with the tide at a typical rate of three knots, for a period of four hours, a single vessel would cover just over 54 acres. Five vessels would cover nearly 273 acres.

3.  Wood, W. (1911) *North Sea Fishers and Fighters.* Kegan Paul, Trench, Trübner & Co. Ltd., London.

4.  Garstang, W. (1900) The impoverishment of the sea. *Journal of the Marine Biological Association of the UK* 6: 1–69.

5.  Wood (1911) *North Sea Fishers and Fighters.*

6.  Cushing, D.H. (1988) *The Provident Sea.* Cambridge University Press, Cambridge.

7.  Carson, R.L. (1943) *Food from the Sea: Fish and Shellfish of New England.* U.S. Department of the Interior Fish and Wildlife Service Bulletin 33. Government Printing Office, Washington, DC.

8.  Ibid.

9.  Ibid.

10. Daniel, H., and F. Minot (1955) *The Inexhaustible Sea.* MacDonald, London.
11. Ibid.
12. Alverson, D.L., and N.J. Wilimovsky (1964) Prospective developments in the harvesting of marine fishes. In *Modern Fishing Gear of the World 2.* Fishing News (Books) Ltd., London.
13. Hardy, A. (1959) *Fish and Fisheries.* Collins, London.

### Chapter 13: The Legacy of Whaling

1. Krasheninnikov, S.P. (1754) *The History of Kamtschatka and the Kurilski Islands, with the Countries Adjacent.* Translated by J. Grieve. Quadrangle Books, Chicago, 1962.
2. Browning, R.J. (1974) *Fisheries of the North Pacific. History, Species, Gear and Processes.* Alaska Northwest Publishing Company, Anchorage.
3. Ibid.
4. Kenyon, K.W. (1975) *The Sea Otter in the Eastern Pacific Ocean.* Dover Publications Inc., New York.
5. Goode, G.B. (1884) *The Fisheries and Fishery Industries of the United States. Section 1. Natural History of Useful Aquatic Animals.* Government Printing Office, Washington, DC.
6. Marsh, J. (2005) *Walleye Pollock*: Theragra chalcogramma. Seafood Watch Seafood Report. Monterey Bay Aquarium, Monterey. www.seafood-watch.org.
7. Springer, A.M., J.A. Estes, G.B. van Vliet, T.M. Williams, D.F. Doak, E.M. Danner, K.A. Fornay, and B. Pfister. (2003) Sequential megafaunal collapse in the North Pacific Ocean: An ongoing legacy of industrial whaling. *Proceedings of the National Academy of Science* (USA) 100: 12223–12228.
8. Hardy, A. (1959) *Fish and Fisheries: The Open Sea; Its Natural History, part II.* Collins, London.
9. Rackham, H. (trans.) (1983) *Pliny Natural History Books VIII–XI.* Harvard University Press, Cambridge.
10. The largest whale species is the blue, which reaches a length of 30 meters or so (100 feet). Olaus Magnus is mistaken in describing whales 300 feet long.
11. Magnus, O. (1555) *Historia de Gentibus Septentrionalibus. Description of the Northern Peoples.* Translated by P. Fisher and H. Higgens. Hakluyt Society, London, 1996.
12. Ibid.
13. Krasheninnikov (1754) *The History of Kamtschatka and the Kurilski Islands.*
14. The identity of kasatki as killer whales is unmistakable from the description that follows: "They [the Kamchadals] never go a fishing for the kasatki, but if this fish is thrown on shore they use its fat like that of the whale. Mr *Steller* says, that, in the year 1742, eight of them were thrown on

shore at once, near the Lopatka; but the distance and the bad weather prevented his going to examine them. He was told, that the largest never exceed four fathoms in length [7.4 meters]; that they have small eyes, a wide mouth, and great sharp teeth, with which they wound the whale; but that they tear up the belly of the whale with a sharp fin which is upon their backs is a false report; for though this fin is about five feet long [1.5 meters], very sharp, and in the sea stands quite upright, yet it is altogether soft, and consists only of fat." Pages 139-140 of Krasheninnikov (1754) *The History of Kamtschatka and the Kurilski Islands.*

15. Goldsmith, O. (1776) *An History of the Earth and Animated Nature.* Volume VI. James Williams, Dublin.

16. In the Carolinas, early settlers benefited from the leftovers of killer whale predation, according to John Lawson's early eighteenth-century description: "Whales are very numerous, on the coast of North Carolina, from which they make Oil, Bone [baleen], &c. to the great Advantage of those inhabiting the Sand-Banks, along the Ocean, where these Whales come ashore, none being struck or kill'd with a Harpoon in this Place, as they are to the Northward, and elsewhere; all those Fish being found dead on the Shoar, most commonly by those that inhabit the Banks, and Sea-side, where they dwell, for that Intent, and for the Benefit of Wrecks, which sometimes fall in upon that Shoar. . . . These Fish seldom come ashore with their Tongues in their Heads, the Thrasher [killer whale] (which is the Whale's mortal Enemy, wheresoever he meets him) eating that out of his Head, as soon as he and the Sword-Fish have killed him." Lawson, J. (1709) *A New Voyage to Carolina.* Reprinted by University Microfilms Inc., Ann Arbor, Michigan, 1966.

17. Cooke, E. (1712) *A Voyage to the South Sea and Round the World in the Years 1708 to 1711.* N. Israel, Amsterdam, and Da Capo Press, New York, 1969.

18. The name "killer whale" is a fairly recent corruption of the original name for this species. Spanish sailors in the eighteenth century called it *asesina ballenas,* "the whale killer." In British Columbia, people of the Haida nation, who had a great reverence for the species, named it *skana,* "the killing demon." In Japan, the written character for the killer whale translates as "tiger fish," while Linneaus in 1758 gave the species its Latin name *Orcinus orca,* meaning "from hell." Orca was the name given to the killer by the ancients, and *Orcinus* came from Orcus, a Roman god of the underworld.

19. Scammon, C. M. (1874) *The Marine Mammals of the North-western Coast of North America.* Dover Publications Inc., New York, 1968.

20. Dudley, P. (1725) An essay upon the natural history of whales, with a particular account of the ambergris found in the spermaceti whale. *Philosophical Transactions of the Royal Society of London (B Biological Science)* 33: 256–269.

21. Comment made by William Scoresby dating from 1810–1820, quoted in T. Stamp and C. Stamp (1983) *Greenland Voyager.* Caedmon of Whitby, UK.

22. Hanna, G.D. (1922) What becomes of the fur seals. *Science* 55: 505–507.

23. Williams, T.M., J.A. Estes, D.F. Doak, and A.M. Springer (2004) Killer appetites: Assessing the role of predators in ecological communities. *Ecology* 85: 3373–3384.

24. Hanna wrote, "If the killer be found the great destroyer of fur seals which is suspected, then methods for its destruction should be devised. In lieu of submarines, it might be made the object of target practice of navy gunners. Or a bounty might be offered, so as to make it profitable for whalers to handle. Or what is probably the best of all suggestions, fully equip whaling vessels to scour the seas, just as sheep men of the west keep coyote hunters constantly on duty." Hanna (1922) What becomes of the fur seals.

### Chapter 14: Emptying European Seas

1. Mitford, W. (1969) *Lovely She Goes!* Michael Joseph Ltd., London.

2. Garstang, W. (1900) The impoverishment of the sea. *Journal of the Marine Biological Association of the UK* 6: 1–69.

3. Graham, M. (1948) *Rational Fishing of the Cod of the North Sea.* Edward Arnold & Co., London.

4. Robinson, R. (1996) *Trawling: The Rise and Fall of the British Trawl Fishery.* University of Exeter Press, Exeter.

5. Reid, C. (2000) From boom to bust: The herring industry in the twentieth century. Pages 188–196 in D.J. Starkey, C. Reid, and N. Ashcroft (eds.), *England's Sea Fisheries: The Commercial Sea Fisheries of England and Wales since 1300.* Chatham Publishing, London.

6. In coastal waters of North America, communities resisted introduction of the trawl until the early twentieth century. After trawling became established, their fisheries pursued a pattern of depletion and species switching similar to that seen in Europe.

7. Robinson (1996) *Trawling.*

8. Ashcroft, N. (2000) The diminishing commons: Politics, war and territorial waters in the twentieth century. Pages 217–226 in D.J. Starkey, C. Reid, and N. Ashcroft (eds.) *England's Sea Fisheries: The Commercial Sea Fisheries of England and Wales since 1300.* Chatham Publishing, London.

9. Graham, M. (1943) *The Fish Gate.* Faber and Faber Ltd., London.

10. Russell, E.S. (1942) *The Overfishing Problem.* Cambridge University Press, Cambridge.

11. Robinson (1996) *Trawling.*

12. Mitford (1969) *Lovely She Goes!*

13. Russell (1942) *The Overfishing Problem.*

14. Coull, J.R. (1972) *The Fisheries of Europe: An Economic Geography.* G. Bell & Sons Ltd., London.
15. Ashcroft (2000) The diminishing commons.
16. Russell (1942) *The Overfishing Problem.*
17. Robinson (1996) *Trawling.*
18. Ashcroft (2000) The diminishing commons.
19. Smylie, M. (2004) *Herring: A History of the Silver Darlings.* Tempus, Stroud, UK.
20. Jennings, S., S.P.R. Greenstreet, and J.D. Reynolds (1999) Structural change in an exploited fish community: A consequence of differential fishing effects on species with contrasting life histories. *Journal of Animal Ecology* 68: 617–627.
21. Jennings, S., T.A. Dinmore, D.E. Duplisea, K.J. Warr, and J.E. Lancaster (2001) Trawling disturbance can modify benthic production processes. *Journal of Animal Ecology* 70: 459–475.
22. Christensen, V., S. Guénette, J.J. Heymans, C.J. Walters, R. Watson, D. Zeller, and D. Pauly (2003) Hundred-year decline of North Atlantic predatory fishes. *Fish and Fisheries* 4: 1–24.
23. The nations were Belgium, the Netherlands, Luxembourg, West Germany, France, and Italy.
24. Pauly, D. (1995) Anecdotes and the shifting baseline syndrome of fisheries. *Trends in Ecology and Evolution* 10: 430.
25. Lotze, H.K. (2005) Radical change in the Wadden Sea fauna and flora over the last 2000 years. *Helgolander Marine Research* 59: 71–83.
26. Ibid.

### Chapter 15: The Downfall of King Cod

1. Major, K. (2001) *As Near to Heaven by Sea: A History of Newfoundland and Labrador.* Penguin Books, Toronto.
2. Crosbie, J. (1997) *No Holds Barred: My Life in Politics.* McClelland & Stewart Inc., Toronto.
3. Rich, W. (1929) *Fishing Grounds of the Gulf of Maine. Appendix III to the Report of the US Commissioner of Fisheries.* Doc # 1059. Government Printing Office, Washington, DC.
4. Murawski, S.A., R.W. Brown, S.X. Cadrin, R.K. Mayo, L. O'Brian, W.J. Overholtz, and K.A. Sosebee (1999) New England groundfish. In *Our Living Oceans: Report on the Status of U.S. Living Marine Resources.* NOAA, Silver Spring, Maryland. http://spo.nwr.noaa.gov/fa2.pdf.
5. It was only in 1953 that a minimum mesh-size regulation was implemented to reduce juvenile bycatch.
6. The redfish is *Sebastes fasciatus,* a member of the scorpion fish family, Scorpaenidae.
7. Bigelow, H., and W. Schroeder. (1953) *Fishes of the Gulf of Maine.* U.S.

Fish and Wildlife Service Bulletin 74 (Volume 53). Government Printing Office, Washington, DC.

8.  Carson, R.L. (1943) *Food from the Sea: Fish and Shellfish of New England.* U.S. Department of the Interior Fish and Wildlife Service Bulletin 33. Government Printing Office, Washington, DC.

9.  Ronald Reagan extended United States territorial waters from 3 to 12 nautical miles offshore in 1988.

10. Warner, W.W. (1983) *Distant Water: The Fate of the North American Fisherman.* Little, Brown, Boston.

11. Charles Philbrook, quoted in Warner (1983) *Distant Water.*

12. Warner (1983) *Distant Water.*

13. Ibid.

14. Kunzig, R. (1995) Twilight of the cod. *Discover Magazine* 16(4). www.discover.com/issues/apr-95/features/twilightofthecod489.

15. From S.G. Goodrich (1845). *Enterprise, Industry and Art of Man.* Bradbury, Soden & Company, Boston.

16. Dobbs, D. (2000) *The Great Gulf: Fishermen, Scientists, and the Struggle to Revive the World's Greatest Fishery.* Island Press, Washington, DC.

17. Murawski et al. (1999) New England groundfish.

18. Research by Bruce Bourque, Beverly Johnson, and Bob Steneck on animal remains from a coastal midden site at Penobscot Bay in the Gulf of Maine indicates that prehistoric Native Americans had significant impacts on shallow-water coastal fish stocks several thousand years ago. Apex predators including cod, sea mink (now extinct), swordfish, and seals dominate bone remains, constituting from 50 percent to nearly 80 percent of bones in levels of 3,500 to 4,000 years ago. Over the following 2,500 years, flounder and associated bottom fish like sculpins come to dominate and cod remains fall to only a few percent of bones present, suggesting cod had been greatly reduced in abundance in the areas fished by these people. This temporal shift from high to low trophic levels in catches is one of the first examples of fishing down marine food webs that is so prevalent in the seas of today. Bourque, B.J., B. Johnson, and R. S. Steneck (2007) Possible prehistoric hunter-gatherer impacts on food web structure in the Gulf of Maine. In J. Erlandson and R. Torben (eds.) *Human Impacts on Ancient Marine Environments.* University of California Press, Berkeley.

19. Matteson, G. (1979) *Draggermen: Fishing on Georges Bank.* Four Winds Press, New York.

20. George Matteson (see note 19) describes one example of the process of trawlers penetrating areas of rough seabed: "There is the story of two brothers who fish off the Rhode Island coast, mostly in a place called the Southwest Hole. One arm of this place is so filled with boulders and snags that it was once considered impossible to fish. But the two brothers went

back again and again. More often than not they would tear up and lose gear but once in a while they got through safely and each time they made a clean tow they carefully wrote down exactly how they had done it. They towed and mended, mended and towed as they explored the labyrinth of safe paths through that part of the Southwest Hole. One by one they discovered the alleys along which their nets might safely be drawn. The fish were plentiful there, and the brothers have recently enjoyed great profit. In the rest of the Hole where the rest of the Rhode Island fleet works, the catches have become smaller and smaller. Those without knowledge of the rocky ground are discouraged and have begun to move away. . . . Likewise on Georges Bank there are many vessels that make a specialty out of fishing rough bottom. Far up among the ridges and gullies of the actual shoals there are plenty of cod and haddock, but the likelihood of tearing up is very great."

21.  Matteson (1979) *Draggermen.*
22.  Bartlett, K. (1997) *The Finest Kind. The Fishermen of Gloucester.* W.W. Norton & Company, New York, 2002.
23.  Bennett, F. (1998) Changes to the seafloor in the Chatham area. Pages 115–116 in E.M. Dorsey and J. Pederson (eds.) *Effects of Fishing Gear on the Sea Floor of New England.* Conservation Law Foundation and Massachusetts Institute of Technology, Boston.
24.  Kaiser, J. (2000) Ecologists on a mission to save the world. *Science* 287: 1188–1192.
25.  Bourque, B.J., B. Johnson, and R. S. Steneck (2007) Possible prehistoric hunter-gatherer impacts on food web structure in the Gulf of Maine. In J. Erlandson and R. Torben (eds.) *Human Impacts on Ancient Marine Environments.* University of California Press, Berkeley.
26.  Harris, L.G., and M.C. Tyrrell (2001) Changing community states in the Gulf of Maine: Synergism between invaders, overfishing and climate change. *Biological Invasions* 3: 9–21.
27.  Hutchings, J.A., C. Walters, and R.L. Haedrich (1997) Is scientific inquiry incompatible with government information control? *Canadian Journal of Fisheries and Aquatic Sciences* 54: 1198–1210.
28.  Rose, G.A. (2004) Reconciling overfishing and climate change with stock dynamics of Atlantic cod (*Gadus morhua*) over 500 years. *Canadian Journal of Fisheries and Aquatic Sciences* 61: 1553–1557.
29.  Rosenberg, A.A., W.J. Bolster, K.E. Alexander, W.B. Leavenworth, A.B. Cooper, and M.G. McKenzie (2005) The history of ocean resources: Modeling cod biomass using historical records. *Frontiers in Ecology and Environment* 3: 78–84.
30.  Carson (1943) *Food from the Sea.*
31.  Canadian Broadcasting Corporation (2003) "The Codless Sea."

*Chapter 16: Slow Death of an Estuary: Chesapeake Bay*

1. Wennersten, J.R. (1981) *The Oyster Wars of Chesapeake Bay.* Tidewater Publishers, Centreville, Maryland.
2. *Scribner's* magazine (1877), quoted in Wennersten (1981) *The Oyster Wars of Chesapeake Bay.*
3. Horton, T. (2003) *Turning the Tide: Saving the Chesapeake Bay.* Island Press, Washington, DC.
4. Wennersten (1981) *The Oyster Wars of Chesapeake Bay.*
5. Captain Davidson, quoted in Wennersten (1981) *The Oyster Wars of Chesapeake Bay.*
6. Wennersten (1981) *The Oyster Wars of Chesapeake Bay.*
7. Kirby, M.X. (2004) Fishing down the coast: Historical expansion and collapse of oyster fisheries along continental margins. *Proceedings of the National Academy of Sciences* 101: 13096–13099.
8. Ibid.
9. Anonymous (1891) Drake's report on the Georgia oyster-beds. *Science* 17: 155.
10. Wennersten (1981) *The Oyster Wars of Chesapeake Bay.*
11. Anonymous (1891) Drake's report on the Georgia oyster-beds.
12. Cooper, S.R., and G.S. Brush (1991) Long-term history of Chesapeake Bay anoxia. *Science* 254: 992–996. Cores drilled through muddy bottom sediments allow scientists to reconstruct the history of the bay and its watershed. Floodwaters deposited layers of mud containing traces of pollen, charcoal, and other materials that provide a detailed picture of conditions prevailing during the last several thousand years and of how conditions have altered. For thousands of years, sediment input from the forested watershed was low and steady. Cores show that land clearance after colonization increased the rate of sediment input threefold.
13. Tilp, F. (1978) *This Was Potomac River.* 2nd edition. Frederick Tilp, Alexandria, Virginia.
14. Grettler, D.J. (2001) The nature of capitalism: Environmental change and conflict over commercial fishing in nineteenth-century Delaware. *Environmental History* 6: 451–473.
15. These expanded salt marshes had another beneficial effect, reducing the discharge of nutrients into the bay by trapping sediments and organic matter. Today, the area of salt marsh is in decline again due to rising sea levels, exacerbating problems of sedimentation and pollution.
16. Cooper and Brush (1991) Long-term history of Chesapeake Bay anoxia.
17. Horton (2003) *Turning the Tide.*
18. Cooper and Brush (1991) Long-term history of Chesapeake Bay anoxia.
19. Horton (2003) *Turning the Tide.*
20. Orth, R.J., and K.A. Moore. (1983) Chesapeake Bay: An unprecedented decline in submerged aquatic vegetation. *Science* 222: 51–53.

21. Goode, G.B. (1884) *The Fisheries and Fishery Industries of the United States. Section I. Natural History of Useful Aquatic Animals.* Government Printing Office, Washington, DC.

22. Simmonds, P.L. (1879) *The Commercial Products of the Sea; or Marine Contributions to Industry, and Art.* D. Appleton and Company, New York.

23. Ibid.

24. Goode (1884) continues: "Among its enemies may be counted every predaceous animal which swims in the same waters. Whales and dolphins follow the schools and consume them by the hogshead. Sharks of all kinds prey upon them largely; one hundred have been taken from the stomach of one shark. All the large carnivorous fishes feed on them. The tunny is the most destructive. 'I have often,' writes a gentleman from Maine, 'watched their antics from the masthead of my vessel—rushing and thrashing like demons among a school of fish; darting with almost lightning swiftness, scattering them in every direction, and throwing hundreds of them in the air with their tails.' The pollock, the whiting, the striped bass, the cod, the squeteague [drum], and the gar-fish are savage foes. The sword-fish and the bayonet-fish destroy many, rushing through the schools and striking right and left with their powerful swords. The blue-fish and bonito are, however, the most destructive enemies, not even excepting man."

25. Goode (1884) *The Fisheries and Fishery Industries of the United States.*

26. Russell, D. (2005) *Striper Wars: An American Fish Story.* Island Press, Washington, DC.

27. Schubel, J.R., and D.W. Pritchard (1971) Chesapeake Bay: A second look. *Science* 173: 943–945.

28. Horton (2003) *Turning the Tide.*

29. Russell (2005) *Striper Wars.*

30. Ibid.

31. Uphoff, J. (2003) Predator-prey analysis of striped bass and Atlantic menhaden in upper Chesapeake Bay. *Fisheries Management and Ecology* 10: 313–322.

32. Catches of striped bass in 2006 suggest that starvation has been less of a problem recently.

33. Roberts, C.M., and J.P. Hawkins (1999) Extinction risk in the sea. *Trends in Ecology and Evolution* 14: 241–246.

## Chapter 17: Ghost Reefs in the Caribbean

1. Lowe, P.R. (1911) *A Naturalist on Desert Islands.* Witherby & Co., London.

2. Ibid.

3. Ibid.

4. Ibid.

5. Beebe, W. (1928) *Beneath Tropic Seas: A Record of Diving Among the Coral*

 *Reefs of Haiti.* Knickerbocker Press, G.P. Putnam's Sons, New York and London.

6. Ibid.
7. Ibid.
8. Hass, H. (1952) *Diving to Adventure.* Jarrolds Ltd., London.
9. Ibid.
10. Ibid.
11. Ibid. Hass went to Curaçao first on this expedition, but the quote refers to his time on Bonaire as well.
12. Dampier, W. (1697) *A New Voyage Round the World.* Dover Publications Inc., New York, 1968.
13. Jane, C. (ed.) (1930) *Select Documents Illustrating the Four Voyages of Columbus.* Volumes I and II. Hakluyt Society, London.

### Chapter 18: Shifting Baselines

1. Grey, Z. (1925) *Tales of Fishing Virgin Seas.* Derrydale Press, Lanham and New York.
2. Ibid.
3. Ibid.
4. Grey refers to the blackfish as "whale killers" suggesting the *Orca,* but his description of the size of the school of these animals implies numbers in excess of the normal pod size of orcas, and their appearance is much more like that of false killer whales (*Pseudorca crassidens*).
5. Grey (1925) *Tales of Fishing Virgin Seas.*
6. Hedges, F.A.M. (1923) *Battles with Giant Fish.* Duckworth, London.
7. Ibid.
8. Ibid.
9. Bancroft, G. (1932) *Lower California: A Cruise; The Flight of the Least Petrel.* G.P. Putnam & Sons, New York and London.
10. Ray Cannon, quoted in G.S. Kira (1999) *The Unforgettable Sea of Cortez.* Cortez Publications, Torrance, California.
11. Ibid.
12. Leopold, A. (1949) *A Sand County Almanac and Sketches Here and There.* Oxford University Press, New York.
13. Kowalewski, M., G.E. Avila Serrano, K.W. Flessa, and G.A. Goodfriend (2000) Dead delta's former productivity: Two trillion shells at the mouth of the Colorado River. *Geology* 28: 1059–1062.
14. Morgan, L., S. Maxwell, F. Tsao, T.A.C. Wilkinson, and P. Etnoyer. (2005) *Marine Conservation Priority Areas: Baja California to the Bering Sea.* Commission for Environmental Cooperation of North America, Montreal, and Marine Conservation Biology Institute, Seattle.
15. Steinbeck, J. (1951) *The Log from the Sea of Cortez.* Viking Press, New York.
16. Morgan et al. (2005) *Marine Conservation Priority Areas.*
17. Ray Cannon, quoted in Kira (1999) *The Unforgettable Sea of Cortez.*

18. Pangas are wooden and fiberglass skiffs of 4 to 7 meters long (13 to 23 feet) that are equipped with outboard engines.
19. Communidad y Biodiversidad.
20. Saenz-Arroyo, A., C.M. Roberts, J. Torre, M. Carino-Olvera, and R.R. Enriquez Andrade (2005) Rapidly shifting environmental baselines among fishers of the Gulf of California. *Proceedings of the Royal Society B* 272: 1957–1962.
21. Sala, E., O. Aburto-Oropeza, M. Reza, G. Paredes, and L.G. Lopez-Lemus (2004) Fishing down coastal food webs in the Gulf of California. *Fisheries* 29(3): 19–25.
22. The gulf grouper is *Mycteroperca jordani*. Saenz-Arroyo, A., C.M. Roberts, J. Torre, and M. Carino-Olvera (2005) Using fishers' anecdotes, naturalists' observations, and grey literature to reassess marine species at risk: The case of the gulf grouper in the Gulf of California, Mexico. *Fish and Fisheries* 6: 121–133.
23. The change in average size of the largest gulf groupers fishers ever caught does not indicate change in the average size of gulf groupers in the population as a whole. Average fish size goes down more rapidly than this as larger animals are fished out.
24. Pauly, D. (1995) Anecdotes and the shifting baseline syndrome of fisheries. Trends in Ecology and Evolution 10:430.

### Chapter 19: Ghost Habitats

1. An excellent account of the history of the abalone fishery is given by L. Rogers-Bennett, P.L. Haaker, T.O. Huff, and P.K. Dayton (2002) Estimating baseline abundances of abalone in California for restoration. *CalCOFI Reports* 43: 97–111.
2. The abalones are the red (*Haliotis rufescens*), green (*H. fulgens*), pink (*H. corrugata*), black (*H. cracherodii*), white (*H. sorenseni*), pinto or northern (*H. kamtschatkana*), threaded (*H. k. assimilis,* considered by many scientists to be a subspecies of the pinto), and flat (*H. walallensis*).
3. Rogers-Bennett et al. (2002) Estimating baseline abundances of abalone in California for restoration.
4. A measure that was later rescinded.
5. Anonymous 1913 observer, quoted in Rogers-Bennett et al. (2002) Estimating baseline abundances of abalone in California for restoration.
6. Croker, R.S. (1931) Abalones. In *The Commercial Fish Catch of California for the Year 1929.* California Department of Fish and Game, Fisheries Bulletin 30: 58–72.
7. Jones, G., (2005) Restaurant seafood prices since 1850 help plot marine harvests through history. Press release from Texas A&M University.
8. Davis, G.E. (undated) *California Abalone.* U.S. Geological service, http://biology.usgs.gov/s+t/SNT/noframe/ca166.htm. Haaker, P.L., I. Taniguchi, J.K. O'Leary, K. Karper, M. Patyten, and M. Tegner (2003) Aba-

lones. In C. Ryan and M. Patyten (eds.) *Annual Status of the Fisheries report through 2003.* Calilfornia Department of Fish and Game, www.dfg. ca.gov/MRD/status/report2003/abalones.pdf.

9. Rogers-Bennett et al. (2002) Estimating baseline abundances of abalone in California for restoration.

10. Thomas Huxley, address to the International Fisheries Exhibition, London, 1883. The Fisheries Exhibition Literature. W. Clowes and sons, London, 1884.

11. Eighteen white abalones were collected by submersible divers in the late 1990s for captive breeding in an effort to save the species. They have reproduced well in captivity, producing hundreds of thousands of off-spring. However, restocking wild populations with what amounts to a genetically highly homogenous population is not a decision that can be taken lightly. Furthermore, the captive abalone have proven susceptible to the withering disease that affects black abalones. A reintroduction pro-gram might do more harm than good at this stage.

12. Hellyer, D. (1949) Goggle fishing in California waters. *The National Geographic Magazine* 45(5): 615–632.

13. The black sea bass, *Stereolepis gigas,* is a separate species from the animal that was normally referred to as a jewfish in the Caribbean and eastern Pacific, *Epinephelus itajara,* before the latter was recently renamed the goliath grouper.

14. Hellyer (1949) Goggle fishing in California waters.

15. Dayton, P.K., M.J. Tegner, P.B. Edwards, and K.L. Riser (1998) Sliding baselines, ghosts, and reduced expectations in kelp forest communities. *Ecological Applications* 8: 309–322.

16. Crooke, S.J. (1992) History of giant sea bass fishery. Pages 153-157 in W.S. Leet, C.M. Dewees, and C.W. Haugen, (eds.) *California's Living Marine Resources and their Utilization.* Sea Grant Extension Program, University of California Press, Davis.

17. Ray Cannon, quoted in G. Kira (1999) *The Unforgettable Sea of Cortez.* Cortez Publications, California.

18. In 1982 California closed both commercial and recreational fisheries for black sea bass.

19. Mistrals are strong, cold, northerly winds that sometimes sweep southern France.

20. The liche is *Trachinotus glaucus.*

21. Cousteau, J.Y. (1953) *The Silent World.* Hamish Hamilton Ltd., London.

22. John Ottaway, quoted in J. Nevill (2006) *The Impacts of Spearfishing,* www. ids.org.au/~cnevill/marineSpearfishing.doc

23. The white sea bass is *Atractoscion nobilis.*

24. Dayton et al. (1998) plotted California catches from the 1930s to late 1990s. Catches through the 1930s to the 1950s ranged from 1,000 to 2,000 metric tons a year.

25. Ray Cannon, quoted in Kira (1999) *The Unforgettable Sea of Cortez*.
26. Dayton et al. (1998) Sliding baselines.
27. Ray Cannon, quoted in Kira (1999) *The Unforgettable Sea of Cortez*.
28. Love, M., M. Yoklavich, and L. Thorsteinson (2002) *The Rockfishes of the Northeast Pacific*. University of California Press, Berkeley.
29. Ibid.
30. Ibid.
31. Ibid.
32. Bocaccio is listed as critically endangered on the World Conservation Union's red list. Many other rockfish species qualify for listing but have yet to be assessed.
33. Graham Gillespie, quoted on page 71 of Love et al. (2002) *The Rockfishes of the Northeast Pacific*.
34. Dayton et al. (1998) Sliding baselines.

*Chapter 20: Hunting on the High Plains of the Open Sea*
1. Samuel Taylor Coleridge (undated) The rime of the ancient mariner. Pages 7-35 in *Selected Poems*. Collins' Clear-Type Press, London and Glasgow.
2. Ibid.
3. Pauly, D., and V. Christensen (1995) Primary production required to sustain global fisheries. *Nature* 374: 255–257.
4. Edwards, P. (ed.) (1999) The Journals of Captain Cook. Penguin Books, London.
5. Dunmore, J. (ed.) (1995) The Journal of Jean-François de Galaup de la Pérouse 1785–1788. Volumes I–IV. Hakluyt Society, London.
6. Ibid.
7. Colnett J. (1798) *A Voyage to the South Atlantic and around Cape Horn into the Pacific Ocean for the Purpose of Extending the Spermaceti Whale Fisheries and Other Objects of Commerce*. N. Israel, Amsterdam, and Da Capo Press, New York, 1968.
8. Ibid.
9. Beebe, W. (1926) *The Arcturus Adventure*. Knickerbocker Press, New York.
10. Farrington, S.K. (1942) *Pacific Game Fishing*. Coward-McCann Inc., New York.
11. Carson, R.L. (1943) *Food from the Sea: Fish and Shellfish of New England*. U.S. Department of the Interior Fish and Wildlife Service. Government Printing Office, Washington, DC.
12. Tsutsui, W.M. (2003) Landscapes in the dark valley: Toward an environmental history of wartime Japan. *Environmental History* 8(2). www.historycooperative.org/journals/eh/8.2/tsutsui.html
13. Myers, R.A., and B. Worm (2003) Rapid worldwide depletion of predatory fish communities. *Nature* 423: 281–283.

14. Baum, J.K., and R.A. Myers. (2004) Shifting baselines and the decline of pelagic sharks in the Gulf of Mexico. *Ecology Letters* 7: 135–145.

15. Ward, P., and R.A. Myers (2005) Shifts in open ocean fish communities coinciding with the commencement of commercial fishing. *Ecology* 86: 835–847.

16. The albatross slaughter has not stopped completely. A large and active illegal fishing fleet roams the high seas. Their crews are unmoved by the plight of wildlife killed by their fishing operations, and they do not bother to use ethical fishing methods. Until illegal fishing is brought under control, wildlife will continue to be destroyed unnecessarily at sea.

17. Worm, B. (2005) Scientists discover global pattern of big fish diversity in open oceans. SeaWeb press release at Communication Partnership for Science and the Sea, http://www.compassonline.org/pdf_files/PR_2005_7_28.pdf

### Chapter 21: Violating the Last Great Wilderness

1. Pechenik, L.N. and F.M. Troyanovskii. (1971) *Trawling Resources on the North-Atlantic Continental Slope.* Israel Program for Scientific Translations, Jerusalem.

2. Ibid.

3. Ibid.

4. Roberts, C.M. (2002) Deep impact: The rising toll of fishing in the deep sea. *Trends in Ecology and Evolution* 17: 242–245.

5. Branch, T.A. (2001) A review of orange roughy *Hoplostethus atlanticus* fisheries, estimation methods, biology and stock structure. *South African Journal of Marine Science* 23: 181–203.

6. Lack, M., K. Short, and A. Willock (2003) *Managing Risk and Uncertainty in Deep Sea Fisheries: Lessons from Orange Roughy.* TRAFFIC Oceania and WWF, Australia. Chaff bags are small cloth bags much used in agriculture for storing seed, feed, and plant waste.

7. Pechenik and Troyanovskii (1971) *Trawling Resources.*

8. Forbes, E.D.W. and R. Godwin-Austin (1859) The Natural History of the European Seas. John van Voorst, London. Pages 26-27.

9. Beebe, W. (1935) *Half Mile Down.* John Lane, The Bodley Head, London.

10. Ibid.

11. Joubin, M.L. (1922) Les coraux de mer profonde: Nuisibles aux chalutiers. *Notes et Mémoires* (18): 5–16. Office Scientifique et Technique des Pêches Maritimes, Paris.

12. Personal e-mail communication from Les Watling, Darling Marine Laboratory (now at the University of Hawaii), 19th May 2006.

13. Anderson, O. (2004) Coral catches in the South Tasman Rise orange roughy fishery. *Waves* 10(1): 7.

14. *Report of the Commissioners Appointed to Inquire and Report Upon the Complaints That Have Been Made by Line and Drift Net Fishermen of Injuries Sustained by Them in Their Calling Owing to the Use of the Trawl Net and Beam Trawl in the Territorial Waters of the United Kingdom* (1885). Eyre and Spottiswoode, London.

### Chapter 22: No Place Left to Hide

1. Alverson, D.L., and N.J. Wilimovsky (1964) Prospective developments in the harvesting of marine fishes. In *Modern Fishing Gear of the World 2*. Fishing News (Books) Ltd., London.
2. Dobbs, D. (2000) *The Great Gulf. Fishermen, Scientists, and the Struggle to Revive the World's Greatest Fishery*. Island Press, Washington, DC.
3. Greenlaw, L. (1999) *The Hungry Ocean: A Swordboat Captain's Journey*. Hyperion, New York.
4. Ibid.
5. Ibid.
6. Rogers, C.S., and J. Beets (2001) Degradation of marine ecosystems and decline of fishery resources in marine protected areas in the US Virgin Islands. *Environmental Conservation* 28: 312–322.
7. Birkeland, C. (2002) Military technologies and increased fishing effort leave no place to hide for fish. SeaWeb press release at Communiucation Partnership for Science and the Sea, www.compassonline.org/pdf_files/ PR_2002_2_17.pdf.
8. Russell, E.S. (1942) *The Overfishing Problem*. Cambridge University Press, Cambridge.
9. Graham, M. (1943) *The Fish Gate*. Faber and Faber Ltd., London.

### Chapter 23: Barbequed Jellyfish or Swordfish Steak?

1. Watson, R., and D. Pauly (2001) Systematic distortions in world fisheries catch trends. *Nature* 414: 534–536.
2. The decline amounted to 0.66 million metric tons per year, excluding Peruvian anchoveta. Catches of anchoveta fluctuate wildly in relation to prevailing conditions in the El Niño cycle. See note 1.
3. Pauly, D., V. Christensen, J. Dalsgaard, R. Froese, and F.C. Torres (1998) Fishing down marine food webs. *Science* 279: 860–863.
4. Radcliffe, W. (1921) *Fishing from the Earliest Times*. John Murray, London.
5. Graham, M. (1948) *Rational Fishing of the Cod of the North Sea*. Edward Arnold & Co., London.
6. Russell, E.S. (1942) *The Overfishing Problem*. Cambridge University Press, Cambridge.
7. Graham (1948) *Rational Fishing of the Cod of the North Sea*.
8. Hutchings, J. (2000) Collapse and recovery of marine fishes. *Nature* 406: 882–885.

9. Steinbeck, J. (1951) *The Log from the Sea of Cortez*. Viking Press, New York.
10. Rose, G.A. (1993) Cod spawning on a migration highway in the north-west Atlantic. *Nature* 366: 458–461.
11. Ames, E. (1997) *Cod and Haddock Spawning Grounds of the Gulf of Maine*. Island Institute, Rockland, Maine.
12. Bigelow, H.B., and W.C. Schroeder (1953) *Fishes of the Gulf of Maine*. Fishery Bulletin of the Fish and Wildlife Service. Volume 53, Bulletin 74. Government Printing Office, Washington, DC.
13. Ruzzante, D.E., J.S. Wroblewski, C.T. Taggart, R.K. Smedbol, D. Cook, and S.V. Goddard (2000) Bay-scale population structure in coastal Atlantic cod in Labrador and Newfoundland, Canada. *Journal of Fish Biology* 56: 431–447.
14. Hutchinson, W.F., C. van Oosterhout, S.I. Rogers, and G.R. Carvalho (2003) Temporal analysis of archived samples indicates marked genetic changes in declining North Sea cod (*Gadus morhua*). *Proceedings of the Royal Society B* 270: 2125–2132.
15. Dwyer, M.J. (2001) *Sea of Heartbreak*. Key Porter Books, Toronto.
16. Chimaera are commonly known as rabbit fishes. They are from the family Chimaeridae and are found in deep-sea environments all over the world.
17. Dwyer (2001) *Sea of Heartbreak*.
18. Hareide, N., D. Rihan, M. Mulligan, P. McMullen, G. Garnes, M. Clark, P. Connolly, P. Tyndall, R. Misund, D. Furevik, A. Newton, K. Høydal, T. Blasdale, O. Børre Humborstad (2005) *A Preliminary Investigation of Shelf Edge and Deepwater Fixed Net Fisheries to the West and North of Great Britain, Ireland, around Rockall and Hatton Bank*. ICES CM 2005/ N:07.
19. Brashares, J.S., P. Arcese, M.K. Sam, P.B. Copolillo, A.R.E. Sinclair, and A. Balmford (2004) Bushmeat hunting, wildlife declines, and fish supply in West Africa. *Science* 306: 1180–1183.
20. Worm, B., E.B. Barbier, N. Beaumont, J.E. Duffy, C. Folke, B.S. Halpern, J.B.C. Jackson, H.K. Lotze, F. Micheli, S.R. Palumbi, E. Sala, K.A. Selkoe, J.J. Stachowicz, and R. Watson (2006) Impacts of biodiversity loss on ocean ecosystem services. *Science* 314: 787–790. The figures in this paper attracted immediate criticism from some academics and members of the fisheries management community, although little from the fishing industry. Perhaps the declines are self-evident to those who fish. Daniel Pauly and colleagues from the University of British Columbia have since used a variety of methods to estimate the time to disappearance of fish populations. All their estimates cluster around the same general date reported in the Worm et al. paper. In the end, criticizing the date does nothing to challenge the main conclusion, that fisheries are collapsing very fast across the world and will soon run out (unless jellyfish are to your taste, that is).
21. Priede, I.G., R. Froese, D.M. Bailey, O.A. Bergstad, M.A. Collins, J.E. Dyb, C. Henriques, E.G. Jones, and N. King (2006) The absence of

sharks from abyssal regions of the world's oceans. *Proceedings of the Royal Society B* 273: 1435-41

22. Knowler, D., and E.B. Barbier (2000) The economics of an invading species: A theoretical model and case study application. Pages 70-93 in C. Perrings, M. Williamson, and S. Dalmazzone (eds.) *The Economics of Biological Invasions.* Edward Elgar, Cheltenham, UK.

23. Rabalais, N.N, R.E. Turner, and W.J. Wiseman (2002) Gulf of Mexico hypoxia, a.k.a. "the dead zone." *Annual Reviews of Ecology and Systematics* 33: 235–263.

24. Diaz, R.J. (2000) Overview of hypoxia around the world. *Journal of Environmental Quality* 30: 275–281.

25. Rogers-Bennett, L., P.L. Haaker, T.O. Huff, and P.K. Dayton (2002) Estimating baseline abundances of abalone in California for restoration. *CalCOFI Reports* 43: 97–111.

26. Sadovy, Y., and W.L. Cheung (2003) Near extinction of a highly fecund fish: The one that nearly got away. *Fish and Fisheries* 4: 86–99.

27. Lane, E.W. (1902) *The Arabian Nights' Entertainments.* Sands and Co., London.

## *Chapter 24: Reinventing Fishery Management*

1. Although guiding principles for the Common Fisheries Policy were developed in 1970, it took thirteen more years before a full agreement was fleshed out among member states and implemented.

2. A few species are considered as groups; for example, skates and rays are lumped together. One adverse effect of lumping is to hide population trends for individual species. A steep decline in numbers of common skate was obscured by increased catches of smaller-bodied species, for example.

3. Within countries, fishing organizations subdivide allocations among individual fishing vessels.

4. Management of northern herring fisheries in Europe has been quite successful following recovery from the crash in the 1970s. There are two good reasons for success where others have failed. The first is that herring and other pelagic schooling fish are real single-species fisheries. They form discrete groups that can be caught in isolation from pretty much all other species. Nor are many herring caught accidentally by fishers targeting other species, so directed catches represent the great majority of total fishing mortality. This makes it far easier for scientists to set, and politicians to implement, sustainable levels of catch. The second reason is that herring were food for dozens of predator species, like cod, that have been massively depleted. Their populations are thus enjoying a welcome respite from nonhuman predation.

5. Norway's fisheries Website, www.fisheries.no/marine_stocks/fish_stocks /haddock/north_sea_haddock.htm

6. Those committees interact very little, even if the targets of their management efforts are as intimately connected as predator and prey. The herring committee deliberates on its species separately from committees that manage a host of herring predators, for example. It is only very recently that concerns over habitat modification and damage by fishing have grown sufficiently for an ICES committee to be formed to investigate. That committee is separate from all the others.

7. Many of these reforms are embodied in the conclusions of the UK Royal Commission on Environmental Pollution's report *Turning the Tide*, published in 2004 (RCEP, London), www.rcep.org.uk/fishreport.htm. The report sets out to address the environmental impacts of fisheries in Europe.

8. Graham, M. (1948) *Rational Fishing of the Cod of the North Sea*. Edward Arnold & Co., London.

9. Many subsistence fisheries in the developing world are still open access, which is one reason that fishers in densely populated regions live in poverty. Open access means that fish populations have become highly overfished and fishing is a hand-to-mouth existence.

10. I heard a British fishery minister interviewed on the late evening news one day state, "We have got to get the stocks in synch with the fishing effort that's there," meaning exactly the opposite!

11. Reid, C. (2000) From boom to bust: The herring industry in the twentieth century. Pages 188–196 in D.J. Starkey, C. Reid, and N. Ashcroft (eds.) *England's Sea Fisheries: The Commercial Sea Fisheries of England and Wales since 1300*. Chatham Publishing, London.

12. Okey, T.A. (2003) Membership of the eight regional Fishery Management Councils in the United States: Are special interests over-represented? *Marine Policy* 27: 193–206.

13. As of 2006, the European Union has failed to ban pair trawling for sea bass in the English Channel, despite clear evidence of the destruction of marine mammals that it is obliged by other legislation to protect. Pair trawls are huge midwater trawl nets towed between two boats, and the porpoises find it hard to avoid them. Bycatch of dolphins is less because there are so few left. In over thirty years of the application of the Common Fisheries Policy, the European Union has introduced only a handful of fishery regulations that are designed to protect nontarget species and habitats, often with great reluctance.

### Chapter 25: The Return of Abundance

1. Roberts, C.M., and J.P. Hawkins (1997) How small can a marine reserve be and still be effective? *Coral Reefs* 16: 150.

2. Hérubel, M.A. (1912) *Sea Fisheries, Their Treasures and Toilers*. T. Fisher Unwin, London.

3. Ibid.

4. Ibid.

5. Ibid.

6. McIntosh, W.C. (1899) *The Resources of the Sea as Shown in the Scientific Experiments to Test the Effects of Trawling and of the Closure of Certain Areas off the Scottish Shores.* C.J. Clay and Sons, London.

7. "A Correspondent" (1899) *Reply to the So-called Criticism and Analysis of Professor M'Intosh on Trawling and Trawling Investigations.* Rosemount Press, Aberdeen, UK.

8. Ballantine, W.J. (1991) *Marine Reserves for New Zealand.* Leigh Laboratory Bulletin No. 25, University of Auckland.

9. Kelly, S., D. Scott, A.B. MacDiarmid, and R.C. Babcock (2000) Spiny lobster, *Jasus edwardsii*, recovery in New Zealand marine reserves. *Biological Conservation* 92: 359–369.

10. Cole, R.G., T.M Ayling, and R.G. Creese (1990) Effects of marine reserve protection at Goat Island, northern New Zealand. *New Zealand Journal of Marine and Freshwater Research* 24: 197–210.

11. Snappers, red moki, and blue cod are, respectively, *Pagrus auratus, Cheilodactylus spectabilis,* and *Parapercis colias.*

12. Babcock, R.C., S. Kelly, N.T. Shears, J.W. Walker, and T.J. Willis (1999) Changes in community structure in temperate marine reserves. *Marine Ecology Progress Series* 189: 125–134.

13. Ballantine (1991) *Marine Reserves for New Zealand.*

14. Babcock et al. (1999) Changes in community structure in temperate marine reserves.

15. Carlos-Castilla, J. (1993) Humans: Capstone strong actors in the past and present coastal ecological play. Pages 158–162 in G.E. Likens (ed.) *Humans as Components of Ecosystems: The Ecology of Subtle Human Effects and Populated Areas.* Springer-Verlag, New York.

16. Most elkhorn corals, *Acropora palmata*, in St. Lucia were dead, killed by a disease epidemic in the 1980s. Their robust skeletons had not disintegrated by this time, often remaining in the original growth position.

17. Black drum, red drum, and spotted sea trout are, respectively, *Pogonias cromis, Sciaenops ocellatus,* and *Cynoscion nebulosus.* They are all species of croaker.

18. Anderson, W.W., and J.W. Gehringer (1965) *Biological-statistical census of the species entering fisheries in the Cape Canaveral area.* U.S. Fish and Wildlife Service Special Scientific Report Series No. 514.

19. Murawski, S.A., R. Brown, H.L. Lai, P.J. Rago, and L. Hendrickson. (2000) Large-scale closed areas as a fisheries-management tool in temperate marine systems: The Georges Bank experience. *Bulletin of Marine Science* 66: 775–798.

20. Gell, F.R., and C.M. Roberts (2003) Benefits beyond boundaries: the fishery effects of marine reserves and fishery closures. *Trends in Ecology and Evolution* 18: 448–455. Gell, F.R., and C.M. Roberts (2003) *The Fishery Effects of Marine Reserves and Fishery Closures.* WWF-US, Washington, DC. 89pp. www.worldwildlife.org/oceans/pdfs/fishery_effects.pdf

21. Russ, G.R., and A.C. Alcala (2004) Marine reserves: Rates and patterns of recovery and decline. *Ecological Applications* 13: 1553–1565.

22. Maypa, A.P., G.R. Russ, A.C. Alcala, and H.P. Calumpong (2002) Long-term trends in yield and catch rates of the coral reef fishery at Apo Island, Central Philippines. *Marine and Freshwater Research* 53: 207–213.

### Chapter 26: The Future of Fish

1. By meat, I mean the meat of land animals and birds. Industrial fisheries sweep up vast amounts of fish to be rendered down into feed for these farm animals.

2. My thanks to Steve Gaines and Alan Hastings for this description.

3. Gell, F.R., and C.M. Roberts (2003) Benefits beyond boundaries: the fishery effects of marine reserves and fishery closures. *Trends in Ecology and Evolution* 18: 448–455. Gell, F.R., and C.M. Roberts (2003) *The Fishery Effects of Marine Reserves and Fishery Closures.* WWF-US, Washington, DC. 89pp. www.worldwildlife.org/oceans/pdfs/fishery_effects.pdf

4. Beets, J., and A. Friedlander (1999) Evaluation of a conservation strategy: A spawning aggregation closure for red hind, *Epinephelus guttatus*, in the US Virgin Islands. *Environmental Biology of Fishes* 55: 91–98.

5. The survey was a random mailing to two thousand households in Britain conducted in 2005–2006. Twenty-five percent of people responded. As with all such surveys, those who respond are likely to hold stronger views on the subject polled than nonrespondents. However, they represent a significant fraction of the population, indicating a high level of support for greater protection for marine life.

6. Balmford, A., P. Gravestock, N. Hockley, C. McClean, and C.M. Roberts (2004) The worldwide costs of marine protected areas. *Proceedings of the National Academy of Science USA* 101: 9694–9697.

7. www.globalsecurity.org

8. Royal Commission on Environmental Pollution (2004) *Turning the Tide,* RCEP, London. www.rcep.org.uk/fishreport.htm.

9. Heyman, W.D., R.T. Graham, B. Kjerfve, and R.E. Johannes (2001) Whale sharks *Rhincodon typus* aggregate to feed on fish spawn in Belize. *Marine Ecology Progress Series* 215: 275–282.

10. Take Gladden Spit, for example. At the time of writing (2006), although it has been declared a marine reserve, people are still allowed to fish the snapper spawning aggregations. And this is the last aggregation of any size still remaining in Belize. The others were fished to oblivion many years ago.

11. Readers of this book can help improve the state of the oceans by choosing only seafoods that have been caught using sustainable methods. The Marine Stewardship Council (www.msc.org) certifies fish caught from sustainable fisheries that cause minimal damage to the environment and other species. Fish from certified fisheries carry the MSC logo. Ask for fish caught this way when you next buy seafood, and avoid species that are from unsustainable fisheries. The Monterey Bay Aquarium (www. mbayaq.org/cr/seafoodwatch.asp), Audubon Society (www.audubon. org/campaign/lo/seafood), Blue Ocean Institute (www.blueoceaninsti tute.org/miniguide.pdf), and Sustainable Seafood Choices (www.sea foodchoices.com) in the United States, and the Marine Conservation Society in Britain (www.mcsuk.org) provide detailed lists of which are the best fish to eat and which to avoid.

# Index

## About Island Press

Island Press is the only nonprofit organization in the United States whose principal purpose is the publication of books on environmental issues and natural resource management. We provide solutions-oriented information to professionals, public officials, business and community leaders, and concerned citizens who are shaping responses to environmental problems.

Since 1984, Island Press has been the leading provider of timely and practical books that take a multidisciplinary approach to critical environmental concerns. Our growing list of titles reflects our commitment to bringing the best of an expanding body of literature to the environmental community throughout North America and the world.

Support for Island Press is provided by the Agua Fund, The Geraldine R. Dodge Foundation, Doris Duke Charitable Foundation, The Ford Foundation, The William and Flora Hewlett Foundation, The Joyce Foundation, Kendeda Sustainability Fund of the Tides Foundation, The Forrest & Frances Lattner Foundation, The Henry Luce Foundation, The John D. and Catherine T. MacArthur Foundation, The Marisla Foundation, The Andrew W. Mellon Foundation, Gordon and Betty Moore Foundation, The Curtis and Edith Munson Foundation, Oak Foundation, The Overbrook Foundation, The David and Lucile Packard Foundation, Wallace Global Fund, The Winslow Foundation, and other generous donors.

The opinions expressed in this book are those of the author(s) and do not necessarily reflect the views of these foundations.